Praise for
The South's Forgotten Fire-Eater

"Chris McIlwain once again sets his critical eye on another Alabamian who led the state to make a series of disastrous decisions during the mid-nineteenth century. David Hubbard started his political career as a firm supporter of Andrew Jackson, but with each new national conflict he emerged as a more radical and uncompromising defender of a separate Southern nation. Much of his success lay in gaining the votes of the non-slaveholders by over appeals to their fears of slave rebellions and to their resentment of the wealthy. At the time, Hubbard was among those north Alabamians pushing for critical economic changes, including industrialization, which McIlwain details in a particularly significant contribution. In short, *The South's Forgotten Fire-Eater* is a fresh look at one road to secession—twists, turns, dust, rocks, and all." — **G. WARD HUBBS, author of** *Searching for Freedom after the Civil War: Klansman, Carpetbagger, Scalawag, and Freedman*

"Chris McIlwain has become one of the leading historians of nineteenth-century Alabama, and this fine volume will only add luster to that reputation. Deeply researched, provocatively argued, and forcefully written, McIlwain's newest work rescues a significant Alabama fire-eater from obscurity. This book unravels a complex but important story of land speculation, banking, railroads, economic development, partisan intrigue, and sectional politics. McIlwain uses David Hubbard's life to probe the actions of Alabama politicians hurtling toward secession and war. A must-read for anyone interested in Civil War-era Alabama." — **GEORGE C. RABLE, Professor Emeritus, The University of Alabama**

"No one would have known about north Alabama's David Hubbard without this well-researched and well-rounded exploration of the man and his times. It's a fascinating account offered by Chris McIlwain to the general reader and serious historian alike, one which describes a man of action who greatly influenced the course of events leading up to the secession of the Southern states and how events played out during and immediately after the Civil War." — NANCY M. ROHR, author of *Incidents of the War: The Civil War Journey of Mary Jane Chadick*

"McIlwain's study of Congressman David Hubbard illustrates the sheer weirdness of the path to secession through one fire-eater's long and varied career. Hubbard went from being one of Andrew Jackson's Indian fighters to a proslavery militant, and his racial animus is the one consistent thing about him. McIlwain provides a troubling look at north Alabama society through the vehicle of this devoted secessionist, a political rebel who lived by the adage, 'it is good to be shifty in a new state.'" — MICHAEL W. FITZGERALD, author of *Reconstruction in Alabama: From Civil War to Redemption in the Cotton South*

"McIlwain's biography of David Hubbard is much more than an engaging account of an overlooked politician from antebellum Alabama; it is a bold reappraisal of the human factors driving the state's secession movement in the late 1850s. Through strong prose backed by extensive research, the author highlights the crucial role that Hubbard played in transforming the region of northern Alabama from one that generally viewed secession with great reluctance into one that became increasingly more receptive to this radical course of action. In doing so, McIlwain rightly accords Hubbard the same level of prominence and agency in bringing about Alabama's secession that historians have long attributed to the more famous William L. Yancey. This book is an important and original contribution to the history of Alabama during the Civil War era." — BEN H. SEVERANCE, author of *A War State All Over: Alabama Politics and the Confederate Cause* and *Portraits of Conflict: A Photographic History of Alabama in the Civil War*

THE SOUTH'S
FORGOTTEN FIRE-EATER

THE SOUTH'S FORGOTTEN FIRE-EATER

David Hubbard and North Alabama's Long Road to Disunion

CHRIS MCILWAIN

NEWSOUTH BOOKS

Montgomery

NewSouth Books
105 S. Court Street
Montgomery, AL 36104

Library of Congress Cataloging-in-Publication Data
Names: McIlwain, Christopher Lyle, author.
Title: The South's forgotten fire-eater : David Hubbard and North Alabama's
long road to disunion / Chris McIlwain.
Other titles: David Hubbard and North Alabama's long road to disunion.
Description: Montgomery : NewSouth Books, [2020] | Includes bibliographical
references and index.
Identifiers: LCCN 2020018836 (print) | LCCN 2020018837 (ebook) | ISBN
9781588384119 (hardback) | ISBN 9781588384126 (epub)
Subjects: LCSH: Hubbard, David, 1792-1874. | Alabama—Politics and
government—To 1865. | Legislators—Alabama—Biography. |
Secession—Alabama. | United States—Politics and government—1849-1861.
| Legislators—United State—Biography. | United States. Congress.
House—Biography. | Kinlock (Miss.)—Biography.
Classification: LCC F326.H77 M35 2020 (print) | LCC F326.H77 (ebook) |
DDC 328.73/092 [B]--dc23
LC record available at https://lccn.loc.gov/2020018836
LC ebook record available at https://lccn.loc.gov/2020018837

Design by Randall Williams
Printed in the United States of America by Sheridan Books

Front Cover: "Portrait of David Hubbard."
Alabama Department of Archives and History.

*The Black Belt, defined by its dark, rich soil, stretches across central Alabama. It
was the heart of the cotton belt. It was and is a place of great beauty, of extreme
wealth and grinding poverty, of pain and joy. Here we take our stand, listening to
the past, looking to the future.*

To my wife, Anna;
my children, Christopher and Elizabeth;
and my grandchildren, Carter, Claire, Jack, and Hunter.

Contents

Preface

This is a biography of antebellum north Alabama with an emphasis on the events that led to its unique economic and political development up to 1861. It is also a biography of a man, David Hubbard, of whom you have probably never heard. He was a lawyer, land speculator, businessman, and politician whose influence is critically important to understanding why north Alabama moved slowly but surely toward secession and civil war.

This is definitely not an homage to Hubbard, but he is a ready vehicle for studying the troubled birth of Alabama, its intermittent economic development, and its lengthy radicalization process. He was born in 1792, the son of an American soldier in the Revolutionary War. Like so many residents of the Eastern Seaboard states, his family emigrated west, first to Tennessee. There he joined Andrew Jackson's army of militiamen and participated in Jackson's efforts to defeat the British and their Native American allies in the War of 1812, thereby bringing a degree of security to the frontier.

Because the financial history of north Alabama and David Hubbard are of critical importance in understanding what happened, the reader should expect a steady dose of that poor relation in the history world: economics. Increased world demand for cotton, and the availability of Native American land for its production, initially caused the white and slave populations of north Alabama to surge well beyond that of south Alabama. Hubbard was active in the postwar land boom in Alabama, as well as one of the thousands of victims of the long depression in cotton prices that followed immediately thereafter. This depression caused many of the debt-ridden landowning class in the South, as well as the manufacturing interests in the upper South and the Northeast, to elevate sectional interests and goals over national needs. Hubbard entered politics as a staunch Jacksonian Democrat and was elected to the Alabama Senate, where he demonstrated extraordinary political skills and influence and was involved in many of the important issues that confronted the young frontier state.

Hubbard was also a trailblazer in the earliest efforts to industrialize Alabama. Among other things, he initiated construction of the first railroad in the entire South, which ran between Tuscumbia, Alabama, and the Tennessee River. This railroad was later extended to Decatur to provide a means of bypassing the Muscle Shoals, which had been a significant and dangerous impediment to commercial navigation of the Tennessee River in north Alabama for decades.

However, as sectional conflict increased and the sinister influence of South Carolina radicals began to metastasize, Hubbard came to be defined for his uncompromising positions on the rights of the South. This began with his surprisingly vocal public opposition to President Jackson's efforts in the 1830s to use force to put down the tariff nullification movement in South Carolina. As slave populations increased, as a member of Congress, Hubbard's fiery opposition continued against the admission of California as a free state as part of the Compromise of 1850, as well as his subsequent efforts to bring about secession. Like-minded south Alabamians praised him for his consistency, but most of his north Alabama constituents did not until after abolitionist John Brown's famous raid on Harper's Ferry in 1859. With the election of Abraham Lincoln in 1860, Hubbard and others succeeded in orchestrating the secession of Alabama and the creation of the Confederacy, which he served in an appointed civilian capacity.

As many north Alabamians had feared, the region where they and Hubbard lived quickly became a battleground, causing all to experience terrible losses in family and property. Hubbard lost his youngest son in battle, and he and his family were ultimately forced to flee until the war finally ended. Through it all, however, Hubbard never lost his faith in the "Cause."

Hubbard has received little mention in recent scholarship regarding the "fire-eaters"—the men who led the South to secession, civil war, and destruction. Eric Walther's *The Fire-Eaters*, for example, discusses at length only one Alabamian, William Lowndes Yancey of Montgomery,[1] seen by most modern historians as the leader of Alabama secessionists.[2] Yancey had an ancestral connection to South Carolina, long the hot spot for anti-federal government and pro-secession sentiment in the antebellum South. He was, in addition, a member of the south Alabama Black Belt's elite, which voted overwhelmingly for immediate secession in December 1860. Along the way, Yancey cultivated a cadre of relatively young newspaper editors who portrayed him as a natural successor to the Southern Rights icon John Caldwell Calhoun of South Carolina and ultimately as a leader of the fight for those rights relating to the institution of slavery. With Yancey's flair for public speaking—he was a classic silver-tongued orator—and staging dramatic publicity stunts, he provided those editors with good copy on a regular basis.[3] He has since been pure catnip for historians of this period.

The reality is, however, that Yancey was not even the most extreme or consistent fire-eater in south Alabama. That designation would have to go to George Washington Gayle, a South Carolina native and Cahaba lawyer.[4] Like Gayle, Yancey's efforts were focused on the area of the state where the slave-to-white ratios were the highest, where former South Carolinians were concentrated, and thus where the seeds he sowed for secession were most likely to take root and bear fruit as sectional tensions over slavery increased in the 1850s.

David Hubbard had none of those traits, advantages, or disadvantages, and, in fact, had every reason to fit the stereotype we have long had of the north Alabama Unionist. He was born in relatively moderate Virginia, not in South Carolina or anywhere else in the Deep South. He fought under the quintessential Southern Unionist, Andrew Jackson, and settled in generally pro-Union north Alabama where Jacksonian Democracy was always strongest. Hubbard was colorful, but not a polished public speaker. An early populist, he portrayed himself as a man of the people and, although he repeatedly achieved (and lost) wealth, he eschewed aristocratic airs. As a consequence, he was in and out of favor with economic elites in Alabama. Hubbard became radicalized long before Yancey did. In fact, there is reason to believe that after Yancey went through a period in which he was a staunch Unionist and a vocal and passionate critic of Calhoun he took some of Hubbard's ideas and rhetoric regarding Southern Rights and, without attribution, made them his own. Despite Hubbard's overt Southern nationalism in a region known for its strong attachment to the Union, he had a much more successful and extensive political career than Yancey.

David Hubbard's story allows us to study the lengthy radicalization process in Alabama from a totally different perspective than before: north rather than south Alabama. It also challenges many assumptions about the secession movement in Alabama. For example, although that movement has traditionally been portrayed as driven by radicalized younger men like Yancey, C. C. Clay, Leroy Pope Walker, and J. L. M. Curry, and opposed by the more conservative older generation, David Hubbard was sixty-eight years old in 1860.[5] In addition, although north Alabama has long been presumed to have been a bastion of Unionism, it was not beyond making threats of disunion to intimidate the North and thereby achieve political goals. Most north Alabamians, for example, voted for Southern Rights Democrat John Breckinridge instead of National Democrat Stephen A. Douglas or Constitutional Unionist John Bell in the 1860 presidential election, thereby unwittingly helping fracture the anti-Lincoln vote nationwide.[6] What or who caused this? In this regard, it is noteworthy that David Hubbard was one of the two statewide electors for Breckinridge.[7]

Since then, Hubbard has been, with a few exceptions, lost to history. Unlike his younger counterparts, he has somewhat surprisingly never been the subject of a biography. This book is intended to correct that and to analyze the life and times of David Hubbard, an important but largely forgotten Alabamian.

THE SOUTH'S
FORGOTTEN FIRE-EATER

1

Yankee Doodle

David Hubbard's genealogy is that of a classic Unionist. His father, Thomas Mortimer Hubbard, was born in Virginia in 1754 and fought in a variety of military units in the Revolutionary War, rising to the rank of major.[1] In 1785 Thomas Hubbard married Mary Blakely Swann, another Virginian, and sired ten children. David Hubbard, the fifth child, was born in Bedford County, Virginia (not Tennessee, as some have written), on February 19, 1792.[2]

Hubbard's early childhood coincided with frightening events occurring in a French slave colony on the Caribbean island of St. Domingue in the 1790s. There a large-scale slave insurrection resulted in the massacre of every white man, woman, and child who did not flee the island.[3] It was the sum of all fears for Southerners in slave states like Virginia where slave-to-white ratios were high.[4] In 1800, 135 miles east of the Hubbards' home, Henrico County, Virginia, slaves reputed to have been inspired by the St. Domingue revolt plotted an insurrection there that was intended to accomplish the same bloody result. The execution of the plot was foiled when some other slaves reported it to their masters and the members of the conspiracy were apprehended and hanged,[5] but rumors of other nightmarish insurrection conspiracies swept Virginia for the next several years.[6]

At the same time, the soil in Virginia was becoming increasingly exhausted as a result of the destructive nature of contemporary agricultural methods. Land farther west was not only relatively virgin but temporarily free of large slave populations.[7] In 1803 President Thomas Jefferson concluded the Louisiana Purchase, thereby assuring that those lands connected by water to the Mississippi River had the ability to use New Orleans as an international port for export of staple crops like corn, wheat, sugar cane, and, increasingly, cotton.[8] The price being paid for cotton at New Orleans was on the rise, meaning those who had fertile land and an adequate labor supply could materially improve their economic situation.[9] Predictably, the westward stream of emigrants from Virginia that had begun before the Revolutionary War became a flood.[10]

In 1804 Thomas Hubbard moved his family west to Rutherford County in fertile Middle Tennessee.[11] The following year, he acquired a one hundred-acre parcel of land described as being "on both sides of the west fork of Stone's River," south of present-day Murfreesboro.[12] The Hubbards were not subsistence farmers. Locating on Stone's River, which emptied into the Cumberland River and ultimately the Mississippi by way of the Ohio, allowed the shipment of agricultural products to New Orleans and beyond.[13] To cultivate those products, the Hubbards used slave labor. The 1810 federal census reflects that Thomas Hubbard owned eight slaves.[14]

Rutherford County had been formed in 1803 and was still a frontier region.[15] In addition to the normal challenges of antebellum life was the threat of bloody reprisals by Native Americans bitter over white settlement on their ancestral lands and years of exploitation.[16] Anecdotal evidence supported the common assumption among the settlers and some political leaders that these attacks were encouraged by foreign powers such as the British and the Spanish.[17] All too often, pleas for federal assistance to deal with these threats went unheeded. As a consequence, white settlers realized that they would have to band together and fend for themselves. This encouraged an important degree of animosity toward, and independence from, the national government.[18]

After the United States declared war against Great Britain in June 1812, Tennessee called for volunteers from among its militia, and Rutherford County residents led by another Virginia native, forty-year-old John Coffee, mobilized to meet the threat presented by the British and their Native American allies.[19] Coffee was appointed by future president Andrew Jackson to command his cavalry regiment.[20] Twenty-year-old David Hubbard, along with two of his brothers, Thomas Hubbard Jr. and Green Kirk Hubbard, were among numerous local young men who enlisted in Coffee's unit of "mounted gunmen." They donned uniforms of blue homespun and went off to war in December 1812.

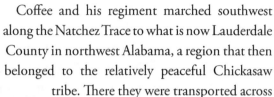

Coffee and his regiment marched southwest along the Natchez Trace to what is now Lauderdale County in northwest Alabama, a region that then belonged to the relatively peaceful Chickasaw tribe. There they were transported across the Tennessee River on the Colbert Ferry operated by a Chickasaw chief, George Colbert,[21] and arrived at Natchez in February 1813. As in many military campaigns, however, it was a matter of hurry-up-and-wait. Over a month later, they were ordered by the ostensibly feckless federal government to return to their Tennessee homes. Jackson then turned his exasperated army around, and they trudged back up the Natchez Trace, arriving in Tennessee in April.[22]

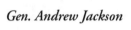

Gen. Andrew Jackson

Although David Hubbard did not yet have any tales of battlefield heroics about which to brag to the home folks, the ordeal was not a total waste. It was actually a seminal event in his life. For one thing he had experienced military life under the leadership of Andrew Jackson, now nicknamed "Old Hickory." He had also seen the natural beauty of what became northwest Alabama, later called by one of the men the "garden of America."[23] Just as important, he was exposed to the seemingly arbitrary nature of the federal government, which had always been considered far too slow in providing military protection to families on the frontier.[24]

Hubbard found real military adventure in just a few short months, however, after a militant faction of the Creek tribe attacked a frontier settlement in what is now Baldwin County, Alabama, on August 30, 1813, and committed what is called the Fort Mims Massacre.[25] This incident

John Coffee

aroused outrage among whites in Tennessee and throughout the southeast who used it, as well as earlier attacks, as a reason for what was in essence a war of extermination and for reparations in the form of vast cessions of land in what is now south Alabama.[26] A public meeting in Nashville called for a force "to be marched to the Creek Nation, that would be sufficient to give immediate check to their ravages; exterminate their Nation and abettors; and save thousands of the unoffending women and children on our frontier."[27] John Coffee issued another call for men to leave their homes and go south to engage in this social gardening on a vast scale.[28] Coffee's regiment, which also included David Hubbard and the then little-known David Crockett, proceeded south to the panic-stricken Madison County, Alabama, town of Huntsville.[29] They then marched ten miles south of Huntsville to the Tennessee River, where they crossed on a ferry at Ditto's Landing and established a defensive position.[30] There they awaited a rumored attack of a large Creek war party that never came. General Jackson subsequently arrived and ordered Coffee to attack a Creek town near present-day Tuscaloosa known as Black Warrior's Town. Residents from there had killed settlers in Tennessee in 1812 and kidnapped a woman, and the Tennesseans were bent on revenge.[31] Following Jackson's directions, Coffee and his brigade returned to the north side of the river and marched west to present-day Limestone County and there forded the river to what was known as Melton's Bluff in present-day Lawrence County.[32]

Melton's Bluff was situated at the beginning of approximately thirty-seven miles of a formidable and oftentimes deadly gauntlet of shoals that created falls and rapids composing what was called the Muscle Shoals. Except following the spring rains, it was an obstacle that significantly inhibited westward commercial river traffic on the Tennessee River in that area during much of the year.[33] But this was a time of the year in which the water was so shallow that David Hubbard and Coffee's other men were able to ride and walk across the river bottom without getting wet.[34] It was then that Hubbard saw Lawrence County for the first time. An early travel journalist, Anne Newport Royall, was later struck by the beauty of the region. "To compare it with the Elysian Fields of the ancients, would give but a feeble idea of it. The diminutive vale of Tempe and their thousand sylvan shades,

Battle of Horseshoe Bend

vanish into nothing, compared with this."[35] According to a contemporary of David Hubbard, it was a scene that caused every soldier's heart to glow "with admiration and covetousness."[36]

But for now they had a bloody job to do. They proceeded south, found that Black Warrior's Town had been evacuated, and burned it.[37] Coffee's brigade then marched east across central Alabama and joined Andrew Jackson's army near what is now Gadsden.[38] Then the war of extermination began in earnest. The bloody, climactic battle occurred on March 27, 1814, at Tohopeka or "Horseshoe Bend" in what is now Tallapoosa County.[39] There almost a thousand Creeks were killed, effectively ending the Creek War. This did not, however, end the threat presented by the British.[40]

As Jackson's army marched back to Huntsville and then Tennessee, England and Spain were rumored to be attempting to inspire and sponsor more attacks by the remaining Creeks, as well as an uprising by Southern slaves.[41] It was at this point that Jackson sought to clear the region of Creeks—both hostile *and* friendly—by way of the Treaty of Fort Jackson. This fateful treaty, which was coerced on August 9, 1814, included a "cession" or transfer by the Creeks to the federal government of millions of acres of land comprising

approximately 60 percent of what is now Alabama.[42] It was a land speculator's dream, but before anyone could take advantage, British and Spanish
influence in the region would have to be permanently suppressed.

While British forces were humiliating the United States by burning the
executive mansion and many other government buildings in Washington,
Andrew Jackson led his army toward Pensacola, which was then a Spanish
possession guarded by British troops and naval forces.[43] The federal government attempted to interfere, ordering Jackson not to attack Pensacola,
but as young David Hubbard observed, Jackson ignored this order and on
November 7, 1814, attacked and forced the surrender of that important
gulf town.[44] Jackson did eventually return the town to its Spanish governor,
but only because he had business elsewhere. It was on to Baton Rouge and
then New Orleans, which was bracing for an attack by British naval and
land forces.[45]

So far, David Hubbard had made it through the war unscathed. But
during a British assault near New Orleans on the night of December 23,
1814, he suffered a serious and painful leg wound when a musket ball frac-
tured his thigh. He was captured, along with several of Coffee's other men,
and was therefore not involved in the subsequent battles there, including
the famous final repulse of the British that occurred on Sunday, January
8, 1815.[46] The true details of Hubbard's experience as a prisoner of war
are unknown, but the lore is quite colorful. According to one tale, he was
placed in a makeshift hospital with British wounded where he played a joke
on his captors. When a British surgeon asked if anyone could play a violin
to distract a British patient who was to undergo an amputation, Hubbard
volunteered—but then began playing "Yankee Doodle." At this the surgeon
supposedly took the violin from Hubbard and broke it over his head.[47]
Another story had Hubbard confronting an arrogant British officer who
had declared that "Gen. Jackson would save the effusion of much valuable
blood by surrendering the City of New Orleans, for we have Lord [Edward
Michael] Packenham, Lord [John] Keen and Gen. [John] Lambert, and
fourteen thousand British regulars, and are certain to beat him." To this
Hubbard supposedly replied that "our cause is just, and we have Lord God
Almighty, Lord Jesus Christ and Gen. Jackson—and to a certainty we'll

Battle of New Orleans

whip you."[48] According to another account, when the British made their attack on Jackson's breastworks "the heart of young Hubbard sank within him. His deep anxiety during the battle was unrelieved until the wreck of the British army fell back on the camp." At that point, "the spirits of young Hubbard then reacted so powerfully that he flapped his wings and crowed." This infuriated one of the British guards, who "assaulted [Hubbard] with the bayonet, but his officer arrested the movement and protected [Hubbard]."[49]

The British began their final retreat from Louisiana on January 18 but did not immediately release Hubbard. Instead he was taken aboard a British ship that was part of a fleet destined to attack an outer fort protecting Mobile Bay.[50] That fort surrendered on February 12, but, fortunately for Hubbard and Mobile, the British then received word that the war was over by virtue of the Treaty of Ghent.[51] Hubbard was released and might have returned to New Orleans where Andrew Jackson's army was still stationed. According to some accounts, Jackson promoted the then-convalescing Hubbard from the rank of sergeant to major and assigned him the task of serving as quartermaster.[52] On March 15, Jackson and his men began the long trip back to Tennessee by way of the Natchez Trace, allowing Hubbard another long look at the lands held by the Chickasaws in north Mississippi and northwest Alabama. They finally arrived home for good in April 1815, where they were discharged and feted as returning heroes.[53]

Jackson's victory at New Orleans was celebrated throughout the young nation, but it was actually a victory for sectionalism rather than nationalism. New Orleans was essential for the economies of the emerging western states and territories, not those original states along the Eastern Seaboard. In addition, Jackson's efforts to clear out the Creeks proved to be a detriment to the east, which soon witnessed a land rush of their citizens to the newly available Creek lands.[54]

Perhaps of even more significance was the example set by Jackson when he disobeyed a direct order by attacking and taking Spanish Pensacola. Federal officials were concerned that such hostility would provoke a war with Spain, then still a military power, but to Jackson, regional security trumped national interests. Spain, Jackson knew, had supplied ammunition to the Creeks and had gotten the punishment it deserved as far as he was concerned. What would happen in the future when regional interests conflicted with those of the nation? The answer to that question came very quickly when the federal government demanded adherence to a provision of the Treaty of Ghent requiring the Creek lands ceded by the Treaty of Fort Jackson to be returned. Jackson was among many on the frontier who denounced that requirement, and as a result, the administration of President James Madison backed down.[55]

It would not be the last time the federal government was cowed by Southern intransigence. However, of greatest significance is that Jackson, today perceived as the ultimate nationalist, had taught David Hubbard and everyone in the region how to deal with that distant government relating to matters of sectional importance, particularly those relating to internal security: defiantly.

2

'A Desperate Speculation'

One significant economic consequence of the War of 1812 was its effect on the demand for cotton. Before the war, cotton fabrics were imported from overseas, particularly the textile industries in Great Britain. That source of supply had been cut off during the war and was replaced by new domestic manufacturers in Massachusetts, Connecticut, New York, New Jersey, and Maryland, who increasingly looked to the South to supply quality raw cotton. This demand, in turn, led to an increase in emigration from the original states to new lands opening farther west where cotton could be grown.[1] When the war ended and the manufacturers in Britain reentered their former markets in the United States and Europe, the demand for cotton products increased, as did the international price of cotton, which spiked upward to twenty-seven cents a pound.[2] This significantly increased demand for land, slaves, and credit, the unholy trinity essential to the efficient and profitable production of cotton.[3]

Becoming rich or richer was the goal. A Virginia newspaper reported that an acre of fertile land could be expected to produce a thousand pounds of cotton on an annual basis.[4] Thus, if a farmer could purchase five hundred acres of this land, *and* cotton prices remained this high, *and* he could ship it to New Orleans, he could expect to gross the princely sum of $135,000 a year. Word of this seductive opportunity quickly spread throughout the nation, encouraging settlers with dreams of wealth to flood into the region, squat on the formerly Native American lands, and await the public auction sales that would take place at Huntsville and other points.[5]

Some in the east attempted to warn everyone that the promise of great wealth in Alabama was all an illusion. According to a North Carolina editor, this "Alabama Fever" was simply a "desperate speculation," and a prescient Virginia editor wrote that "we must lay down for a rule, that where this spirit of speculation rages, some persons are to be benefitted and others are to be bit."[6] Few heeded these warnings. Among those who concocted the fever were several members of the Hubbard family, including David Hubbard.[7]

In addition to cashing in on the cotton boom, David Hubbard aspired to become a lawyer, despite having received only a minimal education. He moved to Huntsville, which had attracted a large number of lawyers from other states, one of whom he probably studied under.[8] However, he did not study very hard. Years later he wrote a young college student that becoming a lawyer "*will* certainly give you more influence in society than any other pursuit," but cautioned that "to become eminent, you must study well and thoroughly before you begin practice." Hubbard warned that "it is an *up hill* business unprepared as did your humble servant."[9]

There were any number of distractions that might have caused young Hubbard to lose focus on his study of the law. There was seemingly more and quicker money in land speculation as the Chickasaws and Cherokees in northwest Alabama were persuaded to make treaties in 1816 to cede most of their lands to the federal government.[10] As one of Andrew Jackson's friends wrote, "Such a field for the acquirement of wealth I have never before witnessed." Speculation in Alabama land, he continued, "is superior to Law and Physick" [medicine] in that regard.[11]

David Hubbard's former commanding officer, John Coffee, was appointed by President Monroe to serve as the chief surveyor for the new public lands in the northern portion of what officially became the Alabama Territory.[12] This position gave Coffee and those working under him the opportunity to determine where the best lands were located so that they could make intelligent purchases at the upcoming public auction sales.[13] The lucrative possibilities inherent in this arrangement obviously interested then twenty-four-year-old David Hubbard. Despite having recently been determined by federal pension authorities to have a 50 percent disability to his body as a result of the wound he suffered during the war, Hubbard wrote Coffee on March 27, 1816, seeking a position as a surveyor, a very physically demanding occupation. Hubbard wisely opened his letter by reminding Coffee of his active military service, stating that "since I have recovered from my wound I have been anxious to get into business where there appears to be a probability of my making a living."[14] This approach apparently worked. Hubbard and his eldest brother, Green Kirk Hubbard, both worked on the survey of what became Lawrence County.[15] It would not be the last time Hubbard successfully made use of his war wound for purposes of personal advancement.[16]

After completing the survey, and while awaiting the auction sales of Lawrence County land scheduled to take place in the summer and fall of 1818,[17] David Hubbard was called back into military service by Andrew Jackson in connection with what became known as the First Seminole War. Jackson appointed Hubbard his assistant inspector general, and off they went to swampy Spanish Florida in what became the most controversial campaign of Jackson's military career.[18] Jackson and his forces not only routed their foes but managed to cause international outrage by executing two British subjects suspected of encouraging violence by Native Americans, and by attacking and taking two Spanish military installations, including—once again—Pensacola. Jackson was later accused of exceeding his authority but, as far as Southerners were concerned, the promotion of their regional interests trumped national concerns.[19] It was another lesson learned for David Hubbard.[20]

In September 1818, Green Kirk Hubbard and David Hubbard separately purchased at auction several hundred acres located in the central portion of Lawrence County just southwest of present-day Moulton, a town named in honor of a young lieutenant killed at the Battle of Horseshoe Bend. Green Hubbard bought over 480 acres,[21] while David Hubbard purchased over 600, some of which might have been acquired for speculative purposes.[22] The price paid for land throughout Lawrence County was very high—from $40–$100 an acre—and was influenced in part by rumors that the Tennessee River along the county's northern border would somehow be opened for continuous, unimpeded navigation,[23] as well as the market price of cotton, which had risen to almost thirty cents a pound in 1817.[24] Farmers with dreams of becoming wealthy cotton planters had competed with land speculators to acquire the choicest cotton lands throughout north Alabama, and as a result the prices paid were far above their true market value.[25] That the purchasers could pay in installments also contributed to this growing bubble.[26] Under federal law, buyers were only required to make an up-front deposit of one-twentieth of their bid amount, which was credited on their first installment payment of one-fourth of the purchase price due forty days later. It was all a perfect storm of supply, demand, credit, and hubris that would have important political implications for decades.

Unknown to all, the price paid for cotton in 1817 was the highest in the antebellum period. In late 1818, *after* the Alabama sales had concluded, it suddenly dropped to twenty-one cents a pound.[27] David Hubbard and others who had budgeted for land costs based on expected revenues from thirty-cent-a-pound cotton were now faced with the impossible task of paying land costs, slave labor costs, and other expenses with a third less than that amount. Dreams of great wealth turned into a nightmare of extended duration. The result was widespread insolvency, a massive number of defaults in payment, very hard times, and economic misery.[28] For Native Americans in the South pressured to leave their ancestral lands in the first of two great diasporas, it must have been pure schadenfreude.

Fear rising from these and other problems made more acute an already existing degree of class conflict, as well as a pronounced anti-creditor bias.[29] Writing of the situation in Huntsville, Anne Royall referred to old-money families and observed that several men were "rich as princes, and are stigmatized, by a few of the vicious, by the appellation of nobility."[30] This important political dynamic was, perhaps unwittingly, empowered when the delegates to Alabama's constitutional convention—most of whom were economic elites and land speculators—met in Huntsville in the summer of 1819.[31] Unlike the voting laws in some older states, which placed political power in the hands of elites by granting the right to vote only to men who owned a certain minimum amount or value of property, the constitutional document adopted in Huntsville on August 2, 1819, made a very broad grant of suffrage rights. Every white man could vote who was at least twenty-one years old, had been a resident in Alabama for at least one year, and a resident of a county for at least three months.[32] Given that elites were in the minority in north Alabama, aspiring politicians would find it to be advantageous to pander to the desires and prejudices of the common man.[33] Thus, in Alabama the politics of egalitarianism and populism actually predated the coming Jacksonian Era.

So did the politics of slavery. This new constitution, which was not submitted to the people for approval, also fatefully authorized and protected the institution of slavery.[34] It was foreseen that this forced labor system, which was ominously being phased out in most of the northeastern states, would bring to Alabama the grave security concerns that had led to the St. Domingue slave revolt.[35] But for land speculators like David Hubbard who recognized that the availability of slave labor was essential to cotton production, which was of critical importance to maintaining inflated land values, the risk was worth it. And, given their debt loads, it was now unavoidable. We will never know whether the non-slaveowners of this period saw it that way.

David Hubbard returned to his legal studies in Huntsville and even worked as a carpenter in his spare time,[36] finally receiving his license to practice law in 1819 or 1820.[37] Huntsville was too crowded with lawyers, so Hubbard established his first law practice in Lauderdale County where John Coffee had also come to reside.[38] The content of his law practice is unknown, but given the times it probably included criminal defense work, representing debtors or creditors in debt collection actions, and any other activities that could earn additional income.

Welcome news from Washington came in 1821 when Congress adopted a bill that gave at least partial relief to those like Hubbard who were land poor as a result of purchases of public land. Those purchasers were allowed to "relinquish" or give back to the federal government any of the lands they had bought at public auction and to reapply the payments they had already made to any land they kept. Like many other Alabamians, Hubbard took advantage of the relief afforded by this law by relinquishing some parcels of his land,[39] but he also retained a considerable amount of acreage. With cotton prices dipping even further in 1822 to eleven cents a pound, however, this meant he would have to keep his nose to the grindstone in his law practice for many years to come in an increasingly competitive market to make the remaining installment payments and keep his other debts current.[40]

Adding to his financial pressures, Hubbard soon also had a family to support. He married Elizabeth Campbell, the daughter of the late Dr. Duncan Campbell of Kentucky, a native of Scotland, and the sister of a Lawrence County lawyer. She was also the niece of George Washington Campbell, a confidante of Andrew Jackson and John Coffee who had served as a U.S. Senator from Tennessee, the secretary of the treasury under President Madison, and ambassador to Russia.[41] In addition to this socially and politically advantageous marriage, Eliza bore Hubbard six children: Mary, Duncan, David Jr., Caledonia, Emma, and George.[42]

Whether Hubbard's marriage within a prominent family had anything to do with his subsequent successful entry into politics is unknown. In December 1823, after the price of cotton dropped again,[43] he was elected by the Alabama legislature to the position of solicitor (the predecessor to today's district attorney) of the Fourth Judicial District, which included Lawrence, Limestone, Franklin, and Lauderdale counties, among others.[44] In this position, Hubbard was responsible for prosecuting those accused of committing crimes and for bringing the guilty to justice.

James Edward Saunders, a contemporary political rival of David Hubbard who wrote an important early history of the region, recalled that there was a public bias against solicitors at the time of Hubbard's election. "There is no sympathy for [solicitors] either amongst the members of the Bar, or the spectators. He is an Ishmaelite indeed; for 'his hand is against every man, and every man's hand against him.'"[45] In many cases, convictions were difficult to obtain because juries were often willing to countenance acts of violence.[46] But Hubbard's service in this position also gave him important opportunities. Among the benefits of this to a young lawyer was that it afforded regular courtroom experience and the opportunity to hone one's ability to speak in public. As Saunders put it, Hubbard was "taught the science of 'thrust and parry' in mental gladiation."[47] Hubbard also had the opportunity to meet men in every county in his multi-county circuit and thereby develop a network of politically valuable contacts. Although the office came with only a small salary, he had the opportunity to earn some incentive fees for convictions.[48]

Whether Hubbard was generally successful in obtaining convictions is unknown, but he certainly made an impressive appearance to a jury. His only known portrait, painted in the early-to-mid-1820s, depicts him as quite handsome and fashionably dressed.[49] He was also tall, a symbol of authority, masculinity, and power. Hubbard was later known for having a

Muscle Shoals

mind "full of vigor and vitality" as well as "shrewdness and tact" that were "proverbial" in Lawrence County.[50] He was not, however, a silver-tongued orator, and he regularly faced off against older, more experienced lawyers who had moved to the area from other states.[51]

Throughout the period David Hubbard lived in Florence, the Muscle Shoals remained a nemesis to safe and reasonably priced commercial navigation of the Tennessee River, and therefore an albatross around the neck of the economies of counties to the east of Florence, like Lawrence.[52] Raising private capital in Alabama to execute any solution was still very difficult as a result of the continuing depression in cotton prices.[53] The few privately owned banks in Alabama would be of no help. When panic-induced runs occurred in Alabama in 1819, most had chosen to cease making specie payments. This had led to a groundswell of support for the state to establish a public bank under state control that would use the state's capital as a basis for making loans.[54] Some touted it as a "people's bank" that would make loans to the small farmer and be free of elite influence,[55] but another argument in favor of the scheme was that the bank could finance the construction of a canal around the Muscle Shoals. The Huntsville *Democrat*, one of the leaders of the public bank movement, called for this to be the first project undertaken. The "Muscle Shoals will remain, to future generations a monument of our *imbecility and folly* if we fail to make it one of strength and wisdom." Noting the ongoing construction of the Erie Canal in New York State, the editor asked his readers whether Alabama would merely "fold her arms and gaze in stupid astonishment, on this splendid achievement of a sister state, surely, surely not."[56]

But there was a significant practical impediment to establishing a new bank funded by money in the state treasury. As a result of the depression, the treasury then held only a little over $22,000 of unearmarked funds.[57] Despite this, the Alabama legislature went ahead and passed legislation in late 1823 establishing the State Bank. It was to be capitalized in part by funds earmarked for education and other purposes, as well as specie borrowed in northern capital markets.[58] However, it took a considerable amount of time to get the bank's operations underway, and even then loans were made for other purposes.[59]

The 1824 presidential election had presented another opportunity for navigational improvement. Andrew Jackson, who also bought land in Lawrence County and therefore had every reason to eliminate this navigational hazard, was a candidate and was strongly supported by most Alabamians, particularly those in north Alabama.[60] Anne Royall wrote from Moulton that the "settlers of this new country love him to idolatry."[61] Jackson ultimately received almost 70 percent of the vote in Alabama—over 75 percent in north Alabama.[62] For the vice presidency many were supporting Secretary of War John Caldwell Calhoun, a South Carolinian who was also backing federal intervention to overcome the Muscle Shoals.[63] Calhoun won his race, but Jackson was beaten by John Quincy Adams of Massachusetts. With the Alabama legislature having adopted resolutions endorsing Andrew Jackson for the next presidential election, it is not surprising that the Adams administration did not make the Muscle Shoals a priority.[64]

Meanwhile, the low price of cotton was joined by drought conditions that produced only short crops in 1826 and 1827, making the lives of all Alabamians even more miserable.[65] In 1827 Hubbard resigned his position as circuit solicitor and established a private law practice and a general store in Moulton.[66] One reason for this might have been the death earlier that year of the incumbent state senator from Lawrence County, Matthew Clay.[67] Hubbard, then thirty-five, ran for that seat and won it in the general election of August 1827.[68]

The Alabama legislature (called the "general assembly" during this period) had decided in 1825 to move the state capital from Cahaba in Black Belt Dallas County farther north to Tuscaloosa.[69] A twelve-foot-wide toll road known as Byler's Turnpike Road had been built through Lawrence County to Tuscaloosa, making Hubbard's journey there even less difficult than during his military service in the war.[70] However, if he assumed he would go to the capital and somehow be an agent of rapid economic change, he was to be disappointed. For starters, there was no state capitol building. In fact, the earlier legislatures had still not decided on a design or even on a location in Tuscaloosa to construct the building.[71] Similarly, although the 1820 legislature had decided to create a public university, it had not yet decided where in the state to locate that potential economic engine, much less provided the funds for its construction.[72] These were just a few of the many unresolved issues the legislature had pending when it convened on November 19, 1827.[73]

Hubbard was appointed to two special committees tasked to focus on economic issues. One was to consider means to extract the state from its financial "distress and embarrassment," and another was to focus on controversial efforts underway in Congress to increase the amount of tariffs on imported goods to protect American producers from foreign competition.[74] He was made chairman of the special committee on financial distress and reported that committee's approval of Governor John Murphy's recommendation for the state to borrow more specie for the State Bank so that additional loans could be made by it to the public. This, according to Hubbard's committee's report, would "prevent the sacrifice of property, and enable a large portion of our worthy and valuable citizens to save their property from ruin and families from distress."[75] A majority of the legislature agreed with this logic and adopted a law authorizing the issuance and sale of up to $100,000 of certificates of stock in the State Bank, but only if the purchasers agreed to accept a relatively low interest rate.[76]

With the state's capital tied up in the State Bank and focused on the relief of land debtors, there was little this legislature could do to address the Muscle Shoals problem but petition the federal government. Hubbard therefore proposed a memorial to Congress requesting that the federal government make a grant to the state of the land in north Alabama earlier relinquished by him and other purchasers.[77] His controversial idea was to have these lands resold, but not initially at public auction. Instead, those who had officially relinquished a parcel of land but then (illegally) remained on it would be given a "pre-emption right" or first right to purchase that land.[78]

Hubbard's support for pre-emption rights proved to be unpopular among some powerful elites in northwest Alabama,[79] but it did not affect Hubbard's growing personal popularity among common folks or others in the legislature. He was elected by his fellow legislators one of two men from the Fourth Judicial Circuit to the board of trustees of The University of Alabama, which during this session was finally located in Tuscaloosa. In fact, he received more votes than John Coffee, who was also a candidate.[80]

While Hubbard was focused on improving the economy of north Alabama, he was also attempting to lay the groundwork for future political support by currying favor with south Alabama elites. Among others, he supported the election of Dixon Hall Lewis, another Virginia native who had made his name in the Alabama House as a champion of Southern rights, to the university's board of trustees.[81] Lewis was an outspoken opponent of protective tariffs that arguably favored northern manufacturers and others while having a disparate negative impact on the South.[82] This legislature adopted a strongly worded remonstrance against tariff increases pending before Congress, condemning the protective concept as a "palpable usurpation of power not given by the constitution" and "a species of oppression little less than legalized pillage on the property of [Alabama's] citizens, to which she can never submit, until the constitutional means of resistance shall be exhausted."[83]

Whether David Hubbard approved all of this wording is unknown because the Senate Journal does not reflect the debates or the roll call votes on the resolution. There is no question, however, that he, like most struggling Alabamians, opposed high tariffs because they diminished competition and increased the price of the goods he and his constituents needed.[84] Some tariff opponents also supported the concept of political resistance to tariff increases within the constitutional framework. The question is where Hubbard stood on the use of *extra-constitutional* means of resistance. The answer to this question for all Alabamians would be revealed in the coming years.

After the legislature adjourned in January 1828, Hubbard began his return to Lawrence County mindful that he would have to run for reelection in August and that he might have opposition from those who disagreed with him over some of the positions he had taken. However, other events in Congress diverted the public's attention. After months of wrangling, Congress significantly increased duties on several imports in what became known as the "Tariff of Abominations," thereby sparking a storm of protest, particularly from increasingly militant South Carolina.[85]

Hubbard was also a political beneficiary of Congress's grant of four hundred thousand acres of the relinquished lands in northwest Alabama to the state on May 23, 1828, for the purpose of constructing the Muscle Shoals canal with the proceeds of their sale.[86] The law making this grant did not address the issue of whether the land should be sold at public auction as many north Alabama planters anxious to acquire adjoining lands preferred, or whether squatters living on the land would be allowed to avoid having to bid against their wealthier neighbors and instead be given pre-emption rights as most yeomen farmers desired.

This issue was tailor made for class conflict and demagoguery, and David Hubbard is said by James Saunders, his opponent in the race for a full term in the Alabama Senate, to have chosen to back the yeomen farmers.[87] Saunders was a highly educated lawyer-elitist who had graduated from Georgia College in 1825 and married into a very prominent planter's family.[88] As Saunders noted with obvious jealousy, Hubbard had sacrificed his own education to serve under Andrew Jackson in the War of 1812, during which he had earned a politically priceless war wound.[89] According to another contemporary, "when some kind-hearted voter would inquire why he limped," Hubbard would "indifferently" reply, "'Oh, nothing but that old wound I got at New Orleans.'"[90] But Hubbard was hardly a plain farmer. As Saunders wrote, Hubbard then "had law, merchandise [referring to Hubbard's store], and politics, all in full blast, at the same time."[91] Hubbard was also a planter and during the legislative session had promoted nothing that would be of any particular interest to the less well off with the exception of pre-emption rights.

That was apparently enough. According to Saunders, Hubbard chose to alienate the planter elites and promote a populist—if not agrarian—program with regard to the method of disposition of the land grant. Saunders wrote that Hubbard "assumed the ground that poor men, who had no land, ought to have pre-emption of these lands, divided into small tracts, and at a cash valuation; and that, where more than one person applied for the same tract, it should be drawn for." Hubbard's stated rationale, Saunders continued, was based on the "trials and hardships of the poor man." Hubbard, he wrote, maintained that the land that the poor had been able to acquire was "'like skimmed milk, for it would not fatten,'" and voiced his desire that "these hard-working men . . . have a chance for a small tract of rich land." All of Hubbard's speeches, Saunders concluded with disdain, "were models of that kind."[92] Hubbard was the original little man's big friend. One critic accused him of being a "mobocrat in principle" who was "incessantly railing against what he called the aristocracy of the country."[93]

Hubbard's decision to advocate a populist position affected him politically for better and for worse for the rest of his political career. For now, however, his strategy worked like a charm. As Saunders later wrote, Hubbard was unbeatable and was "triumphantly elected over him." Saunders was certain that even if "George Washington had been alive, and [Hubbard's] competitor, he [Washington] would have been disgracefully beaten as the advocate of the rights of the planters."[94] One can certainly understand Saunders's desire to save face. He did not reveal in his memoir that Hubbard trounced him 1098 to 233.[95]

Between Hubbard's reelection and the meeting of the Alabama legislature, Andrew Jackson succeeded in his run for the presidency. One reason Southerners loved him was his military prowess against Native Americans, the British, and the Spanish, which inured to the benefit of the South. Another was that he was not a political "trimmer"—one who would set his principles and their interests aside to advance his political career.[96] During the campaign, however, Jackson had taken no public position on the increased tariff.[97] His running mate, John C. Calhoun of South Carolina, was also uncharacteristically mum, but had secretly proposed a procedure to avoid tariff duties that became infamously known as "nullification." He instructed a committee of the South Carolina legislature that the enforcement of this or any other allegedly unconstitutional law could be "nullified" by a specially convened state convention, which would be followed by a convention of all the states. If that national convention approved the law by at least a three-fourths vote, each state then had the choice of submission or secession.[98] Support for this concept in South Carolina, although not the identity of its author, became public shortly before the election but too late to affect its outcome.[99] Afterwards, the South Carolina legislature met to consider its plan, and a special committee subsequently reported what was titled the "South Carolina Exposition and Protest" that advocated the nullification doctrine.[100]

The reaction of the Alabama legislature and Governor Murphy can be discerned from the mode of dress of some when it convened on November 17, 1828. According to the Tuscaloosa *Chronicle*, Murphy and "a number of the members of the Legislature had evidenced a practical opposition to the present Tariff by appearing in full suits of Homespun."[101] Murphy's message to the legislators was very critical of the tariff but did not flatly declare that it was unconstitutional. Instead, he encouraged Alabamians to "commence manufacturing ourselves" using slaves and "needy and in-

John C. Calhoun

digent persons" as laborers. At the same time, he recommended that the legislature call for relief from the tariff by adopting a "free but temperate" memorial to Congress. Murphy was certain that Alabama could count on the effectiveness of the "ordinary means of redress under the constitution," and he opposed anything that might "disturb the harmony of the Union."[102]

Given the state's continuing capital shortage, this was prudent advice. Conventional wisdom throughout the antebellum period and beyond likened capital to a skittish animal. Potential political upheaval in the South undermined its ability to attract capital from its primary source: northern money markets.[103] Alabama had already been unsuccessful in its effort to borrow more specie at a reasonable interest rate to inject new capital into the State Bank.[104] Any threat to secede, even if only intended as a bluff to extort tariff revision, would make this problem even more insoluble. Moreover, there was a common belief that tariff reform would follow Andrew Jackson's inauguration.[105] As a consequence, that issue was placed on a back burner by Alabama legislators while efforts were made to address other pressing matters.

One major issue was the procedure by which the land grant for the Tennessee River canal would be sold and how the proceeds of that sale would be used. This question, according to James Saunders, was the "prominent one of the session" and for it, he continued, the "Communists mustered in force."[106] Governor Murphy sided with David Hubbard and others who were opposed to selling the land at public auction to the highest bidder. He also favored the idea of giving a right of pre-emption to squatters currently residing on the land to purchase that land at values assessed by commissioners selected to make appraisals.[107] Hubbard was appointed chairman of a special committee of the senate tasked with assessing the governor's program and preparing legislation[108] and, after some wrangling, a bill giving pre-emption rights was unanimously adopted by the senate and sent to the house for its consideration.[109]

Clement Clay of Huntsville, a member of the lawyer-planter elite who opposed the bill, had been selected speaker of the house. He was therefore theoretically in a position to impede the bill's progress and force amendments as a condition of its adoption.[110] According to one of Clay's critics, Clay "used his best exertions to screw out of us, the last cent our partialities, necessities, or fancies [for land he] could wring from us."[111]

While the house debated the senate's land sale bill, David Hubbard was engaged in another very controversial populist measure relating to the Alabama Supreme Court. That court had ruled in favor of creditors in connection with efforts by debtors to recover interest they had paid on loans made at ruinous interest rates during the boom period before the Panic of 1819. Outrage over this ruling had fueled efforts to amend the Alabama constitution to limit the terms of judges to six years—as opposed to their lifetimes—and to impeach certain members of the court for alleged corruption. While William Kelly of north Alabama pushed for impeachment, Hubbard was the floor leader in the senate for the constitutional amendment.[112] He and all but one of the other senators voted to concur with amendments made by the house to a joint resolution calling for a public referendum on a constitutional amendment to this effect.[113] This might have effectively mooted the issues raised in the impeachment trial of the judges, but that trial was allowed to play itself out. David Hubbard ultimately voted with a majority of the other senators who agreed that the charges against the judges were "not sufficiently sustained by proof."[114] However, when one of the senators offered a resolution that these judges were "entitled to the unimpaired confidence of the community," Hubbard joined the majority in its defeat.[115]

The matter of the tariff finally resurfaced on January 27, 1829, just two days before the legislature was scheduled to adjourn.[116] A special committee of the senate chaired by a south Alabama senator submitted a joint resolution declaring the tariff impolitic, unjust, without constitutional authority, and "too well calculated to disturb the harmony of the union." The proposed resolution did not adopt the nullification remedy, but it did not expressly rule it out or condemn armed resistance to the tariff's enforcement either. Instead it maintained the "legitimate mode of opposition becoming the dignity of a sovereign state is by respectful remonstrance, and that *open and unqualified resistance should only be the dernier resort*."[117] Evidencing that David Hubbard was not totally radicalized against the federal government at this point, he voted for an amendment eliminating the clause regarding "unqualified" resistance. Without his vote that amendment would have been defeated. Interestingly, when another amendment was proposed seeking to table the resolution until the next session of the legislature, Hubbard joined a minority of senators in its support.[118] After the anti-tariff resolution was adopted as amended, it was sent to the house for concurrence. That body voted to add back the deleted language regarding unqualified resistance and the senate concurred on a voice vote.[119] Hubbard's vote is not identified in the senate's journal.

This legislative session lasted eighty-one days, primarily because of the debate over the land grant.[120] Despite criticism from the Huntsville press and Clement Clay's opposition, David Hubbard had succeeded in fulfilling his campaign promise by bringing home the land grant sale bill.[121] Those then illegally occupying and farming a parcel of relinquished land would not have to outbid others to acquire ownership of that land. Moreover, the appraised price they would be required to pay was closer to their reach and would be set by at least some men they knew, not all outsiders.[122] It was a boon for the less well off, but not necessarily for those interested in the construction of the Muscle Shoals canal. The question whether the gross proceeds of the sale would be adequate to fully fund that project remained open.

It is likely that David Hubbard recognized the real possibility that he would be blamed if the canal project failed because of inadequate funding. He could not afford the political fallout, for he intended to make a run for the United States Senate in 1830. This may explain his involvement in the commercial activities for which he has heretofore been best known by most historians.[123] Furthermore, given his later stance on sectional issues, it was very ironic that at this point Hubbard looked to the North for a potential solution to this conundrum.

3

'His Magic Influence'

For the past few years the national press had been full of reports about the construction and operation of a railroad of sorts in eastern Pennsylvania being used to transport coal from a coal mine to a nearby river for shipment to Philadelphia. Specifically, the Mauch Chunk Railroad ran approximately 8.5 miles from the mine atop Summit Hill down to Mauch Chunk, Pennsylvania, which was situated on the Lehigh River. The cost of construction had been only $5,000 a mile, far less than the cost of canal construction. It used gravity for the iron cars on iron wheels to travel down Summit Hill, and a special braking system operated by a single employee to govern the speed and to stop. Once the tons of coal carried in the cars were off-loaded at the river, mules or horses pulled the empty cars back up the hill for reloading. The cars did not roll on iron or steel rails, but instead used wooden rails inserted in oak sleepers laying in a bed of rocks. An iron plate was nailed to the upper surface and inner edges of the wooden rails.[1]

Ever since the road opened in 1827, thousands of tourists had flocked there to see this new wonder, many to examine how it worked and gauge its viability for their own locale and others simply out of curiosity. Local lore has it that David Hubbard began a trek from Florence to Pennsylvania,[2] where he examined this relatively new innovation to determine whether it might be effective in hauling cotton in Alabama. By all accounts, Hubbard concluded that it would, and he returned to Alabama with a plan of building America's first railroad west of the Allegheny Mountains between Tuscumbia and Decatur to circumvent the Muscle Shoals.[3] The key would be convincing local men of means to contribute toward the cost of constructing the road and purchasing the necessary equipment. This would not be easy given Hubbard's earlier rhetorical assaults on the aristocracy, as well as the novelty of the technology, the continuing depression in the cotton market (cotton sold at less than nine cents a pound in 1829), and the belief that the construction of the Muscle Shoals canal might render the road obsolete in just a few years.[4]

The latter problem would soon be eliminated, however, at least in the minds of many canal promoters. Appraisals of the federal land grant found that their value was only $500,000, considerably less than the expected two-million-dollar construction costs. This set off a major political firestorm, with those who had favored auction sales instead of pre-emption rights to maximize the sales proceeds and fully fund canal construction alleging corruption in the legislature.[5] The Huntsville *Democrat* was certain there was "something rotten in Denmark." Without naming Hubbard, the *Democrat* denounced the land law as the work of "a few artful, designing, electioneering politicians—we had almost said, *demagogues.*"[6]

With the completion of the canal now doubtful, the need for a railroad was slowly becoming more apparent. By this point, Hubbard had somehow convinced one very wealthy and influential local planter, Benjamin Sherrod, that it was worth a try, at least on a limited, experimental scale.[7] Their plan was initially to construct and operate a railroad from Tuscumbia 2.1 miles north to the Tennessee River at present-day Sheffield to demonstrate that the technology was feasible and the cost of construction reasonable. They hoped this would interest potential investors in the longer road from Tuscumbia to Decatur.[8] In support of the longer road Hubbard requested United States Senator John McKinley of Florence to make arrangements to have federal engineers conduct a survey to locate the best route. McKinley, who supported construction of the canal, did not accomplish this, a failure Hubbard would not forget.[9]

In November, Hubbard was off to Tuscaloosa to, among other

John McKinley

things, obtain passage of a law granting a corporate charter for what would be called the Tuscumbia Railway Company. That would be difficult given the continuing animosity of elites toward Hubbard regarding his land bill. He circumvented this by using surrogates as floor leaders in the senate and the house. His railroad bill was adopted by the senate, approved in the house,[10] and signed into law by recently elected Governor Gabriel Moore on January 18, 1830.[11]

Related to this victory were the results of the election by the legislature of officers and directors of the State Bank, a potential source of loans for the construction and equipment of the road. Dr. John Lewis Tindall of Tuscaloosa was reelected president of the bank with Hubbard's support. Three other men backed by Hubbard were elected to the bank's board of directors.[12]

This legislative session also saw the fruition of Hubbard's efforts to strip the state's supreme court judges of lifetime tenure in office. With a majority of voters in Lawrence County and elsewhere voting in favor of a constitutional amendment, and this legislature ratifying that vote, the Alabama Constitution was amended for the first time, limiting judicial tenure to six years.[13] That is still the limit today.

Months later, another step was taken toward transforming the dream of a railroad in north Alabama to a reality when the stockholders of the Tuscumbia Railway Company met to elect directors and officers of the new corporation. Twelve prominent local men were elected to the board, including a Pennsylvania-born civil engineer, David Deshler.[14] Hubbard continued to remain in the background and was not selected as an officer or director. While Deshler began surveying to identify the best route to locate that road, Hubbard already had his mind on the future. Most immediate was the challenge of financing construction of the much longer road east to Decatur.

One possibility was to seek a loan from the State Bank, which had finally succeeded in obtaining the long-sought specie loan of $100,000 in New York.[15] Another involved Chickasaw land in north Mississippi. Most saw it as only a matter of time before they were "treatied" out of it, especially after Congress adopted the Indian Removal Act of 1830.[16] Then those lands could potentially be purchased by the railroad's investors and sold at a profit to raise funds for railroad construction.

But objections were being raised by some in Congress to any further land sales until all land that had already been surveyed and put up for sale was sold. If this policy were adopted, purchasing Chickasaw land in Mississippi would not be possible for years. But neither of Alabama's senators, north Alabamian John McKinley and William Rufus King of south Alabama, expressly condemned it. On the contrary, over the objection of several Southern senators, McKinley sought to have the issue referred to the Public Lands Committee, of which he was a member, rather than voting to kill it outright.[17]

It was not long after this that word of a possible challenge to the aristocratic McKinley began to spread across the Tennessee Valley. McKinley would be before the 1830–1831 Alabama legislature seeking reelection (at this time United States senators were elected by state legislatures), but the Huntsville *Democrat*, which was one of his most vocal supporters, expressed disbelief that anyone would have the temerity to challenge him.[18] At least initially the identity of McKinley's challenger remained a mystery, but the fact that the *Courtland Herald* was attacking McKinley should have been a clue.[19] The *Herald* ended any suspense when it reported the endorsement of thirty-eight-year-old David Hubbard for McKinley's seat. The *Democrat's* editor ridiculed Hubbard's candidacy and called him a lightweight. "Mr. Hubbard is kicking at the moon, if he really intends to oppose Mr. McKinley." If Hubbard expected to be elected, he taunted, "it must be upon the ground of superior talent; but from what we know of him, he has too much common sense, to wish an enquiry to be instituted on that ground." The editor even dismissed Hubbard's military service as a relevant factor, asserting that Hubbard had already gotten his seat in the state senate as recompense and deserved nothing further on that account.[20]

Despite this, McKinley, who was then fifty years old, was vulnerable to the right candidate. Before moving to Alabama from Kentucky, he had been a Federalist, the now discredited political party that had opposed the United States' decision to go to war with Great Britain in 1812. He had also chosen not to fight in that war, and after coming to Alabama had lived the life of an elite and a lawyer representing creditors.[21] But he had subsequently reinvented himself from a political standpoint, and his support for

Andrew Jackson had led to success as a politician and his election to the United States Senate in 1826.[22]

Hubbard might have expected that President Jackson would endorse his candidacy. After all, Hubbard had served under Jackson in the war, had been wounded in the process, and had certainly never been a Federalist. One of Hubbard's Moulton supporters charged that while Hubbard was in the war, "McKinley was 'kicking at the moon' in Kentucky trying to get the people to oppose our struggling government; and on one public occasion, he drank [to] King George, Bonaparte, and Thomas Jefferson!!"[23] Hubbard had also been a consistent supporter of Jackson in his quest for the presidency and had not publicly criticized Jackson for his failure to seek tariff reform up to this point. By contrast, McKinley had not only broken with all except one Southern senator to vote for a controversial bill that President Jackson vetoed—to expend federal funds to build a road between Lexington, Kentucky, and Maysville, Kentucky, on the Ohio River—but had also voted with supporters of Jackson rival Henry Clay in an unsuccessful effort to override Jackson's subsequent veto of a similar bill regarding a road in Maryland.[24] Certainly Jackson would not countenance such disloyalty, or so Hubbard might have reasonably assumed.

After McKinley made a speech in defense of his record on July 5 in Florence, Hubbard went on the attack in a controversial speech at Tuscumbia.[25] He denounced McKinley as a Federalist and an elitist, an opponent of pre-emption rights for the common man, an instigator of the assault on the system of land sales adopted during the last Alabama legislative session, an opponent of federal efforts to remove Native Americans to the west, a supporter of terminating public land sales, and of Henry Clay's "American System" of protective tariffs and federally funded internal improvements, and an enemy of President Jackson.[26] However, for some reason, Jackson stuck with McKinley. Hubbard would not forget this, especially after he was left swinging in the wind and subjected to fierce editorial assaults by the Huntsville *Democrat* and other pro-Jackson newspapers supporting McKinley.

Therefore, as the legislative session approached, Hubbard convinced Governor Gabriel Moore to enter the race in his stead.[27] Moore, then forty-five years old, was a more formidable candidate, having been elected governor without opposition in 1829.[28] He also did not necessarily mind crossing Jackson over the Senate seat, especially after Jackson failed to appoint Moore's nephew federal marshal of north Alabama.[29] Jackson was convinced that the nullification movement was behind the challenge to McKinley, and that Governor Moore had defected to that cause.[30] Most historians have accepted this interpretation without question.[31] They cite no supporting authority, however, and a careful review of the available evidence does not reveal any convincing support for it. Instead, contemporary observers blamed the result of the race on Hubbard, thereby cementing his growing renown as one of Alabama's formidable politicians.

The Alabama legislature convened in the still-unfinished capitol in Tuscaloosa on November 15, 1830. Governor Moore submitted his annual message the following day, and in it he touched on a number of issues. But what Moore finally said about tariff reform would not have pleased any committed nullifier. Moore pointedly advocated only "constitutional means" to obtain reform. He went even further and discouraged the legislators from adopting provocative resolutions—he called "measures calculated to add to the state of excitement which already exists upon this subject"—and instead suggested "a temperate, though firm and decisive appeal to the justice and magnanimity of the General Government" and, meanwhile, the development of a "system of domestic industry" in Alabama.[32] These were hardly the words of a radical and were, instead, seen as consistent with the views of Andrew Jackson and John McKinley.[33]

On December 13, 1830, after several attempts, both houses of the legislature finally went into a joint session to elect a United States senator for the term beginning in 1831. In a handbill earlier submitted to the legislators, Governor Moore had framed the crucial issue between him and McKinley to be which of the two was a better Andrew Jackson man.[34] Moore claimed that honor, and apparently a majority of the legislature agreed; Moore prevailed 49–40.[35] The contemporary post-election analysis did not attribute the outcome to nullification politics, probably because the support for Moore included several members from north Alabama where opposition to that dogma was strongest. The *Tuscaloosa Inquirer* believed that "this election may be regarded as an evidence of the strong attachment to State sovereignty, and the principles of the [Maysville Road] veto message by President Jackson."[36]

A disappointed correspondent to the Huntsville *Democrat,* however, saw it as having nothing to do with "principles and measures." He blamed it all on anti-McKinley sentiment, that "there has been political juggling here that would embarrass even a Talleyrand," and that this intrigue had created a "down with him! down with him" spirit. He did not identify the juggler, instead referring generally to McKinley's "malignant, black-hearted uncompromising enemies, whose object was, to put him out of office, at every hazard."[37]

A Franklin County correspondent was more bold. He expressed outrage that the legislative delegation from his county had been elected based on their "sacred pledges" to vote for McKinley but had instead voted for Moore. He blamed this on David Hubbard and, to a lesser extent, on Hubbard's lieutenant in the house, Thomas Benton Coopwood of Lawrence County, another veteran of the War of 1812 who had served under Jackson. "The will of the people of Franklin [was] grossly neglected and perverted, and the will of Capt. Coopwood and Davy Hubbard obeyed," he charged. "We frankly concede to Davy the right to vote against Col. McKinley," he continued, "but we do not think, he ought to exercise his magic influence, over the minds of our *poor little Representatives.* For Davy knows very well that our members are innocent little fellows—easily alarmed and bewildered by bugbears and goblins, and such other non-existences, as Davy is capable of conjuring up in their little imaginations."[38]

This correspondent also expressed grave concern that Hubbard might be endorsed by Gabriel Moore for the office of governor. If Hubbard were elected, he predicted, "we will be getting a goorily [*sic*] set of 'The Peoples' Men' in office. O, what a triumph of Democracy! The Peoples' Men are carrying their point in every contest. The people instructing their representatives to vote one way; and Davy H.—instructing them to vote another; the voice of the latter obeyed, that of the former disregarded. A triumph of principle truly! And an increase of republicanism indeed!"[39]

Even the young assistant secretary of the senate, future Black Belt arch-secessionist George Washington Gayle, publicly blasted Hubbard in the newspapers. Gayle, who was then an ardent Jackson man, accused Hubbard of being "politically and morally dishonest." Hubbard, Gayle alleged, acted "mild, and somewhat dull and harmless" while on the floor of the senate, but showed his true colors at night. Hubbard was actually a "cruel and un-relenting tyrant, and one who would 'smile and murder when he smiles.'" Hubbard's method was to make use of "trick, of juggle, and low intrigue, to which an honest and highminded man would never stoop." When the legislature adjourned for the day, Gayle continued, Hubbard was "instantly animated and active, and can be seen at all times of the night flitting from room to room of the members."[40]

As most legislators knew, however, Gayle had an axe to grind because Hubbard was the leader of a group of them who had censured Gayle for authoring an article for a Selma newspaper ridiculing James Abercrombie, a pro-nullification south Alabama senator, for his remarks in opposition to a memorial to Congress requesting a land grant for improvements to another Alabama river.[41] If Hubbard had been as Machiavellian as Gayle claimed, Gayle's position with the senate would have been terminated. But he was not. Yet Gayle's remarks do accurately reflect Hubbard's develop-ment as a master of the legislative process. Despite, as Gayle put it, "inces-santly railing against what he called the aristocracy of the country" at the beginning of his political career, Hubbard had learned the art of coalition, consensus building, horse-trading, compromise, and working behind the scenes.[42] Furthermore, he was not picky about whose support he sought to achieve his goals. Aristocrats, commoners, and nullifiers were all welcome to join his crusades. And as James Saunders later wrote, Hubbard became a "dreaded adversary."[43]

John Coffee also blamed Hubbard for McKinley's defeat. He wrote President Jackson that the election "has been one of the most corrupt, and intrigueing [sic] elections, ever had in this state, or I hope any other—and I am sorry to say that your long professed friend, David Hubbard has been one of the most prominent men in the dirty work." Coffee too was struck by the number of legislators who pledged to support McKinley, but then voted for Moore.[44] Coffee did not, however, accuse Hubbard or Moore of

being nullifiers, but by this point Jackson saw Calhoun and his nullification followers behind every exercise of independent judgment, every honest
disagreement with his policies, and every bush. He wrote Coffee that "this
has been a secrete [*sic*] intrigue of the great *nullifyer* [*sic*]" and predicted
that Moore would come to Washington as an opponent of his administration and a "perfect nullifyer [*sic*] & supporter of the So. Carolina nullifying
Doctrine."[45]

In any event, this episode appears to have cooled David Hubbard's
ardor for Andrew Jackson, who had failed to endorse his candidacy for the
United States Senate. No longer would he blindly support Jackson or his
policies. He would, instead, subject them to a critical analysis. By doing
this, however, he risked alienating his constituents, thereby possibly ending
what seemed to be a promising political career.

4

'Squinting at Nullification'

The race to complete a canal around the Muscle Shoals before the completion of a railroad quickly proved to be no race at all when canal construction stumbled out of the block in early 1831. Official estimates finally received in January revealed the cost of construction to be a staggering $1.4 million, almost three times the proceeds of the sale of the federal land grant.[1] This revelation renewed and increased the bitterness among canal supporters toward David Hubbard and others who had orchestrated the adoption of the pre-emption bill relating to the land grant. John McKinley, still smarting over his defeat by Gabriel Moore, wrote that this bill had defeated "this great national improvement"—the canal—and predicted that the reason for its adoption was "a question which must, and will frequently be asked; not only by the present generation but posterity also." The editor of the Huntsville *Democrat* declared that "upon the heads of those, who brought such calamity and disgrace upon the state, be the frowns of the living, and the execrations of posterity."[2]

Nonetheless, the railroad project Hubbard was pushing remained essential to most of north Alabama's commerce and now to Hubbard's political future.[3] Construction of the first leg of that project from Tuscumbia to the Tennessee River began with great fanfare on June 29, 1831.[4] "The ground was broken on Wednesday last, amid the roar of cannon, and in the presence of a number of our citizens both from town and country," wrote the excited editor of the *Tuscumbia Advertiser*. The crowd had "attended to witness the commencement of a work which we doubt not will be extended through the Tennessee Valley to some point above the Muscle Shoals," he continued, "and if we may hazzard [*sic*] an opinion it will be an improvement of greater utility than any hitherto undertaken in the western country."[5] Enough of the road was completed by July 4 that a demonstration of the operation of a train of cars pulled by a horse was a well-received, central feature of the area's annual celebration of the nation's independence.[6] Optimism was so high that the road would turn Tuscumbia into a great metropolis that many in the region began to relocate there.[7]

Meanwhile, railroad promoters in the Eastern Seaboard states made plans to project roads to the eventual Tuscumbia, Courtland, and Decatur ("TC&D") to reach Memphis and tap into the Mississippi River trade.[8] First, however, Hubbard and his backers would have to obtain a corporate charter for the longer and more ambitious railroad to Decatur, and then convince prominent persons along the proposed line to buy corporate stock to finance the immense cost of constructing and equipping the road.[9] The price of cotton had increased only slightly from nine to ten cents a pound, meaning that most planters had little disposable income, if any, above their costs.[10] Theoretically the State Bank in Tuscaloosa was a possibility, but competition for the dwindling loan capacity of that institution was great.[11] It was, therefore, decided to try to have the legislature establish a branch of the State Bank with its own capital in north Alabama to meet the railroad's needs.[12]

David Hubbard's three-year term as a member of the senate expired in 1831, and it appears that he initially decided to leave these legislative goals to Thomas Coopwood, who entered the race for Hubbard's seat.[13] Then, however, supporters of the canal in Lauderdale County convinced John McKinley to run for the Alabama House.[14] It was foreseeable that McKinley would set up obstacles to this railroad project, which threatened Lauderdale County's economic supremacy at the foot of the Shoals by potentially drawing shipping from the north side of the Tennessee River to the south side. The *Florence Gazette*, McKinley's organ, was already accusing the railroaders of scheming to divert the canal fund to the TC&D in the next legislative session, and the Huntsville press joined that chorus.[15] This charge was untrue, but McKinley had every reason to try to block whatever Hubbard supported.[16]

Hubbard, therefore, decided to run for legislative office to, among other things, help shepherd bills for the railroad and the branch bank through the legislature. He sought and received a seat in the house. This would permit him to serve a single year, just long enough to secure the bills, and then allow him to focus solely on his private interests.[17] In fact, it is possible that Hubbard intended this to be his last political race. If so, events were already conspiring against him.

The brewing sectional dispute over abolishing slavery reared its head to new heights in 1831 with the publication in Boston of a pro-abolition newspaper, *The Liberator*. To landowners in the South, and particularly Southern land speculators like David Hubbard, the abolition of slavery, which would cripple the ability to produce cotton, would be the death knell of land values. Several months later, this abolition agitation was followed by the bloody but ultimately unsuccessful Nat Turner-led slave rebellion in Virginia. The possible connection between these two events was easy for Southerners to imagine.[18] So were the dangerous implications with regard to Alabama's 73,208 slaves (44,176 of whom were in north Alabama) of the apprehension in Mobile a few weeks later of a slave who had alleg-edly been sent from North Carolina to distribute what Mobile authorities termed "seditious publications" authored by a New Yorker who advocated the abolition of slavery. It was feared by Alabamians that other Nat Turners were already at work encouraging other mass slave insurrections in their state.[19] Fears of more slave insurrections, possibly sponsored by Northerners, compounded the existing dispute over the tariff, which itself was exacerbated by the approaching 1832 presidential election. After publicly breaking with President Jackson, Vice President John C. Calhoun had thrown down the gauntlet in July 1831 when he publicly embraced the nullification doctrine he had earlier secretly authored. Now nullifiers who had argued that federal power to enact protective tariffs might one day be used to abolish slavery did not seem so crazy.[20]

Promoters of the Tuscumbia-to-Decatur railroad attempted to refocus the public on their project by conducting what became known as the "Valley Railroad Convention" in Courtland on October 8.[21] By this time word had spread of plans being made in Memphis, Tennessee, and Charleston, South Carolina, to construct railroads to connect with the Alabama road.[22] The delegates to the Courtland convention, who were from Franklin, Lawrence, and Morgan counties, and who included future Alabama governor Reuben

Chapman of Decatur, resolved that Decatur ought to be connected by rail with Memphis.[23] The delegates also appointed a committee to prepare an address to the public, and that address, which was drafted by David Hubbard, also favored a connection with the Atlantic Ocean. "To the Southern planter and merchant, to the farmer raising live stock and provisions, to all within reach, Charleston presents greater advantages than any other sea port in the union."[24] The potential for investors was great, but so were the risks. Significantly, connecting local fortunes with those of increasingly militant South Carolina might force elites in one region or the other to alter their political views to maintain commercial harmony. Given the relatively greater economic power of South Carolina, it was most likely that any such changes would occur in north Alabama.[25]

That this might be the case was demonstrated after the Alabama legislature convened in Tuscaloosa on November 21, 1831. The agenda of pro-Jackson forces in the legislature was to suppress the expression of nullification sentiment and to obtain an endorsement of Jackson's reelection. Ironically, newly elected South Carolina-born governor John Gayle's inauguration address to the legislators forcefully argued that nullification was unconstitutional and that its exercise would bring on a civil war. "The strife of blood would commence, and the government would perish amid the perils and horrors of civil discord."[26] Hubbard did not necessarily disagree with this, but he had to have support from somewhere to enact his legislative agenda. On November 22 he submitted a petition signed by the supporters of the TC&D to the house and by the next day he was clashing with John McKinley over an unrelated procedural matter.[27] Those legislators from north Alabama who had supported McKinley in his bid for reelection to the United States Senate were likely to support McKinley in his obstructionist endeavors, so Hubbard fatefully looked for votes among house members from south Alabama.

One of those was Moseley Baker, the editor of the pro-nullification Montgomery *Alabama Journal*.[28] The day after a north Alabama member introduced a resolution supporting President Jackson's reelection, Baker offered a controversial resolution calling for appointment of a committee on "state and federal relations," which all knew was intended to criticize the tariff. It was tabled, however, on the motion of an anti-nullificationist. Later that day, Hubbard called up Baker's resolution for a vote and was among the twenty-seven-man minority who voted in its favor.[29] In an editorial titled "Squinting at Nullification," the Huntsville *Southern Advocate* criticized Hubbard and other north Alabamians who had supported Baker's motion and participated in the ensuing "animated debate."[30]

Less than two weeks later, a majority of the house was mysteriously convinced to go into a committee of the whole to consider the tariff.[31] The meetings of this committee, which first convened on December 6 and met on several subsequent occasions during the session, were the scene of a high level of animosity. Some of this was from Jackson supporters who charged that Hubbard was a nullifier and a disunionist. According to an account in the Tuscaloosa *Alabama State Intelligencer*, Hubbard indignantly replied that "some gentlemen seemed disposed to boast of their devotion to President Jackson, but that he [Hubbard] had been with [Jackson] in those days of darkness and gloom, of savage warfare, surrounded by impenetrable forests, when the tomahawk and scalping knife were crimsoned with the innocent blood of defenseless women and children, when danger lurked in every path, and death in every ambush." Moreover, he continued, even before this "that beautiful Tree of Liberty which has been spoken of in such heart-felt strains, was watered by the blood of my father." Hubbard's remarks, according to the correspondent, "created the deepest sensation."[32]

The Huntsville *Democrat* was not impressed. "Some mighty pretty speeches have been made upon the Tariff, about watering the Tree of Liberty with blood, and all that kind of stuff, but nothing is done for the community." The editor declared that "we can't, for the life of us see what purpose can, or was intended to be, subserved by all those declamatory flourishes on the Tariff, that have burthened the Tuscaloosa presses for the last two or three papers."[33] However, as Hubbard might have intended, the continuing uproar in the house over tariff reform was a perfect distraction from the activities in the senate. There Thomas Coopwood had quietly reported a bill incorporating the TC&D on December 7, and by December 29 the senate had adopted a revised version despite obstructionist efforts by James Jackson of Lauderdale County.[34]

By the time that bill went to the house, word had reached Alabama that

President Jackson had finally called for a reduction in tariff duties in his annual message to Congress, thereby calming the issue somewhat.[35] Hubbard attempted to shove the senate's TC&D bill through the house without the necessity of having it first read three times as required by the Alabama Constitution under those circumstances, but that required a supermajority in its favor that he was unable to achieve. Nonetheless, his motion received the support of a simple majority that tellingly included Moseley Baker and thirty-seven other house members, thereby assuring that the bill's passage over John McKinley and the minority was only a matter of time. It was, indeed, adopted on January 7 despite McKinley's dilatory tactics.[36]

Hubbard's efforts came up short, however, in terms of having a branch of the State Bank established in the Tennessee Valley. Baker and other south Alabama legislators wanted a state bank in Montgomery and were successful in acquiring it,[37] and under the Alabama Constitution, only one bank could be established during a legislative session.[38] Hubbard's apparent loss on the bank issue, however, might have actually been part of a backroom deal. In a span of three days at the end of the session, the report and resolutions on the tariff were tabled, a resolution recommending President Jackson's reelection was adopted, and Montgomery was chosen for the new bank branch.[39]

It would have been only natural for Hubbard's political enemies to charge that he had joined the nullification movement and to try to use this to ruin him as a political force in north Alabama in the coming years. Near the end of the legislative session, however, he attended public meetings at the capitol designed to rally support for Andrew Jackson's reelection in 1832. But then one such meeting was hijacked by Moseley Baker and his followers, who proposed resolutions supporting Jackson for president but a Southern Jacksonian, Philip P. Barbour of Virginia, for vice president rather than pro-tariff Northerner Martin Van Buren, who was Jackson's choice.[40] Hubbard went along with Moseley and, to those who agreed with Jackson even when he was wrong, it was another act of disloyalty.[41]

Not long after the legislature adjourned, Hubbard was given a final opportunity to prove his loyalty to Jackson, albeit at the expense of a friend. The occasion arose out of a vote in the United States Senate regarding Jackson's nomination of Martin Van Buren to serve as minister to Great Britain. Gabriel

Moore voted against confirmation of Van Buren, whom Jackson was indeed grooming to be his running mate, creating a tie that was broken when Calhoun as president of the Senate likewise voted against him. This caused a political firestorm.[42] Jackson was so incensed that he, among other things, set out to have Moore politically ruined by requesting John Coffee to organize public meetings in Alabama to denounce him.[43]

John McKinley

Among the first such meetings was one on February 10 in Courtland. There Hubbard offered a widely reported preamble and resolutions that expressed "deep mortification and regret" regarding Moore's vote, and declared that Moore had "acted in violation of the will of the people of Alabama" and in "opposition to the President contrary to the known feelings of the people of Alabama and against the interest of the people of the United States."[44] Unlike some resolutions adopted in similar meetings conducted across north Alabama in the following weeks, however, Hubbard's resolutions, which were adopted unanimously, did not call for Moore to resign.[45] Moore was merely instructed to support Van Buren if he were renominated, "unless the most substantial causes yet unknown to us, should imperiously require him to act otherwise."[46] The anti-Van Buren press had praised Moore for his vote and suggested that he was merely acting in accordance with the wishes of Alabamians who, it was contended, opposed Van Buren. But the Huntsville *Democrat* subsequently cited Hubbard's resolutions to demonstrate otherwise and highlighted the fact that Hubbard had been Moore's "warm and efficient friend, in his election to the Senate over Col. McKinley." The "people are indignant," its editor concluded, and even the "Governor's best friends have deserted him."[47]

The true reason Hubbard turned on Moore is unknown, but one possibility is that the circumstances were such that Hubbard could not then say no to John Coffee. On the day before the Courtland meeting the board of directors of the TC&D had met to take the next steps toward construction of the railroad to Decatur. In addition to appointing David Hubbard corporate secretary, they directed engineer David Deshler to begin making surveys of the route and estimates of the cost of construction.[48] All assumed that cost would be immense. A Memphis newspaper had reported the Alabama legislature's grant of a charter to the TC&D, and that it looked forward to that railroad's extension to Memphis, but it also noted that this "may be delayed until the settlement of the Chickasaw nation" to areas west of the Mississippi River.[49] Coffee, Hubbard certainly knew, was heavily involved with ongoing treaty negotiations with that tribe and would likely have some role in the survey of ultimately ceded Chickasaw land in north Mississippi.[50] As was the case with the sales of land in north Alabama in 1818, access to information from the surveyors regarding the quality of particular tracts would be of critical importance to speculators and other purchasers in making buying decisions. Thus, complying with Coffee's request might eventually prove to be profitable. If this was Hubbard's motivation, it was certainly not the first or last time his politics were driven by his personal economic interests.

The TC&D's need for capital was more immediate. Over the next several months, it advertised for bids to perform the first ten miles of grading work and began ordering materials and entering into construction contracts.[51] Its promoters, therefore, sought to solicit more investors to buy stock. This effort was aided by the completion of the Tuscumbia Railway on June 12, 1832. A mass celebration was held, beginning with the firing of a cannon—"seven rounds for the seven valley counties." The *Florence Gazette* reported that a "large concourse" assembled "to witness the operation of the first railroad in Alabama." An estimated four thousand curious onlookers were treated to free rides on cars drawn by a horse, and the Huntsville *Southern Advocate*'s correspondent remarked that it was "truly novel and interesting to witness the rapid and graceful flight of the 'majestic cars' in a country where but yesterday the paths of Indians were the only traces of human footsteps."[52]

A local historian later claimed that this demonstration, which was followed by an outdoor dinner and a ball, had the desired effect: it "fired the planters in the valley to the east with an enthusiasm for a railroad to connect a point above the Shoals to a deep water point below."[53]

Subscriptions for stock in excess of $300,000 were made, and enough capital was paid in to at least begin the work.[54] However, stock subscriptions did not guarantee that all of the subscribers would actually fully pay for their stock. It was typical during this period for subscribers to give their promissory notes instead. To obtain cash, the TC&D could assign these notes to a bank as collateral for a loan or sell them to the bank outright. Given the diminishing specie reserves and lending capacity of the State Bank at Tuscaloosa, however, the loan amount needed by the TC&D could not be met by that institution. Hence, obtaining a bank with its own capital for the Tennessee Valley during the 1832–1833 legislative session was even more important.

However, with the upcoming presidential election and the continuing controversy over the tariff, the dynamics of the Alabama legislature would again be disrupted by extraneous factors that would make business as usual even more difficult. As expected, Martin Van Buren received the vice-presidential nomination at the Democrats' national convention in Baltimore, but many Southerners in Alabama and elsewhere could not forget that he had voted for the Tariff of 1828.[55] However, the opposition, led by Henry Clay of Kentucky, provided no real alternative. Clay's economic program, called the "American System," fully supported protective tariffs as well as federal funding of internal improvements.[56] As a consequence, no electoral ticket supporting him was named in Alabama.[57] The apparent absence of a choice in the election caused hopelessness in some and defiant radicalism in others. There were concerns that, unless Congress rolled back the tariff duties, South Carolinians would nullify the tariff and use force to prevent its enforcement in that state. The radical *Charleston Mercury* urged its readers to do just that and to disregard fears that the federal government might, in response, use force to collect the duties and thereby spark a civil war. Its editor assured that such coercion would not occur because the government knew that Georgia, Alabama, and Mississippi would side with South Carolina and that "the first gun fired would sound the funeral knell of the republic."[58]

The nullification movement in Alabama suffered a setback when it was discovered that Moseley Baker, editor of the Montgomery *Alabama Journal*, had used a forgery scheme to defraud the State Bank of almost $20,000 and then fled the state. Baker was captured in New Orleans, brought to Tuscaloosa in chains, and lambasted by the still generally anti-nullification Alabama press. Before he was brought to trial, Baker managed to escape by drugging his guards and made his way to Texas, then part of Mexico.[59]

Some Alabamians were sympathetic to South Carolina, where soil exhaustion had led to lower yields and where higher overhead costs resulting from the tariff were therefore relatively more painful.[60] Nevertheless most political leaders in Alabama opposed nullification and were hopeful that efforts ongoing in Congress to reduce tariff duties would resolve the growing political crisis.[61] Those efforts, which led to the adoption of the Tariff of 1832, were only partially successful, however, and fears of a federal-state confrontation in South Carolina continued to grow.[62] If nullification occurred any time soon, the next Alabama legislature would be forced to decide how the state would respond.

David Hubbard was reelected to the Alabama House in August 1832, but his primary goal was to obtain a branch of the State Bank in north Alabama to serve as a consistent lender for the TC&D and his other business interests.[63] Under normal circumstances, that would not have been too difficult. John McKinley did not seek reelection and, in any event, support for obtaining a bank was shared by all factions in north Alabama.[64] It was possible, however, that those legislators from other parts of the state who were sympathetic to South Carolina might extract a pledge of support for the Palmetto State in exchange for their vote on the bank issue. Some also wanted a state convention to be called regarding the tariff.[65] South Carolina's legislature met in special session and, a few days later, adopted a law calling for the meeting of a convention in that state in November 1832 whose delegates were required to "devise the means of redress" regarding the tariff.[66] This was widely assumed to mean that the convention would nullify the tariff, thereby increasing the possibility of civil war.[67] Alabama legislators who accepted President Jackson's stance wanted the legislature to publicly denounce South Carolina's course.[68]

A third group, of which David Hubbard was a part, rejected both of those positions. They maintained that the protective tariff was unconstitutional because it imposed disparate tax burdens on the South, and that South Carolina, therefore, had good cause to be dissatisfied. However, as they tactfully put it in a written declaration to the Alabama legislature, "South Carolina may have mistaken her remedy." In other words, nullification was not the appropriate course, and the use of force by South Carolina or the federal government was also improper. Whatever Alabama did, they cautioned legislators against being perceived as taking "the part of congress in its unauthorized oppressions," reasoning that it "will only serve to strengthen the arm of the general government, already too strong for the people and the states, and would induce the majority of congress, to view with contempt the dissatisfactions of our people." The danger of this was clear to all slaveowners: if Congress could pass an unconstitutional law imposing a protective tariff, it could also adopt an unconstitutional law abolishing slavery directly, or indirectly by imposing a confiscatory tax on slaveholders.[69] Given the population growth in the North, there would not always be a slaveowner in the White House to veto such a law. Hence, Southern solidarity—not division—was absolutely essential to Hubbard and those who shared his views.

It is certainly possible that David Hubbard's political position was, as usual, also shaped by his economic interests. In the short run, if a bank branch were located in the Tennessee Valley, initial capitalization would necessarily have to be sought in Northern money markets, and the potential for civil war would scare away potential lenders.[70] Moreover, in the long run, connecting the TC&D to Charleston, South Carolina, would require harmonious relations with that state. Denouncing it in the midst of its crisis would likely permanently cripple those budding relations.

As had been his practice during the last legislative session, Hubbard again used surrogates to advance most of his agenda. Dr. Henry W. Rhodes, a Morgan County physician and planter who was both a legislator and a member of the TC&D board of directors—as well as the chairman of the house committee on the State Bank—served as the floor leader in the house to bring a State Bank branch to the Tennessee Valley.[71] Thomas Coopwood was the floor leader in the senate.[72] By November 15, a satisfactory bill providing for one million dollars in capital had been adopted by both houses, and on November 16 they met in a joint session to select the town where it would be placed.[73] The Huntsville press assumed that Huntsville was the only logical choice because it was by far the largest commercial town in north Alabama. But Decatur, then a tiny hamlet in Morgan County that was not even the county seat (it was then in Somerville), won the prize. The *Democrat* was apoplectic and unsuccessfully urged the legislature to reconsider putting it in what it described as a "small village in N. Alabama, on the Tennessee river, with two stores and a population of 50 persons."[74]

What the editor overlooked was that Decatur was the future eastern terminus of the TC&D. Huntsville was the very last place David Hubbard wanted the bank to be located—where the *Democrat* and several of his political enemies resided.[75] He wanted it close enough that he could influence its lending policies and practices regarding that one million dollars in capital.[76] Such manipulation was facilitated when the president and board of directors were later elected by the legislature. John Southerland, a member of the board of directors of the Tuscumbia Railway and a promoter of the TC&D, was selected president of the bank. James Fennell, a major stockholder in the TC&D, and J. T. Sykes, another member of the TC&D board, were elected to the bank's board of directors. So were three other promoters of the TC&D: Jesse W. Garth, Horace Green, and Isaac Lane of Morgan County. Furthermore, when the sole director from Huntsville resigned, he was replaced by Sykes's brother.[77]

The *Democrat*, which was unaware of the connections between the TC&D and the Decatur bank, predicted—quite correctly—that the bank was doomed to fail. It would necessarily be subject to "that universal tendency in small bodies of men to make the control of money subserve other purposes than purely the public." It warned that "if our money should be borrowed and squandered, the Legislature which meets ten years hence, when our first [loan] installment [on the bonds sold to capitalize the bank] becomes due, will be apt to feel some reluctance to sustain burdens [through increased state taxes] whose benefits their constituents never felt." In other words, by putting the bank at Decatur, the state's creditworthiness, and its taxpayers, were being placed at great risk.[78]

A more important question remained. Would the nation survive for ten years? On November 24, the convention in South Carolina crossed the Rubicon and adopted an ordinance declaring the Tariff of 1828 and the Tariff of 1832 "null, void, and no law, nor binding upon this State, its officers or citizens," and directing the South Carolina legislature to adopt legislation to "prevent the enforcement and arrest the operation" of the tariffs after February 1, 1833. Any use of force by the federal government was to be resisted "at every hazard" and was also grounds for secession.[79]

That very day, Alabama House Speaker Oliver assigned the tariff issue to a special committee chaired by a Jackson man, John J. Ormond of Lawrence County, and composed of six other legislators who had supported Oliver.[80] Meanwhile, news of Andrew Jackson's reelection by a landslide reached Tuscaloosa, prompting Ormond to propose a resolution that the capitol be illuminated that night "as a manifestation of our pleasure on the happening of this auspicious event." Before that resolution could be voted on, however, a Franklin County legislator moved that the resolution be amended to include Martin Van Buren, the vice president-elect. After what one onlooker described as "much warm and vehement debate," this amendment was adopted, but by only one vote, with David Hubbard surprisingly voting with the majority. Once amended the resolution was adopted unanimously.[81]

This degree of unity quickly disappeared once news of President Jackson's threatening proclamation of December 10 reached Alabama. In words that would inspire Abraham Lincoln less than thirty years later, Jackson declared to South Carolina that federal law would be enforced, that any "forcible opposition" constituted "TREASON" and would be punished, and that he would "preserve the Union by all constitutional means."[82] It is debatable whether the saber-rattling by the South Carolina convention and President Jackson was actually necessary at this point to resolve the dispute over the tariff. Jackson had been reelected and was, therefore, finally free from political considerations to boldly push Congress for reform.

Given this, it was pointless to David Hubbard and some other legislators for the Alabama legislature to enter the fray. After all, as Governor Gayle had predicted, Northern public opinion did appear to be changing, and with President Jackson now able to openly push for reform, it was only a matter of time before acceptable changes were made. But that did not satisfy a majority of Alabama's legislators, who were anxious to show their strong support for Jackson by openly condemning South Carolina.[83] They adopted five resolutions on January 2, 1833: (1) that the protective tariff was unconstitutional; (2) but that the Tariff of 1832 was a pledge by Congress to eventually abandon the principle of protective tariffs; (3) that nullification was not only unconstitutional but dangerous and revolutionary; (4) that Alabamians should trust the justice of the federal government and reject nullification, but that Congress should avoid the exercise of "dubious and constructive" powers; and (5) that as a last resort to avoid civil war, a national convention should be called by the states to meet in Washington on March 1, 1834, to amend the Constitution.[84] David Hubbard voted for the first resolution, which was adopted with only one dissenting vote, but he and several others voted against the rest because they appeared intended to condemn South Carolina and to support the Tariff of 1832.[85] Hubbard and the others offered resolutions that expressed their concerns about the growing power of the federal government, but they were "indefinitely postponed" by the majority on the motion of John Ormond.[86]

Not long thereafter, President Jackson raised tensions even further when he requested Congress to pass what some Southerners called the "Bloody Bill" or "Force Bill" providing military support for tariff collection.[87] This threat appears to have brought most of Alabama's legislators over to David Hubbard's position, which was in opposition to the use of force.[88] The day the legislature adjourned, January 12, 1833, the senate adopted the resolutions to which he was opposed, but both houses also adopted a very conciliatory special address to South Carolina, Congress, and President Jackson. It "affectionately and solemnly" appealed to Congress and South Carolina to resolve the crisis by modifying the tariff to eliminate its protective features, and called for a constitutional convention to amend the federal constitution to expressly prohibit adoption of a protective tariff in the future. South Carolina was also "earnestly" recommended to suspend its nullification ordinance and "urgently" recommended to abstain from the use of military force. Then, "with equal earnestness," the legislators recommended to "the government"—Jackson's name and position were not used—to "exercise moderation, and to employ only such means as are peaceful and usual to execute the laws of the Union."[89]

Despite this, news from Washington was not initially encouraging in terms of progress on tariff reform.[90] The deadline imposed by South Carolina came and went without any movement by Congress. Then came sensational reports of a surprising proposal made by Henry Clay consistent with previous suggestions for a gradual reduction of tariff duties over a period of years.[91] At least on this occasion the editor of the Huntsville *Democrat* spoke for most north Alabamians when he wrote that Clay's proposal "has created much excitement in the political world in this peculiar season of high excitement," and that the "surprise, has not been greater than the pleasure, to those who long to see the lowering clouds which portend the wild fury of a coming tempest, quietly dissipated and driven from our sky."[92]

There was still the matter of saving face.[93] Neither President Jackson nor South Carolina nullifiers wanted to concede that they had been intimidated into a compromise—even though they had. Congress adopted a new tariff, but the next day pointlessly adopted the enforcement bill requested by Jackson. South Carolina's convention subsequently rescinded its nullification ordinance, but then just as pointlessly nullified the enforcement bill.[94] In any event, the crisis was finally over and, as the Huntsville *Democrat* declared, "Nullification is stone dead."[95] Perhaps, to many still smoldering South Carolinians, the idea of secession was not.

Ironically, one of the most vocal critics of those nullifiers and John C. Calhoun during this period was nineteen-year-old South Carolina resident and future Alabama fire-eater William Lowndes Yancey. While studying law there, he gave a number of public addresses and, as a newspaper editor, authored several fiery editorials, in which he scorched Calhoun as a disunionist and traitor, selfishly motivated solely by political ambition rather than the good of the citizens.[96] Hubbard's conciliatory course in Alabama during this crisis would have fared no better in Yancey's young eyes. Indeed, it is likely most of Hubbard's constituents would have agreed with Yancey in this early period.

At about the time Hubbard returned from Tuscaloosa, a number of

Lawrence County residents met in a mass meeting in Moulton to, among other things, show their support for President Jackson. They adopted a resolution vowing to sustain him "in all constitutional means to preserve the Union." They also affirmed it to be "a duty we owe to ourselves, to that band of patriots who fought, bled and died, that we may be free, and to our posterity to whom we should transmit the liberty we enjoy as an inheritance above all price, to declare to the world" that if South Carolina "persist in her mad career (which heaven forbid) . . . we will never take the field unless the star spangled banner waves over us."[97] Whether this was intended as a rebuke of Hubbard for his defense of South Carolina in the legislature is unknown, but it is noteworthy that he did not run for any political office again for several years.

On the other hand, Hubbard no longer had any real need for political office. The Tuscumbia Railway was busy efficiently hauling huge amounts of cotton to the portion of the Tennessee River below the Shoals. According to a Rhode Island newspaper, "seventy bales of cotton, weighing 31,500 lbs. were recently drawn by one horse from Tuscumbia (Alabama) to the river, a distance of 2 1/8 miles, in 14 minutes, on the Rail Road."[98] The road to Decatur, however, was still far from completion. At this point it needed much more capital. Acquiring control of the new bank in Decatur was a coup, but that bank had not yet been successful in obtaining specie capitalization. The Alabama legislature had selected George Strother Gaines of Mobile to go to northern or European money markets to attempt to sell more bonds to obtain $2.5 million in specie to capitalize the Decatur bank and a new branch in Mobile, and also to recapitalize the Montgomery branch.[99] Many expected this would be relatively easy and that the bonds, which paid an interest rate of 5 percent, would be sold at a premium. But reports of the very few pro-nullification meetings that had occurred in Alabama had reached the North, and money markets there remained jittery over the sectional drama. As a result, Gaines was only able to sell a portion of them at par to a single commercial banking house in New York, J.D. Beers & Co.[100] Thus, the Alabama branch banks would get capital, but the state of Alabama lost approximately $472,000 on the transaction.[101] This would not be the last adverse economic consequence that would befall Alabama as a result of sectional crises.

Old State Bank Building

The Decatur bank's board of directors met to select officers and employees to operate the bank, and it was expected that the bank would finally open its doors and begin making loans at some point in July.[102] This made the 1833 Independence Day celebration in Tuscumbia that much more joyous. At sunrise the TC&D reportedly began the festivities with the "firing of cannon, which was conveyed on a car and discharged at short intervals" on the eight-mile portion of the road that had been completed. The crowd drawn in this manner was treated throughout the day to free rides on horse-drawn "pleasure cars" and lumber cars.[103]

The Decatur bank finally opened on July 31, 1833,[104] and the TC&D's stockholders immediately began borrowing heavily to pay for construction.[105] As David Hubbard later put it, "We were constant borrowers from the Alabama Banks."[106] In fact, the demands of borrowers were so great that an injection of another million dollars of bank capital had to be sought during the Alabama legislature's 1833–1834 session.[107] With the TC&D now in a position to make large capital expenditures, Hubbard was dispatched to Baltimore, Maryland, to place an order for the road's first locomotive engine. He succeeded in negotiating the purchase of an engine of British manufacture for delivery in November, just in time for the fall cotton crop. It would not arrive until much later. Meanwhile, the TC&D was completed to Leighton on August 20 and would reach Courtland and Decatur in 1834.[108] Sooner or later, however, the loans being made for construction and equipping the road would have to be repaid. That would prove to be much more difficult than Hubbard or anyone else could have foreseen.

5

The 'Feast of Reason and the Flow of Soul'

Speculating in Chickasaw lands in north Mississippi to raise cash was still not an option for David Hubbard and his associates,[1] but another opportunity presented itself in 1832 when the Creeks entered into the Treaty of Cusseta regarding their remaining lands in the newly created east Alabama counties of Benton (now Calhoun), Talladega, Randolph, Coosa, Tallapoosa, Chambers, Barbour, Russell, and Macon. All signs indicated that this presented a somewhat lucrative target for speculators. Approximately twenty thousand settlers from South Carolina, Georgia, and other states on the Eastern Seaboard (where soil exhaustion was increasingly prevalent) were flooding into this region and squatting while awaiting government auction sales—despite a provision in the treaty prohibiting this.[2]

Efforts to remove some of those squatters by the United States deputy marshal for the Southern District of Alabama were resisted, prompting him to call for a squad of federal troops from Fort Mitchell in Russell County to aid him. On July 31, 1833, the soldiers shot and killed a Russell County man when he resisted them. Then a Russell County grand jury indicted the soldiers for murder. Efforts by the Russell County sheriff to arrest the soldiers were resisted, at which time the circuit judge there requested newly reelected governor John Gayle to call up the state militia to aid in making the arrests. Rather than acceding to clear authority to enforce the federal treaty, the heretofore anti-nullification governor sought to have the Jackson administration cease its use of force in squatter removal efforts and to require those who sought to oust them to instead use the Alabama courts established there during the last legislative session to obtain that remedy. This clash between federal and state authority caused yet another national controversy that raged for several months, prompting some to again fear civil war.[3] To many, Gayle's action smacked of a new form of state nullification of federal law. He was criticized for this not only by Northerners but also some north Alabamians.[4] Hubbard was certainly not among Gayle's critics on this issue or its resolution.

As had ultimately occurred with regard to the tariff, however, the federal government finally backed away from a potential military conflict and compromised on terms that potentially benefited Hubbard.[5] Most significantly for his purposes, the process of surveying the Creek lands was expedited so that allotments of parcels of land could be made to the Creeks and the remaining land sold as soon as possible at public auction. Cotton prices were, by this time, gradually rising and would eclipse fifteen cents a pound, ushering in the period in the Deep South historians have called the Flush Times.[6] This was destined to drive up demand for fertile land even further and thereby increase the profits of speculators. Hence, this prompt resolution, which was made in December 1833 shortly before the 1834 planting season, was very timely.

However, the manner in which it was effectuated was less advantageous to speculators than on previous occasions. Among other things, rather than using a malleable civilian political appointee (like John Coffee) to oversee the survey, a military topographical engineer, John James Abert, was assigned.[7] Not only did Abert acquire knowledge of the best lands, but he had the power to allot them to the Creeks and thereby prevent them from being sold at auction to the public. In addition, on December 17, 1833, President Jackson ordered that the public auctions begin on January 13, 1834, giving little time for speculators to learn of his order and travel to the auction sites, much less to make arrangements to obtain funds sufficient to make the purchases.[8] As a skeptical Georgia editor observed: "Five millions of acres of land offered for sale at about ten days notice!"[9]

All of this caused many speculators to opt to forego the auction and to instead make purchases directly from individual Creek Indians of their allotments. David Hubbard, Hubbard's brother Green, and several men associated with the Decatur Bank—including its president and a member of its board of directors—entered into a joint venture agreement with others to begin speculating in Creek land.[10]

The Creeks had been devastated by Andrew Jackson's troops during the War of 1812, and observers noted that they had still not recovered economically from that holocaust.[11] They were in desperate need of money and, as a result, would be easy prey for sharp-talking whites even under normal circumstances. The terms of any sale of an allotment had to be approved and certified by federal agents, but the effectiveness of this mechanism was dependent on the vigilance of the agents and their ability to see through some of the frauds practiced on them by some speculators and other buyers. The historiography regarding these transactions, which is primarily based on anecdotal evidence, suggests that some of these agents were easily fooled, if not corrupt.[12] On the other hand, engineer Abert could not be bought. He rejected multiple offers from Hubbard and others to join in the speculations.[13] Thus, speculating in Creek lands might not have been as lucrative as hoped. Meanwhile, land sales were chilled when hysteria swept east Alabama after the circuit court clerk of Russell County was murdered by Creeks in Macon County.[14] Land speculators and settlers were unlikely to receive more favorable treatment at their hands.

The TC&D was a different story. It had awarded a contract for construction of its last leg toward Decatur, and had also offered to extend the road to Huntsville if investors there subscribed to $80,000 in TC&D stock and obtained the necessary rights of way.[15] Railroad promoters in Memphis, Tennessee, were increasing their efforts to marshal support for a railroad from that town to the Atlantic Ocean at Charleston, South Carolina, using the TC&D as a link in the chain of that mammoth project.[16] This, and the completion of the TC&D to Courtland, was cause for great celebration.[17] A huge Fourth of July shindig in Courtland sponsored by the road, wrote the editor of the Tuscumbia *North Alabamian*, drew "the largest collection of persons I ever witnessed."[18] This is not surprising. Featured at this gathering was Alabama's first locomotive engine, called the "Fulton," which weighed in at 4½ tons. With a light load, wrote David Deshler to a national railroad journal, this state-of-the-art engine of British design was capable of reaching a speed of forty miles an hour.[19]

Completing the TC&D was only one part of Hubbard's business plan. To succeed in having it connected with the proposed road from Memphis

The Fulton

would require the resolution of the impediment presented by the Chickasaw tribe in north Mississippi through which that road was projected. In 1834, the final details to the Treaty of Pontotoc with the Chickasaws were finally agreed upon, thereby laying the groundwork for their eventual removal and putting over 6.7 million acres of land in north Mississippi in play for speculators during this period of increasing cotton prices and demand for cotton land. This land was in the present-day north Mississippi counties of DeSoto, Marshall, Benton, Tippah, Alcorn, Tunica, Tate, Prentiss, Tishomingo, Quitman, Panola, Lafayette, Union, Pontotoc, Lee, Itawamba, Yalobusha, Calhoun, Chickasaw, Clay, and Monroe, and the northwest Alabama counties of Franklin (later Colbert) and Marion.[20] As under the treaty with the Creeks, allotments were first to be made to members of the tribe and the balance of the ceded lands later sold at public auction in 1836.[21]

Hubbard put together the Chickasaw Land Company, a joint venture capitalized with $180,000 to purchase Chickasaw allotments. This group included Dr. John Tindall, the president of the State Bank in Tuscaloosa who served as the company's treasurer and one of its principal financial backers. Governor John Gayle was also an important early member. Rather than relying on locals to serve as intermediaries with the Chickasaws, Thomas Coopwood was tasked to move to Aberdeen, Mississippi, to undertake that role.[22] The company ultimately succeeded in contracting for thirty thousand acres of land from the Chickasaws.[23]

The reason for the failure to use the branch of the State Bank at Decatur as the primary institutional funding source of this new venture is unknown. One possibility is that, by this time, the Decatur bank only had slightly less than $200,000 in specie while its notes and bills issued totaled a staggering $1.8 million. The bank, nonetheless, was surprisingly later found by three state banking commissioners who conducted an annual audit to be operating in accordance with its charter. Noteworthy in this regard is the fact that one of the commissioners who signed the official report to the Alabama legislature, future Alabama governor Reuben Chapman, was a promoter of the TC&D.[24] In reliance, during its 1834–35 session the legislature increased the Decatur bank's capital by another $500,000.[25]

By this time the TC&D was planning another grand celebration, this to commemorate the completion of the road to Decatur scheduled for December.[26] The party began on December 15, 1834, in Decatur where throngs had gathered to enjoy the spectacle. According to the *Decatur Clarion*, "at precisely ½ past 1 P.M. the welcome visitant made its appearance with a train of three pleasure cars. The 'Union,'" he continued, "was freighted with the most *precious* product of the country, the lovely FAIR of Franklin and Lawrence—enough within themselves to have made the scene one of enchantment. The other two cars were crowded to overflowing, by gentlemen from Courtland and Tuscumbia." Everyone had a wonderful time that afternoon, leading the happy editor to conclude that the "proprietors and the stockholders [of the TC&D] may well have whispered to themselves, 'This is the feast of reason and the flow of soul.'"[27]

It was characteristic of the Flush Times that everything seemed possible. From a national standpoint, the federal government's debt was paid in full for the first time, and the government was running a budget surplus.[28] In Alabama, the legislature would soon be repealing almost all state taxes with the idea of operating state government primarily from the surging interest income of the state-owned banking system.[29] For these and other reasons, including increasing cotton prices, Hubbard had to be optimistic. A visitor to the Chickasaw Cession reported what Hubbard and others had observed. "I have never in my life seen such a rush for land." Another wrote of the consequence of that demand. "People here are run mad with speculation" and did business in "a kind of phrenzy."[30] They "thought of nothing but the purchasing of land and negroes, and at high prices," wrote another.[31]

When that frenzy caused the Chickasaw Land Company to run low on operating capital, Hubbard was able to convince Joseph D. Beers, the owner of the commercial bank in New York that had purchased Alabama's last bond issue, to form a consortium of businessmen in the Northeast to partner with Hubbard's land company in making purchases on a speculative basis. This led to the formation in 1835 of a joint stock company called the New York and Mississippi Land Company, of which the president of New York City's Phoenix Bank, John Delafield, was elected president.[32] Hubbard, Benjamin Sherrod, and other locals became stockholders, but Hubbard was no passive investor.[33] He was instructed by his Northern partners to proceed to Mississippi, examine the land, and identify the most valuable parcels.

One can probably guess how he managed to gain the trust of the federal government's agent to the Chickasaws, Benjamin Reynolds, who permitted Hubbard's crew to assist in speeding up the otherwise slow process of making allotments to the Chickasaws. This, of course, gave Hubbard access to critically important first-hand knowledge of not only the best lands, but also the identity of those Chickasaws to whom those lands were allotted.[34] Then Hubbard could negotiate with the individual Indian allottees to purchase their allotments and have some degree of confidence that federal authorities would, as required by the treaty, certify the transactions as fair.[35] The company's plan was to sell this land during the government's first auction in January 1836, so acquisition and certification before then were imperative. Through Hubbard's efforts, the New York and Mississippi Land Company was able to contract for 206,787 acres in allotments to Chickasaw tribesmen. The secret of Hubbard's success was his ability to endear himself to those Chickasaws and their families by providing for their minimal living expenses until the closing of the sale.[36]

The ultimate success of this venture, however, would also depend on other factors. Cotton prices, which were driving demand, needed to remain high. At least for the time being that was happening, although some were already predicting they would soon fall.[37] These warnings were ignored as purchasers paid over $30 million during the period from 1834 through 1836 to buy more slaves.[38] By the same token, other sources of land needed to remain as limited as possible. Creek land in east Alabama remained available, but in 1835 the national press was filled with reports of more attacks by Creeks on settlers there, giving rise to significant security concerns.[39] Many Americans were also headed to the Texas portion of Mexico where land was still relatively inexpensive. A Mobile correspondent of a Northern newspaper reported that "to this last land of promise, thousands are now wending their way."[40] However, this land of promise was also a land of extreme danger, explaining why land values there had not appreciated as much as land in the United States. Most significantly, settlers were subject to the laws of Mexico, some of which conflicted with their interests. Among others was Mexico's prohibition of slavery, to which Texians were objecting.[41] Based on reports from Texas, it was foreseeable that friction between the Texians and the Mexican government would bring them to the brink of war.[42]

War did break out in Texas on October 1, 1835.[43] Some militia companies of young Americans, including one from Courtland—the ill-fated "Red Rovers" led by TC&D director Dr. Jack Shackelford[44]—responded to appeals for men and weapons by the Texians.[45] There is little doubt that some volunteers were attracted by promises of liberal bounties of land made by Sam Houston, who had left Tennessee, moved to Texas in 1832, and become a leader of the opposition to Mexican ruler Antonio Lopez de Santa Anna.[46] Those looking for land on which to plant a cotton crop at the beginning of 1836 prudently shunned this zone of a war of unknown duration and outcome.[47] So far, so good.

Then, Hubbard's land company suffered a setback. In response to objections about the fairness of dealings between speculators and Chickasaws, the Jackson administration ordered that no transactions predating April 1836 would be certified. As a consequence of this order, which was issued by Secretary of War Lewis Cass in December 1835, the land company was unable to sell any of that land as planned during the government auction sales at Pontotoc in January 1836 and was forced to renegotiate the purchase contracts with the Chickasaw sellers.[48]

Having missed the prime selling season before the 1836 crop year began, the company decided to wait until the second public auction in September 1836 to put its acreage up for sale to those seeking land for the 1837 crop year.[49] The potential problem with this strategy was that the factors that had affected supply and demand could change radically during that period of time, just as had occurred from 1818 to 1819 in Alabama. From a supply standpoint, however, it appeared that the conflict between the Creeks and white settlers in east Alabama was intensifying despite reports in February of a peace accord.[50] It would be just a few months before war broke out there.[51] Thus the lands of the Creek cession in east Alabama remained a dangerous option for those in search of cotton land. The same could be said for Texas. A Mississippi newspaper reported that Santa Anna and his Mexican army were marching into Texas and predicted that "the campaign will be protracted, as the war on the part of the Texians will, for the present, be entirely defensive."[52] Then came horrifying news of the fall of the Texian fortifications at the Alamo and Goliad, and the massacre of a captured Texian force that included the Red Rovers from Lawrence County.[53] It was believed that if Santa Anna were successful in defeating the Texians, further emigration of Americans to Texas would be prohibited.[54]

Not long after receiving these reports, David Hubbard wrote confidently to his Northern partners of the "total destruction of all hopes of obtaining cotton lands in Texas."[55] But his assessment initially appeared to be premature. A few weeks later, a Huntsville, Alabama, newspaper reported what it called "glorious news" of an "unparalleled victory" at San Jacinto by a Texian force led by Sam Houston. Not only was Santa Anna's larger army routed, but Santa Anna was taken prisoner.[56] Reports conflicted, however, regarding whether Santa Anna's defeat would end the war. Mexican forces under other generals remained on Texas soil.[57] Although Santa Anna signed an accord that required the withdrawal of those troops, the government of Mexico did not ratify that agreement, and the threat of further hostilities continued.[58] Mexican soldiers were not the only danger to settlers. The Mexicans had stirred up the Comanches and other hostile Native Americans to attack the

Texians, and they had done so from the beginning of the conflict.[59]

As a result, a question remained whether what became the Republic of Texas could defend itself. Some advocated that Texas be annexed into the United States so that federal troops could be sent in to bolster its defenses,[60] but former president John Quincy Adams, then a United States congressman from Massachusetts, spoke for an increasing number of Northerners when he denounced this idea because it would add another slave state to the Union.[61] Texas would, therefore, have to fend for itself. It was reported in the Southern press that its provisional president was calling up every man over the age of sixteen and under fifty for military duty, but even with this the Texas government could not guarantee prospective emigrants that they or their slaves would not be molested.[62]

The same uncertainty continued to prevail in east Alabama. What became known as the Second Creek War finally ended during the summer of 1836, but the process of actually removing the estimated seventeen thousand Creeks from that region to the West would take several more months.[63] Until that was accomplished, Creek attacks continued and the danger of a third war remained.[64]

With the supply of competing lands thus still artificially restricted, and the price of cotton remaining relatively high, everything seemed to point to great success for David Hubbard's land company.[65] In the interim before the September sales, Hubbard took the opportunity to take his family to New York and Philadelphia for a well-deserved summer vacation. At age forty-four, he undoubtedly believed that, in a short while, he would be able to retire from active business life—just as he had done with politics—and enjoy the fruits of his labors. However, multiple forces were already at work to deny him that pleasure.

6

Changing 'the Politicks of the Union'

During David Hubbard's trip to the Northeast, he could not have missed the predictions of gloom and doom in the press regarding the national economy. Much of this was politically motivated—an effort by an increasingly influential opposition Whig Party to defeat Democratic presidential nominee Martin Van Buren by attacking the financial policies of Andrew Jackson, including his opposition to federal funding for infrastructure, his extermination of the Second Bank of the United States, and, most recently, his issuance of the "specie circular."[1] The stated reason for this executive order was to make it more difficult for speculators like Hubbard and his associates to outbid members of the general public at auction sales of public lands. It attempted to accomplish this by requiring only the speculators to pay for those lands in specie.[2] Even the Whig press, which objected to the order, agreed that thwarting the speculators was "highly praiseworthy in itself."[3] Indeed, the nation seemed unanimous that the schemes of what some demonized as "land sharks" should somehow be curtailed, and that their gambling in land values would catch up with them.[4]

More than one editor predicted that market forces would eventually burst the speculative bubble, citing the debacle in Alabama in 1819 when an unexpected decline in the cotton market caused the collapse of real-estate values and a lengthy depression in the South.[5] The editor of the Washington *Globe*, a pro-Van Buren newspaper, was sure that history would soon repeat itself and that land values would plummet. "THEY CANNOT LAST," declared the editor, and "a revulsion is near at hand, if it has not already commenced."[6] He was right.

As is the case today, the financial system of this period was international and interlocking. Alabama's banks were operating on specie from money markets in the Northeast, principally New York, which had acquired much of that specie from overseas, particularly England.[7] Specie flows from England over the last several years had been used to fuel the United States' now-roaring economy and indirectly to capitalize local banks like those in Alabama that used them as a basis for lending. "Capital," David Hubbard wrote in 1836, was offered to "anybody who will take it—knave or fool can now fill his pockets." This easy money had been used to, among other things, speculate in everything from Indian land, railroads, and canals, to slaves and cotton.[8] As a result, wrote one Alabama planter in 1836, "Everybody is in debt neck over ears."[9]

So much specie had left the Bank of England's vault in 1836 that the amount remaining was insufficient to safely support England's paper currency.[10] As a consequence, beginning in July, the Bank of England (BOE) made the first of several hikes in the interest rate charged to commercial borrowers. Then, in late August, the BOE decided to stop lending to several commercial entities that did a significant amount of cotton-related business in the United States but, in response to appeals by them, subsequently adopted a policy of granting only limited credit.[11]

Hubbard had returned south before news of the BOE's decisions reached the United States. He attended the auction at Pontotoc that began on September 5, where his land company began selling off much of its land holdings on credit to unsuspecting buyers still optimistic about the cotton economy's future.[12] These sales were unaffected by the "specie circular," which required only speculators in lands owned by the government to pay federal land offices in specie.[13] The prices obtained in the government auction sales were nonetheless record highs.[14]

Interestingly, these sales at Pontotoc were used by the Whig press throughout the nation in an unsuccessful campaign to defeat Martin Van Buren.[15] A few weeks before the presidential election, they alleged that Van Buren was involved in the speculation and that he had assisted David Hubbard to obtain specie to make purchases while Hubbard was on his family vacation.[16] A Massachusetts editor was certain that "a BONUS probably constituted [Van Buren's] fee for lending the influence of his name, and commending Mr. Hubbard to the Democratic mammoth land speculators of Boston. Remember, at the polls, Martin Van Buren, the land speculator."[17] The Whigs also falsely alleged that the specie circular had caused the prices paid at the auction sales to be artificially low.[18]

In an October 13, 1836, letter to the editor of the Pontotoc *Chickasaw Union* that was reprinted in pro-Van Buren newspapers across the nation, Hubbard categorically denied having received any help from Van Buren, or even meeting with him in 1836. "I never had any communication with Mr. Van Buren, verbal or written, on the subject of the public lands; nor did I ever hear the subject mentioned in his presence." Hubbard also took this opportunity to blast the critics of land speculators. "If it is wrong to over-bid a settler for a piece of public land, the fault is with those who, by legislation, have ordered the lands to be sold for the highest bid." It was "hypocritical—it is worse—it is attempting to practice a fraud upon the public, for *either* political party to bring the land question into the election for President, until such party can show that they made an *honest* exertion to give the lands, at a cheap rate, to the occupants."[19] The Pontotoc newspaper, which might have been underwritten by speculators like Hubbard's company, also rebutted the claim about depressed prices for public land sold at the sale. "The amount received for the two weeks," wrote the editor, was "somewhat above $290,000," and this "at an average price of $1.90 per acre!" By comparison, it noted, land sold in January before the issuance of the specie circular "averaged $1.68 per acre."[20]

Then came news of tightening credit markets and a decline in cotton prices. Even before this, Hubbard had expressed concern to his Northern partners that the Flush Times would soon, in essence, become the Bust Times.[21] Those concerns were justified. American businesses connected to the international cotton trade were the first to fail. Hubbard was again in Philadelphia with his family when the financial panic began in the Northeast and news of the collapse of the major New York firms began to circulate.[22] Hubbard wrote Washington Miller, a student at The University of Alabama from Lawrence County, regarding the growing crisis after he learned that some university students had contemplated quitting school and trying to strike it rich through land speculation.[23] Hubbard admonished Miller to "avoid speculating of every class and stay in school." Speculations, he continued, "may make [you] enormously rich but never add to permanent happiness. They come too sudden to a conclusion even if successful to supply that constant existing desire which must be gratified" and, even worse, "if unsuccessful are overwhelming in their consequences."[24]

Southerners did not know what had triggered the widening disaster. One editor thought there was "some deepseated disease in the body commercial."[25] However, as before the 1836 presidential election, which was narrowly won by Martin Van Buren and the Democrats,[26] the Whig press and Whig candidates began the campaign for the upcoming off-year congressional elections by blaming it all on the Democrats' fiscal policies.[27] As both parties put blame on the other, reports of business failures of cotton brokers and factors in Mobile and New Orleans were circulating in Alabama, Mississippi, and New York.[28] It was most importune timing for north Alabama planters who had expected to receive top dollar for their cotton but were now shipping it to New Orleans and hoping not to take a loss.

Low cotton prices meant that those like David Hubbard who had incurred debt during the heyday of the Flush Times in reliance on high cotton prices would be unable to pay that debt as it came due unless prices rallied. However, as one of his land company's other agents wrote, "Cotton has taken a perpendicular fall."[29] A correspondent in New Orleans reported in April that "Cotton was a complete drug, and several lots of fair Tennessee and North Alabama cottons were offered at 5 cents per lb. without finding buyers."[30] Prices did increase later in the year, but only slightly to nine cents.[31] The cotton land in the Chickasaw Cession would, therefore, no longer be a cash cow. It, too, took a "perpendicular fall."[32]

Hubbard and others nonetheless remained on the hook for over $340,000 borrowed from the State Bank at Decatur for the construction and operation of the TC&D, which was having significant problems due to breakdowns of its engines.[33] He had also spent countless sums of borrowed money for land. As a Richmond editor wrote of the speculators, their investments were "now locked up in lands, which are not cultivated, and cannot be sold without a sacrifice."[34] Hubbard was not alone. Alabama banks that had earlier liberally extended credit were now extremely cautious and, instead, demanding payment. A bitter loan customer of the State Bank branch at Decatur invoked Shakespeare's lines from *The Merchant of Venice* about the vengeful Jewish moneylender, Shylock, when he complained of that bank's hard line toward its debtors: "We of this fair and fertile valley, called on our *Decatur Bank friends*—and what is the reply? 'The bond!—the bond!!—or the pound of flesh!!'"[35]

Alabamians owed banks alone approximately $20 million for short-term loans.[36] Their inability to pay put banks and other creditors at risk, as did an ensuing run by those who held bank paper and demanded the issuing banks to fulfill their legal duty to exchange it for specie.[37] No bank, however, had sufficient specie to redeem all of its paper. At this point the total note issues outstanding for the entire State Bank system was over $5.5 million, but specie reserves amounted to only $751,772.[38] Every dollar of specie paid out devalued the paper that had not been redeemed, and hampered the banks from making new loans by issuing new paper.[39]

To protect their remaining specie reserves from total depletion, each of the branches of the State Bank, like virtually all banks nationally, chose to suspend specie payments in May 1837.[40] This potentially placed the state and its citizens in even greater financial jeopardy. A bank's failure to redeem in specie on demand was grounds for its charter's forfeiture. If that occurred, the loan customers of that bank would be required prematurely to pay their debts in full during the winding-up process. Because of the downturn in the economy, however, those customers were now cash-poor and would have to sell their property at a loss to try to pay those debts.

The failure of the State Bank would also deprive the state of funds with which to operate, most state taxes having been repealed in early 1836. New taxes would have to be imposed for this purpose, as well as to pay the state's bonded indebtedness, which had earlier ballooned to $10 million to capitalize the banks and permit them to make loans.[41] Hence, farmers and others who had borrowed no money could eventually be required to pay crushing property taxes for those who did borrow, or else lose their property in tax sales. It seemed that only the already dirt poor could avoid this fate. A Georgia editor wrote that "Poor folks may now bless their poverty, and give thanks that they had no credit."[42]

For some, the fear of this bleak future outweighed security concerns about hostile Mexicans and Native Americans in Texas. What was described as a "tremendous rush" to Texas was underway. "Vast numbers are gone, going, or preparing to go, with their money and their domestic slaves, even from the fertile lands of Mississippi and Alabama," wrote one editor.[43] By 1840, the population of Texas had increased by over one hundred thousand.[44] In that foreign country, they and their mobile assets such as slaves would, they hoped, be shielded from creditors' claims.[45] In addition, it was reported in the Alabama press that, if they arrived and applied before October 1837, they would be entitled to a grant of free land by virtue of a Texas law enacted to bolster that country's population.[46]

Suspension of specie payments was always a very controversial and potentially dangerous measure. It enraged those who were holding notes issued by the banks and made an already suspicious public even more critical of the power of banks, whom some began to blame for the financial crisis.[47] To protect the banks from a possible backlash from the public, some petitioned Alabama Governor Clement Clay to call a special session of the legislature to enact legislation legalizing the suspension.[48] This move, which was being proposed in virtually every Southern state, was equally controversial. According to the editor of a New Orleans newspaper, the banks had caused the problem in the first instance when they "lavishly discounted the notes of a few rotten aristocrats," thereby giving them the means to speculate. "The very cotton which was purchased by them *two years ago*, and paid for at the same time, has fallen over 50 per cent in value, and cannot be sold even at that, simply because there is no money in the country to pay for it."[49] Therefore, he concluded, legislation "calculated to afford some relief to those who are now suffering from their own wild system of over trading" was the "greatest humbug of all." "The monopolizers have got themselves into the mire," he continued, and "now call upon the legislature, like the wagoner in the fable upon Hercules, to extricate them from it. Let them alone. They know the road which led them into difficulties, let them now find one leading out."[50]

This same sort of populist, anti-bank, and anti-bank-debtor sentiment appears to have been increasing in Alabama as well.[51] The editor of the Whig organ in Tuscumbia opposed a special legislative session and charged that the "present disastrous state of things owes its origin to wild speculation and reckless extravagance, engendered and kept alive by the ease with which money has been procured from the Banks."[52] This sentiment would have an important influence on state politics in the next decade. Nonetheless, on May 13, 1837, Governor Clay did what some had requested by calling a special session of the legislature to convene during the second week of June.[53]

Hubbard was not among those who absconded to Texas. He returned from Philadelphia to Alabama and then went to Pontotoc where the next round of auction sales was to take place in late May. He undoubtedly hoped that demand might be sufficient to permit disposal of the remainder of his company's lands, but the sale reportedly drew few purchasers and the best lands were knocked off at $1.25 an acre.[54] This was no surprise. "Everyone is aiming to get out of debt, by selling everything and buying comparatively nothing," one Huntsvillian observed.[55] Even worse for Hubbard, many who had earlier purchased land on credit from the New York and Mississippi Land Company remained in default and had to be sued.[56]

He, nonetheless, received some very good and, perhaps, unexpected news from Tuscaloosa. When the Alabama legislature met in special session, a law was passed that not only approved the suspension of specie payments and permitted it to continue for three years but also provided for the issuance and sale of even more state bonds to obtain an additional $5 million in specie to replenish the reserves of the state-owned banks. The branch at Decatur was to receive $1 million of the new specie.[57] As a quid pro quo, the law also required the banks to permit borrowers to renew unpaid loans and thereby postpone the due dates of those loans.[58]

As would be noted in future political campaigns, this relief legislation was a good deal for the state banks and bank debtors like David Hubbard, most of whom were still among the wealthiest on paper. It was a very bad deal, however, for the state and its less well-heeled, who composed a majority of the electorate.[59] The wealthy few who were debtors of the state banking system should have been required to pay their debts even if it meant selling their property. In this fashion, the state could have used the funds collected to pay off the state's bonded indebtedness. As critics would later charge, however, this legislature was composed of far too many who were either bank debtors or connected to bank debtors or directors interested in maintaining the status quo.[60] The upshot was that, with the inevitable erosion of the value of assets held by debtors—and the fact that many of those assets were portable and therefore subject to movement across state and international lines—an increasingly large amount of the debt would later be uncollectible. Unless the price of cotton rebounded fairly quickly, the state's newly augmented bonded indebtedness—over $15 million—would ultimately have to be paid by *all* of the remaining people through taxes. Thus were the seeds of future political strife sown in Alabama.[61]

Despite these objections, which were voiced by many at the time, Governor Clay signed what was known as the "Relief Law." One can only speculate whether his unanimous selection by the legislature during this special session to fill an open seat in the United States Senate was somehow connected.[62] Thus, Clay would not be forced to face the voters or stand for reelection as governor in the fall of 1837, but he would never again hold elected office.[63]

The bank and debtor relief legislation enacted in the 1837 special session was predicated on the assumption that, like some previous economic down-

Clement Comer Clay

turns in the United States, this one would be over in two or three years and (for Democrats) certainly before the 1840 presidential election. Despite frantic efforts by the nation's politicians and financiers to right the economic ship of state, however, the price of cotton remained low and David Hubbard's investments would go in the same direction as Martin Van Buren's reelection hopes.[64] One wonders whether the Native Americans being pushed off their ancestral lands to the West during this period felt some degree of satisfaction in the whites' misery.[65] Some had been transported across north Alabama by boat and then on the TC&D, but many had been compelled by military force to walk, resulting in hundreds of deaths.[66] It would have been difficult for them to miss the irony of the white man's persistent efforts to forcibly remove them to the West, only to follow them to a region where Native Americans again constituted the vast majority of the population.

The Relief Law gave Hubbard and other bank debtors in Alabama the right to defer loan payments until the spring of 1838. At that point, however, 25 percent of the balance would be due. Two more installments, including the final payment, would be due later. The failure to make any installment on time would cause the entire debt to be immediately due. Thus, Hubbard had some breathing space, but it would not last long.[67]

Even this was potentially jeopardized. The Whig Party and its congressional candidates in Alabama and elsewhere were advocating the resurrection of the Second Bank of the United States, whose charter had expired in 1836 as a consequence of Andrew Jackson's veto of a bill that would have extended it.[68] If recharter occurred, and the Bank of the United States again became the depository of the gold and silver holdings of the federal government, its note issues would become the most secure and, therefore, most desired of all banks. With a national bank armed with this economic power and the ability to establish branch banks that could make specie payments in each of the states *and* require state banks to redeem their notes with scarce specie, state banks would eventually fail.[69] Liquidation of those banks would potentially include collection of all of the debts due by Hubbard and each of the many other debtors.

President Van Buren and many Democrats were opposed to the creation of another national bank, or even depositing federal funds in any bank. Instead, Van Buren called Congress into special session and advocated that the Treasury Department itself maintain those funds in its own vaults. None other than John C. Calhoun of South Carolina surprised and delighted many Southern Democrats when he supported this "subtreasury" or "independent treasury" plan.[70] According to his biographers, Calhoun's primary motivation was the same as always: the presidency. In the long run, he also feared that an all-powerful bank based in the North would control the nation's politics to such an extent that Congress might eventually endanger Southern rights, particularly with regard to slavery.[71] On October 3, he and Alabama's senators joined in passing a treasury bill in the United States Senate.[72] Although it failed in the House, the Pontotoc *Chickasaw Union*, which was a Democrat organ, praised Calhoun and welcomed him back to the party of Andrew Jackson with open arms. With the issue of nullification "put to rest, if we find a man of Mr. Calhoun's powers battling by the side of the democratic party, from which he has been so long estranged, in support of one of the most important measures which can engage the attention of a public man, we see no reason why he should not be welcomed."[73]

Hubbard undoubtedly agreed with this sentiment, but of equal if not more importance to him was Calhoun's seemingly vacillating stance on the direction of a railroad to be built west from South Carolina. Early plans to run it to Memphis using the TC&D as a link appeared to have been replaced by a project to connect Charleston by rail to Louisville, Kentucky, and Cincinnati, Ohio. As often occurred with railroad initiatives, opinions differed regarding the precise route to be used, and Calhoun's disagreement with the chosen route through North Carolina rather than Tennessee was so adamant that he ultimately ended his involvement with the project.[74] However, even before that occurred Calhoun appeared to be a man who could be convinced to back the original plan through north Georgia, north Alabama, and north Mississippi to Memphis. If that project were undertaken, it might inject new life into the now financially struggling TC&D and spur demand for the remaining land of Hubbard's land company.[75] At the behest of his Northern partners, Hubbard went to Washington in the fall of 1837, purportedly to market that land to members of Congress and lay the groundwork for similar solicitation efforts when the various legislatures of the Southeastern Seaboard states convened in the coming months. Because of the continuing depression of cotton prices, however, he was unsuccessful in making any sales.[76] It is likely that Hubbard first met Calhoun during this visit to the capital. Hubbard took this opportunity to pitch the north Alabama route for a railroad from Charleston and the significance of connecting with Memphis. After returning to Pontotoc to attend the January 1838 auction sales, Hubbard wrote Washington Miller that he was to confer with Calhoun again in February.[77]

Hubbard's experience in the nation's capital was impactful, if not transformative, because it was there Hubbard saw firsthand the growing power of Northern abolitionism in action. They had changed tactics from the direct mail propaganda campaign of the early 1830s to petitioning Congress to end slavery, and a few mainstream, influential Northern politicians such as Senator Daniel Webster of Massachusetts, a presidential aspirant, were supporting their right to do so.[78] Calhoun was leading the opposition to this, arguing that if Congress agreed to receive the petitions, it might ultimately debate their merits, and if that occurred slavery might eventually be abolished in the District of Columbia over which Congress had exclusive power. This, Calhoun feared, would ultimately lead to abolition in the South or destruction of the Union.[79] Hubbard shared this concern and felt an irresistible urge to help Calhoun.

Hubbard returned to Philadelphia, where his family was still somewhat curiously residing,[80] and over the next several months took on the role of a political hatchetman, writing attack pieces targeting Daniel Webster and other leading Whigs for publication in that state's primary Democrat organ, the Harrisburg *Pennsylvania Reporter*.[81] With few exceptions, only Hubbard's reports of these activities to Calhoun's Alabama lieutenant in the House of Representatives, Dixon Hall Lewis, still survive. In April 1838, Lewis wrote Hubbard enthusiastic letters reporting that Hubbard's articles were "producing great impression in our circles here and are much sought for." Lewis also told Hubbard, "Don't stop your efforts for your blows tell with appalling effect."[82] Hubbard was not about to stop. He requested that Lewis send him copies of the *Congressional Globe* "relating to Mr. Webster's course in Congress during the late War [of 1812]." Webster, as Hubbard knew, had been a Federalist as well as a vocal opponent of that war and had even suggested that the New England states might nullify federal wartime economic policies. Hubbard bragged to Lewis that, "I have it [in] my power with this aid to finish Webster's public character as completely and much more effectively than was done to [John] Sergeant," Henry Clay's Pennsylvania running mate in the 1832 presidential election. Hubbard vowed that "Clay and [Nicholas] Biddle" would "come next."[83] When Hubbard received those materials from Lewis, he expressed rage regarding Webster's declarations of "baseness and treasonable feeling." Hubbard wrote Lewis in righteous indignation that "I can scarcely forgive any Republican of the day who was a witness to their treachery for ever having treated any one of this nest of vipers with ordinary respect." Hubbard sent his draft article to Lewis for him to "scrutinize" it before publication, "lest my feelings should have betrayed my judgment."[84]

Hubbard did expand his "blows" to include Nicholas Biddle, the very controversial former president of the Second Bank of the United States who was then serving as president of a large, state-chartered private bank in Pennsylvania. Biddle's stewardship of the Second Bank, as well as this more recently chartered bank, was held up by Whigs as the model for a national banking system.[85] However, because Hubbard was also then trying to solicit Biddle to purchase his land company's properties in north Mississippi, he used a newspaper editor in Washington as a cat's paw.[86] He wrote Dixon Hall Lewis requesting that he have Richard Cralle, the pro-Calhoun editor of the new *Washington Reformer*, publish an expose claiming—correctly—that "Mr. Biddle's Bank was insolvent and that now they are wholly unable to resume [specie payments], that all his parade about conscious strength has been utterly false; [and] that those men who have heretofore relied on him can rely upon him no longer."[87] Sending this message to the South, Hubbard maintained, was essential. "Mr. Biddle on his part is to operate on the South and Southwest where it is supposed that the people and Banks being largely indebted will more readily respond to his sentiments" unless they were aware "he is unable to pay and that New York and Boston know it and have given him up."[88] This attack journalism might have had some effect: Biddle's new bank delighted Democrats when it failed a few months later.[89] Moreover, Democrats won Pennsylvania in the fall 1838 elections, seen by political pundits as foreshadowing the outcome of the 1840 presidential election.[90]

Hubbard's dedication to Calhoun's cause looked like it might also pay off for him personally. He wrote Calhoun urging that the interstate railroad under contemplation in South Carolina connect with a Georgia railroad being constructed to Chattanooga and that this be joined with the TC&D

and ultimately with Memphis. Calhoun replied that he agreed with Hubbard regarding the route "you so strongly recommend." Calhoun added
that he took "the deepest interest in the work, not only in a commercial
but a political point of view. It will do more to unite & conciliate the slave
holding States, than can be effected by anything else; and will change not
only the commerce, but the politicks of the Union."[91] And so it would.

7

'A No-Account Locofoco'

Rumors were circulating that the incumbent congressman from Hubbard's district, Joshua Lanier Martin, was planning to resign.[1] Perhaps Hubbard, too, could help change "the politicks of the Union" if he could win Martin's seat. Things did not go quite as smoothly as Hubbard and others anticipated. Martin did finally decide not to run, but the Alabama Democratic State Convention, which had met in Tuscaloosa in late December 1838, did not endorse anyone for that race. Instead it was decided that the Democrats of the congressional district would meet and decide whom to support. Yet, when they met, they endorsed no one.[2]

It was clear that David Hubbard had many negatives to overcome in his return to politics. He had represented the farmers of Lawrence County quite well in the legislature but had upset Jacksonites by defending South Carolina during the nullification crisis.[3] Hubbard also had helped bring railroad transportation to northwest Alabama but was seen as an opponent of, and obstacle to, the never-completed canal around the Muscle Shoals. In addition, there had been strong rumors that the branch of the State Bank at Decatur was in financial trouble, and then a report of the state banking commissioners revealed that those associated with the now-insolvent TC&D owed a huge sum—$344,433—to that bank.[4] Finally, Hubbard was not only known to be a major land speculator—a land shark—but was suspected of having used money borrowed from the Decatur bank to fund his purchases in Mississippi.[5]

The Whiggish editor of the Huntsville *Southern Advocate* even teased that Hubbard was running for Congress as a member of the Whig Party. This incensed Hubbard and led him to write a lengthy public letter of protest to the editor. Hubbard prudently used the first few paragraphs of that letter to remind the public of his military service against the British and that he had "suffered from the insolence of that haughty and tyrannical power which had arrayed itself against us for the purpose of overturning our Republican Government." He also contrasted this with the antiwar activities of the Federalists who were now prominent in the Whig Party and, like the British, favored a "strong central government" to "enable the few to plunder the many, by sponging up the earnings of labor without immediate and direct accountability; and hence the anxiety of such to degrade State sovereignty and to exalt federal power." The protective tariffs still promoted by Whigs were, according to Hubbard, simply intended to "enable a few capitalists to charge double as much for manufactured articles as the articles were worth," and for the government to use the money "dishonestly extorted from labor upon extravagant works of internal improvements, many of which were useless." Hubbard also used populist rhetoric to pound away at the Whigs' goal of a national banking system. To him it was a "contrivance" by which "Congress takes a few wealthy men into partnership with the federal Government, and agrees for twenty years to come, to tax the residue of our citizens, however needy and poor, and lend those taxes, without interest, to the Bankers, however affluent and rich."[6]

Then Hubbard finally addressed the issue of his loyalty to the Democratic Party. "I supported Gen. Jackson three times as a candidate for the Presidency, and supported most of the measures of his administration." However, he conceded, "I opposed publicly and openly the Proclamation and Force Bill, as tending to too strong a central Government." Yet Hubbard bravely—seemingly foolishly—declared that he "would do so again under the same impressions." He was "delighted" with Jackson's opposition to a national bank and he also "consequently" supported, and would continue to support, Martin Van Buren for that reason.[7]

The editor of the Huntsville *Democrat* was quite satisfied with Hubbard's manifesto. He was "gratified that Mr. Hubbard has thus promptly repelled the imputation that his politics were of the 'Whig Order.'" But he stopped short of recommending Hubbard's election. He instead called on the Democrats to avoid any "division in their ranks" that would result from promoting multiple candidates. To Whigs, Hubbard was now merely a "no-account Locofoco," a term of derision applied to Democrats who supported Van Buren and the concept of an independent treasury instead of the charter of national banks. The editor of the Huntsville *Southern Advocate* expressed hope that there would be a division, and encouraged the Whigs of the fourth district to "select their strongest man" to enter the race.[8] The new pro-Whig *Decatur Register* also encouraged the Whigs to "awake from their lethargy, and come forward, fired with that zeal which is now required to break the brittle thread of locofocoism" in the district.[9]

David Hubbard was undoubtedly pleased with the choice made by the Whigs to oppose him: Moulton lawyer David Greenhill Ligon. Ligon had earlier served with Hubbard in the legislature, but since then had suffered from alcoholism. As one contemporary put it, Ligon had "allowed the indulgence of his appetite for stimulants to put the brakes on his otherwise promising future." Social prejudice against the consumption of alcohol had existed for some time in Alabama, as evidenced by the formation of a temperance movement several years earlier. Ligon had undergone a religious conversion and, in 1837, tried to make a political comeback in a race for the congressional seat, but it was handily won by Joshua Lanier Martin.[10]

Whether that defeat was due to concerns that Ligon might fall off the wagon is unknown, but the issue made him vulnerable. So did Ligon's support for a national bank during this period when banks were blamed by many for causing the nation's economic ills.[11] The mood of some segments of the public toward banks was graphically illustrated by the destruction in Decatur, Mississippi, of a private bank, which was set on fire by an angry mob. When the president of that bank attempted to escape to Texas, he was reportedly "pursued, overtaken, and hanged."[12]

Ligon's chances against Hubbard did not improve when the bottom fell out of the cotton market once again in the summer of 1839, heralding several more years of economic depression.[13] This may explain why Ligon's supporters attacked Hubbard so vociferously in the weeks leading up to the state election in August 1839. Most of those accusations against Hubbard related to the manner in which he acquired the funds used to speculate in Chickasaw lands. Some believed he got them from Martin Van Buren and that the two were partners. Others charged that he borrowed it from the State Bank in Decatur. In addition, David Ligon issued a "circular" alleging that Hubbard desired to be elected to Congress to obtain some advantage in the purchase of more public lands.[14]

Hubbard recognized the potential power of Ligon's argument regarding the public lands. He had earlier written to President Van Buren advising him that the settlers and squatters in the newer states "turn the scale of public opinion in all elections" and supported those who promised pre-emption rights. These "country people," Hubbard explained, whether "waking or sleeping [,] eating [,] or working never think of anything but 'Land.'" As a consequence, a man like the late David Crockett, who Hubbard judged as being "without talent," was "enabled to maintain his popularity for years against Genl. Jackson and every other member of Congress from Tennessee solely on the ground of his wanting rights of pre-emption to that portion of his constituents who were termed squatters." Ironically, Hubbard also advised Van Buren to end "this odious scheme of fraud and speculation practiced at public sales by monopolizing combinations" who outbid settlers, and assured Van Buren that if he did this he would secure for himself "a name in the West which will never be forgotten."[15]

As Hubbard recognized, the converse of this was also true. If settlers and squatters believed that he was a champion of that "odious scheme," public opinion would be against him. He was, therefore, forced to issue his own circular, which was published in newspapers throughout the district. In it he explained his source of funding and his relationship with the New York investors, and denied receiving anything from the Decatur bank for the purchase of Chickasaw lands. He did not, however, volunteer any information regarding his investments in Creek lands in east Alabama or the purpose of his loans from the Tuscaloosa bank. Those aspects of the question had apparently not been raised. Hubbard also rebutted Ligon's charge regarding an ulterior motive for going to Washington. In his circular, Hubbard conceded that he was "on account of the public lands, desirous of a seat in Congress," but he claimed that his true goal was to "aid in giving pre-emptions to the occupants and none others, and to graduate and reduce the price of such as have been long on hand, so that they may be settled on and cultivated."[16] He did not mention the opportunities it would give him to market Mississippi land to wealthy men in and out of Congress.[17]

Hubbard also vaguely and obliquely alluded to Ligon's drinking habit when he proposed a "test of qualification for office" based on which of the two was most able to accomplish this goal: "when you confer a trust on an individual, *knowing his habits*, you have a right to expect all the care and attention, skill and fidelity which he exercises in the management of his own affairs, and no more." On this score, Hubbard reminded that he had not only been successful in his private endeavors, but while in the legislature had been instrumental in having pre-emption rights granted to hundreds of families in the lands granted to the state by Congress in connection with the Muscle Shoals canal. Hubbard encouraged the voters to "Try Mr. Ligon by the same rule," suggesting that "You have a right to expect of him all the care, prudence and attention which he exercises in the management of his own affairs, and you have no right to expect more."[18]

The only recorded reply by Ligon to these not-so-subtle aspersions was apparently issued after the results of the election of August 5 were made known. Ligon quipped that it was the "first time he had ever heard it suggested that 'the bell cow' should be sent to put *up* the fence."[19] In any event, Hubbard was victorious even though Ligon edged him in Lawrence County.[20] Hubbard was one of three Democrats from Alabama elected to Congress at this time, the other two being incumbents Reuben Chapman of the Huntsville District and Dixon Hall Lewis. Two south Alabama Whigs were also elected.[21]

Regardless of party affiliation, the victors had their work cut out for them. The interim period between the election and the meeting of Congress was full of signs of social unrest as the economic depression deepened. The business district in Mobile was beset with a series of highly destructive fires that were set by a militant element who resorted to arson. A deadly yellow fever epidemic there added to the people's misery and led one editor to wonder if Mobile was a "doomed" city. "Have we not drank deep enough of the bitter cup of adversity and affliction? When and where will our calamities end? Alas! Heaven only knows!"[22]

Just as disturbing to Southerners of both parties was the increasing politicization of the abolition movement as evidenced by the organization of what was called the Liberty Party. Its members convened in New York in November and nominated former Huntsville, Alabama, lawyer James Birney as their presidential candidate for 1840.[23] Birney had no chance, but, as Hubbard would later note, the heightened involvement of the anti-slavery movement in the political realm necessarily gave it the potential for traction among members of the two mainstream parties. Politics is, in essence, a game of addition; those candidates who can attract any blocs of voters have a greater chance to succeed.

Hubbard proceeded to Washington in the late fall of 1839, arriving on November 23.[24] He took a room in a popular boarding house near Capitol Hill known as the "Old Capitol."[25] This three-story red brick building had been constructed after the British burned the capitol in the War of 1812, and it was where Congress had met until the capitol was rebuilt.[26] Among Hubbard's messmates were several other Southern congressmen, including South Carolina extremist Robert Barnwell Rhett. The dominant topic of political discourse revolved around the election of the Speaker of the House, which would occur after Congress convened on December 2.[27] Given that 1840 was a presidential election year, this was destined to be a very contentious issue in a very contentious session. Democrats held a small majority of seats, at least on paper,[28] but party discipline was poor. David Hubbard supported Dixon Hall Lewis, who was initially spoken of as a strong candidate for the Democrats, but, after several days of balloting, a young nominal Whig from Virginia, Robert M. T. Hunter, finally won the contest.[29]

Despite this, Hubbard received the committee assignment he needed: a place on the House Committee on the Public Lands.[30] However, many saw the speakership election as a harbinger of the outcome of the presidential election. The Whigs had nominated William Henry Harrison, who had the qualifications to attract large blocs of votes. He was a native of Virginia, but now resided in Ohio. Unlike Martin Van Buren, Harrison was also a war hero. He, in addition, had the benefit of the nation's continuing economic miseries, which the Democrats had so far been unsuccessful in resolving.[31]

Democrats attempted to distract the public and divide the Whigs by agitating the slavery issue. Harrison, they alleged, was in favor of abolition and so were most Northern Whigs.[32] Democrats made frequent use of blood-curdling tales of the St. Domingue slave insurrection less than fifty years earlier, calling the massacre of whites there the "first fruits of abolition."[33] Twenty-seven-year-old William Yancey's pro-Democrat Wetumpka newspaper, the *Wetumpka Argus,* was also critical of Southern Whigs, lamenting that there was a "large party, in the South, who are using every endeavor to elevate to the Presidency, a man, who hopes to see the day, when the sun will not shine upon a North American slave."[34] To undermine this perception, a Whig member of the House from Maryland advocated the adoption of a permanent rule further restricting the reception of anti-slavery petitions by the House. This so-called "gag rule," which required all such petitions to be "laid on the table, without debate or further action thereon," was adopted with Hubbard voting with the rest of the Alabama delegation in the affirmative.[35] This, however, would eventually backfire on slavery perpetualists of both parties.

Hubbard recognized that the Democratic Party was in trouble. He wrote James K. Polk, who had recently won the governor's race in Tennessee and then attended a public dinner in his honor in Courtland,[36] urging Polk to seek election as vice president and thereby defeat the incumbent, Richard Mentor Johnson of Kentucky.[37] Johnson had committed the cardinal sin of Southern politics of this era by openly living with his mulatto mistress and their two children, and many Southern Democrats were anxious to dump him in favor of someone whose racial and social mores were orthodox. Polk replied to Hubbard, whom he had known for some time, that he would only do so if he received the nomination to that position at the upcoming Democratic National Convention in May.[38] Hubbard responded by noting that this was the accepted procedure under normal circumstances, but that these times were not normal. "The whole union is in a state of fermentation and effervescence growing out of the derangements produced by paper money." This excessive expansion of the currency, Hubbard continued, produced "extravagance & indebtedness," and now "contraction . . . produces poverty, ruin and distress" among "the prudent & cautious as well as [the] extravagant & profligate." The "masses," as a result, "are ready to lend a ready and willing ear to the federalists who are ready to ruin our country to advance their own principles."[39] As a consequence, the nation faced more danger than it had "since our Government was set on foot." Not only must

Polk run, Hubbard urged, but he must tell the people that the importance of the outcome of this election was "second only to the Revolution itself." They must also be told, Hubbard concluded, that "monopoly, priveledge [*sic*], monarchy or aristocracy & all the other forms in which plunderers can be bound together by common cement (love of power & a desire to enjoy the fruits of labor without undergoing its fatigues) compose his forces & upon all of these questions the people should be advised forewarned & guarded."[40] Polk remained reluctant, however, to breach traditional party protocol.

Regardless of who was to blame for the economic devastation and suffering, Hubbard recognized that the people would support the party they perceived to have the ability to implement a successful plan for relief. On February 10 and March 9, he offered resolutions calling for the House Judiciary Committee to "inquire into the expediency of establishing a uniform system of bankruptcy in the United States."[41] In addition to giving debtors a fresh start by discharging their debts, this system would put a stop to collection lawsuits that had sometimes led to bloodshed in Alabama and elsewhere.[42]

The United States Constitution had always authorized Congress to adopt a system of bankruptcy, but Congress had exercised this power only once despite several earlier economic downturns. One reason was the adverse effect on creditors of discharging debts owed to them.[43] However, the national economy was in such bad shape that those creditors were already at risk. Several months earlier one perceptive Alabamian wrote that "Our Banks are likely to fall to pieces."[44] If that occurred, they would take all of their loan and deposit customers with them, including Hubbard. As a consequence, Alabama's congressional delegation was receiving petitions and memorials from every strata of society in Alabama praying for the adoption of a federal bankruptcy law,[45] but Hubbard and others were unable to overcome opposition and pass that law during this session.[46] Hence, the Democrats and Van Buren, who was blamed by the Whigs for the failure of the bill, would have nothing other than their Independent Treasury idea to offer the public, and no one even pretended that it would actually stimulate the economy.[47]

This forced the Democrats to intensify their attacks on the Whigs.

Shortly before he attended the Democratic National Convention in Balti-more, Hubbard issued a lengthy and sometimes technical public letter to his constituents criticizing the portion of the Whig platform advocating the creation of a national banking system. He, among other things, appealed to anti-British sentiment when he pointed out that this concept originated in England with the Bank of England, and quoted extensively from a report by commercial interests there blaming that nation's current economic problems, as well as those of the South, on the policies of the Bank of England. He then requested his constituents not to "re-engraft a branch thereof into the Tree of Liberty, which was planted by our fathers, and watered with their blood, that your children may gather like fruit!"[48] Hubbard's letter, however, offered nothing that might right the economy.

Neither did the Democratic National Convention, where he served as a member of the resolutions committee. On the contrary, the delegates es-sentially confirmed that the party Andrew Jackson had built was the party of "no." No to federally funded internal improvements; no to the assumption of the debts of the states; no to protective tariffs; no to a national banking system; and certainly no to abolitionists. Despite efforts by Hubbard and others, the Democrats could not agree to dump Richard Johnson and nomi-nate James K. Polk as the vice-presidential candidate. At least they voted to make no nomination at all for that position, as Hubbard then urged, thereby allowing each state to back Polk or Johnson.[49] Hubbard wrote Polk that "this is better than to have to carry such a load as would have been laid upon us had we" nominated Johnson.[50]

David Hubbard, Dixon Hall Lewis, Reuben Chapman, Clement Clay, and William R. King, the Democrat members of Alabama's congressional delegation, then issued a circular on May 14, 1840, calling on party leaders in Alabama to organize at the county level, select strong candidates for the upcoming state election, and begin collecting funds to pay for the dissemina-tion of political propaganda. Such funds, they explained, were necessary to counter the "immense funds, collected from [the Whig] party numbering in their ranks a large majority of the mercantile and professional classes, and backed by the banks."[51]

Hubbard, meanwhile, attempted to fulfill his main campaign promise when he made a lengthy speech in the House on May 24 advocating the adoption of a bill granting pre-emption rights to settlers on public lands. The text of his remarks, which were made in an effort to rebut arguments against the bill made by members from Massachusetts and Kentucky, reflects a mixture of logic, advocacy, and ridicule.[52] Hubbard obviously thought well of his effort. According to the *Congressional Globe*, he declared that he had "triumphantly answered every objection, and had 'squared off' with both of his opponents." A large majority of the House apparently agreed; the bill passed by a vote of 126 to 64, although it later failed in the Senate.[53]

The following month Hubbard became even more flamboyant—and not a little hypocritical—when he took the floor in support of the Independent Treasury bill. "The world had been governed by priestcraft, and then by kingcraft," he declared, "but this was the age of bankcraft, the age of corrupt men, who make money without capital." He then reportedly "gave a vivid picture of the system of modern banking, and its ruinous effects upon the country" and "showed the great superiority of the present measure, which would operate as a check upon excessive imports, and may prevent a recurrence of the disastrous scenes of former years."[54] Unlike the pre-emption bill, the Independent Treasury bill was not only passed by the House, but on July 4 it was signed into law by President Van Buren.[55]

After Congress adjourned on July 21, David Hubbard, his wife, and one of his children began the long journey back to Alabama, perhaps hoping they would finally have some restful family time aboard the series of coaches, railroads, and steamships that the trip entailed. However, when they boarded the SS *North Carolina* at Wilmington, North Carolina, on July 25, they were joined by several other Southern congressmen who were also on their way home, including Hubbard's friend Dixon Hall Lewis. Politics would continue to rule, or so they thought.

At one o'clock on the morning of Sunday, July 26, after reaching a point approximately sixty miles south of Wilmington on its way to Charleston, South Carolina, the *North Carolina* was struck in her larboard cover by her sister ship, the SS *Governor Dudley*. Within ten minutes the *North Carolina* reportedly sank down "to the water's edge in eleven fathoms" of water. Fortunately the Hubbards and all of the other passengers (surprisingly including the grossly obese Lewis) and crew were able to scamper aboard yawl boats that conveyed them to the crippled *Governor Dudley* before the *North Carolina* keeled over and sank seventy feet to the ocean floor approximately eighteen nautical miles east of present-day Myrtle Beach, South Carolina. They had not had time to retrieve the bulk of their luggage or other valuables, and, according to one of the many newspaper reports around the nation about this incident, David Hubbard's "loss in money was larger" than that of any other passenger. The approximate amount exceeded $15,000, but the reason he was carrying so much is unknown.[56]

At least Hubbard and his family were not killed or injured in this near disaster, and they eventually made their way home. The sinking of the *North Carolina* was an omen of sorts. When they reached Alabama, Hubbard learned that the Whigs had made gains in the Alabama legislative races in August. This was particularly the case in south Alabama. The Democrats, however, succeeded in hanging on to majority control of the legislature, but their prospects of retaining the White House were not good.[57]

In September David Hubbard wrote a group of Democrats in Tennessee declining their invitation to attend a public dinner because of "sickness now in my family," but also taking a shot at the enemy. In that letter, which was published in newspapers far and wide, Hubbard declared that "Could your citizens—could every disinterested voter in our once happy country, see Whiggery as it has appeared to me in days of excitement in Congress, they would not give it countenance, but would look upon it as a 'Hideous Monster,' to be dreaded by the whole Union." That "monster," Hubbard continued, had a head composed of "monarchy, called federalism," and a body "formed of the Bank-paper credit-usury-taking system." His right arm, he asserted, "is Abolition," and his left "composed of disappointed ambition." His "legs and feet" and path to power, Hubbard alleged, consisted of "the want and distresses of the country, produced by his own former *ravages*, and now falsely charged to Democratic principles, and magnified for present effect. Such is Whiggery as it appeared to my vision," Hubbard maintained. Given this, he concluded, "the voters of the Union ought by their voices expressed through the ballot boxes (not cartridge boxes), in November to shiver [the Whig monster] in pieces and scatter him to the four corners of the Union, the captains of his Hosts and their misguided followers."[58]

With Hubbard's support and that of what was becoming known as the "avalanche" counties of north Alabama, Democrats were able to preserve Alabama for Van Buren in the presidential election of 1840 by a 54.4 percent to 45.6 percent margin. But Van Buren garnered only 60 out of 294 electoral votes nationwide.[59] Thus for the first time the "Hideous Monster" of Whiggery would control the presidency. If Hubbard assumed times could not get worse, he would be sadly mistaken.

8

'A Man of the Masses'

David Hubbard soon learned that the victorious Whig Party had also captured a majority of both houses of Congress, which convened on December 7, 1840. Although he was nonetheless assigned to the prestigious Ways and Means Committee, the reality was that Henry Clay and the Whigs now seemingly had nothing to stop them from systematically dismantling the brand of government erected by the Democrats during the Jacksonian Era.[1] Often haughty with their newfound power, the Whigs were frequently disrespectful to Hubbard and other Democrats when they spoke, and typically ignored their input.[2] As a consequence, even the normally courtly, calm, and collected William Rufus King of Alabama challenged Henry Clay to a duel.[3]

Hubbard was particularly incensed at the hypocrisy of the Whigs for their change of tune regarding the spoils system, which they had denounced while the Democrats were in power. In a letter to an Alabama Democrat, Hubbard predicted that once president-elect Harrison was inaugurated in March, Democrats would be removed from "all offices having a salary worth having." The Whigs, he continued, "will prove by their acts that they are the spoilers. Their rapacity has not been equaled since the Government was organized [;] nothing has ever come near it." Hubbard even compared them to the "English at N[ew] Orleans," whose "watchword" was "Beauty [and] Booty."[4] Even worse, news of Harrison's probable cabinet appointments demonstrated that he was moving toward what Hubbard called "an amalgamated coalition" consisting of former Federalists, Whigs, and anti-slavery zealots and sympathizers. In light of this growing abolition influence within the Whig Party, Hubbard warned that "if Southern men hold on [to that party] after this, no one can predict *how soon* they are doomed to destruction, for doomed they certainly are if they arouse not from their present lethargy."[5]

Hubbard also had concerns back in Alabama. His wife, Eliza, was several months pregnant and due to give birth in the spring.[6] Furthermore, with the price of cotton still depressed at seven cents a pound, Hubbard's financial situation was not improving.[7] Moreover, if political trends in the state continued, it could become even worse and possibly politically embarrassing. With the nomination of a south Alabamian, Benjamin Fitzpatrick, for governor on December 21, Alabama Democrats signaled their intention to make the eroding condition of the State Bank system a major issue in the upcoming state election.[8] Their plan was to blame Whig legislators for corruptly using their positions to obtain loans. To demonstrate this, the Democrats' state organ, the Tuscaloosa *Flag of the Union*, published a chart revealing the loan amounts owed by current members of the legislature, and that a majority of the borrowers were members of the Whig Party. However, this strategy potentially cut both ways. Democrat Benjamin Fitzpatrick could honestly tell the voters—as he did—that "I never borrowed a dollar from a Bank—neither was I ever President or Director of one. I am a tiller of the earth, and look to that as the only true source of our prosperity and wealth."[9] Many other Democrats could not truthfully make that representation.[10]

Hubbard certainly could not. Indeed, of the one million dollars classified as bad debt owed to the Decatur branch of the State Bank, he owed a very large amount.[11] The debts owed regarding the TC&D, and the fact that its stockholders were on the bank's board of directors, had already become a major issue in the Alabama legislature.[12] The Whig press was certain to hold up Hubbard and others as examples of Democrat hypocrisy during the upcoming congressional elections. Even worse, if Democrat leaders decided to double down on the bank issue by pushing for the aggressive collection of outstanding debts to avoid a painful tax increase to pay the roughly $859,000 principal and interest payment due in 1842 on the state's bonded indebtedness, Hubbard would be sacrificed and financially and politically ruined.[13] If that occurred, his now burning desire to be elected to the United States Senate would never be fulfilled.[14]

All of these family, business, and political considerations led Hubbard to consider not seeking reelection in 1841. He might have intended to delay any final decision until after Congress adjourned in March when he would

George S. Houston

have time to ponder it and, if necessary, identify a possible successor whose political views were consistent with his own. On February 24, 1841, shortly after his forty-ninth birthday, he wrote his eventual successor, thirty-year-old George Smith Houston, from snowy Washington, encouraging Houston to throw his hat in the ring, and explaining why he could not "possibly continue in public life." It was "the present deranged state of my affairs."[15]

Houston was born in Tennessee in 1811, became a lawyer, and, like Hubbard, served in the Alabama legislature and as a circuit solicitor. The reason why Hubbard picked Houston is unclear, but it might be that he saw much of himself in the younger man. Their relationship had been testy at times. Possibly alluding to the nullification crisis, Hubbard noted in his letter that "there was a time that things did not go well between us." Hubbard rationalized this as solely a function of Houston's youth and inexperience. Hubbard also forgave Houston for his error in judgment, and assured him that "my feelings toward you are as if it never had taken place," and that "I feel toward you as toward one having the same sentiments with myself [and] the same purposes in view." Hubbard expressed hope that "you feel sufficiently confident in your own exertions that you don't need any system of *Government Charity* to enable you to make a support of yourself and family," and if "you have too strong a sense of meum and tuum [mine and thine], to desire that Government shall step in between us and take that which belongs to me and was intended for the support of mine, and give it to *thee* for the support of *thine*–If this is your feeling," Hubbard concluded, "you are in heart a Democrat, and we are 'brothers in the faith.'"[16] Houston certainly believed in conservative economic and racial policies,[17] but whether they were also "brothers in the faith" in terms of extremist Southern sectionalism remained to be seen.

Hubbard's timetable to publicly announce his intentions had to be accelerated when President Harrison issued a call for Congress to convene in special session on May 31, 1841, to consider pressing economic problems. Because the terms of Alabama's congressmen were to expire when Congress adjourned in March, and the general election was not until August, Alabama's governor Arthur Bagby had to call the legislature into a special session to enact legislation setting a special election to fill those seats. That election was set for May 20.[18] Thus, if Hubbard instead chose to seek reelection, he would have very little time to spend with his wife or to address his financial concerns before having to campaign and, if elected, return to Washington.

Hubbard privately chose to wait until the district nominating convention on April 5 in Courtland before revealing his decision to the public. After the delegates praised his service and unanimously nominated him for reelection, he appeared at the convention and announced that he could not accept that nomination. The excuse he reportedly gave was that his "agent, who for several years" had attended to his "large business," had written him a letter "which was received yesterday, stating that he could no longer manage it without the aid" of Hubbard's "personal attention." This, he concluded, made it his "duty to decline." The identity of this so-called agent is unknown, but Hubbard might have been referring to his brother, Green, who would eventually emigrate to Texas.

All of this might have been a charade orchestrated by Democrats to avoid embarrassing Hubbard. After he gave a speech discussing his past military and public service, and warning all of the various harmful elements of the Whig program, the delegates recessed for only thirty minutes before unanimously nominating George Smith Houston to replace Hubbard.[19] Two days later, Houston issued an acceptance letter that, with one exception, basically parroted everything Hubbard had said in his speech. That exception was that Houston declared himself "unwilling to condemn any administration in advance of its measures."[20]

By this time the entire nation had learned that President Harrison had died on April 4, and that Vice President John Tyler, a conservative Virginia Whig, was the president. Some hoped that Tyler would block enactment of Henry Clay's American System, and so it was logical that Houston announced he would take a wait-and-see approach on Tyler.[21] This relative moderation, in turn, might have endeared Houston to many Whigs in the district. In any event, Houston easily defeated his Whig opponent and, as Hubbard would later discover, would prove to be popular and almost unbeatable.[22]

Hubbard had little time to ponder this. On June 11, 1841, his wife Eliza died and was buried in a cemetery at the Hubbard's homeplace, which was then in Courtland.[23] Just over a month later, Hubbard also lost his father, Thomas.[24] Then, on August 13, the centerpiece of President Van Buren's economic program—the Independent Treasury bill—was repealed by the Whig-controlled Congress.[25] There was, however, some solace in the fact that Congress also finally adopted a bankruptcy law despite opposition from Alabama's congressional delegation.[26] With Benjamin Fitzpatrick easily winning the governor's race, that could come in handy if Hubbard's creditors came after him.[27] As a precaution, Hubbard had previously applied for and, after examination, received a license to practice law in Mississippi in case leaving Alabama with his property became necessary.[28]

President Tyler shocked most observers and enraged many Whigs when he vetoed bills that would have established a national bank.[29] Hubbard was so happy about the resulting split between pro-Tyler Whigs and Clay Whigs that he took time away from his personal affairs to write two of the men expected to be potential Democrat nominees for the presidency in 1844, James K. Polk and John C. Calhoun. To Polk he wrote from Washington that "Tyler desires to profit by [the split] & intends running for the Presidency & expects to so shape his course as to compell [sic] our party as a choice of evils to take him up." Hubbard disclosed that he had told Tyler "in the plainest language" that Democrats would first "require of him works faithfully performed in advancing our principles before we confide in him."[30] In October, Hubbard wrote to Calhoun from New York of the rumors of Whig infighting and political trends in that region.[31]

It is apparent that by this point Hubbard was missing political life in Washington. However, George Houston now had Hubbard's seat in Congress, and William Rufus King and Clement Comer Clay seemed safely ensconced in their Senate seats for years to come. All of a sudden, however, word reached Alabama that Clay had given notice of the resignation of his seat. Clay cited "obligations which cannot be cancelled"—code words for overwhelming debt—as the reason for his decision. Like Hubbard, Clay also took this opportunity to warn Alabamians of the growing strength of the abolitionists in Congress and the fact that they had formed a coalition in the Senate with unnamed "Southern Whig leaders."[32]

Hubbard was already aware of this and anxious to return to Washington in Clay's place to fight this evil coalition.[33] Alabama Whigs in the legislature had other ideas. They coalesced behind Dr. David Moore, a north Alabama Democrat and former Alabama governor who had opposed the Independent Treasury concept. In response, most Democrat legislators ultimately backed Governor Arthur Bagby to finish Clay's term.[34] Thus, Hubbard would remain on the outside looking in from a political standpoint until that term came to an end.

With the Alabama legislature in session and considering options for bank reform, it paid to also keep an eye on that body. By this time the Whigs were citing the woes of the State Bank system in Alabama as evidence of the Democratic Party's fundamentally flawed economic approach, and were calling for all of those banks to be placed in liquidation. This forced Alabama Democrats to address the undeniable problems in the system.[35] The New York *Tribune* reported that the Alabama legislature was "engaged in the pleasant business of overhauling the remains of their State Bank and Branches, which emit an odor of rascality and rottenness strong enough to turn the stomach of a 'Bank Whig.'" The *Tribune* added that the "Branch Bank at Decatur will have to be wound up; and some others ought to be."[36] The Tuscaloosa *Flag of the Union* specifically referred to the "large debt" due from the TC&D, "which has so long hung like a dark cloud over the [Decatur] institution," although it also noted that Benjamin Sherrod had recently stepped forward and personally guaranteed that debt in an effort to save the bank.[37] Yet this left that bank with a circulation of over $1.5 million in note issues compared to only $439,000 in specie—still an unhealthy ratio.[38]

Nonetheless, this legislature was unable to agree on any measures to be taken, a function according to some of the fact that there were still so many legislators who were indebted to the banks and preferred the status quo.[39] Far from liquidating the Decatur branch, they elected a TC&D stockholder,

James Fennell, to be its president.[40] Nevertheless the problems with the banks would not go away. Specie payments were still suspended and public confidence in the banking system's notes had led to their discount by 30 percent in some money markets.[41] As a consequence the banks were increasingly becoming a political liability for the Democrats that would have to be eliminated, certainly before the 1844 presidential election.[42]

As the 1842 state election approached, more and more Democrats saw the first step in reform and political survival would be the election of legislators who were not indebted to the banks. Only a legislature freed of their influence, they asserted, could bring about the necessary reforms. The Democrats' ulterior motive was, of course, to defeat the Whigs who were bank debtors, but this strategy would also undermine similarly situated Democrats.[43] Despite this, Hubbard chose to run for a seat in the legislature. Some charged that he intended to promote an economic program that included repudiation of the state's bonded indebtedness, as had shockingly occurred in Mississippi. But Hubbard denied this in a public letter to the Tuscumbia *Franklin Democrat*.[44] Instead, his primary motivation evidently related to his personal debt load. Some of his land in north Mississippi would soon be sold for nonpayment of the property taxes.[45] If he had insufficient funds to prevent that, he certainly did not have enough to repay his approximately sixteen-thousand-dollar personal debt to the Decatur Bank, which had already filed suit against him on one of his outstanding promissory notes.[46] Moreover, as a legislator Hubbard would be in a position to attempt to block liquidation of the banks—particularly the Decatur bank—as the Whigs advocated and, if liquidation were imposed, to make sure that the debt collection process was extended as long as possible, rather than rapid as some Democrats preferred.[47] This would allow him precious time to raise the money to pay his debts. In addition, bank officials would be more likely to renew his loans when they came due, or at least less likely to aggressively pursue him for repayment.

To be elected, Hubbard had to somehow overcome the growing public prejudice against bank debtors. As Governor Fitzpatrick later put it, the banks were the "absorbing and exciting topic" in the canvass.[48] The method Hubbard used to finesse the bank issue was very clever. He declared that when the state had repealed property taxes in 1836 every property owner in effect became a bank debtor. "Have they not for five years been borrowing of the Banks to support the Government, rather than pay their annual tax upon their property?" he asked. "Do they not as justly owe these borrowed sums as any other borrower?" To this Hubbard added a populist appeal. While property owners had been relieved of their taxes, the "poor white laborer" remained "burdened with great personal services. He is compelled to work ten days on the road, and to serve six days in the militia, making sixteen days of personal servitude in each year." The legislature "did not take any thought of the laborer to relieve him of these heavy personal services."[49] Now, he continued, if taxes had to be reimposed to pay for government operations and the state's bonded indebtedness, they should not be imposed on the "poor white laborer." The legislature, he declared, should not "lay a feather's weight upon him, until all of the borrowed money with its interest has been paid back."[50]

Hubbard recognized the power of appeals to class envy and knew that the yeoman farmers among his constituents who leased land from elites would be appreciative. As one put it, Hubbard was "truly and emphatically a man of the masses, and he worked for the masses." The "great aim of his life has been to meliorate and improve their condition—to strengthen their love of country by giving them a home to fight for, and to excite their pride by the evidences of his rise and the encouragement of his example."[51] Hubbard's strategy worked. In fact, he received more votes that year than any other candidate for the legislature in Lawrence County.[52] For at least one of his supporters who wrote a letter to the editor of a Huntsville newspaper signed "Justice," Hubbard deserved more: Governor Bagby's seat in the United States Senate. Clement Clay's term, which Bagby was serving, would soon come to an end. As his replacement, "Justice" maintained, the Democratic Party should not select a mere party operative. Instead, it should back a man who had served the party, the state, and the Union; one "whose patriotism and fitness" had been tested "in the tented field" and "by the display of a courage which made the lion of Old England crouch." David Hubbard, according to "Justice," was that man.[53]

Hubbard certainly agreed with those sentiments even if he was not actually "Justice." In furtherance of his quest, he published a pamphlet of his ideas regarding policies to be adopted by the party and sent copies to most of the legislators who were members of the Democratic Party. Solving the bank question without placing burdens on the poor was, Hubbard wrote, the key to defeating the Whigs in future elections. The solution to that question was reform, but his list of proposed reforms did not include aggressive collection efforts against bank debtors. Moreover, he advocated that only banks that had not been "honestly conducted" should be placed in liquidation.[54] Hubbard also urged that the party had to remain harmonious as it dealt with lesser issues, such as laying off the state in new congressional districts as a consequence of the 1840 census and choosing the right man in the senatorial election. Seemingly selflessly, Hubbard suggested that if "we cannot harmonize the party upon the Senatorial Election, we can put if off until another year."[55] As Hubbard well knew, it would be easier to defeat Bagby during the 1843–44 legislative session, after Clay's term had expired and while the Senate seat was open, than during the upcoming session while Bagby was an incumbent.

The hostile response by a recipient of Hubbard's pamphlet who had supported Bagby made it apparent that Hubbard had his work cut out for him. This legislator, John S. Kennedy of Lauderdale County, blasted Hubbard's plan on the bank question because of his failure to make bank debt collection a precondition for the imposition of any taxes. "I cannot subscribe," he wrote in a letter to the *Florence Gazette*, "to the doctrine that the Bank debtors ought to be indulged with longer time, and the great body of the people taxed to redeem the circulation." Kennedy also expressed regret "to see a man [like Hubbard] who will carry so much weight into our Legislative Halls, take a stand so firmly on the side of the Bank debtors."[56]

Kennedy saved his severest cut for last. With regard to the senatorial election, he asserted that "whoever may be selected, should have been long identified and connected with the democratic party."[57] This had reference to Hubbard's stance during the nullification crisis and his connection with John C. Calhoun, who had gone through a period where he opposed Andrew Jackson and, as one historian put it, "acted *with*" but "never *of* the Whig party."[58] Even though Calhoun was now acting with the Democrats, some among the Jacksonian element of the party in Alabama still saw him as an apostate whose loyalty would always be suspect. As Hubbard recognized, no matter how much he railed against the Whigs, his own loyalty would still be doubted and remain an obstacle to party advancement.[59] This, he knew, was simply human nature. He had earlier written James Polk that "men remember injuries longer than favors. They hate stronger than they love & whenever the feelings have been once trampled upon they require more than merely saying I won't do so again. They require atonement for injuries which they know have been wantonly inflicted."[60]

Despite this, Hubbard received good news in late November when it was announced that Bagby would not seek reelection to the Senate.[61] Thus, when the legislature convened on December 5, 1842, Hubbard probably assumed that his chances for that seat had improved. But then Bagby changed his mind, which set the stage for a candidate to be selected in a Democratic legislative caucus. Bagby, rather than Hubbard, received the nomination. According to a contemporary of both, the "same reasons which influenced the Jackson Democracy in withholding their support in former days from the men who came over with Mr. Calhoun [and back to the Democratic Party], operated against [Hubbard] in these aspirations."[62] Not wishing to again appear disloyal to the party, Hubbard voted for Bagby, as did an overwhelming majority of the legislature.[63]

Hubbard's loyalty, however, proved to be short-lived when some Democrats failed to follow Governor Fitzpatrick's recommendation that only the Mobile branch of the State Bank be placed in liquidation. The House Committee on the State Bank and Branches, which was chaired by John Archibald Campbell of Mobile, reported bills to liquidate the bank branches at both Mobile and Decatur.[64] During the ensuing debate, bank debtors were reportedly "openly denounced as 'robbers and swindlers,'" at which point the "Hon. David Hubbard participated in the Debate with his usual ability." For this he was praised by the correspondent of the Democrat organ in William Yancey's legislative district. This correspondent, who might have been Yancey himself, hailed Hubbard's "sterling, old-fashioned common sense," his "sagacity, rarely if ever, at fault," and his "intellect, on the whole, which is quick, penetrating and bold." Hubbard was unable to stop the proposal of Campbell's committee using normal dilatory tactics. He therefore used surrogates to put the other three banks at risk to intimidate their protectors in the legislature. He did this by using a poison-pill strategy: if they were going to put the Decatur bank in liquidation, their banks would be wound up too.[65] To the shock of most everyone in the state, particularly Huntsville residents and their freshman legislator, Clement Claiborne Clay (also known as C. C. Clay Jr.), a majority of the legislators, composed of Hubbard and the Whigs, ultimately voted to put all of them in liquidation.[66] The angry editor of the Huntsville *Democrat* declared that "we are mortified, deeply mortified, at the ruinous and unexpected course which has been taken in relation to our banks." There was, he continued, a "contagion which seems spreading through the whole community of just and honest indignation at such acts of reckless legislation."[67]

Hubbard's handiwork can also be seen in some of the provisions of the liquidation bills, as well as the bill reimposing taxes. The banks could make no new loans, but they were expressly allowed to renew and extend any outstanding loans—such as his. Moreover, there was no requirement that those loans be immediately collected.[68] Thus, Hubbard would potentially have his breathing room. Taxes were reimposed even before collection efforts against the bank debtors were made, and for the first time income taxes were imposed, but only on the wealthy. Property taxes were also imposed, but on an ad valorem basis, meaning they would fall more heavily on the wealthy, particularly those who owned property in the Black Belt where the most valuable land in the state was located.[69]

These controversial measures caused great consternation among several Democrats in the house as they worked their way through the legislative process.[70] Democrat James M. Calhoun of Black Belt Dallas County, a nephew of South Carolina's John C. Calhoun, was among those who were particularly incensed.[71] He reportedly called Hubbard a liar during a house session on January 4, 1843, and Hubbard replied by punching Calhoun. Other legislators broke up this fight while John Archibald Campbell proposed that a special committee be appointed to investigate the disturbance. This incident made national news, with some Whig editors referring to it as a disgraceful "pugilistic set-to."[72]

Lest anyone might question Hubbard's party loyalty after all of this, he also enraged the Whigs by pushing for the congressional redistricting and apportionment of the state to be made on what was called the "white basis," instead of the "mixed" or federal basis as was the existing practice. By virtue of the 1840 census, Alabama was entitled to two more congressional seats. Each of the districts had to have essentially the same population and Hubbard proposed that only the white population be counted in drawing district lines. This would result in more seats in heavily Democratic north Alabama than in pro-Whig south Alabama, where the slave population was now much larger. The Whigs preferred the mixed basis in which all whites and three-fifths of the slaves would be counted. Despite Whig protests, however, the Democratic majority shoved the white basis down their throats in both houses.[73]

The editor of the Tuscaloosa Whig organ, the *Independent Monitor*, subsequently published a pamphlet describing each of the leaders of the 1842–43 legislative session. In it he lampooned Hubbard at great length for his failure to consistently adhere to the line of either party. Other than evidencing a solicitude for the poor that the editor believed was excessive, Hubbard was difficult to "delineate" accurately. "He has intellect and experience enough to make a good subject for the political artist; but when the outlines are drawn, and the features must be worked in, with the proper light and shade to give them animation and relief, there is a mass of expression so admirably zigzag—so like cross-eyes, which look one way and see another, that we are almost tempted to throw down our pencil in despair." The editor did at least give Hubbard left-handed praise for his military service. "Mr. H. was a good soldier under Gen. Jackson, and had the felicity of being wounded, like a brave man, at the battle of New-Orleans, in 1815." Hubbard's "military laurels," he noted, were "of twenty-eight years' growth," implying that the tall tales Hubbard told about his military exploits during that period had been growing far beyond the truth with every passing year.[74]

Some Alabama Democrats were no less upset. One north Alabama editor predicted that the legislative "session of 1842–3 will long be remembered with bitter curses by many, very many, upon whom it will bring utter ruin."[75] Some accused Hubbard of demagoguery and intentionally trying to depreciate the value of the notes of the State Bank even further so he could use them to pay his debts.[76] This furor may explain why Hubbard declined to run for his former seat in Congress that year.[77]

At least Alabama now had a relatively solid—yet barely sufficient—source of revenue with which to try to make the upcoming interest payments on its $9.8 million bonded indebtedness.[78] As the elections in August approached, the value of the white basis apportionment of the congressional districts to the Democratic Party came into focus.[79] Democratic success then would provide a springboard for more success in the all-important 1844 presidential election. So would a new, extremely controversial issue that few saw coming.

9

'Northern Fanatics'

B y this time, the nation's economy had somewhat improved as capital flows from England finally began to increase.[1] Even though this did not translate into higher cotton prices for the South, initially it did lead many Alabama Democrats to join the groundswell of national support within the party for the nomination of Martin Van Buren as the Democrats' 1844 presidential candidate.[2] Given Van Buren's defeat in 1840, and questions regarding his stance about the increased Tariff of 1842, concerned Democrats in Alabama and elsewhere sought to entice the Calhoun faction to help defeat the all-but-anointed Whig candidate, Henry Clay. Those Calhounists who agreed to back Van Buren could expect Democrats to advance them to position and place.

David Hubbard, who had been reelected to the legislature along with a Whig, Leroy Pope Walker,[3] was one of those prominent Alabama Calhounites approached in the weeks leading up to the State Democratic Convention in December 1843. He was requested to define his position publicly by a group of his constituents who were attempting to orchestrate his selection as a presidential elector. Hubbard did so from Kinlock in a public letter that was praised from one end of the state to the other.[4] In that letter, Hubbard admitted his continuing belief that,

Martin Van Buren

in light of the need to again reduce tariff rates, Calhoun was "better qualified from the place of his location and other causes combined to stop the
extravagance and waste of public money than Mr. Van Buren; because the
State in which Mr. Calhoun lives (a State like our own) feels this waste in a
much greater degree than does New York, where the money is spent." Hubbard declared, however, that he was willing to sacrifice his "first choice" in
the "battle for public good." Hubbard also assured that his support for the
Democratic nominee would be full; he would not "act reluctantly" or "be
an unwilling servant." He referred all "to my past life and ask you if you ever
knew me [to] attempt things by halves?" Hubbard did, however, place one
important condition on that support. He announced that he would back
whomever was nominated by the national convention "unless the members
of that Convention shall yield our rights in some respect to secure to our
Ticket the support of Northern fanatics." He warned that "if any thing is
demanded of the south on this subject no Southern man ought to yield,
but should instantly withdraw from the Meeting."[5] This boycott threat was
a tactic others would plagiarize later.

Despite placing section over party, Hubbard was selected as one of two
presidential electors for the state at large when Alabama Democrats met in
Tuscaloosa for their state convention.[6] The pro-Van Buren organ in Mobile
praised him as a "strong-minded mountain democrat" who was "for the *cause*,
and for the nominee of the national convention, with no other reservation
than that the man shall be true and trustworthy on the slave question."[7]
Similarly, Hubbard's old nemesis, the Huntsville *Democrat*, declared that his
letter "breathes the spirit of a patriot and a statesman; it holds the doctrine
of one who loves his principles for their own sake, and who cherishes his
country because it is his mother."[8]

Ominously, the proceedings of that same state convention revealed the
existence of an issue that could have produced the walkout about which
Hubbard warned. One of the delegates offered a resolution stating that it
was "most essential to the interests of the South, that the Republic of Texas
should be annexed to the United States."[9] Earlier in the year, John Quincy
Adams and several other Northern congressmen had issued a widely publicized address to the "people of the Free States" declaring that the annexation

of Texas would justify dissolution of the Union.[10] It was the same saber-rattling strategy that Southerners had occasionally used to get their way. For reasons that are not apparent, the resolution proposed at the Alabama convention was withdrawn, but the divisive Texas issue would not go away. For that the United States could thank Republic of Texas president Sam Houston, who had married one of David Hubbard's south Alabama cousins, Margaret Lea of Perry County, in 1840.[11]

Sam Houston

Ever since the Texas Revolution, Houston had been attempting without success to convince the United States to annex Texas. Even Andrew Jackson had been reluctant to press the issue because of fear that the addition of another slave state would incite those "Northern fanatics" about whom Hubbard had written and possibly cause a sectional split in the Democratic Party. Jackson's successor, Martin Van Buren, followed his lead.[12] After several bloody invasions of Texas by Mexico, Houston changed tactics. Stated very simply, the new strategy was to make it known that Texas was flirting with Great Britain and might give up slavery and become a British protectorate if Britain resolved Texas's security concerns with Mexico. Houston and his closest advisers—among whom was Hubbard's friend, Washington Miller—believed that the United States would annex Texas to prevent the British from obtaining a foothold on its southern border. It was a brilliant plan, and Miller was a key member of the Texas team that began to put it in motion in 1843, beginning with two carefully crafted letters sent by Miller to President John Tyler apprising him of diplomatic overtures by Great Britain toward Texas and the possibility of an alliance.[13] Word of this threat reached Alabama in the fall of that year and caused quite a stir.

So did reports that John Quincy Adams and his "fanatical crew" remained vehemently opposed to annexation of Texas as a remedy.[14]

It was in the immediate wake of this controversy that Hubbard issued his previously mentioned letter referring to "Northern fanatics." But if one were to judge from the proceedings of the Alabama legislature, which also convened on December 4, it seemed as if Democrats and Whigs were attempting to avoid the Texas issue for fear of a sectional split in both their respective parties. Hubbard was there in attack mode, but primarily against the attorneys hired by the banks to collect debts, not against abolitionists.[15] Even after he was appointed to chair a new standing committee on federal relations, Hubbard showed continued, uncharacteristic restraint on the issue of Texas.[16] He was tested, however, when Governor Fitzpatrick presented for consideration resolutions adopted by the legislatures of other states, including two from Massachusetts. One of these resolutions called for an amendment to the federal constitution deleting the three-fifths clause, which augmented slave state representation in Congress. The other resolution opposed the annexation of Texas.[17] A copy of the resolution opposing annexation had also been sent to Congress, where Tennessee congressman Andrew Johnson reported that it "set the Southern delegation ablaze."[18] However, the only counter resolution Hubbard's committee reported related to the proposed constitutional amendment.[19] Alabama, it said, considered the three-fifths clause "one of the terms upon which the Union was formed" and warned that any attempt to change it was an act of bad faith that would "disturb the confederacy" and "weaken the bonds of mutual interest and good feeling which has [sic] hitherto bound us together."[20]

For reasons that are unclear, however, Hubbard's approach changed in the weeks after the legislature adjourned.[21] This coincided with the arrival of word from Nashville that Andrew Jackson had made public his support for the annexation of Texas, and rumors that the Tyler administration was close to reaching an agreement with Texas on a treaty of annexation.[22] The press reported that a group of "citizens of Lawrence and the adjoining counties in Alabama, without distinction of party," met in Moulton on March 18, 1844, and adopted a series of what were called "strong resolutions" favoring the "incorporation of the people and Territory of Texas into the Union of the United States, as soon as practicable." According to those resolutions, this was required by, among other things, "justice to Texas, security to ourselves, and humanity to relations, friends, acquaintances and countrymen in Texas," and should occur regardless of whether it was accomplished by "annexation, purchase, cession, gift, restoration, conquest, acquisition, or any other name."[23]

There were at least four additional reasons why the citizens of northwest Alabama were so zealous for the acquisition of the Lone Star Republic. Anglophobia arising from the Revolutionary War and the War of 1812 remained strong. In addition, this was the region from which the ill-fated Red Rovers had been recruited, and there were more than a few interested in payback for the Mexicans if annexation sparked a war. Third, the soil of much of north Alabama was moving toward exhaustion.[24] Fourth, and connected with this last reason, there was increasing sentiment that the only way to get rid of the growing, increasingly redundant slave population in a depressed cotton economy—and to eventually reach lily-whitehood—was to diffuse them to new lands in the west. Otherwise, when the land became totally infertile, whites would be overrun by a black population of slaves released by their owners for economic reasons.[25] In his letters back to Alabama, Washington Miller had cleverly played on the desire for fresh lands by portraying Texas as the biblical promised land.[26]

President Tyler, still hopeful of receiving the nomination of one of the political parties for another term, was attempting to fulfill these aspirations.[27] So was Sam Houston,[28] who, in early 1844, had dispatched Washington Miller to confer with Andrew Jackson in Tennessee and then proceed to Washington as Houston's personal representative on a team of Texans negotiating a treaty of annexation with the United States.[29] Miller's efforts ultimately bore fruit. On April 12, 1844, after Calhoun received the appointment as Tyler's secretary of state, a treaty was finally signed. Ten days later it was submitted to the United States Senate for ratification as a thinly veiled pro-slavery measure.[30]

This, and the Northern furor that erupted, forced both Henry Clay and Martin Van Buren to state their respective positions on the annexation question.[31] In April they issued separate but, in the end, equally politically suicidal public letters announcing their opposition to immediate annexation. Van Buren's letter stressed the neutrality requirements of international law and the likelihood of war with Mexico if the treaty were adopted without Mexico's consent.[32] That did it for Hubbard, who was in Pennsylvania at the time Van Buren's letter was issued. In a public letter, Hubbard wrote back to Alabama that he would not support the New Yorker if he were nominated.[33]

Henry Clay's fateful letter made the further mistake of not only implying the illegality of groups of Americans such as the Red Rovers participating in the Texas Revolution in 1836, but recognizing the legality of Mexico's continuing claim to the region won by their blood. Adding insult to injury, Clay expressed fear of war with Mexico and Great Britain, and empathy for objections by Northern abolitionists that Texas would add to the political power of the slave states. Concluding with words that would dismay Whigs in Alabama to no end, Clay wrote that "I consider the annexation of Texas, at this time, without the assent of Mexico, as a measure compromising the National character, involving us certainly in war with Mexico, probably with other foreign powers, dangerous to the integrity of the Union, inexpedient in the present financial condition of the country, and not called for by any general expression of public opinion."[34] Clay nonetheless received his party's nomination for the presidency.

The majority of Democrat politicos, however, had no intention of risking a walkout of their party's Southern wing at their national convention in Baltimore. They would not, in the words of David Hubbard, attempt to placate "Northern fanatics" by nominating Van Buren or any other candidate who opposed the immediate annexation of Texas. After several ballots they, instead, nominated Hubbard's friend, James K. Polk of Tennessee, who had recently issued his own Texas letter stating that "I have no hesitation in declaring that I am in favor of the immediate re-annexation of Texas to the territory and Government of the United States."[35]

A few days after Polk's nomination, the United States Senate decisively rejected the treaty with Texas, thereby further infuriating pro-annexation Southerners who were convinced that the vote was simply another example of the federal government's increasing tendency to appease anti-slavery Northerners at the expense of Southern interests.[36] Word of the Senate's

decision arrived in Alabama at about the same time
as shocking news that the General Conference of
the Methodist Episcopal Church had adopted a resolution at its annual meeting
in New York instructing a Southern
bishop to cease from serving as such
because he was a slaveowner. This
would ultimately lead to a sectional
split in that denomination.[37]

Support in Alabama for annexation continued to grow. As recently appointed (due to the resignation of
William Rufus King) United States
Senator Dixon Hall Lewis put it, "To

James K. Polk

the North it is a question of interest—to the West, one of feeling—while,
to the down-trodden, tariff-ridden and Abolition-bedeviled South, it is a
question of existence!"[38] Polk's surging popularity in north Alabama and
Clay's unpopular position on Texas threatened to sound the death knell for
the Whig Party in the Tennessee Valley. The Whigs in Lawrence County
had steadily built a political base that had, among other things, led to the
election of Leroy Pope Walker to the legislature, and he was standing for
almost certain reelection in August 1844. In the wake of these develop-
ments, however, Whigs began defecting to the Democrats in large numbers
in the face of the "Polk and Texas" steamroller, which Polk elector David
Hubbard supported with fiery, divisive rhetoric that (falsely) linked Clay
to the abolitionists and the British, and called on men "of both parties, as
patriots and Southerners to rally in behalf of Polk and Texas, as a measure
of deliverance from and security against the mad efforts of England and
Northern Abolitionists."[39]

The resulting depth of feeling in Lawrence County at this time came
to national attention once again when a resolution was adopted during a
routine battalion militia muster in Moulton in late June or early July 1844.
Apparently responding to the disunion threats of John Quincy Adams and
other abolitionists, the resolution stated that "the possession of Texas is

infinitely more important to us of this section of the Union, than a longer connexion [sic] and friendship with the north eastern States, and if we have to yield either it cannot and shall not be Texas—because the people of Texas are more nearly allied to us in blood and congeniality of institutions, their territory more convenient in locality and infinitely more valuable in fertility of soil and commercial advantages, than the north eastern States themselves, from whence now proceeds the present unfriendly opposition to our wishes."[40]

In desperation, Moulton lawyer Thomas Peters, who was a Clay sub-elector, and other Alabama Whigs had written to Henry Clay informing him of the rapid evaporation of support for his candidacy in north Alabama due to the dispute over Texas, and pleading with him to issue a statement favoring annexation. On July 1 Clay finally replied to the editor of the pro-Whig Tuscaloosa *Independent Monitor* meekly stating that "I could have no objection to the annexation of Texas, but I certainly would be unwilling to see the existing Union dissolved or seriously jeoparded for the sake of acquiring Texas."[41] This first of Clay's controversial "Alabama Letters" only made the situation worse. It provided no ammunition to Southern Whigs and offended many Northern Whigs who thought Clay was beginning to cave in to pro-slavery interests. As a result, the rout was seemingly on, and Whig defections to Polk and the Texas movement in north Alabama became like a flood.[42] For example, Leroy Pope Walker announced that he too would support Polk and Texas, and went even further and renounced his membership in the Whig Party.[43]

On July 29, Hubbard made another controversial speech in Moulton that drew more national attention. In it he expressed a more radical stance than ever before. According to the Tuscumbia *North Alabamian*, Hubbard "declared, both in his speech and private conversation, that he was fully prepared to see the Union rent asunder unless the northern portion of the Confederacy would consent to let us have Texas."[44] Some in the Whig press attempted to use the extremism orchestrated and expressed by Hubbard in Lawrence County against Polk. A Georgia editor declared that "with such repeated evidences before the people of the treasonable inclinations of the supporters of the Loco-foco nominees, it will be in vain for the editors of that party to deny that *Polk* and *Disunion* are almost synonymous terms." He called on the "sturdy old 'Union Men' of Georgia" to reject "this bold preaching up of disunion" and cease to be "co-workers with such men in the cause of 'Polk and Texas.'"[45]

As a consequence, Democrats were somewhat forced on the defensive and had to spend time denying an absence of patriotism within their ranks,[46] but this had no ascertainable effect in Alabama when voters went to the polls to elect legislators who would select someone to complete Dixon Hall Lewis's term in Congress. Particularly after the defection of so many prominent Whigs, Democrats retained control of both houses of the legislature.[47] In addition, twenty-nine-year-old William Lowndes Yancey won Lewis's old House seat in Congress in a district that had given a 655 vote majority for William Henry Harrison in the 1840 presidential election. It is noteworthy that Yancey did not adopt Hubbard's Texas-or-disunion extremism during his campaign and won the race by only sixty votes. Yancey, who had been a staunch Unionist, would not err on the side of moderation again and would instead eventually adopt much of Hubbard's tactics and rhetoric.[48]

The date Hubbard and Yancey first met is unknown, and we can only wonder what he thought of the much younger (by twenty-two years) upstart who was already becoming a favorite of Democrat organs around the state.[49] Yancey had never served in the military and never would. As previously mentioned, he had also been a vocal opponent of John C. Calhoun and the nullification movement while a resident of South Carolina. Moreover, Yancey was a hothead who sometimes acted rashly and without thinking. This trait was on display when he shot and killed his wife's uncle in South Carolina in the 1830s during an argument, criminal conduct for which he was convicted and jailed before moving permanently to the Alabama Black Belt to reinvent

William L. Yancey

himself.[50] As a former prosecutor, Hubbard could not have been impressed.

Unlike Hubbard, however, Yancey was from a very prominent South Carolina family, had received a college education, and, as a result, effortlessly displayed an aristocratic public image of the sort deeply admired by south Alabama elites of similar background. Moreover, when he arrived in Alabama he was already a member of the clubby newspaper fraternity. This allowed him to cultivate strong and lasting relationships with the new generation of influential editors who were taking up their pens in the 1840s and 1850s. With a few notable exceptions, they would support him in his political career, cover for his faults (he abused opiates and alcohol), and perpetuate his memory.[51] In return he gave them friendship, attention, and colorful quotes for their readers.

Not long after the state election was concluded, Hubbard went to what was billed as a "Union Democratic Convention" in Nashville that was attended by a large number of party leaders from around the country as well as a huge crowd. The primary goal of this meeting was to dispel the image Hubbard and others had helped create that Polk's supporters were disunionists. It was, Hubbard reported to Calhoun, a series of "'Union loving' demonstrations" consisting of speeches in which the idea of disunion for any cause was denounced.[52] Hubbard did not indicate whether he considered this a personal rebuke, nor did he reveal to Calhoun that he had also addressed the crowd.[53]

Hubbard had another reason for visiting Nashville: Rebecca Stoddert. She was the forty-seven-year-old, Maryland-born daughter of the late Benjamin Stoddert, the nation's first secretary of the navy. He had served in the cabinets of John Adams and Thomas Jefferson and, after leaving that post, lost his fortune in land speculation before his death in 1813. Rebecca's sister, Harriet, was married to George Washington Campbell, the uncle of Hubbard's late wife.[54] Thus, it is likely Hubbard had known Rebecca for many years. Unfortunately, the details of their courtship are lost to history.

While Hubbard was now focused on his soon-to-be second wife, Alabama Whigs were facing less-promising prospects. The pro-Whig Huntsville *Southern Advocate* acknowledged with disdain that the "Texas flag waves over the State in triumph," but called on Whigs to remain loyal to Clay. "Steady,

Whigs! Steady! Strike earnestly from this to the election in favor of the good cause. Do your duty and leave the result to Providence."[55] Providence, however, was not smiling on Henry Clay, who committed yet another gaffe with his pen. He wrote a fourth letter, this time making even more explicit his objections to the annexation of Texas, denying any intention "in either of the two letters which I addressed to Alabama, to express any contrary opinion," and reaffirming his opposition "as long as any considerable and respectable portion of the confederation should continue to stand out in opposition to the annexation of Texas."[56]

Clay's flip-flopping did not escape the notice of Democrat organs or Southern voters.[57] Hubbard, who was traveling in east Alabama in the fall after making his last speaking engagement in Russellville, wrote Polk of reports he was hearing regarding the promising results in the Georgia state elections.[58] "We have beat them in Georgia, carrying 5 certain and 6 probable of the Congressmen, and an estimated popular majority from 5,000 to 8,000."[59] Predictably, Polk won Alabama, Georgia, and every other Deep South state on the way to victory.[60] His election did nothing to dampen the ardor of Hubbard's "Northern fanatics." On the contrary, this election cycle was pivotal in the growth of political abolition in the North. Indeed, Clay was its first national victim when he lost the election as a consequence of thirty-six decisive electoral votes in New York being won by James Gillespie Birney, the only truly pro-abolition candidate in the race.[61]

From this, Northern politicians seeking to promote themselves or their party for national office learned that they could no longer ignore the growing political power of the anti-slavery movement. By the same token, they could not appear to pander to what some Northerners now called the "Slave Power" among arrogant Southerners like the now nationally famous (or infamous) David Hubbard, who threatened disunion if they did not get their way. Evidence that they learned this lesson came very quickly after Congress convened in December. The recognized leader of the "Northern fanatics," John Quincy Adams, followed his annual practice by giving notice that he would be introducing yet another resolution to rescind the House gag rule against the receipt and consideration of anti-slavery petitions. The House had repeatedly rejected Adams's resolutions in all previous sessions and, with Democrats still in the majority, Southerners might have assumed that it would fail once again. This time, however, enough Northern Democrats voted aye on December 3, 1844, to adopt Adams's resolution 108 to 89.[62] Henceforth, Congress would not only receive thousands of calls for an end to slavery, but would now have nothing to prevent their debate, or the hard feelings those debates would engender between Northern and Southern politicians of both parties.

The vote on the gag rule also confirmed the fears of pro-Texas Southerners that, despite the election of Polk, the efforts to have the annexation treaty ratified by the requisite two-thirds majority of the Whig-controlled Senate would again fail.[63]

Even a change of tactics by pro-annexation congressmen to instead adopt a resolution—which required approval of only a bare majority vote in both houses—seemed doubtful of success. The situation was made even worse by a speech in Congress on the Texas issue given in January 1845 by Yancey. He made a personal attack on a North Carolina Whig that led to a duel, and also criticized as unpatriotic threats of disunion that had come from the New England states, and particularly "the manifesto put out by certain members of Congress at the head of which was Mr. John Quincy Adams, threatening a dissolution of the Union in case Texas was admitted into it."[64] The Whigs countered young Yancey's holier-than-thou thrust by reminding him of the threats of disunion that had been made by pro-Texas Southerners like David Hubbard. Even the pro-Democrat Washington *Globe* suggested that Yancey should have also rebuked that "spirit of revolt."[65]

It appears that Hubbard's extremism also cost him when the Alabama legislature convened and the Democratic caucus met to decide on a candidate to fill the remainder of William Rufus King's term in the United States Senate. Hubbard was rumored to be seeking the seat even though it was still held by Dixon Hall Lewis.[66] Those rumors were accurate, and Hubbard, along with King and Lewis, were put in nomination. However Lewis, despite his own strong connection to Calhoun, had not publicly supported disunion. He reportedly received "nearly nine tenths" of the votes in the caucus and was ultimately elected over a Whig challenger.[67]

The Alabama Democratic caucus did honor Hubbard for his service as a Polk elector by advocating his selection by Polk to a position in his government, that of commissioner of the General Land Office. For some reason, however, Polk was not so sure. Hubbard later wrote that he went to Columbia, Tennessee, to meet with Polk and that Polk told him "he could not determine appointments until he reached Washington; but politely invited me to accompany him and a few friends, stating, that, it was very probable I would get the office I desired, or one as good.'" Hubbard said he, instead, returned to Alabama and "on looking at my affairs, became convinced that I could not at that time leave my business without ruin." He "then went to Nashville and told Mr. Polk that I desired no office." Nevertheless Hubbard did go to Washington to attend Polk's inauguration.[68] Perhaps to save face, Hubbard issued a public letter in which he declared that "I would not accept the office, if offered to me, from considerations personal to myself," but would continue to support Polk.[69]

Hubbard would not be bringing his fire to bear in support of annexation. In the end, however, that was unnecessary. Setting a precedent Democrats would later regret, a resolution skipping the territorial stage and making Texas a state was finally adopted by Congress in late February 1845.[70] Hubbard was certainly pleased with that, but by this time his financial situation had taken another turn for the worse. A few months earlier he had written one of the stockholders of the New York and Mississippi Land Company pleading to be compensated for the expenses he had incurred while acting in its behalf. "I am now on the very verge of Bankruptcy & must have something—I have relied upon the Company to do me justice & hope that it will be done."[71] Perhaps before the company learned of his efforts in behalf of the annexation of Texas, it agreed to compensate Hubbard to a limited extent. But whether any payment was ever actually made is unclear. After all, with the United States placing its protective umbrella over Texas, land there was even more attractive.[72] By supporting that, Hubbard had arguably acted contrary to the company's interests.[73]

David Hubbard married Rebecca Stoddert on July 1, 1845, but whether this improved his finances is unknown.[74] The fact that he did not seek the Democratic nomination for governor that year after being endorsed by Lawrence County Democrats suggests that his finances had not improved.[75] So

Kinlock

does the fact that Hubbard and his new wife did not live in Courtland, but instead took up residence at Kinlock, a small plantation adjacent to the Byler Road in south Lawrence County approximately twenty miles south of Moulton. It had been established many years earlier by Green Kirk Hubbard before he moved to Texas, and the two-story, four-room house there was much more rustic than the home at Courtland.[76]

Kinlock was served by a natural spring that fed Hubbard Creek and its fall line at Hubbard Falls. One observer wrote that at the falls, Hubbard Creek "booms over a rock shelf in a gorge so deep and narrow that it is like a gash of a giant knife."[77] This provided not only an excellent source of drinking water, but also water power. Hubbard was thereby able to generate some cash by using that power to begin a grist mill, a cotton mill, a tannery, and a shoe factory, and for the operation of all he had his twenty-four slaves instructed.[78]

While Hubbard and his new bride set up their household, the most significant governor's race in Hubbard's political career was playing out.

The primary burning issue was Alabama's huge debt. At this time, the total debt owed by all debtors to the State Bank was $13,139,974.97 while the state's bonded debt and other liabilities totaled $13,146,765.57. The problem was that, as property values had decreased with cotton prices, more and more debtors absconded to Texas and elsewhere. As the banks renewed and extended old loans, the collectibility of the bank debt had eroded significantly over the years. To pay the ever-increasing shortfall between the collectible bank debt and the state's debt, collections would have to be accelerated and/or taxes would have to be increased even further.[79] As a consequence, this election cycle in Alabama was billed as one pitting bank debtors against taxpayers.[80]

The Democrats met in a state convention and, nonetheless, foolishly nominated a bank debtor, Nathaniel Terry of Limestone County, who pledged to seek a revision of the bank debtor law to make the requirements for loan renewals less onerous.[81] Disgruntled Democrats and Whigs coalesced behind a Democratic bolter, former Alabama congressman Joshua Lanier Martin, who supported the very aggressive collection of the debts of the banks to avoid another tax increase. Martin ran and won as an independent "Peoples" candidate,[82] becoming Alabama's first overtly populist governor.

Despite Martin's demagogic attacks on bank debtors, Hubbard was reelected to the Alabama House along with Thomas Peters.[83] He certainly recognized the distinct possibility that Governor Martin would veto efforts to repeal or even modify the bank-debtor law. In his inaugural address, Martin denounced the manner in which defaulting bank debtors had been coddled by the banks and the legislature, all to the great prejudice of the taxpayers who would have to pay the state's bonded indebtedness through higher taxes unless the bank debtors paid their debts. Martin adamantly opposed any tax increase unless all of the collectible debts were collected.[84] Newspapers throughout the state reported that Hubbard, according to one observer, "attacked with uncommon fury" immediately after the governor's message was read. He called it an "extraordinary document, wrong in its conclusions and suggestions."[85] Hubbard was incensed that bank debtors were being "offered up" as "political scape goats, to propitiate that public vengeance which has been aroused against us for our past follies and delusions," especially when the state and its citizens were also complicit. "Why did not the Governor also tell the people that it was the public policy of the State" to borrow money to be lent out, he asked. Why did not the Governor tell them that they had, in essence, borrowed money from the banks in lieu of paying taxes? "Why did he not own this, and bear his share of this weak and foolish policy, of which the State, the public, as well as citizens, have been guilty?" Turning to those in the legislature who shared Governor Martin's views, Hubbard admitted he was a debtor of the State Bank, but also noted that he had "paid you thousands by way of interest, and tens of thousands by way of principal, and am not yet through." As a consequence, Hubbard concluded, "I may hold up my head among you until each of you render back what you have taken out of the bank to pay your taxes and interest thereon. If you do this, and I fail, then will I deserve the denunciations contained in the message."[86]

Martin's opposition was not the only hurdle Hubbard faced in obtaining debt relief. This legislature also addressed several other very controversial and time-consuming measures, particularly the issue of whether the state's capital would be removed from Tuscaloosa. Hubbard made a spirited op-position to the move, but Montgomery ultimately won the prize.[87]

Another issue that would have repercussions for Hubbard's political future involved efforts by Yancey to obtain legislative relief from a law requiring all persons elected to state or local office to give an oath swearing that they had never been involved in a duel. There was a difference of opinion regard-ing whether the legislature had the power to grant such relief, and in any event Hubbard had long been opposed to such relief laws because of his personal opposition to dueling. He, therefore, voted against the bill, but it was passed over Governor Martin's veto.[88] Yancey and his south Alabama friends would not forget Hubbard's snub.

As the session neared its close, debate over a bank bill and a tax bill inten-sified.[89] A breakthrough finally resulted in a bank bill in part orchestrated by Hubbard that gave him and some other bank debtors a modicum of relief. Those debtors who had complied with the prior law by paying one-third of their outstanding debt were permitted another extension to June 1, 1847, if they paid one-half of the balance owed plus interest by June 1, 1846.[90]

The following day a bill raising taxes a modest amount on the wealthy was adopted.[91] Neither bill was vetoed by Governor Martin.

The result did not satisfy everyone. Some were very concerned that this approach would not produce sufficient revenues for the state to pay its debt. A Jacksonville, Alabama, editor complained that rather than taking a hard line and "striking out a bold and comprehensive policy" that would avoid a default on the state's bonded indebtedness, the legislature had adopted "a base, unmanly piece of moral cowardice." The legislators had, "like time-serving politicians as they were, legislated only for the moment, thinking more of some plausible hobby for the next canvass than of the credit, honor, and prosperity—the great future of our young State."[92] Others, however, were upset that taxes were increased at all.[93] Hubbard's support of tax increases for the wealthy likely ended any real chance he ever had to be elected to the United States Senate.

If there was to be a backlash by the voters against their legislators, it would have to wait until August 1847. This legislature ratified a constitutional amendment providing for biennial rather than annual legislative sessions. In conjunction with this, a bill was passed that assured that neither Hubbard nor any other legislator would be forced to face the voters for almost eighteen months.[94] Much would happen before then, thanks to more Northern and Southern fanatics.

10

The 'Alabama Platform'

Those who had predicted that war with Mexico would follow the annexation of Texas were quickly proven to be correct. News of the clash of arms between Mexican and American troops near the Rio Grande first reached north Alabama in May 1846.[1] There were few, if any, expressions of regret in Alabama or elsewhere in the South, particularly after the steady series of American victories as the U.S. army penetrated Mexico.[2]

To David Hubbard, success in achieving annexation was all a function of the threats of disunion that had emanated from Lawrence County and elsewhere during the debate on annexation. He was requested to speak to the residents of Lawrence County during the Fourth of July celebration in 1846, and during that address replied to what he called the "sneers that have been cast upon the 'Moulton Meetings'" held on the Texas question. "If the sneering was a ridicule of the resolutions," he said, "we can reply that the wisdom of the nation, after months of deliberation, have come to the same conclusion, and done no better than we did." If, on the other hand, "the ridicule has been intended for our place or people," he continued, "we can only say that humble as may be our pretensions compared to our more favored fellow-citizens, to advise or consult with them, in relation to our public affairs, yet each of us have a vote, a voice in this mighty Union, which counts one; and who is the man, on his *personal* account, or by reason of the place he lives at, that presumes to count his voice for two."[3]

Hubbard's primary theme related to the benefits that were to accrue from the war. "There is no power upon earth," he declared, "which can prevent the extension of our settlements to every part of the continent." Moreover, the continent, he made clear, would not limit American influence or empire. "Nor can any power on earth prevent our hardy seamen and skillful merchants from sailing upon every sea, where a fish can be caught, or trading with every people, with whom bargains can be made, and from whom things of value are to be had." "We want commercial locations, marts and strong holds—'positions on the globe'—as a great nation, and we must and will have them." For this, "savage and weaker nations must give way to civilization, and the strength which good government creates by that law of necessity which our expansion calls into existence."[4]

Interestingly, however, although Hubbard praised the patriotism of those who were volunteering to fight in the war against Mexico, he did not expressly support the imperial aims of the Polk administration. In this he was consistent with Calhoun, who worried that Mexico, many of whose people were opposed to slavery, would be subjugated through conquest, that the twenty Mexican states would become territories of the United States, and that their later admission to the Union would lead to the passage of a constitutional amendment abolishing slavery.[5] "Mexico is to us the forbidden fruit," Calhoun later declared, and "the penalty of eating it" would be to subject "our institutions to political death."[6]

Imperial thrusts for lands like Texas where slavery was well established and legal was a different matter altogether. In his Moulton speech, Hubbard singled out Cuba, still a Spanish possession, where slavery was legal, as the next piece of territory important for the nation's expansion. "No rival commercial nation [read: Great Britain] should be permitted to take possession of Cuba," he declared to the cheering crowd. "They can only desire it for the purpose of annoying us and blocking up our 'right of way' through which the untold millions, destined to inhabit the Mississippi Valley, must carry their products to the markets of the world and receive their supplies from other countries in return." Hubbard compared the loss of Cuba by Southern interests to a farmer who had given "a mischievous and troublesome neighbor the keys of his corn crib and meat house." Before Cuba was lost, Hubbard said to more cheering, "we should bury our last soldier—sink our last ship, and expend our last dollar."[7]

Hubbard also warned his listeners of impediments to this Southern-style manifest destiny, all of which were political in nature. First, "our Chiefs, civil and military, are ambitious and envious, and their rivalries and dislikes, threaten to do our armies more injury than the common enemy." Second, these evils "are greatly aggravated by combinations or cliques of office-seekers throughout the land, who seek office not altogether to promote or gratify a laudable ambition, or as a means of subsistence and support but as a means of getting hold of public moneys and thereby enriching themselves and families." Third, "these train-bands of office-seekers often own a public Press [and] hire an editor, whose duty it becomes to praise every man who will assist, and defame such as are likely to oppose their schemes."[8]

Hubbard was likely unaware of the influence some of these factors were having on an obscure Pennsylvania Democrat, David Wilmot. This freshman congressman had broken ranks with the pro-tariff Pennsylvania delegation and voted contrary to instructions from the Pennsylvania legislature in favor of a Democrat tariff measure that reduced the duties elevated by the Whig-backed protective tariff of 1842. As a consequence, Wilmot had been subjected to significant criticism in his home state, and his reelection chances in October 1846 were placed in great jeopardy. To demonstrate that he was not controlled by Southern interests, Wilmot offered a very controversial amendment to an appropriation bill intended to provide funds for use during treaty negotiations with Mexico. That proposed amendment, which became known as the Wilmot Proviso, prohibited slavery in any lands acquired from Mexico in those negotiations. Ominously, almost all of the Northern congressmen of both political parties voted for the proviso when it was adopted in the House, although it died in the Senate on August 10 when Congress adjourned. Wilmot, however, went on to win reelection and his tactic quickly gained traction in the North.[9]

It is noteworthy that there was initially little mention of Wilmot's proposed amendment in the Alabama press or among the state's politicians. Hubbard, who was being encouraged by some to challenge George Smith Houston for his seat in Congress, was more than happy to remedy this curious omission. During a public meeting at Russellville, Alabama, in the fall of 1846, he was "called for by acclamation" to address the threat presented by the possible exclusion of slavery in the West and, according to the *Franklin Democrat*, "handled the subject with decided ability; and dwelt upon the injustice of taxing the slave States, to purchase territory, and then prohibit the citizens thereof from carrying their property into the newly acquired country. He said the principle was unjust and deserved public condemnation." Hubbard was also selected to serve on a committee at this meeting, which subsequently reported resolutions condemning any exclusionary proviso as a "direct usurpation of the rights of all the slaveholding States and citizens thereof." These resolutions, which were unanimously adopted, also advised the South to "require pledges from all seeking their votes for high offices, that our rights in the Southern States should be protected, and that we should not vote for any man, as President, who would withhold such pledges."[10]

It should be noted that Hubbard's stance of requiring presidential candidates to expressly pledge their support for slaveholders' rights as a precondition to receiving Southern votes for nomination predated William Yancey's move in that direction by over a year. Given the widespread publicity the Russellville resolutions garnered in the interim, it is very possible that Yancey was influenced by them.[11] Most of the Democrat press in Alabama took very positive notice of Hubbard's resolutions. The editor of the Tuscaloosa *State Journal and Flag of the Union* heartily approved and endorsed them.[12] Resolutions to this effect were later adopted at what was called a "Great Southern Meeting" that met in Cahaba, Alabama, in March 1847.[13] Similar resolutions had also been adopted by the Virginia legislature in February 1847, and these, in turn, were concurred with by the delegates to the Alabama Democratic Party's state convention, which met in Montgomery on May 3, 1847, to select a gubernatorial candidate.[14] The following month the Georgia Democratic Convention did likewise.[15]

The Huntsville *Democrat* published Hubbard's resolutions but never endorsed his candidacy for Congress. On the contrary, it praised George Smith Houston's service and saw no reason for him to be challenged.[16] Hubbard probably expected nothing less and simply moved forward with his campaign. It was a fierce fight. The editor of the pro-Whig Huntsville *Southern Advocate* wryly quipped that "Hubbard and Houston have waged a ferocious warfare upon each other—and have no doubt perfectly satisfied the people that neither ought to go to Congress."[17]

Hubbard's candidacy was undermined by his connection to Calhoun, who in March 1847 had called on Southerners to quit the Democratic Party because of the continuing support of Northern Democrats for the concept of the Wilmot Proviso. This was compounded by Calhoun's differences with President Polk over war policy and aims.[18] Consistent with the views of a majority of his constituents, George Smith Houston had been loyal to the Democratic Party and to President Polk, and an opponent of Calhoun's influence. Moreover, he used Hubbard's relationship with Calhoun to good effect,[19] so good that Hubbard dropped out of the race, albeit temporarily. At a public meeting in Franklin in July, fifty-five-year-old Hubbard reportedly "took the stand, and stated that as many reports were in circulation throughout the District prejudicial to him, and his health would not permit his traversing the District and correcting them, he withdrew from the canvass."[20] A few days later, however, Hubbard announced his return to the race. For this he was given the rhetorical equivalent of a kiss of death when his candidacy was endorsed by the Huntsville *Southern Advocate*.[21] Houston promptly routed him in the August election in every county in the congressional district except Lawrence.[22]

More bad news was on the way. After several years of litigation, the barely operational TC&D was sold at public auction on September 22, 1847, to satisfy a judgment obtained against the corporation by its creditors. The purchasers were a group of north Alabamians who received a charter for a new entity called the Tennessee Valley Railroad Corporation, and who intended to continue the railroad in operation.[23] They, however, lacked the funds necessary to make essential upgrades, such as the replacement of the old wooden rails with iron.[24] Hubbard could only wonder how all of this might affect efforts to generate support for a railroad between Charleston, South Carolina, and Memphis, Tennessee, that Calhoun had renewed at a large commercial convention in Memphis in 1845.[25] Now there was no certainty it would even cross north Alabama, much less Lawrence County.

Making matters worse, the price of cotton remained very low. At the conclusion of the 1847 crop year, a north Alabama editor lamented that "our people have been buying negroes, horses, stock, pork, groceries, etc., besides paying foreign debts, and they calculated upon getting *eight* or *ten* cents for their cotton, to cause a return of the money-tide—but cotton won't bring more than five cents if that, and is not saleable at present at all.

The consequence of all is general and severe pecuniary pressure throughout the classes of the community, which is felt in every branch of business."[26] This made even more painful the news from Montgomery in March 1848 regarding the adoption of a significant tax increase to fund payment of the state's debt.[27]

This increase did not mean, however, that the state would no longer pursue bank debtors like Hubbard to collect debts still owed to the State Bank. This, in turn, may explain why no evidence has been found indicating that Hubbard was politically active during the 1848 presidential election cycle. But his Russellville resolutions lived on in the so-called "Alabama Platform," adopted by the Alabama Democratic Party in February 1848. Yancey secured approval of platform planks opposing any effort by the federal government to exclude slavery in the now-ceded Mexican lands unless by way of the extension of the Missouri Compromise line. Alabama delegates to the national convention were also instructed not to vote for any presidential or vice-presidential candidate who did not "unequivocally avow" themselves to be opposed to restrictions on slavery.[28] Yancey also invoked (again without attribution) Hubbard's 1843 suggestion regarding withdrawing from any party convention that yielded Southern rights "to secure to our Ticket the support of Northern fanatics."[29] At their national convention in Baltimore, Maryland, the Democrats nominated United States Senator Lewis Cass of Michigan as the party's presidential candidate even though Cass did not express opposition to bans by territorial legislatures on slavery as Yancey and some others demanded. Then the delegates overwhelmingly rejected Yancey's proposed resolution prohibiting congressional interference with slavery moving into the territories. In protest, Yancey got up and walked out of the convention hall, but only one other delegate followed him.[30]

Yancey received widespread criticism from mainstream Democrats in and outside Alabama for his display of party disloyalty. A Mississippi editor thought the country would be better off if he were dead.[31] Hubbard's reaction to this is unknown, but there was initially some solace in the fact that John Quincy Adams had finally died in February 1848,[32] and that the Polk administration initiated negotiations in July to fulfill Hubbard's dream of acquiring Cuba.[33] Those negotiations failed, however, and what was becoming known as the "Free Soil" movement did not die with Adams. Defeating that movement, and assuring that at least a portion of California—with its recently discovered gold deposits—was open to slave labor, became even more of an imperative to what Free Soilers called the "Slavocracy." To Hubbard it was essential that slaveowners long suffering from low cotton prices be allowed to sell or take their slaves to the gold fields there to be put to work mining gold.[34]

Much would depend on who was elected president of the United States in 1848. To face non-slaveowner Lewis Cass, the Whigs ironically nominated a slaveowner, Mexican War hero General Zachary Taylor.[35] At least superficially, Taylor seemed to be the obvious choice of other slaveowners. However, Taylor had too many disturbing connections with Free Soilers.[36] Hence, most north Alabama Democrats stuck with their nominee, Cass.[37] Taylor, however, won Lawrence County and the election.[38]

Not long after the election, Free Soilers in Congress began what a Mobile editor called the "great 'Anti-Slavery Crusade,' which they design, shall not terminate until all the peculiar institutions of the South are broken down and this section of the Union is blasted in all its agricultural and domestic interests."[39] After Congress convened in December, several Northern Whigs introduced anti-slavery measures. If adopted, the slave trade and slavery itself in the District of Columbia, an area over which Congress had exclusive control, would be prohibited.[40] Congress would also exercise its exclusive control over the territories to ban slavery in the lands acquired from Mexico, including gold-rich California.[41]

In response, Calhoun and several other Southern senators and congressmen established an informal committee to prepare an address to the South to encourage Southern solidarity and resistance. That address, which was adopted on January 22, 1849, predicted that if the South would unify, the North would be "brought to a change of measures and the adoption of a course of policy that may quietly and peacefully terminate this long conflict between the two sections of the country." The address also warned Southerners of the baneful consequences of their failure to unite:

> To destroy the existing relation between the free and servile races at the

South would lead to consequences unparalleled in history. They cannot be separated, and cannot live together in peace, or harmony, or to their mutual advantage, except in their present relation. Under any other, wretchedeness, and misery, and desolation, would overspread the whole South.

Abolition and its dystopic outcome, the address continued, could occur only under one set of circumstances:

It can then only be effected by the prostration of the white race; and that would necessarily engender the bitterest feelings of hostility between them and the North. But the reverse would be the case between the blacks of the South and the people of the North. Owing their emancipation to them, they would regard them as friends, guardians, and patrons, and centre, accordingly, all their sympathy in them. The people of the North would not fail to reciprocate and to favor them, instead of the whites. Under the influence of such feelings, and impelled by fanaticism and love of power, they would not stop at emancipation. Another step would be taken—to raise them to a political and social equality with their former owners, by giving them the right of voting and holding public offices under the Federal Government. * * * But when once raised to an equality, they would become the fast political associates of the North, acting and voting with them on all questions, and by the political union between them holding the white race at the South in complete subjection. The blacks, *and the profligate whites that might unite with them*, would become the principal recipients of federal offices and patronage, and would, in consequence, be raised above the whites of the South in the political and social scale. We would, in a word, change conditions with them—a degradation greater than has ever yet fallen to the lot of a free and enlightened people, and one from which we could not escape, should emancipation take place (which it certainly will, if not prevented), but by fleeing the homes of ourselves and ancestors, and by abandoning our country, to our former slaves, to become the permanent abode of disorder, anarchy, poverty, misery, and wretchedness."[42]

Calhoun and the others behind this movement did not receive the degree of support from the 121 Southern congressmen they had expected. Seventy-three, including both congressmen from north Alabama, George Smith Houston and Williamson R. W. Cobb of Jackson County, declined to sign it.[43] When Houston returned to Alabama after Congress adjourned without enacting any Free Soil legislation, he was confronted at a Democratic Party meeting in Athens by those who disagreed with his course.[44] Although this reaction was not unanimous, it was not long before Houston announced he would not seek reelection.[45]

One reason Houston and Cobb were met with criticism was concern that north Alabama might lose in the now fierce competition to have the Memphis and Charleston Railroad come through that region. The route for that vitally important project had not yet been decided and would not be until October 1849.[46] Moreover, it was still undetermined whether South Carolinians would provide the degree of financial support essential for its construction.[47] Huntsville's business community desperately wanted the road to come through their town, and C. C. Clay Jr., Jeremiah Clemens, and its other politicos dutifully gave speeches praising the Southern Address and denouncing all who had withheld their signature.[48] Then Calhoun wrote a widely publicized letter in May 1849 to the promoters of a planned railroad convention in which he made clear the connection between support for his Southern solidarity movement and the route of the road.[49]

In a matter of weeks, Jeremiah Clemens announced that he would challenge Williamson R. W. Cobb for his seat in Congress.[50] David Hubbard then entered the race for George Smith Houston's seat.[51] He had begun laying the groundwork for his candidacy a few months earlier by issuing a lengthy public letter addressing the state's ponderous debt load. It was an impressive primer on public finance and tax policy, and in it Hubbard proposed a plan that would lead to the payment of the debt without high taxes through a complicated arrangement involving mutual concessions with the holders of the state's bonds. Perhaps the most important passages in this letter were those assuring protection to the less affluent—particularly the non-slaveowners who represented a majority of the voters in his congressional district.[52] This would prove to be beneficial against his two well-heeled younger opponents, both of whom were from Florence. One,

Edward Asbury O'Neal, was a Democrat who was a close friend and political supporter of Houston. The other, William Basil Wood, was a Whig.[53]

Hubbard had another advantage. For the first time, his perceived connection with Calhoun appears to have been seen by some in his district as a plus rather than a minus. Houston worriedly wrote Georgia congressman Howell Cobb in June predicting that "a rabid Calhoun man" who was "an old nullifier and an enemy of mine" would likely be elected.[54] Houston and his friends tried their best to prevent that. Among other things, they wrote anonymous letters published in one of Houston's organs, the *Florence Gazette*, accusing Hubbard of opposing the Mexican War after not receiving a patronage appointment from President Polk; attempting to divide north Alabamians along class lines when he advocated that state and local taxes should be borne by slaveowners (many of whom were Whigs), but not non-slaveowners; and being a political opportunist loyal only to himself and not the Democratic Party.[55] Hubbard issued his own public letter denying these charges and stressing his military service and later accomplishments during his last term in Congress, particularly the passage of a pre-emption bill.[56] He also gave a speech in Moulton emphasizing the need to stand up to Northern aggression.[57]

Hubbard, then fifty-seven, was victorious on election day, albeit by a plurality of the vote cast. To the chagrin of George Smith Houston, however, Hubbard won every county in the fifth congressional district except Lauderdale County, the home of Hubbard's two opponents.[58] The Memphis and Charleston Railroad had seemingly "changed the politicks" of northwest Alabama, but the question remained whether it changed that of the Union as Calhoun had predicted to Hubbard years earlier. Northeast Alabama had maintained its support for Williamson R. W. Cobb,[59] but despite this, the decision was made that the route of the Memphis and Charleston Railroad would be through north Alabama.[60] It would not, however, pass through George Houston's Limestone County. Perhaps as South Carolina's influence strengthened in northeast Alabama with the construction of the railroad, and the Free Soil forces in the North became even more aggressive and threatening, attitudes would change even there. With aid from a surprising source, Free Soilers would soon show their aggression even more. So would David Hubbard.

11

'Disunion Davy'

B y the time Congress met in December 1849, it was evident that proponents of the desires of slaveowners to expand and protect slavery had no friend in the White House. This was graphically illustrated in August when President Zachary Taylor issued a proclamation declaring illegal an effort then underway by an irregular band of American "filibusters" to take Cuba by force, and calling out the U.S. military to put down the invasion before it was fully underway. As Hubbard likely knew, however, planning for another attempt to take Cuba and have it made into one or two slave states was already underway.[1]

Startling news from the West made Cuba's acquisition even more imperative. The gold-plated California version of Alabama Fever had drawn over a hundred thousand hopeful emigrants to the region in 1848 and 1849, more than enough to qualify for application for statehood. In the fall of 1849, a constitutional convention in California unanimously adopted a constitution containing a provision stating that "neither slavery, nor involuntary servitude, unless for punishment of crimes, shall ever be tolerated in this State."[2] For good reason, many Southerners suspected that President Taylor had orchestrated this attempt to propel the region directly to statehood without slavery and without passing through a territorial stage.[3]

For men like Hubbard, allowing the motley assortment of newcomers to California to decide the slavery issue for the portion of the region south of the Missouri Compromise line was intolerable. Not only would slavery be banned from the gold fields, but the balance between free and slave states in the United States Senate would end. The time to fight was now, not later, wrote a like-minded editor in Montgomery.[4] Pursuant to a plan that appears to have been conceived over a period of several weeks if not months, the fight began in Congress with an attempt to block California's admission to the Union. The strategy used by Hubbard and others in the House of Representatives was to paralyze its proceedings as long as possible, and then to raise the threat of disunion to intimidate Northerners in connection with the vote on California's admission. Despite claims to the contrary, there was no consensus among Alabamians over the South's next move if this strategy failed. That, Calhoun and others maintained, was to be decided at a convention of delegates from the Southern states scheduled to take place in the late spring of 1850.[5] The pro-Memphis and Charleston Railroad Huntsville *Democrat* was already in lockstep with Calhoun and other South Carolina radicals in its opposition to further compromise by Southerners on the issue of slavery, and its support for secession if the North pushed the Wilmot Proviso through Congress or took any other action resulting in the restriction of slavery's extension.[6]

This outcome could be avoided if Congress were frozen into gridlock and unable to adopt anti-slavery legislation or admit California. To do any business, the House was required by federal law to first elect a Speaker, administer to him the oath of office, and then have the Speaker administer the oath to each of the House members.[7] Thus, Hubbard and other Calhounite Democrats first attempted to prevent this election. They were successful for almost three weeks by splitting their votes among several candidates and obstinately refusing to vote for Democrat Howell Cobb of Georgia—the Democratic caucus nominee, the owner of over a thousand slaves, and the eventual winner—because Cobb had not signed Calhoun's Southern Address earlier in the year. Cobb, they believed, was too moderate and party-oriented and not sufficiently radical in support of Southern interests.[8]

During the election process, Hubbard reported back to Alabama disingenuously placing the blame for the delay on the Free Soilers. In a joint public letter to recently elected Alabama governor Henry Watkins Collier that received wide national notice, Hubbard and some other Democrat and Whig representatives from Alabama declared that the "affairs of the Government have reached a crisis of no ordinary moment" because the "Free Soil Party" was refusing to organize the House "unless they can secure from the presiding officer, whose duty it will be to appoint committees, some pledge [in advance] to aid them in their purpose of directing the legislation of Congress against the interest and honor of the slaveholding States. For the first time in our history," the letter continued, "these men have acquired sufficient strength to enable them seriously to affect the action of the Government."[9]

Hubbard did not subsequently report that Democrats and Whigs finally combined to put an end to the impasse created by him and others in Congress. A majority of the House, in response to great public criticism, voted to elect a Speaker by a plurality vote, thereby allowing Cobb to be elected on December 22. Ironically, David Hubbard and Southern pariah David Wilmot both voted against allowing the election by plurality vote, although Hubbard did finally vote for Cobb.[10] Then Cobb assigned both to serve together on the same unimportant committee, the Committee of Claims.[11] The response in Alabama to Hubbard's efforts was, nonetheless, initially positive. Even the *Florence Gazette* appeared to be coming around. Its editor, Mathew Gallaway, wrote that "we are rejoiced to see the bold and patriotic stand which the representative from this district has taken in behalf of Southern rights." He "is watchful and vigilant" and "unwilling to bestow power on any one whose position on the Wilmot Proviso is the least equivocal."[12]

Gallaway's opinion of Hubbard began to resume its former low level, however, after President Taylor's annual message was read on December 24. Taylor favored the admission of California, opposed the taking of Cuba by force, and pledged, Jackson-like, to defend the Union.[13] Hubbard's reaction was swift. He wrote a public letter to a Whig editor in south Alabama advocating that all Southerners eschew political parties and instead form a solid phalanx against the abolition threat. "Let there be no more wrangling among the factions of *Hunker* and *Chivalry,* or either 'Whigs' or 'Democrats.'" A unified assertion of the South's independence was the only way to prevent abolition. Northern politicians, he maintained, recognized that, once independent, the South "will be an overmatch for them in everything—having a larger export and surplus—more willing both to turn out as soldiers or to pay soldiers for going into service."[14] Hubbard's advice was well received in Dallas County and other portions of south Alabama where slave populations were high, but in north Alabama a desire to again compromise sectional differences rather than risk a civil war was growing.[15]

Hubbard then wrote the first of several public letters to his north Alabama constituents in an effort to arrest this current of feeling. He still complained that Congress had been "nearly six weeks in session without being able, as yet, to elect its officers," and again blamed this "extraordinary delay" on the fact that the "Halls of Congress, up to this date, have more resembled abolition conventicles than legislative assemblies acting for a Republic of States." He warned that the "Northern people intend to abolish slavery as fast as they can induce the Southern people to endure the measures intended to effect that object," and to do so would "deceive, coax, and threaten." To those opposed to disunion, Hubbard declared that the North had already "*broken* the covenant of Union by their attacks upon the character, the property, and the institutions of the South; by their incendiary publications, their meetings, teachings, and preachings, whereby the value of slaves has been reduced millions of dollars, our lives endangered, by trying to give the negroes a right to vote and control elections, and, by the encouragement given every other imaginable mode of injury known to these agitators; and lastly, by their constant disturbances and hindrance to the legislation of Congress."[16]

Hubbard's recommendations regarding a course of action were initially vague, but it is clear that he was attempting to plant the seeds of secession, not compromise. He urged his constituents to disregard pleas that they compromise for the sake of the Union, for to do so "we become as silly as the sheep in the fable, which, listening to the cajoling of the wolves, sent away their 'guard dogs,' and let the wolves among them as 'family friends' and 'were devoured.'" Encouraging financially struggling north Alabamians to begin calculating the value of the Union, Hubbard reported that "it is admitted here, that 'the cotton, sugar, rice and tobacco of the slave States has built up the commerce and cities of the North, and that *were the South to declare ourselves independent* of these abolition assemblies [sessions of Congress], we would soon exceed them in prosperity, wealth and power.'" His concluding paragraph declared that "it is time to take a stand and to maintain it," and he advised that his constituents "consider among yourselves as to the choice you will take between submission to wrong, or the assertion (*in some form*) of the independent right of self-protection."[17]

Some Southern Whigs in Congress, however, began to break ranks and concede that another compromise was possible. Most notably, Kentucky senator Henry Clay introduced several resolutions on January 29, 1850, one of which supported the admission of California to the Union. Clay's other resolutions called for the establishment of territorial governments for the balance of the Mexican Cession with no Wilmot Proviso; sought to establish the border between Texas and what would become New Mexico, and to pay some of Texas's pre-annexation debt in exchange for Texas's relinquishment of all of New Mexico; abolished the commercial slave trade, but not slavery, in the District of Columbia; and strengthened the federal fugitive slave law.[18]

A correspondent to the Huntsville *Democrat* wrote from Washington that "Mr. Clay's infamous proposition, which he calls a compromise, will do us great harm." Already, he continued, the "drooping spirits of Northern men begin to revive, and men who ten days ago never spoke of the slavery question without trepidation are now boldly urging its renewed agitation. They were just coming to their senses when this infernal scheme made its appearance, and coming as it does from a Southern man, gives the North ground to believe that we are not in earnest about resistance, and that when the time of trial comes we will falter in our duty."[19] Even worse for those like Hubbard who had been attempting to at least create the illusion that the South was a unit in its uncompromising opposition to all anti-slavery measures, many Southern Whig organs announced their support for Clay's proposals and portrayed those who voiced resistance as traitors to the Union.[20] Among those newspapers favoring compromise was the *Moulton Sentinel.*[21]

Further evidence of moderation in Alabama was revealed when the legislature was unable to reach agreement on whether to schedule an election of delegates to the Nashville Convention. As a consequence, a group of legislators selected the delegates in a caucus, meaning those delegates would have no official authority to act for Alabama.[22] At about the same time, the Whig-dominated Tennessee legislature resolved against sending any delegates, and pledged to defend the Union "at all hazards and to the last extremity."[23]

Hubbard correctly diagnosed the situation. At least for the time being, the people valued a peaceful Union over anything else, particularly as cotton prices improved slightly and made the need to move to the West less acute.[24] In a letter to a Montgomery newspaper he warned that expressions of acquiescence and submission would only encourage aggression, and the North would "need not more than four or five weeks in abolishing slavery in the States." Echoing the 1849 Southern Address of the now dying John C. Calhoun, Hubbard prophesied that "the negroes would be put upon equality and voting at the next election, holding offices and exercising all other acts of citizenship." Hubbard urged the South to, instead, "unite all the friends of our institutions, regardless of former differences, and success is certain." In fact, he assured that if the South would use its economic power and deny the North and England even one of its cotton crops, textile workers there would revolt. "It would break up, starve, and lay waste more country than three of Bonaparte's campaigns." Then Hubbard went a step further: "If the south would assert its own *independence* and its *equality*—for it should assert the first if the latter is longer withheld—these agitators north would be hung in four years."[25]

Hubbard's radical rhetoric was then reinforced by Calhoun's dramatic and highly provocative last speech in the Senate on March 4. In that speech, which had to be read by another because of Calhoun's terminal illness, he declared that the South would compromise no further on the issue of slavery. Instead, it was the North's turn. It must, he declared, terminate agitation of the slavery issue, afford equal rights to slaveowners in the Mexican Cession, enforce the fugitive slave law, and adopt a constitutional amendment giving the slave states equal power with the North in Congress. Otherwise, Calhoun instructed the senators, "let the States we both represent agree to separate and part in peace. If you are unwilling we part in peace," he warned, "we shall know what to do."[26]

Calhoun's speech did little to reassure or unite the South. "Mr. Calhoun, in our judgment, has completely thrown off the mask, and stands before the country an avowed DISUNIONIST," wrote the editor of the *Richmond Whig*.[27] However, it was not just the Whig press that expressed disapproval. The Democrat organ in Alabama's largest city, the *Mobile Register*, did also.[28] Not long after a very conciliatory and influential speech in the United States

Senate by Senator Daniel Webster of Massachusetts, editorials endorsing Henry Clay's compromise measures began to appear in other Democrat Alabama newspapers.[29]

At about the same time, the *Florence Gazette* began attacking Hubbard. It published an anonymous letter in its March 23 edition criticizing "the fanatics North and South" in Congress for failing to reach an accord based on Clay's compromise measures, and ridiculing Hubbard's letters to his constituents. "By infusing into us uncompromising dislike to the North and to Congress, and stimulating our Southern interests, pride and valor, he seeks to prepare our minds through our passions for his suggestions and manufacture public opinion to support his destructive objects," which included a "dismemberment of the Union" that would be "destructive to the best interests of the common country." The author of this letter, which was signed "A Friend to Constitutional Union, and a voter in the 5th Congressional district of Alabama," advised a different course of action that was as a past life to Hubbard. "The means by which we should endeavor to maintain our rights, ought not to be violent abuse and invective which generally injures a cause instead of aiding it, but by mild and persuasive reasoning, urging with good temper constitutional guaranties; common interests; love of country; strength of union; weakness of disunion; and the calamities which must befall us all by dismemberment. These topics urged with gentleness and persuasion would be listened to in a kindly spirit by the most of Northern members, and harmonious and wise legislation would result, yielding justice to all according to the spirit of the Constitution, uniting us as one people, glorying in the preservation of that union which has made us great and prosperous."[30]

This letter, which might have been written by George Smith Houston, was the opening shot in the campaign leading up to the 1851 congressional election in Hubbard's district. The next came a week later when the *Florence Gazette's* editor, Mathew Gallaway, declared in an editorial that "cherishing as we always have done a strong attachment for the Union our feelings involuntarily revolt at the prospect of a dissolution." He called instead for "a patriotic conciliatory course" and "the spirit of patriotism to preside over our own actions and the councils of the nation." Citing Webster's speech and pro-compromise rallies in the North that took place in the ensuing days, Gallaway concluded that "a more national conservative spirit is being exhibited—and we hope and expect in a few weeks to announce to our readers the gratifying intelligence that this fearful question is peaceably adjusted with satisfaction to all parties." This would include, wrote Gallaway, admitting California with her present constitution even though it prohibited slavery.[31] As if on cue, sixty-eight-year-old John C. Calhoun died the very next day.[32]

On April 19, the Senate appointed thirteen senators, including William Rufus King of Alabama and Henry Clay, to a special committee to develop a plan of compromise to be submitted to Congress.[33] This made those who favored an amicable resolution even more hopeful. David Hubbard attempted to counter this sentiment in a third letter to his constituents, which appeared in the *Florence Gazette* two weeks before the Nashville Convention. He denied that the threat to the South had passed. Insofar as the "determination and purpose" of the abolitionists in Congress, "I cannot discover any change for the better." Referring to the speech of a Northern Whig four years earlier, Hubbard declared that, regardless of their form, the measures being supported by the North were "with the view of hemming us in, and making a wall of free States around you, thereby forcing emancipation of slaves, and putting the negroes and whites upon an equality." The North, he declared, would use any means necessary to accomplish that goal. Responding to jeers that his cries of "wolf" had so far proven unfounded, Hubbard reminded his readers that in the fable, "'the wolf *did* come at last,' and if you go on as heretofore, quarreling about party schemes, he will find you off your guard and helpless." Knowing that South Carolina planned to send a very aggressive, pro-secession delegation to Nashville, Hubbard urged his constituents to send delegates to the convention and "let them consult with those from other Southern States, and see whether the South *can* give ground any further, and remain in the Union with *safety* to their institutions. If they think not, let them say so. If they think we can give ground, let them say how far and having fixed the limit of Northern aggression, let them, in a plain, firm, and friendly manner, tell the North that 'we cannot remain together if the power which Union gives is longer used to despoil us of our rights to property justly ours.' Do but this," Hubbard assured, "and I stake my life upon the result that much as the Northern men hate slavery, their love *of the advantages* which Union already give them over us, will make them agree to our terms." Defiantly, Hubbard warned that if "my constituents desire to submit to aggressions, and to fall at the feet of that power which abolition and the lust of power and dominion combined have threatened to use against them—if they have become alarmed at the threat of marching Northern regiments against them so frequently made—then *they must look up another Representative* to make the degrading submission."[34]

Not long after the Senate Committee of Thirteen reported a bill that would admit California and resolve several other slavery-related issues, the *Florence Gazette* began laying the groundwork for that very eventuality. It published a call signed by fifty-two men for a public meeting to rally support for compromise scheduled to take place just days before the Nashville Convention was to convene.[35] Although a majority of those who attended the meeting were Whigs, most notably Leroy Pope Walker's brother, Richard Wilde Walker, several, including Mathew Gallaway, were Democrats.[36] This was a troubling sign to Alabama's Democratic Party leaders concerned that the threat of secession and civil war was causing a political realignment in the heretofore Democrat "avalanche" counties of north Alabama whose support had been absolutely essential to Democrat supremacy in the state since the beginning of the Jacksonian Era.[37]

When C. C. Clay Jr. and other Democrats promoted a meeting in Huntsville to rally support for the Nashville Convention and continuing resistance to the admission of California, only 132 men out of the 23,000 Madison County voters showed up. Even more embarrassingly, despite spirited speeches by Clay, Huntsville attorney David Campbell Humphreys, and other Democrat leaders, fifty-three of those in attendance voted against pro-convention resolutions offered by Clay.[38] Not to be denied, Clay then reportedly waited until all of his opposition left the meeting before moving again for the adoption of his resolutions, which were later dutifully reported in the Huntsville *Democrat* as having been adopted "unanimously" by the people of Madison County.[39] Tricks like this would not paper over growing Unionist sentiment in north Alabama, and Williamson Cobb would make Clay regret those tricks in 1853.

On May 28, 1850, Hubbard attempted to check the budding Union political movement in a public letter to Mathew Gallaway. He derided this "new scheme of President making—called union, compromise, concession, adjustment, fraternity and equality between North and South, black and white." Concession for party reasons, he warned, would not only result in the accomplishment of each of the immediate goals of the abolitionists, but was the path to complete abolition. "Fanatical Abolition would vote to break up slavery tomorrow, and put black and white upon equality at once," he warned. He continued, "political abolition" would reach this goal over the next several years in stages through successive compromises and concessions by the South. "Nothing is easier, plainer or more direct than such a result after you get out upon the road; the road to mill or market will not be plainer."[40]

In the days leading up to the Nashville Convention, however, opposition to it and support for the compromise bill in the Senate continued to grow, especially in north Alabama. In Mathew Gallaway's next editorial on the subject, which was published two days before the Nashville Convention, he argued that the compromise deal already on the table was "the best the South can get" and "we prefer to take [it], sweetened by the other ingredients of the compromise, though there is a precious little of the sweet, and a good deal of the bitter in all." To do otherwise would permit "the ultra free-soilers, and the abolitionists," who were also opposed to the compromise, to simply "bring California in by itself" and then "New Mexico, and next Utah, as free States, as they successfully apply for admission." That the compromise would disappoint and defeat them "is a strong recommendation of the measure."[41]

Gallaway did not make specific reference to Hubbard, but an anonymous, widely reported letter purporting to be addressed to Hubbard and published with Galloway's editorial certainly did. It was a funny litany of ridicule apparently written by the same classically educated author of one of the preelection letters unfavorable to Hubbard. With regard to Hubbard's service in Congress, the author, who signed the letter "Civis," flatly declared that "after the most thorough investigation of your whole congressional life, I can find no solitary act that claims my gratitude or applause." Referring to Hubbard's "silly and incendiary despatches" to his constituents, Civis observed that "history informs us that the midnight cackling of a goose saved one Republic from desolation and ruin, and it should be a subject of congratulation that we have an equally vigilant, if not a more sagacious '*Sentinel upon the Watchtower*.'"[42]

But, Civis warned Hubbard, he was in danger of the "horrors of a political death—possibly from infamy" by "pledging your constituents to the blighting and unholy cause of treason and disunion" and thereby dishonoring "in the eyes of the world and of posterity forever" the "attachments and integrity to the sacred institutions of their country" held by his constituents. "What better evidence of this could you ask," queried Civis, "than the universal scorn and disapprobation with which they have received the so called *Nashville Convention*, upon which you seem to build your greatest hopes for the triumph of treason. The day is just at hand, and yet, not one solitary motion of the *People* has given it countenance and support. The miserable manakin [*sic*] is already dead and buried beneath a mountain of popular ridicule and contempt. If any appear at Nashville, to revive the exploded humbug, be assured they will require nothing more to give immortality to their name."[43]

The day was "not far distant," Civis continued, "when from the last extremity of forbearance *the People* will be roused into action, when a wave of popular indignation will roll toward the Capitol at Washington, which will free the land from the withering, blighting, and damning influence of these earth-scourging and heaven-defying demagogues, who have already tarnished the escutcheon of our country's glory." Civis urged Hubbard to, therefore, "consult both your *interest* and future happiness by returning at once to the legitimate duties with which you are charged, and assuming the virtues, tho' God has denied you the abilities of a statesman."[44]

Proving Civis's last point most emphatically, Hubbard followed a very conciliatory pro-Union, nationalistic speech by Williamson Cobb in Congress on June 3 with one of the most divisive, hateful attacks on the North witnessed during this session of Congress.[45] Hubbard began his rambling speech by demanding that Congress "at once" give Southerners part of the Mexican Cession and then threatening that, if they did not, "you will repent it." Later in his address, Hubbard coldly explained that "California accounts state that an able-bodied negro man is worth in the mines five thousand dollars, and hires readily for one thousand dollars a year. Now, it is clear that had our people been allowed freely to carry their negroes to that country without hindrance, at this day negroes throughout the Southern States would have been worth three hundred dollars more each than they are—at least one thousand millions of dollars beyond the present value of the whole—a sum sufficient to raise and pay an army ten times the size of the army of the United States; to construct all of the canals and build all of the railroads needed in each of the Southern States. All of which we are required to lose, give up, and part with, to quiet your pretended conscientious objections to the extension of African slavery, which you assisted in bringing to this country, and the price of which sin is now in *your pockets*. I am not willing to make such sacrifices, nor do I think my constituents will disagree with me upon this subject."[46]

It was not Hubbard's intention to persuade his colleagues to join his position, or any other that might be acceptable to radical Southerners. At the time, he was probably aware that the few delegates who were in attendance at the Nashville Convention (Leroy Pope Walker was among the twenty-one Alabama delegates who went, while fifteen others who had been selected stayed at home) that was then in its third day of deliberations were hopelessly divided. If it appeared that the proposed compromise legislation was on the verge of being adopted, the convention would not issue any strong ultimatum, much less announce plans for secession and the formation of a Southern confederacy.[47] Increasing the level of sectional animosity in Congress held the possibility of assuring that no mutually agreeable compromise would be reached. Thus, virtually all of Hubbard's speech was an insulting attack on the North and an effort to incite Southern nationalism. He asserted that the abolition movement was a hypocritical conspiracy by the rich and powerful "to break down our Constitution" and eliminate "liberty regulated by law" to create classes consisting of "wealth, office, power, and a privileged few on one side, and labor, toil, subjection, and degradation of multitudes on the other." He also questioned Northerners for their lack of "charity," "humanity," and spirit of Christianity toward the underpaid working classes living in their allegedly crime-ridden, poverty-stricken major cities. By contrast, lectured Hubbard, Southern slaves were not only better fed, clothed, and cared for than "the sewing women of Philadelphia," but since being brought to this country as "a cannibal and heathen . . . his descendants now are humanized christians." "I will venture my life," said Hubbard, "that I can find a greater number of scoffers and infidels and unbelievers in the Divinity of the Savior within sight of the highest church-steeple in Boston, than can be counted among the three millions of slaves in the Southern States, and their owners, put together." As if this were not enough, Hubbard added that "if Northern people think Christ worth preaching about, or praying to, then all of these pretended abolitionists, on Christ's account, are nothing but hypocrites and blasphemers."[48]

Hubbard finally concluded his lengthy address by attacking the loyalty of Southern leaders who were favoring the compromise measures. He also again challenged Southerners to unite, using an anecdote from the bloody conflict centuries earlier between oppressed Scotland and oppressor England:

It is our own divisions which had enabled the northern section of the union to encroach upon the rights of our constituents. And our conduct here for the last ten years reminds me of an incident reported in history, where England was trying to reduce Scotland to submission by arms. Sir William Wallace was the patriotic leader of the Scots, and England, like our Northern opposers, had seduced many of the Scottish leaders into her armies, Robert Bruce among others. In these contests, it is related that one day, after a hard-fought battle, Bruce sat down to his meal with the English nobles, with his hands all besmeared with the blood of his own countrymen slain in the battle; upon seeing which, a haughty English earl could not conceal his disgust. 'Look,' said he, 'at that Scot; see how he eats his own blood.' This insulting taunt, although true, cut Bruce to the heart. He could not eat another morsel, but quietly arose from the table without uttering a word. That night Bruce joined the standard of his countrymen, and never rested or slept quietly until every hostile foot had been driven far beyond the 'Scotish [sic] border.'

I, sir, never hear a Southern man speak against his section of country, or read a Southern paper opposed to us, but I think that some cool, calculating Northerner, like the English nobleman, is expressing his disgust 'for the fellow who eats his own blood.'

When will every true-hearted southron, like Bruce, leave the camp of the oppressor, and join the standard of his own country? Until then, the North will never regard our rights, nor respect our feelings."[49]

One Southerner to whom Hubbard might have been referring was Thomas Ritchie, a veteran newspaperman from Virginia who was the editor of the Democrat organ in the nation's capital, the *Washington Union*. "Father" Ritchie, as he was sometimes known, had been the target of much criticism by Southern extremists for his efforts to encourage moderation and compromise to save the Union. A few weeks earlier, Hubbard and other members of Congress had organized support for the launch of a competitor, the *Southern Press*, to encourage anti-compromise sentiment.[50] Like most newspapermen who become the brunt of criticism, Ritchie would have his revenge.

Someone sent Ritchie copies of a letter from David Hubbard to Mathew Gallaway attacking the provisions of the compromise, as well as Gallaway's spirited reply to Hubbard. Gallaway referred to "this healing, patriotic and equitable compromise" and to Hubbard's criticisms as "an insult to the intelligence and understanding of his constituents." Opposition in Congress to the compromise was a product of what he called an "'ominous conjunction,' between the extremists of the North and the extremists of the South-Northern agitation embracing Southern ultraism." It was "David Wilmot and David Hubbard gracious and loving yoke-fellows. An '*ominous conjunction* truly!' And one which the people of the South will not fail to mark and *to recollect*."[51] Perhaps with some degree of satisfaction, Ritchie promptly published both in the June 25 edition of the *Union* to demonstrate that Hubbard's constituents publicly disagreed with his course. Hubbard attempted to limit the damage to his credibility by writing a letter to the editors of the *Southern Press* ridiculing Gallaway as "one of those kind, obliging men, whose opinions are formed from impulses, without much tax upon his judgment," but who "will be ready to change them whenever he finds himself in error, as he is in this instance."[52]

Nonetheless, the divisive and disorganizing efforts of Hubbard and those like him to prevent resolution of the crisis seemingly bore fruit.[53] President Taylor died on July 9,[54] some solace for the failure of a second attempt to take Cuba by force a few weeks earlier.[55] Then, despite the backing of Alabama senators King and Jeremiah Clemens, amendments to the compromise bill embracing the Missouri Compromise line were soundly defeated in the Senate on June 28 with every Northern senator voting against them.[56] Moreover, despite widespread support in north Alabama for the compromise bill even after the Nashville Convention,[57] it too went down to defeat on July 31, primarily at the hands of Democrat senators and House members.[58] King wrote a letter back to Alabama lamenting that "nothing short of divine interposition can prevent a dissolution of the Union."[59]

Hubbard was likely among the opponents of the compromise in Washington who celebrated their great victory, but the thrill of victory would be short-lived. Democrats led by Illinois senator Stephen A. Douglas began an effort to revive the essence of the compromise.[60] Meanwhile, Alabama Unionists moved quickly to shape public opinion against secession and civil war. "The Union is in danger," warned Mathew Gallaway, "and no man with an American heart can fold his arms and say to the winds of faction, blow on!" On the contrary, "a grave and imperative duty is imposed upon every citizen of the country and so far as we are concerned, we intend to discharge that duty faithfully and fearlessly, and in such a manner as to aid in preserving our glorious confederacy."[61]

Perhaps the most remarkable and widely reported display of Unionism in north Alabama took place at Patton Springs in Lauderdale County on August 31, 1851. A mass meeting was called by Leroy Pope Walker to orchestrate the adoption of resolutions denouncing the resurrected compromise measures, which were seemingly, through the "divine interposition" to which Senator King had referred, independently moving toward passage. According to Mathew Gallaway's account of the meeting, "Gen'l Walker was called upon and spoke about one hour in defence of the Nashville Convention, . . . attacked the Compromise bills . . . and boldly declared that the

Union was not worth the sacrifices which the friends of the Compromise required of the Southern people." Walker spoke, Gallaway continued, "with confidence—but loosely and unguardedly and apparently without thinking that his statements and appeals to the passions and prejudices of the people were noted by an able adversary who was fully prepared to meet and scatter his sophistries to the winds." That "able adversary" turned out to be Leroy Pope Walker's own brother and former law partner, Richard Wilde Walker, who rose and made what Gallaway described as "an eloquent, powerful and patriotic appeal to his fellow-citizens in behalf of the Union," and challenged each of his brother's contentions regarding the effect of the compromise bills. After his brother sat down, Leroy Pope Walker attempted a rebuttal argument for approximately thirty minutes, and then competing resolutions were submitted for adoption by those in attendance. Apparently realizing that his resolutions might suffer an embarrassing defeat, Leroy Pope Walker reportedly moved that the meeting adjourn.[62]

Meanwhile, led by Stephen Douglas, the compromise measures were working their way piecemeal through Congress. Most significantly, the bill to admit California as a free state was adopted in the House by a vote of ninety-seven to eighty-five on September 7, despite opposition by Hubbard.[63] The entire package of bills comprising the Compromise of 1850 was adopted and signed into law by Millard Fillmore, the late president's successor, by September 17, 1850.[64] None adopted the Wilmot Proviso or banned slavery in the District of Columbia. Hubbard's reaction to this turn of events is unknown. The *Florence Gazette* reported that "strenuous efforts have been made to drive old Lawrence [County] into the disunion ranks," but if Hubbard still favored secession, that would be very difficult if not impossible to accomplish any time soon.[65] The amendment of Alabama's constitution to provide for biennial rather than annual legislative sessions meant that the next regular session would not convene for over a year.

Governor Collier had the authority to call for a special session to meet, but public opinion did not appear to favor that.[66] When a group of south Alabama radicals led by George Washington Gayle petitioned the governor to issue the call, they were ridiculed in an editorial in the *Athens Herald*, George Smith Houston's hometown newspaper. "Speaking of a called session of the legislature," wrote the editor with his tongue firmly planted in his cheek, "we *would* like to see a squad of those South Alabama 'fire-eaters' assembled together. The way they would cavort, and snort, and rave, and rant, and pant and blow and swell, and drink and smoke, and pass funny resolutions, and kick the government into pieces with their high-heeled boots, and froth and foam—would be some, it would. We expect they would even fight some, if they could get any body to 'come to the rescue.' You must pay your own expenses, though, boys, understand that before you start."[67] Governor Collier recognized the trend of public opinion and announced his refusal to convene the legislature.[68]

A "Union Party" coalition of Democrat and Whig moderates was then forming in preparation for the August 1851 congressional elections.[69] As Hubbard well knew, he was among those being targeted for defeat. He also knew that the only important press in north Alabama that shared his views was the increasingly extremist Huntsville *Democrat*.[70] "[Hubbard's] bold, zealous and independent course in defense of the South against her abolition enemies, entitled him to the gratitude of every true Southerner," wrote its editor.[71] However, all members of the press in his own district—Democrat and Whig organs—would be against him, making reelection a distinctly uphill battle.[72]

After adjourning in September, Congress reconvened on December 2, at which point Hubbard was appointed to the Committee on Manufactures.[73] From then to the final adjournment of the Thirty-First Congress on March 3, 1851, Hubbard was noticeably quiet, even during the uproar in the North over the profoundly aggressive federal enforcement of the newly revised fugitive slave law. Gone were his divisive speeches. Gone were his radical letters to his constituents. Part of this was due to a health setback, which the press initially reported to be so severe that "for some days his life was considered in imminent danger."[74] As the *Florence Gazette* recognized, however, part of Hubbard's uncharacteristic silence was strategic.

> The disunion fuglemen have ceased their clamor and resorted to stealth
> and strategem to accomplish their treasonable objects. They have seen enough
> to satisfy them that certain and inevitable defeat awaits all those who openly

avow disunion doctrine. From motives of policy they have temporarily hushed their disunion cry, and are not so bold in proclaiming and endeavoring to propagate their infamous principles, while many of them have taken down the treasonable banner which they so bravely flung to the breeze; but not withstanding all this they are stealthily endeavoring to fan the flames of discord and disunion—while they are making loud professions of devotion to the Union, they are at the same time denouncing in fierce terms the friends of the Union and those patriots who have aided in calming the storm. Let us not be deceived by these specious professions, for the disunionists are only preparing for renewed action which will develop itself as soon as they think there is the least prospect of success.[75]

This editorial did not mention Hubbard directly, but it anticipated his ultimate reelection campaign tactics with great precision. The race drew national attention but, at least initially, Hubbard's only opposition was Francis H. Jones, a young planter and Union Democrat from Lauderdale County.[76] Although Jones was a relative political newcomer, one Mobile Whig newspaper assured that with his status as a Unionist, "there is no doubt about his licking the hind sights off of Disunion Davy."[77] Similarly, a Tuscaloosa Whig newspaper opined that if Hubbard won, it would be "because of his extensive acquaintance, demagogueism and chicanery." It predicted that Hubbard could not succeed in a canvass because, due to his "misdeeds," he "is too vulnerable on many points."[78] Certainly with no Whig candidate in the race to split the Unionist vote, that seemed like a sound prediction. Jones wisely played to his strength by focusing almost exclusively on Hubbard's actions in Congress and disloyalty to the Democratic Party and the Union.[79]

The Huntsville *Democrat* tried to defend Hubbard's actions in Congress. He had stood "with his feet planted on the rock of Southern Rights," wrote its editor.[80] Charges of irrational extremism and support for disunion continued to dog him. Hubbard responded by suddenly trimming his sails in a way that reminds one of the famous credo of the fictional Alabama con man, Simon Suggs, immortalized by Alabama lawyer-editor-humorist Johnson J. Hooper: "It is good to be shifty."[81] Hubbard announced that he now supported the "Georgia Platform," which pledged acquiescence to the Compromise of 1850, but resistance to any further encroachments on Southern rights. "The Major is an old stager," jeered the Huntsville *Southern Advocate*, and "with surprising but characteristic agility, has jumped upon the Georgia platform."[82] Hubbard's political aspirations later forced him to retreat even further from the position he had taken just a year earlier. In a speech in Athens in May, he reportedly "declared he would be opposed to secession or disunion even if the north should repeal the fugitive slave law—he did not think the repeal of that law would be sufficient cause for such action on the part of the South."[83] Upon reviewing this report of what he called "A Late Summerset," an incredulous editor in south Alabama remarked that "when Hon. Davy 'goes a catting he goes a catting,' and does nothing by halves."[84] Another editor saw it as a product of Hubbard having the "sensation [in his back] of a vigorous antagonist after him with a piece of scantling sharpened to a tickling apex."[85]

His surprising feat of political gymnastics made some see him as the probable winner.[86] It also appears to have worried Hubbard's opposition strategists enough to draw George Smith Houston into the race.[87] It is possible that Jones had actually been a stalking horse all along for Houston, who might have wondered whether his refusal to sign the Southern Address in 1849 would still be held against him, and who was gauging public opinion in the district as the battle between Unionists and Southern Rights candidates raged across Alabama. Like Hubbard, Houston would have noted that the vast majority of the north Alabama press, regardless of party affiliation, was quite active in shaping public opinion toward support for the compromise and opposition to secession. The *Florence Gazette* had gone so far as to praise President Millard Fillmore, a Whig, for his administration's steadfast enforcement of the revised fugitive slave law.[88] The Huntsville *Southern Advocate*, whose editor had been appointed by President Fillmore to the post of register of the Land Office at Huntsville, had threatened that if south Alabama Southern Rights activist William Yancey and his followers ever succeeded in orchestrating the secession of Alabama from the Union, "North Alabama will, in that event, secede from the new kingdom and petition to be admitted again into the Union and attached to Tennessee or

Georgia."[89] Houston would have also observed the warm reception received by Alabama's Senator Jeremiah Clemens, who had joined Senator King in support for the Compromise, as he campaigned through the district laying the groundwork for his own bid for reelection during the upcoming legislative session.[90]

Houston's supporters were careful not to portray his entry into the field less than a month before the August election as a calculated move. According to the *Athens Herald,* Houston was "*forced* into the canvass against his own predilections and wishes by the Union men of the District" who "have 'demanded' his services *now* for the favors conferred upon him in times *past,* and he *could not* refuse." Frances Jones, it was said, had too limited an "acquaintance in the District" (read: lightweight nobody) "to insure success, and *success* now, above all things, is what the Union men of the District most desire. Upon it—success, *now*—depends every thing—upon it hangs all our hopes of peace—all our hopes of prosperity for the future; and upon it hangs the very existence of this Union *itself.*"[91] Perhaps somewhat embarrassingly to Jones, his hometown newspaper, the *Florence Gazette,* concurred and predicted that with "General Houston" as the Union candidate, "we may cast our votes with an assurance that he can be triumphantly elected over the late incumbent who holds opinions [at] war with the best interest of the country."[92] Even the Huntsville *Southern Advocate* caught the Houston fever, despite the fact that it was not even published in his district. "Were we entitled [to] vote in the District, [we] would willingly walk twenty miles under the broiling sun to vote for him as the *champion of the Union.*"[93]

Houston did not actually sail to victory. Less than a week after his entry into the race became public knowledge, word came that he had withdrawn from the race. However, not long thereafter the *Florence Gazette* happily announced that "his withdrawal [had] been withdrawn."[94] The reason for this turnabout is unclear, but it is possible that Houston's withdrawal was simply a public relations gesture to Jones to draw his Lauderdale County supporters by giving Jones the opportunity to withdraw from the race without appearing to have been forced from the race by Houston's entry. Nonetheless, even after Houston's reentry, the now fervently pro-Hubbard Huntsville *Democrat,* which was the anti-Compromise organ of the Clay family, continued to report that Houston was no longer a candidate. "Hubbard's election is a fixed fact," wrote its editor. "His defence of [the people's] rights and the rights of the South is too highly appreciated by his constituents, to allow him to be defeated. Houston found this out in his brief circuit among the *farmers*, and hence, he is *forced in*."[95]

Despite such tricks, Hubbard's reelection was anything but a fixed fact. His debates with Houston at the various county seats in the district are said to have drawn crowds in the thousands, many of whom enjoyed Houston's superior ability to use anecdotes, wit, repartee, and satire.[96] Moreover, Houston's strong suit, Unionism, was in the ascendancy among Democrats and Whigs in north Alabama. All of this would be graphically illustrated in the election returns.[97] As the Tuscumbia *North Alabamian* would proudly observe, "not a single individual who openly avowed his belief in the abstract right of secession, or was even suspected of entertaining such heretical views, has been elected either to the State Legislature or to Congress."[98] Among the biggest losers of that stripe was Hubbard, who only managed to achieve small majorities in Franklin, Marion, and his home county of Lawrence.[99]

The overall outcome of the 1851 election in Alabama was attributed by pundits to the use of the threat of secession by men like Hubbard to try to force the North to accept Calhoun's final ultimatum. This, according to a south Alabama editor, had been a mistake. It had caused "many of the Union men to take stronger ground in favor of the Union, than they would otherwise have done." He expressed hope that the "signal defeat of the ultra Southern Rights men, in the recent election" would "have the effect of *checking their ultraism*" and, in the end, "*strengthen* the cause of the South."[100]

Hubbard's defeat meant the end of his second and final term in Congress, but it did not eliminate his belief in secession as the only effective means to preserve slavery and the South's way of life from continued Northern aggression. As he had repeatedly warned his constituents, political abolitionism would gradually acquire more political power in the coming decade, and this would ultimately force the South to either make more significant concessions or fight. By that time, however, the North would have also acquired even more men and wealth than the South to wage war. No one could accuse David Hubbard of failing to give fair warning.

12

The 'Viceregent of Old Fogy-Dom'

N ot long after the 1851 election, Lawrence County residents wearied from the turmoil of this particularly heated political battle finally received the answer to their prayers for economic development. Word leaked that the board of directors of the Memphis and Charleston Railroad had officially decided to build that road south of the Tennessee River, rather than north, using the original right of way of the old TC&D.[1] Although the 1850 federal census for Lawrence County had disclosed a paltry twenty-four manufacturing establishments, and a free population of only 8,406 (including sixty-three free blacks), boosters could now dream of a Northern-style quantum economic leap.[2] Even Hubbard, now licking his electoral wounds, had something to rejoice given that the road would eventually pass through north Mississippi, making his remaining land there more attractive and valuable to planters.[3]

Despite repeated calls on stock subscribers to pay in their capital commitments, however, lack of money to construct the road was still a problem. The cost savings from selecting an acquired and already graded road bed probably explains in part why a "south side" route was selected using the TC&D right of way. Supporters of the Memphis and Charleston went to Montgomery intent on seeking financial aid, but the state remained in a shaky financial condition.[4] In his message to the legislature, Governor Collier enthusiastically supported economic diversification, but recommended instead that Congress be petitioned to make land grants to assist construction of the roads.[5]

Moreover, the battle between Unionists and Southern Rights activists thought to have been decisively settled in the 1851 elections threatened to resume when Senator William Rufus King sought to lure Southern Rights Democrats back to the Democratic Party in preparation for the 1852 presidential election. This undermined the Unionist coalition and unwittingly further complicating mutual logrolling efforts by Whigs and Democrats in the legislature supportive of state aid for railroad construction.[6] This controversy spilled into the debate over what was known as the "Internal Improvement Bill," which would have provided aid for several railroad projects by permitting the state to guarantee corporate bonds to be issued and sold by the railroads, including those of the Memphis and Charleston.[7] Tempers became so heated that a Lawrence County legislator introduced a bill to move the state capital from Montgomery to Selma.[8] The railroad aid bill was ultimately killed in the house when a vote on its passage was indefinitely postponed.[9]

Railroad promoters throughout the state were stunned and frustrated by this turn of events, leading one newspaper correspondent to muse that although "Solomon says 'in the multitude of counselors there is wisdom...' this maxim, I opine, applies only to assemblages under the Jewish dispensation. Certainly, if the rule be general, the present General Assembly is an exception thereto."[10] No doubt many others had strong opinions about who ought to be the first inmates for the state's first insane asylum, which was authorized during this session.[11]

The upshot of divisive presidential politics was that neither the legislature nor Congress would be forthcoming any time soon with financial aid for railroad construction. The promoters of each project were, therefore, forced to fend for themselves in a free market still wary of another flare-up in sectional tensions. Southern Rights activists had earlier adopted resolutions asserting that the Compromise of 1850 was, from the North's standpoint, simply a temporary truce and not a final settlement of the issue of slavery.[12] Not long thereafter resolutions approving of the compromise legislation had passed the United States House of Representatives by votes of 101 to 64 and 100 to 65, with most of the negative votes coming from Northern congressmen.[13] As a result, despite the fact that Northern and international money markets were reportedly flush during this period, Memphis and Charleston Railroad promoters and other Alabama railroaders were forced to attempt to attract capital by selling unguaranteed bonds and thereby incurring debt at much higher interest rates, if at all.[14]

North Alabama Union Democrats also reached out to Hubbard during the process of healing their party. He was selected a delegate to the 1852 Democratic National Convention in Baltimore, and while there he was picked one of dozens of honorary vice presidents of the convention. However, there is no evidence that Hubbard took any active role in the proceedings, much less the formation of the party's generally pro-Southern platform.[15] The fact that Alabama's pro-Compromise United States Senator William Rufus King was selected as the party's candidate for vice president may explain why there is no evidence that Hubbard campaigned or even voted for the ticket in November.[16] By contrast, Yancey actively campaigned for the Democrat ticket headed by Franklin Pierce, and C. C. Clay served as a Pierce elector. Pierce and King swept each of the Tennessee Valley counties.[17] The Southern Rights presidential ticket, reluctantly headed by George Troup of Georgia, received only thirty-nine votes in all of north Alabama (four of which came from Lawrence County), a strong indicator of the weakness of the radical secession movement in that region at that time.[18] Whether Hubbard was one of the few that voted for Troup is unknown.

Hubbard did not publicly renounce his connection to the Democratic Party after the election. For now he needed it to reach some of his goals. For example, he attended a local Democratic Party meeting on March 25, 1853, and later announced his candidacy for a seat in the Alabama legislature. He had a clever plan to draw the support of yeoman farmers and deflect criticism of his pro-secession activism while in Congress: opposition to financial aid by the state to railroads. It was no coincidence that Hubbard's announcement occurred when the Alabama Whig Party made support for state aid to railroads one of the key planks in its political platform for the state elections of 1853, and nominated Richard Wilde Walker to head its ticket.[19]

The Democrats nominated forty-year-old Sumter County state senator John Anthony Winston, who had family ties to northwest Alabama. Winston, like Hubbard, had supported the Southern Rights faction of the Democratic Party in 1850 and 1851, seemingly making him vulnerable to Richard Walker among north Alabama Unionists.[20] Winston, who also owned a cotton commission house in Mobile, had also been an early supporter of the Mobile and Ohio Railroad project, which would bring cotton from east Mississippi and west Alabama to that port city,[21] while also enhancing the value of Hubbard's real estate in north Mississippi and Alabama.[22] Mobile leaders certainly assumed that Winston would, therefore, support their request for state aid to their railroad.[23] As evidenced by the defeat of the general state aid program in the 1851–52 legislature, however, there was no unanimity within the Democratic Party on the issue. Thus, in his carefully worded letter accepting the Democratic Party's nomination, Winston attempted to finesse it. He alluded to the collapse of the state banking system, which had necessitated a painful tax increase to prevent the state from defaulting on the bonded indebtedness incurred as the "necessary result" of what he called "hasty and visionary legislation." However, he did not totally rule out state aid for railroad construction. Instead, Winston declared quite ambiguously that such aid would be acceptable only if it did not again involve the state in "*heavy* debts before we are free of those of the past."[24] Winston did not explain what he meant by "heavy debts," but this strategy achieved its initial goal, as the *Moulton Democrat* and virtually all of the Democrat press in north Alabama ultimately fell into line behind Winston.[25]

A twist of fate caused the Whig campaign to disintegrate before their opponents' eyes. Richard Walker wrote from New York on June 28 that he had been "compelled to submit to an operation on my throat which will disable me from speaking at all prior to the [August] election, and which renders the time of my return wholly uncertain." Therefore, he announced his withdrawal from the race.[26] Winston won Lawrence County and the state,[27] and Democrats also prevailed in the north Alabama congressional races. George Smith Houston was reelected without opposition,[28] and Williamson Cobb thoroughly trounced C. C. Clay Jr. (who subsequently referred to Cobb as an "ass"), even beating him in Madison County by over two hundred votes.[29]

Hubbard also succeeded in gaining election to the Alabama House, but he had his sights set on higher office.[30] Both of Alabama's United States Senate seats were up for reelection in the upcoming legislative session, and it was reported across the country that Hubbard was one of the aspirants

along with George Smith Houston, Leroy Pope Walker, who had also been
elected to the legislature, and C. C. Clay Jr., among others.[31] The Democrat
leadership decided that one of the party's nominees would be from north
Alabama, and that both nominees would be chosen in a caucus composed
solely of Democrat legislators from throughout the state.[32] This process
ostensibly gave the advantage to Hubbard and Clay, who were life-long
Democrats and who also had support among south Alabama legislators
who were members of the Southern Rights faction. The caucus method was
most definitely to the disadvantage of Houston, whose failure to support
Calhoun had not been forgotten by that faction. So too with Leroy Pope
Walker, given that his devotion to the Democratic Party dated back only
to his party switch in 1844.[33]

Walker sought an edge when he announced his support for a new "central"
railroad project that would link north and south Alabama by a line running
from Nashville through Athens, Decatur, and Jefferson County.[34] Approximately a week after the legislature convened, Hubbard realized that what he
had assumed was a two-man race between himself and the younger, aristocratic,
and somewhat sickly C. C. Clay Jr., might actually be a two-man race between
Clay and Walker. On the night of November 22, approximately twenty-four
hours before the senatorial caucus was scheduled to meet, Hubbard attempted
to prevent the meeting and force an adjournment of the legislature for several
weeks by raising a panic about the supposed return of a yellow fever epidemic
to Montgomery.[35] His dilatory motion to adjourn filed the following morning, however, lost in the house by two votes.[36] When a younger member of
the house suggested that Hubbard's motion related to the election, Hubbard
indignantly denied it. He maintained that he had "electioneered as little as
any man for the United States Senate, and if the gentleman thought that that
was the way to electioneer, he was green sure enough."[37] Hubbard did not,
however, deny that a delay would afford him more time to electioneer. The
Montgomery correspondent of a Mobile newspaper reported that some also
suspected Hubbard's effort to seek adjournment related to his opposition to
state aid. "They look with suspicion on every movement of Mr. Hubbard, his
opposition to works of the kind being so inveterate and uncompromising, as
to impel him to resort to every expedient to defeat them."[38]

Meanwhile, C. C. Clay Jr., who, of course, received the endorsement of his family organ, the Huntsville *Democrat,* had assiduously lobbied caucus Democrats for the nomination, especially touting his loyalty to Southern Rights principles.[39] Despite these advantages, however, Leroy Pope Walker's showing on the first of fifteen ballots of the caucus vote revealed a horse race. At that point, Clay led with twenty-one votes to Walker's thirteen. To Hubbard's chagrin, he was in fifth place behind both George Smith Houston and Reuben Chapman.[40] Clay prevailed in the end and was seemingly on his way to becoming Alabama's youngest United States senator up to this point.[41] The Democrats had a majority in both houses of the legislature, making the caucus vote tantamount to the election.[42] However, because Richard Walker was nominated by the Whigs to oppose Clay, the outcome was not necessarily certain. Fortunately for Clay, however, Leroy Pope Walker made his next family get-together most interesting when Walker voted for Clay instead of his brother, joining with Hubbard and the balance of his Democrat brethren.[43]

Leroy Pope Walker did not discard his Central Railroad hobby horse once his bid for the Senate was lost. He proposed and supported it with several speeches that received praise in numerous newspapers.[44] A bill incorporating the "Tennessee and Alabama Central Railroad Company" was enacted, but financial aid for construction of the project was a different matter altogether.[45] At about the same time as the Central Railroad was incorporated, the legislature also adopted legislation incorporating several other railroads, including the North-East and South-West Alabama Railroad Company,[46] and the South and North Alabama Railroad Company.[47] These and other existing railroads were fighting over the same legislative largesse,[48] as were the proponents of a bill proposed by one of Leroy Pope Walker's other brothers, Percy Walker of Mobile, that would establish the state's first public school system.[49]

Supporters deemed all of these projects essential to Alabama's future, but their funding would require from the legislators the wisdom of Solomon and the patience of Job. Those biblical figures had never met David Hubbard. Obviously bitter about his defeat in the race for the United States Senate, Hubbard became the house floor leader of a movement in the legislature to block aid to Leroy Pope Walker's Central Railroad project, as well as every other bill proposing financial aid by the state to railroads.[50] As a result of his very effective scare tactics about higher taxes, and his surprisingly populist demagoguery against railroads, the legislature prematurely adjourned from December 20 to January 9 for Christmas and for legislators to seek guidance from their constituents.[51]

Hubbard's defiant stance had an important effect on Governor Winston. On the day of adjournment Winston gave his inaugural address denouncing the "railroad mania" prevalent in the state, and announcing his opposition to any railroad aid until the state had paid off its entire bonded indebtedness,[52] which was then estimated to be slightly less than $4.5 million.[53] Winston's more conservative stance on state aid stunned even many Democrats, and Hubbard's influence predictably drew fire from every direction, especially the Whig press. The *Mobile Advertiser* declared that Hubbard "may be regarded strictly as the viceregent of 'old fogy-dom' in this State, as his hand is turned against everything progressive in its character; and like a huge mass of inertia, he stands stock-still upon the present, *as it is*, unmoved and immovable. A step forward in company with the great line of improvement will not be in keeping with the way our fathers did, or as [Hubbard] may have done almost an age past, and consequently he sets his hand against it."[54]

Hubbard did not back down in the face of this withering criticism. He resumed his anti-railroad aid crusade as soon as the legislature reconvened in January, and during the ensuing weeks he and Leroy Pope Walker jousted in highly publicized debates. The Whig press left little doubt regarding who it believed the winner ought to be. "With the grace of Saladin and the strength of Richard, the blazing brand [Walker] wields is felt by all within its reach. With a commanding appearance, courteous bearing, eloquence of the highest order, nerve to carry him through all emergencies, he is well adapted by nature and education to exert a deep influence upon his generation."[55] For Hubbard, however, there was only ridicule and contempt. "He is a speaker *sui generis*," wrote a Whig editor. "It would be impossible to give a faithful portraiture of the style, manner and matter of the Major, without the invention of a daguerreotype which can transfer to its plate the gesture, words, and expression. Strong, rasping, cutting is his style. The man who is the subject of his satire, his hard knocks, and his quaint sayings, is fully competent to describe the operations of a flax brake." The editor did not stop there: "They call the Major an old fogy. He tells them that nick names are the sure indication of conscious weakness in those who use them. He throws back stubborn facts, in reply to beautiful theories, and holds up the experience of the past as a warning for the future."[56]

Hubbard had promoted the first railroad in Alabama and ultimately became one of the largest borrowers and defenders of the state banking system. Although he now owned no stock in any railroad, he was no "old fogy" in an economic sense.[57] He recognized that if Alabama became a part of a Southern confederacy, it was essential to maintain its creditworthiness in the eyes of foreign money markets. Furthermore he knew what issues to push when it came to motivating the common man in or outside of the legislature. Those "stubborn facts" and bad "experiences of the past" regarding legislative aid to create a banking system to finance the wealthy (including men like Hubbard) were recalled every time the tax collectors gathered their harvest from the common man's earnings or property. Hubbard was truly gifted at harnessing the resulting class conflict bubbling below the surface of Alabama society to persuade Alabama legislators, especially those from the more rural north Alabama counties, to join his crusade against this new form of rich man's welfare. Indeed, with many of the proposed railroads not projected to enter most of their counties, it was not terribly difficult. When the house and the senate finally voted on a general aid bill in early February, Hubbard's forces won by fourteen in the house and two in the senate.[58]

Governor Winston would later earn the moniker of "Veto Governor," but it did not happen during this legislative session. On the contrary, a few days after Hubbard seemingly killed railroad aid for this session, the legislature passed a single bill providing a $400,000 loan for two years to the Mobile and Ohio Railroad, albeit on very onerous terms.[59] Winston, it was later revealed, had personally lobbied for the enactment of this bill. The outrage expressed by the *Florence Gazette*, the Huntsville *Southern Advocate,* and several other north Alabama newspapers who supported aid to the Memphis and Charleston Railroad, and their renewed advocacy that north Alabama seek to be annexed to the state of Tennessee, was certainly no endorsement of Winston's apparent hypocrisy or Hubbard's retaliatory intransigence.[60] The Huntsville *Democrat* shared the desire to join with Tennessee, a state that had been much more liberal in providing aid for railroad construction, but with obvious reference to Hubbard, its editor expressed doubt that Tennessee would be agreeable because it "may not wish such public men in her councils."[61]

The adverse impact of the legislature's failure to provide sufficient financial aid for completion of railroad projects that were arguably keys to Alabama's economic future was made more acute by the furor over the controversial adoption by Congress in May 1854 of bills creating the Kansas and Nebraska territories and repealing the Missouri Compromise. Congress's tumultuous debates and passage of those bills created national political instability that would worsen with each coming year, and further discourage the flow of capital to the South. As the Huntsville *Southern Advocate* lamented, "the Northern money markets have been tried, but the money cannot be obtained there *at any price within reason.* There is a reluctance among Northern capitalists, even in flush times, to investing in *Southern roads*; they give the preference to those in the West and in their own midst."[62]

C. C. Clay's behavior in the United States Senate that year did not help matters.[63] As a stockholder of the Memphis and Charleston Railroad, Clay knew the importance of transportation to opening markets and creating much-desired trade. Thus, in the Senate he had initially attempted to obtain passage of bills providing additional land grants for Alabama railroads, perhaps explaining in part why he and Senator Benjamin Fitzpatrick made no speeches during the debates over the Kansas and Nebraska bills.[64] However, as the ensuing furor in the North increased exponentially with each passing day, and Northern Senators quite predictably began denouncing slavery and pushing for a repeal of the Fugitive Slave Act of 1850 and the Kansas and Nebraska Acts, Clay's better judgment was overcome by emotions, youthful exuberance, a need to grandstand, or all of the above. On June 28, 1854, he rose in reply to one of Massachusetts Senator Charles Sumner's anti-slavery harangues and gave what the approving *Montgomery Advertiser and State Gazette* headlined as "The Speech of the Senate." Clay called Sumner a "sneaking, sinuous, snake-like poltroon" who should be "shunned like a leper, and loathed like a filthy repul." Clay also compared Sumner to "Uriah Heap," a two-faced character in Charles Dickens's *David Copperfield*. "Uriah was mean, yet affected honor; was malignant, yet feigned benevolence; presumptuous, yet pretended humility; instigated others to violence he dared not commit, yet assumed an air of meekness; suggested crimes and incited others to their commission, yet bore himself with studied amenity of manners, and choice expressions of benignity."[65] Other than gaining publicity for himself, and perhaps admiration from Hubbard, however, Clay's tirade did nothing but antagonize those whose support was essential to passing the land grant legislation Alabama needed.[66] Not a single railroad land grant was made during this session of Congress, and as a consequence, Alabama's economic future was coming to depend more and more on financial aid from—thanks to David Hubbard—a very fiscally conservative state government.[67]

The nation, meanwhile, continued its spiral toward civil war. The national Whig Party was disintegrating because of internal division over the repeal of the Missouri Compromise, and was unlikely to resuscitate itself before the 1856 presidential election.[68] Many Northern Whigs and Democrats who opposed that repeal were gradually moving into the newly forming Republican Party, attracted by its populist rhetoric against the Southern "Slave Power."[69] Southern Whigs were initially reluctant to coalesce with their ancient enemy, the Democratic Party.[70] By process of elimination, the only national party vehicle left for Southern Whigs was the also recently formed "American Party." In addition to being new, its principal attractions for Southern Whigs were its initial, high profile victories in some local elections in the North against Democrat candidates, and its ability to attract the support of disaffected Democrats. As one Alabama editor observed, "it cuts like a trenchant sword into old party lines, and may create a total change in the politics of the country."[71] To Southern Democrats like Hubbard, however, it was yet another impediment to Southern solidarity. C. C. Clay called the American Party a "new order,—a bastard, begotten in darkness, conceived in iniquity, and not yet brought forth to the light of noon-day—a child of many fathers and bearing different names."[72] That Democrats and their organs in Alabama had admitted their concern for what they dubbed the "Know-Nothing" Party only made it even more enticing to some.[73]

The American Party not only gained the support of a majority of the electorate in Lawrence County,[74] but also had some success in attracting prominent north Alabama Democrats to its fold, especially those who were opposed to Governor Winston's policies on state aid to railroads.[75] The new party nominated Shelby County Circuit Judge George David Shortridge, a Union Democrat who supported state aid, as its gubernatorial candidate in 1855.[76] Shortridge was an incorporator and stockholder of the Tennessee and Alabama Central Railroad, making him attractive to residents of Limestone County as well as other counties on its projected line.[77]

Hubbard's anti-aid rhetoric during the 1853–1854 legislative session had made him popular among the large yeoman farmer element of the Democratic Party who were opposed to even higher taxes if the railroads, like the State Bank, proved to be a financial bust.[78] However the Democrats had to be careful not to totally alienate members of their party who were willing to consider state aid in limited circumstances. In a public letter Hubbard, therefore, declined to run for governor and announced his support for governor Winston's reelection. Hubbard explained that, like himself, Winston was "opposed to endorsing the bonds of railroad companies, by reason of which the citizens become liable for their debts."[79] No mention was made by Hubbard of *loans* to railroads such as that to the Mobile and Ohio Railroad. Similarly, in his own public letter on the subject, Governor Winston reiterated that he opposed "the endorsement or issue on the part of the State, of bonds to build railroads," but he also made no mention of the issue of loans. Winston also went so far as to remind the proponents of state aid that if he happened to veto a state aid bill passed by a majority of the legislature, the Alabama constitution permitted that same simple majority to override his veto.[80] Likewise, in another carefully worded letter, Winston declared that it was his intention to canvass the state and to portray to the people the dangers of a general policy of state aid to railroads of "endorsing bonds or *borrowing money* for the purpose of loaning it to private companies."[81] Again, Winston did not foreclose the possibility of loaning money from the state's reserves. He was, therefore, able to stump south Alabama portraying himself as a fiscal conservative and Shortridge as a tax-and-spend liberal.[82] In north Alabama, Winston finally announced that he "was in favor of loaning the surplus funds of the State to railroads when the loan could be supported by 'undoubted security.'"[83]

As in south Alabama, Southern Rights Democrats in north Alabama also made use of the Kansas controversy to draw Democrats back to the fold. At a political meeting in Morgan County on July 7, 1855, for example, David Hubbard, Leroy Pope Walker, David Campbell Humphreys, and Oakley H. Bynum engineered the adoption of a preamble noting the existence of "matters of grave importance" that were "pressing themselves upon the earnest attention of Southern men," and that "are of such nature as to require cordial and fraternal concert of action" by Southerners within the Democratic Party. Resolutions were adopted essentially embodying the line-in-the-sand policy of the Georgia Platform of 1851, and denouncing "the combined forces of Know-Nothingism and Absolutism" that were jointly seeking the repeal of the Kansas-Nebraska Acts.[84] With Democrats returning, Governor Winston swept north Alabama—with the notable exception of Lawrence County, which Shortridge won by 173 votes.[85]

Notwithstanding the result in Lawrence County, north Alabama had come through for Winston and now it was time to pay the fiddler. In particular, the Memphis and Charleston Railroad was, according to the Huntsville *Southern Advocate*, one of two railroads (the other being the Alabama and Tennessee Railroad) that qualified to be "assisted by the Legislature under the rule laid down by Gov. Winston; and which the people have sanctioned by his reelection."[86] Given that their support for Winston had virtually destroyed the Whig Party in north Alabama,[87] pro-Winston Whigs in particular would not be denied this just reward. Or so they assumed. At first, everything appeared to go according to plan. The state's bonded indebtedness had been decreased to $3,431,888, and the next bond payment would not be due until January 1858, when $584,888 would have to be paid.[88] In addition, Hubbard did not seek reelection and a majority of the legislators favored state aid.[89] When the legislature met in mid-November, Governor Winston's message to it included an acknowledgment that "it may be proper" to loan surplus state funds to "such enterprises as are considered of public utility . . . provided the parties borrowing guarantee by security both personal and real, the prompt payment of principal and interest, at some early date."[90] Not taking any chances, a delegation consisting of Clement Clay Jr., Leroy Pope Walker, and several officials of the Memphis and Charleston Railroad went to Montgomery to personally lobby for the loan.[91] No doubt expecting smooth sailing, the Huntsville *Southern Advocate* noted that all the company wanted was "a little *present* help. That help the State will, we believe, grant at once."[92]

However this train was headed for a derailment. Opposition in the house caused the loan amount requested by the Memphis and Charleston Railroad to be reduced during debates from $500,000 to $300,000.[93] Then Governor Winston foreshadowed his future actions when he vetoed a bill that would have permitted Limestone County to levy a local tax to purchase $200,000 of stock in the proposed Tennessee and Alabama Central Railroad. His veto was quickly overridden, however.[94] On January 8 and 9, 1856, before the final decision on a loan was made, the "Democratic and Anti-Know Nothing" Party convention met at the capital in Montgomery.[95] In the morning session on January 9, Leroy Pope Walker and William Yancey were unanimously selected as presidential electors for the state at large, and J. L. M. Curry, a Southern Rights activist and legislator from Talladega, was chosen as one of several district electors.[96] Hubbard was selected one of four delegates at large to the National Democratic Convention in Cincinnati, Ohio.[97]

In retrospect, everything up to the evening session on the final day of the convention appears to have been choreographed with the intention of fostering good will between men who had been political enemies for most of their adult lives. But then south Alabama secessionist George Washington Gayle offered a series of resolutions reported as being "laudatory of the action of Gov. Winston during his Gubernatorial career, and desiring him to veto every bill or resolution passed by the present legislature, loaning the public moneys to private corporations."[98] Governor Winston then proceeded to release his veto messages regarding not only the bill for the loan to the Memphis and Charleston Railroad, but also a bill authorizing the renewal of the earlier loan to the Mobile and Ohio Railroad.[99] Although the veto of that loan renewal was quickly overridden,[100] a fight over the loan to the Memphis and Charleston Railroad and another for the Central Railroad ensued, temporarily causing a major logjam on several other matters. The *Montgomery Advertiser and State Gazette* came to Winston's defense, warning that "a system has now been fairly inaugurated that will throw the whole financial interests of the State into the hands of incorporations. By the time money loaned falls due, powerful combinations will have been formed, strong enough to control the elections, and which will force from the Legislature any measures for their benefit they may fancy," an allusion to previous efforts to maintain the State Bank. "In the meantime the present high rates of taxation will be kept up, and we shall be lucky if they do not have to be materially increased."[101]

With the 1856 presidential election just over ten months away, however, Alabama Democrats could not afford to permanently alienate Whigs connected to railroads. Party leaders, therefore, engaged in damage control as the issue of overriding Winston's other vetoes was voted upon. Their efforts were not entirely effective. Both loans were approved, but with an important proviso that the railroads provide collateral and other security for repayment sufficient in the eyes of Governor Winston.[102] In essence, the bills effectively gave Winston an insurmountable veto power, and he made it known that he had no intention of allowing either of these loans to be funded.[103] Thus, when the legislature adjourned in February 1856, the Memphis and Charleston Railroad was still without state financial aid.

Governor Winston had continued Hubbard's policies, and thereby betrayed and incensed key north Alabama political and business leaders, while disingenuously claiming that his action was not politically motivated.[104] He declared that it was "an honest endeavor to do my duty to the State," and he attacked "those who looked to the State treasury for the means of advancing their private speculations—and . . . aspiring men who seem willing, by the financial ruin of the State, to attain preferment."[105] Once again, however, the Democratic Party was in trouble. Historically under these circumstances, they had always fallen back on the old reliable slavery issue to reunite the people, especially during presidential elections. They did so once again.

13

'I am a Radical Democrat'

"Kansas," wrote the editor of *Montgomery Advertiser and State Gazette,* "is to be the battlefield between the North and the South on the slavery question. If the fanatics succeed in keeping slavery therefrom, they will nearly have succeeded in throwing around us a 'cordon of free states,' our institutions will be hemmed in, and the total destruction of our vital institution, and that at no distant day, is inevitable."[1] This was followed by a series of "Kansas Meetings" in Alabama ostensibly intended to drum up financial support for settlement of the Kansas Territory by pro-slavery forces.[2]

David Hubbard was a leader of these efforts in north Alabama. On March 18, 1856, for example, he gave one of several speeches in Moulton encouraging slaveowners to contribute two dollars for each slave they owned to an "emigrating fund to aid Southern emigrants to Kansas."[3] South Carolinians, who were also using the slavery-in-Kansas issue,[4] exercised their growing influence over north Alabama by coming to the financial rescue of the Memphis and Charleston Railroad and purchasing $250,000 of its bonds.[5] This final injection of capital permitted the completion of the Alabama portion of that militarily significant railroad in the spring.[6]

Agitation of the Kansas issue by Hubbard and others led to less productive results in that embattled territory. A few weeks before the National Democratic Party met in its nominating convention in Cincinnati, violence erupted in Kansas when pro-slavery forces that included some Alabamians sacked the town of Lawrence, triggering a cycle of guerrilla violence by both sides that seemed endless.[7] Kansas-related violence entered Congress when pro-abolition United States Senator Charles Sumner was beaten with a cane by South Carolina congressman Preston Brooks on the floor of the Senate. Demonstrating the influence of South Carolina in north Alabama, the editor of the usually moderate Huntsville *Southern Advocate* approved of Brooks "in the *cause* and *manner* of his rebuke to Mr. Sumner," although he could not "acquit him of censure for the *place* and *time* chosen to inflict it."[8]

The convention in Cincinnati was free of violence, though not of controversy. The Kansas imbroglio had given rise to hope among secessionists that the time for uniting the South for secession had finally arrived, but the nationalistic influence of the Democratic Party during this election year was, once again, a potential impediment. Hubbard was selected as an at-large delegate and attended the convention, but once again did not subsequently campaign for the nominee, Pennsylvania Democrat James Buchanan.[9] Buchanan was a man behind whom mainstream Southern Democrats could unite, and he was enthusiastically supported by William Yancey, C. C. Clay and J. L. M. Curry. Buchanan was elected over his two opponents, but ominously only by a plurality of the popular vote.[10]

Hubbard resumed his quest for Southern unity at the Southern Commercial Convention that met in Savannah, Georgia, in December 1856.[11] This conclave was designed to lay the groundwork for Southern economic independence, and Hubbard took a very active role in its proceedings. Among other measures, he successfully advocated the creation of a "select committee of three" to report to the next meeting in August 1857 regarding a "system of detectives, police in the Southern States," and the "propriety of incorporating a planter's union." When that measure was adopted, Hubbard was appointed a member of the committee. The purpose of the force of detectives, Hubbard later explained, was to guard against the threat of abolitionists and to maintain a firmer grip on the slave population. "It will enable us to detect and punish all abolitionists, negro stealers and incendiaries who come among us for mischief." In addition, he continued, "it can easily detect and punish all unlawful trading with slaves by free negroes and white traders base enough to deal in stolen property—whereby immense sums are saved to the owners, and the morals and habits of the slaves improved; while the evil doers may be punished or expelled from among us, giving security and strength to the structure of society with us."[12] What Hubbard did not express is that his proposal implied the existence of a widespread threat to the internal security of the South. As he well knew, fear was a very powerful motivator. Coupled with the ongoing violence in Kansas, this threat was gradually radicalizing an increasing number of Southerners mindful of the dark tales of white annihilation at St. Domingue.[13]

This all increased Hubbard's profile and popularity in Alabama. Nelson White, the editor of the *Moulton Democrat*, then an American (or "Know-Nothing") Party organ, became one of Hubbard's most outspoken supporters. In 1857, he even suggested Hubbard as a candidate for governor. "We are cheek-by jole as regards Internal Improvements—the acquisition of Cuba—the tariff—U.S. Bank, &c., &c." Hubbard, he continued, "has more of the Jackson Democracy and less of the bogus Van Buren, than we usually meet with now-a-days—a purely Southern man in feeling and principle."[14] Then newspapers across the state reported that a convention of Lawrence County Democrats had formally nominated Hubbard for the position.[15]

It is doubtful Hubbard was actually interested in becoming governor at this point. He was then white-haired and sixty-five years old, an advanced age for this period. He also knew that he could use the attention he was receiving as a vehicle to encourage Alabamians to think of the creation of a Southern nation as the only means available for the South to reach its full potential. He, therefore, wrote a public letter to Lawrence County Democrats agreeing to run if nominated by a state convention, but also outlining an attention-grabbing campaign platform. To understand Hubbard's comments, one must know that in the last year the Republican Party had succeeded in electing one of its members Speaker of the United States House, thus foreshadowing the possible denial of admission of Kansas as a slave state.[16] More recently, Southern designs in Central America that depended on the ability of William Walker, an embattled Southern filibusterer, to retain control of Nicaragua, were being stymied by a British-backed alliance of countries in the region.[17] Thus, it appeared that the spread of the Southern way of life might be impossible and that the region was doomed by the twin evils of a growing, redundant slave population, and soil exhaustion.

Hubbard prefaced his comments with the declaration that "I am a radical Democrat." Then he outlined an ultra-radical plan reminiscent of those conceived and executed by Andrew Jackson before he trimmed his sails to become and remain president: the declaration of war against the

British.[18] England, Hubbard asserted, was behind the attack on slavery in the United States by the "abolition and free soil alliance; *they* were doing the "bidding of English Statesmen." Rather than contending with these domestic British surrogates in "annual and quadreannual [elections]," Hubbard advocated "another theatre for the conflict." That, he continued, would be "Central America or some other foreign spot." Hubbard explained what he saw as his plan's many advantages. First, "you thereby divide the Devil's forces." Second, the South would "get clear of the influence of his hypocritical parsons and strong minded women—together with all who wish to establish a character for respectability with a mere shadow of title" and "all ostentatious pretentions to charity, now numerous and noisy." Third, without this interference, "the issue will depend upon the effect of well aimed rifles" shot by "true patriots of every section" as well as "ambitious aspirants and filibusters, and all who want excitement, and love a fight." Ignoring the Clayton-Bulwer Treaty with the British, Hubbard expressed amazement that the Buchanan administration had not already pursued this policy. "No man, it seems to me, is fit for public control who cannot see this." Hubbard made clear that he had no desire to be Alabama's governor unless a majority of the people supported his plan. "I have no ambition for the station of a Minority Governor of the sovereign state of Alabama, with only power to pardon and release convicts and remit fines and forfeitures." If nominated, Hubbard concluded, "I shall as far as I can, push forward the policy indicated; glorying in such symptoms of regeneration as would be manifested by the act."[19]

Hubbard's plan resonated with at least one member of the Alabama press. "This letter," wrote the editor of the Huntsville *Southern Advocate*, "is worthy of the profound consideration of the People of not only the State of Alabama, but of the *entire* South. [Hubbard] has, in our opinion, struck the keynote, to which the Southern heart should vibrate and respond." The "tendency of events, the course of our empire, is toward Central America. There is the region of the Cotton, Sugar, Coffee, and tropical productions. There is the home of our Slaves, where their elevation will go on and their usefulness increase. There is the battlefield to destroy abolitionism and drive fanaticism back to Great Britain, its chosen home."[20]

Hubbard might have had a very different purpose for his letter: to distract the business community from his record on state aid to their railroads. The Memphis and Charleston Railroad had recently been completed without financial aid from the state of Alabama, but other railroad projects were still searching for funding in what was then a recessionary economy.[21] The Democrat organ in Montgomery published Hubbard's letter but also asked "what is his position in regard to State aid and the Central Railroad? The Party at large, and especially the State Convention, *ought and must know*."[22] Not surprisingly, Hubbard's views on that issue had not changed since his time in the legislature, thereby probably eliminating any real possibility of his receiving the Democratic nomination.[23]

Hubbard displayed no malice when a younger man and native of South Carolina, Andrew Barry Moore of Perry County, received the nomination.[24] He announced to the delegates at the nominating convention his ratification of the nomination and his support for Moore.[25] Yet, Hubbard also took this opportunity to agitate the slavery issue once again. Rather than Central America, however, Hubbard's target was Kansas and the ongoing intrigue by abolitionists and Free Soilers there. He called on the delegates to rebuke "this Kansas movement" and to cut ties with "submission Democrats south" and the Northern faction of the Democratic Party that were favorable to Free Soilism.[26] Hubbard recognized that the issue whether Kansas would be admitted to statehood as a slave state would come before Congress when it convened in December,[27] and he had little or no confidence that George Smith Houston—in Hubbard's eyes a "submission Democrat" of the worse sort—would fight for Kansas's admission contrary to the wishes of Senator Stephen Douglas, who was predicted to be the National Democratic Party's nominee for president in 1860. Douglas, who had supported the concept of "popular sovereignty" of the citizens of a territory to determine whether they would allow slavery, was certain that pro-slavery forces in Kansas had committed fraud in procuring the adoption of the "Lecompton" constitution that authorized the existence of slavery there.[28]

At Hubbard's age, however, he might have left this problem to the two younger men who were already running against Houston. One of them, William A. Hewlett of Walker County, was a States Rights Democrat and one of Hubbard's nephews. A supporter of Hewlett's denounced Houston in an anonymous letter to the *Moulton Democrat* and declared—in words suspiciously similar to those commonly used by David Hubbard—that "the South has no use for Compromise or *Union Savers* now."[29] Then Hubbard learned that the *Washington Union* had published an article praising Houston and incorrectly stating that he had won the 1851 election against Hubbard "by the almost unanimous vote of the people of the District." After this article was republished in the *Athens Herald*, Hubbard wrote the editor of the *Union* a fiery letter contesting that statement and, to the delight of the extremist press in south Alabama,[30] announcing that he was entering the race against Houston. Shortly thereafter, Hewlett withdrew from the race and the national press almost immediately took notice of the contest.[31]

Houston and his supporters accused Hubbard of disloyalty to the Democratic Party and being the candidate of the American Party. Hubbard denied this in a pamphlet distributed throughout north Alabama, and also challenged Houston's dedication to the South and its interests. He asked whether the voters who had opposed Hubbard in 1851 now believed that they had "accomplished any desirable good." He declared that "you are compelled to answer no." Anti-slavery agitation had not ceased; "abolition has got possession of the House of Representatives, and the public purse has fallen into its hand." Hubbard cleverly reminded Jacksonian yeoman farmers that "British Abolition" intended the "subjugation of the White" man, and to do so, "both races must be put on an equal footing, and Black and White promiscuously hold office and vote." The result, Hubbard warned, would be the end of democracy and the republican form of government for which they and their forefathers had fought the British. This, he maintained, would be followed by a "military despotism and monarchy." In conclusion, Hubbard declared that Houston had been ineffective in stopping this conspiracy from advancing its agenda, and asked, "why continue him?"[32]

One reason to do so was Hubbard's health. When he announced his candidacy, he was still trying to recover from a bout with pneumonia and was unable to actively canvass for election.[33] This, coupled with the fact that Houston vowed to support the admission of Kansas with the Lecompton Constitution, led to Hubbard's defeat. In fact he embarrassingly lost every county in the district, albeit by less than nine hundred votes.[34]

Hubbard did not tarry long in Lawrence County following the election. He was off to Knoxville for the 1857 Southern Commercial Convention where he served as chairman of the Alabama delegation.[35] At its conclusion, he was named chairman of the committee to determine the agenda for the next convention, which was scheduled to take place in Montgomery in May 1858.[36] Hubbard had one last mission before the end of 1857. Supporters of outgoing Governor Winston were seeking to replace C. C. Clay with Winston in the United States Senate, and it was rumored that supporters of George Smith Houston planned to use this opportunity to put their man in instead. Hubbard, therefore, traveled to Montgomery armed with evidence that Houston had not been loyal to Southern interests, and began lobbying legislators against him.[37] Thomas Peters reported to Houston in December that a Lawrence County legislator "told me the other [day] that Maj. Hubbard has a letter written to him by Col. [O]akley H. Bynum in which *you* are denounced as a *freesoiler*. This letter Hubbard reads against you whenever he can get a crowd that will listen to him. I suppose that the letter is an *old* affair; but the old Major makes it the occasion of pitching into you with a will just now, and no doubt it has its effect in some quarters."[38] It certainly did. Clay was reelected for a term that would not end until March 4, 1865.[39] George Smith Houston did receive a consolation prize of sorts. Perhaps proving Hubbard's charge of Houston's treason to the South, Houston was appointed by the Republican Speaker of the House to serve on the prestigious House Judiciary Committee.[40]

This legislature also honored the late John C. Calhoun by renaming Benton County for him.[41] Perhaps also in his honor, it adopted a joint resolution requiring Governor Moore to call for the election of delegates to a state convention if Congress refused to admit Kansas with the pro-slavery Lecompton constitution.[42] It was, wrote the miffed editor of the Tuscaloosa *Independent Monitor,* the "beginning of the new War in Alabama for dissolving the Union."[43] As debate over the fate of Kansas raged in Congress through the spring of 1858, editorials that might have been authored by David Hubbard began appearing in the *Moulton Democrat* encouraging the delegates to attend the upcoming Southern Commercial Convention in Montgomery to debate the question of a Southern Confederation. "We hold that, NOW is the time to sever the ties that bind us to support a Union whose burdens are awarded the South, and whose blessings are bestowed upon the North. NOW is the time to assert, as our fathers did, our Independence! Delay brings us no strength. Procrastination is the thief, who has stolen our rights—let us, therefore, not loiter longer, and exhaust our energies in empty gasconading, but hasten to rescue the downtrodden South. The Black Republican is at your door, demanding your last *Nigger!*"[44] Governor Moore had appointed Hubbard to serve as one of Alabama's six delegates at large to this convention, and there is no doubt Hubbard firmly embraced these sentiments.[45]

A few days before the delegates convened, however, Congress finessed the Kansas issue by adopting a bill admitting Kansas, but only on the condition that its residents agreed to accept less land within its borders than its application for admission had requested.[46] Nonetheless, Hubbard, Yancey, and a full contingent of Southern secessionists gathered in Montgomery for the convention in May to meet and confer on future strategy, but not about economic issues. According to the moderate editor of the Montgomery *Confederation*, "every form and shape of political malcontent" was present and "ready to assist in any project having for its end a dissolution of the Union, immediate, unconditional, final."[47] The editor likely had the apparently inebriated Yancey in his mind's eye, but judging from Hubbard's widely published address to the delegates, Hubbard certainly fit that description as well. He declared that the "Union Saving Party"—a reference to the National Democratic Party—had "wholly failed" in its efforts to prevent the growth of the abolition movement. As a consequence, Hubbard continued, "abolition has now got possession of the House of Representatives, and has such an influence in all departments, that [the federal government] is in truth now, and has for some time been very nearly an Abolition Government." Several Northern legislatures had, meanwhile, "nullified" the federal fugitive slave law by adopting personal liberty laws to frustrate its enforcement. Yet, Hubbard pointed out, unlike the situation years earlier when South Carolina had attempted to nullify the tariff, "our Union Savers South are very quiet." Given this demonstrated impotence of the National Democrats to protect the South and secure its rights, "we say 'go out.'"[48]

The published accounts of the proceedings of this convention provide little evidence of Hubbard's other activities or what went on behind closed doors.[49] But a letter written by Yancey after the convention adjourned was consistent with Hubbard's recommendation. Yancey wrote of a plan to "precipate the Cotton States into a revolution" when the "next aggression" by the North occurred.[50] There were leaders in Alabama and elsewhere in the South—to Hubbard, "Union Savers"—who were very critical of the convention's work. However, one of Hubbard's former north Alabama critics, Mathew Gallaway, was no longer among them. Now ironically editing the extremist Memphis *Avalanche*, which he had begun in early 1858, Gallaway called the delegates "Southern patriots," more evidence that the radicalization process initiated by Hubbard and others was taking deeper root.[51]

Other events in 1858 and 1859 played into the hands of men like Hubbard. A former resident of Tuscumbia who lived in Pennsylvania was arrested, charged with kidnapping, and jailed there for capturing a fugitive Alabama slave in Missouri and returning him to north Alabama. To many Alabamians it was simply another example of the North obstructing enforcement of the federal fugitive slave law.[52] In November 1858, news reached Alabama that the likely Republican nominee for the presidency in 1860, William Henry Seward, had given a provocative speech in which he declared the existence of an "irrepressible conflict" between supporters of free labor and those of slavery that would determine whether the country became "entirely a free-labor nation."[53]

A large number of north Alabama Democrats pinned their hopes to save the Union on Illinois Senator Stephen A. Douglas, who had recently achieved reelection over his relatively little-known Republican opponent, Abraham Lincoln, and who projected as the probable Democratic nominee for president in 1860.[54] Douglas was, therefore, targeted for abuse as a "Union Saver" by secessionists. Hubbard, who had earlier written Douglas listing radical, untenable demands that he would have to meet to win the support of Southerners in the upcoming election,[55] was among those adamantly opposed to Douglas's nomination. However he recognized that undermining Douglas in the eyes of north Alabamians fearful of civil war would require a subtle approach.[56] Thus, when a south Alabama secessionist wrote Hubbard in early 1859 inquiring of the mood of north Alabamians regarding the upcoming presidential election, Hubbard did not expressly mention Douglas in his reply. He sought to demonstrate that no candidate could possibly improve the South's perilous position in the Union. "What interest then have the people of the Southern States in making the President?" he asked.[57] Once again, Hubbard's letter was published with approval in newspapers in and outside Alabama.[58]

Hubbard was subsequently appointed by Governor Moore to serve as a delegate to yet another Southern Commercial Conference, this one in 1858 in Vicksburg.[59] The nature of his activities there are unknown, but it is likely that he and other delegates to this lightly attended gathering (Yancey was not there) privately discussed the mechanics by which the states would secede. Hubbard had earlier written Virginia Governor Henry A. Wise regarding whether his critically important state was planning to secede. Wise, who had served with Hubbard in Congress and later espoused Hubbard's plan to go to war against the British, replied that the Union would be dissolved but gave no specifics regarding timing.[60] The delegates with whom Hubbard met in Vicksburg were probably also unsure about when their own states would act. Hence, it was deemed essential to success that each state secede separately—called "separate state" secession—rather than waiting on other states that might be lagging behind. They might have also agreed that secession was unlikely if the Democratic Party's nominee—who would be selected in 1860—won the presidential election, but very likely if the Republican candidate prevailed.

The problem that presented for Alabama secessionists was that the Alabama legislature would not meet in a regular session until over a year after that election, and there was no guarantee Governor Moore would call the legislature into a special session unless he was required to do so. Aware of this logistical problem, the editor of the party organ in Montgomery noted that the next legislature, which would convene in the late fall of 1859, "will be a most important body." For this reason, Hubbard sought and was elected to a seat in the Alabama House during the August 1859 election.[61]

Hubbard's election was of great significance to south Alabama secessionists who recalled that north Alabama Democrats had stopped the secession movement in its tracks in 1850 and 1851. For secession to occur, it would take the efforts of popular men there to lead the way. Hubbard's influence was, therefore, deemed crucial to success. As a consequence, he suddenly became the darling of the Southern Rights press in south Alabama, who endorsed him for such positions as Unites States Senator and speaker of the Alabama House.[62] One newspaper correspondent summarized Hubbard's most important qualification: "with him the rights of the South are paramount to the harmony of the National Democratic party, or the preservation of the Union."[63]

Unless some new variable came into play, it seemed that everything was finally possible for David Hubbard after toiling for so many years in behalf of a minority cause. He was finally being given the statewide recognition he believed he had always deserved. Then an unexpected but ultimately welcome event outside Alabama suddenly changed everything.

14

'The Race Is Over'

"**P**rovidence sent us John Brown," wrote the editor of the Montgomery *Mail* following Brown's terrorist attack on the federal arsenal at Harper's Ferry, Virginia, on October 16, 1859. It was subsequently discovered that this was a prelude to a raid through the South freeing and arming the slaves for a bloody reenactment of the scenes of St. Domingue.[1] Abolitionist Brown was seen as a godsend for secessionists, because he finally gave them graphic and undeniable evidence of a plot to violently interfere with slavery where it already was, and not just where it might go. No longer could the "Union Savers" about which David Hubbard had railed undermine secession dogma by claiming that the Union was a dependable shield for the way of life many Southerners preferred.

This shocking event changed not only the calculus of disunion, but also Hubbard's political future. When the legislature finally convened on November 14, 1859, he was not elected speaker of the house. He was, however, appointed chairman of the House Committee on Federal Relations, which now had much more importance than ever before.[2] Among other things, Hubbard's committee reported on John Brown's raid and recommended the adoption of bills funding the militarization of the state.[3] The focus of those interested in replacing moderate Democrat Benjamin Fitzpatrick in the United States Senate was not on Hubbard, but William Yancey and the now somewhat more moderate Douglas supporter, John Anthony Winston.[4]

Hubbard likely anticipated this. Many of the same, generally young, south Alabama editors who had recently praised him were supporters of Yancey, and in their plaudits to Hubbard had cleverly also reminded their readers of his unpopular position on aid to their railroads and of his age. The editor of the *Tuskegee Republican* described him as an "old politician" who had "grown gray in the cause of Democracy." Hubbard, continued the editor, was "also quite hump-shouldered, and has a singular knot on his forehead that looks as if it might contain a pistol ball."[5] Others deprecated his common airs. "With more than ordinary talents, yet in our opinion from the want of proper culture in early life," sniffed the editors of the *Montgomery Advertiser and State Gazette* in a profile piece published shortly before the legislature had convened, "[Hubbard] does not show them to the same advantage as others [read: Yancey] who enjoyed the benefit of better educational training." He was, they continued, "self-taught and self-made," meaning he was not the product of a prominent, aristocratic family that could afford to give him every advantage necessary to prepare him as the ideal of a Southern statesman. Finally, Hubbard's manner of public speaking, which seems to have been a regular target of his most aristocratic political opponents in north Alabama, simply would not do to represent Alabama in the august national Senate where John C. Calhoun had strode. The Montgomery editors wrote that the "rapid succession of his arguments, which sometimes hinders their effect, is owing to the manner in which his thoughts crowd upon him."[6]

This criticism did not cause Hubbard to lose sight of his main goal: secession. He dutifully entered the fray on behalf of the younger Yancey, intending to prevent Benjamin Fitzpatrick from representing Alabama in the Senate following secession and possibly facilitating a Union-saving compromise with what secessionists called the "Black" Republicans. In the process, Hubbard produced some of the most humorous incidents in this very serious legislative session.

One occurred in connection with a dispute between supporters of Fitzpatrick, Yancey, and Winston over whether the election of a senator ought to occur at this time even though Fitzpatrick's term would not expire until 1861. Fitzpatrick's supporters sought delay, but the supporters of Yancey and Winston did not. During the debates, Hubbard clashed with Alexander Clitherall, a Pickens County judge-lawyer-politico who supported Winston as well as Stephen A. Douglas for the presidency. After Clitherall remarked to Hubbard that he had "heard a sermon which made him feel like fighting the Devil the remainder of his life," Hubbard quipped that "the sermon must have been a good one which could make [Clitherall] fall out with so old a friend." According to Hubbard, Clitherall "handed me his hat, which I politely returned to him, and thought no more of the matter." Tempers flared between the two again a few days later during debate over the timing of the senatorial election when Yancey supporters changed their strategy and attempted to stall by discussing the upcoming presidential election instead. Clitherall declared that, "as between Douglas and Seward, I would prefer Douglas; that I always had a choice between evils, and as the lesser evil I would take Douglas." "With all due deference to his Satanic Majesty," he continued, "if the DEVIL were to die and a new Devil had to be elected, I would have a choice between the candidates for the successorship." Hubbard later claimed that he had understood Clitherall to say "he might be placed in such a situation as to make him vote for the Devil himself. Somewhat surprised at so sudden a change in forty-eight hours," Hubbard continued, "and hearing him propose re-entering the service of one he but so recently had declared hostility against for life, I wondered what *motive* could have so influenced him." Hubbard almost literally brought down the house by interrupting Clitherall to ask "What position he expected to occupy in his Satanic majesty's dominions." Not to be outdone, the always witty Clith-erall replied that he "desired the position of Door Keeper that he might let [Hubbard] in." Hubbard was apparently not quick enough to come up with an immediate reply, but the next day he renewed this repartee by giv-ing a half-hearted apology to the house—not Clitherall—for his "breach of parliamentary custom, imputing motives to others for sudden changes, and I promise not to offend again." In his next breath, however, Hubbard did just that: "The Judge [Clitherall] having selected for himself the office of 'Devil's Door Keeper,' has shown his accustomed modesty. We all know his fitness for higher station; in fact, I question if his majesty would trust one as well fitted for his rival, so near his person, and should I be doomed to spend my time in his dominions (for which I have no desire) I very much fear my friend, the Judge, would be in such a *high position*, he like other dignitaries of whom we sometimes hear, would not want to see his former friends."[7]

While Hubbard engaged in dilatory tactics, Yancey's supporters realized that Yancey did not have enough votes to prevail if the election occurred. They, therefore, decided to oppose the election altogether.[8] Hubbard was also a leader of that new movement in the house.[9] He now argued that the election ought not be conducted because "the whole South [was] in a transition state," and "new issues are now just emerging from the womb of events." As a consequence, the "man now elected [may] happen to misrepresent the state." Therefore, he maintained, the "political necessities of the country" should not be "put to hazard, not for the sake of any principle, but simply to gratify the personal wishes of any man, however strong those wishes may be."[10] Hubbard could not resist this opportunity to take a final jab at Fitzpatrick, whose moderate stance on the issue of slavery in the Western territories was rumored to be motivated by a desire for national office. Hubbard blamed the South's loss of political and economic strength over the decades on the "suicidal policy" of "giving up of the material interests of the South, compromising away her territorial possessions, and yielding the proper fiscal arrangements for popularity, that her vanity might be gratified by the promotion of her sons to places of distinction, on the other." The South would be foolish, Hubbard maintained, to continue to play the North's rigged game of what he called "President-making." Hubbard illustrated his point by analogizing to a crooked card game:

> Would any of us who had a young friend or son, who at the gambling table had lost four-fifths of his estate, advise him to go back and risk the remnant which is left, amongst gamblers who had swindled him, and divided the spoils—and to play at the *same* game—with the *same* old stocked cards, and the *same* hands to stock them?[11]

To Hubbard, the answer was an emphatic "no." Instead, the North, which he maintained had breached the covenants contained in the federal constitution, must be given an ultimatum: "Nothing but a fair share of lands, and jurisdiction, in proportion to population, will answer." In addition, the North must give "proper pledges" to stop interfering with the enforcement of the fugitive slave law. "If however, they refuse such reasonable and just demands," Hubbard declared, "we will be free to seek association with such States only as will keep and perform what they bind themselves to do, and no longer associate with the perjurer, and covenant-breaker, who glories in his shame."[12]

The pro-Yancey *Montgomery Advertiser and State Gazette* praised Hubbard for his speech. "He has been fighting the enemies of the South too long to now be made to believe that the progress of Northern tyranny can be arrested by reasoning and submitting." "The facts stated by Major Hubbard sufficiently illustrate the folly of the time-serving policy, heretofore pursued by the South," an obvious reference to Fitzpatrick's mature, diplomatic style in Congress.[13] Despite Hubbard's efforts, the house adopted a resolution to conduct the election and that resolution was sent to the senate where the tactical maneuvering by the three principal factions continued. Ultimately, however, this resolution was defeated there by a vote of fourteen to eighteen.[14]

In January 1860, during the Christmas recess adjournment, the State Democratic Convention met to select delegates to the fateful national convention in Charleston, South Carolina, and electors for the presidential election. There the secession faction engineered the adoption of resolutions requiring the national convention to approve a platform plank that required Congress to protect slavery in the territories from local opposition. As the secessionists well knew, neither Northern Democrats generally nor Douglas would ever agree to this. Its rejection, they also knew, would give Southern Democrats an opportunity to bolt and conduct a convention where a presidential candidate agreeable to this pro-slavery platform would be selected.[15] This strategy, if successful, had the potential of splitting the Democrat vote nationally and handing the election to the Republicans. Secessionists knew that if the Republicans won, Southerners were much more likely to opt for disunion.[16]

Hubbard played an important role in the adoption and execution of this strategy. He had earlier been selected by Lawrence County Democrats to serve as a delegate to the state convention, and he brought his influence to bear in connection with the adoption of the key resolutions.[17] Among other things, he made a fiery speech that the radical *Charleston Mercury* praised as "manly" and sure to have "smote the consciences of younger men!" It was actually a crass reminder of Hubbard's long-standing position:

> Whenever the North made aggressions upon the South, and the latter
> talked about resistance, immediately someone went to calculating the number

of children that would be made fatherless, and the number of widows that would be made; and so, in the crying of the women and children, and the fear of shedding blood, principles and rights were lost sight of. [I am] for maintaining our rights at all hazards.[18]

As newspapers across the nation soon reported, Hubbard was then selected one of two presidential electors for the state at large, the other being south Alabama secessionist John Tyler Morgan.[19]

Douglas supporters immediately cried foul.[20] One Selma editor who was a Douglas supporter pointed his editorial sword at Hubbard, declaring that he was a "regular old political reprobate, a perfect disorganizer in his own county." "There has not been an election in Lawrence County for years unless this old sinner was a candidate against some regular Democratic candidate either for the legislature or for Congress. It is a fixed rule with old Davy Hubbard never to support Democrats when there is an opposition candidate to support, yet he is put on the disunion electoral ticket for the state at large and held up as a pure and true democrat. 'Old Davy,'" he concluded, "is an out and out disunionist, and of course will support the disunion candidate for the Presidency, the bolters from the Charleston Convention may nominate."[21]

Hubbard and other secessionists had one more very important legislative task in Montgomery: the adoption of a resolution requiring Governor Moore to call for a convention of elected delegates to meet when the Republicans won the presidential election. This legislature had been elected before John Brown's raid, and many of the legislators had originally been sent to Montgomery to obtain state aid for railroads that would serve their constituents. This aid, the secessionists knew, was potentially effective bait for obtaining support for the convention resolution as well as other measures that would ready the state for war. For the legislature to provide aid for railroads, however, they would have to go through Hubbard.

Before the Christmas recess, Hubbard had announced that his opposition to financial aid from the state would continue, declaring that he "would in no event vote for any scheme for State aid, as it is called, giving State bonds to be used by the Railroad Companies for their benefit, and whereby the citizen having no interest in the Road may become liable to pay the debts should the company fail to do so."[22] Subsequently, however, he offered the railroaders a ray of hope: "if they will offer but one bill at a time, and take the vote of the House on a single proposition, and make that fair and just, whereby the credit of the whole State can be used for the work, and then make the State secure," he would feel "very differently toward such schemes of improvement." Almost as an appetizer to tempt the desperate, Hubbard announced the following day that he would vote for a bill to extend the time for payment of the debt due the state from the Mobile and Ohio Railroad. That bill had passed the house on December 10,[23] and while it was pending in the senate, that body debated the resolution that would require the governor to call a convention if a Republican were elected.[24] Two days after that resolution was unanimously adopted and sent to the house,[25] the bill extending the loan to the Mobile and Ohio Railroad was adopted by the senate.[26]

When the legislature reconvened after the Christmas recess, it passed several more bills of significance that also appear to have been a product of logrolling between commercial interests and secessionists. On February 23, 1860, a bill was adopted requiring The University of Alabama to establish a "military department."[27] On February 18 and 24, the legislature adopted three bills authorizing loans of unprecedented amounts of money to certain specified railroads, including the North-East and South-West ($200,000), the Alabama and Tennessee ($225,000), the Selma and Gulf ($140,000), and the Tennessee and Alabama Central ($173,940).[28] Also on February 24, it adopted another bill that appropriated an equally unprecedented sum ($200,000) for the state militia and raised taxes to fund it.[29] On the same day that the militia bill and two of the railroad aid bills were passed, the house adopted the convention resolution, which stated that upon the "election of a President advocating the principles and action of the party in the Northern States calling itself the Republican Party, it shall be the duty of the Governor, and he is hereby required forthwith to issue his proclamation," to call for an election of delegates "to a Convention of the State to consider, determine and *do whatever* in the opinion of said Convention, the rights, interests and honor of the State of Alabama requires to be done for their protection."[30]

As secessionists had hoped, the ensuing focus of the Alabama press was on the aid provided to railroads rather than this much more important resolution. The editor of the *Montgomery Mail* declared that "this series of measures" had reversed "in a moment, as it were, the whole internal policy of Alabama."[31] The Tuscaloosa *Independent Monitor* rejoiced that "the liberal and progressive policy of the present Legislature has inaugurated a new era in the State's legislation" and, perhaps referring to Hubbard, that "old-fogyism dazzled by the splendor of [the legislature's] progressive policy has retreated to its den, there to mourn that its days of stay-as-it-were-ism have passed away."[32]

After the legislature adjourned, Hubbard returned to north Alabama and awaited the outcome of the National Democratic Convention that met in Charleston on April 23, 1860. As expected, a majority of the delegates refused to adopt the pro-slavery platform plank dictated by Alabama's convention, at which time the delegations from Alabama and six other states walked out of the convention hall.[33] Before the end of June there were three candidates who would fatally split the vote opposing the Republican nominee, Abraham Lincoln: Stephen A. Douglas, Vice President John C. Breckinridge of Kentucky, and Tennessee Senator John Bell.[34] Breckinridge, who was the advocate of the pro-slavery doctrine of protection, would receive Hubbard's support, but Hubbard likely recognized that Breckinridge had no chance of winning. That did not matter. As most political pundits recognized, secession was made probable if Breckinridge drew the vote of enough Southern Democrats from Douglas, thereby assuring Lincoln's election.[35]

To prevent this, Unionist leaders in Alabama attempted to replicate the same strategy that had proven so successful in 1850 and 1851. They intensified their attack on Hubbard and other Breckinridge Democrats, accusing them all of aiming for secession.[36] Hubbard denied reports by the Douglas and Bell press in Alabama and throughout the nation that he had declared: "Resistance! Resistance! To death against the government is what I want now."[37] Hubbard's recurrent theme on the hustings around the state was actually a version of that the late John C. Calhoun had enunciated before his death, but which had acquired much more practical significance to Southerners since John Brown's raid: "Protection by the Union Government in, or protection out of it." It was bedrock dogma as old for Alabamians as the conflict with Native Americans. Closely related was his message to non-slaveowners. Southerners needed to choose between "emancipation and equality of races" or protection against such an apocalyptic end.[38]

Judging from reports in the north Alabama press, however, one might have thought the Breckinridge campaign was not gaining much momentum in north Alabama. According to an unidentified correspondent of the pro-Douglas Huntsville *Southern Advocate* who had attended the September 1860 term of the circuit court in Moulton:

> The disunion Breck leaders—David Hubbard, L. P. Walker, Gen. [Edward Asbury] O'Neal, Sterling Wood, Wm. Cooper and Jno. S. Kennedy—expected to have every thing their own way at the commencement of the week, but lo and behold to their utmost confusion before the close of the week—when the people's advocates, such men and long tried and sterling Democrats as R. B. Lindsey, O. H. Bynum, Jos. Bradley and James E. Saunders, with the aid of Judge [Thomas] Peters, who has lately come out for the Democratic cause, took the stump for the old Democracy and defended it nobly. These same fireeating and disunion speakers left the court grounds one after another, and looked as if they had been doing something politically wrong all their lives, and the present week in particular.[39]

The results of the election, however, revealed a very different picture. Breck-inridge lost Lawrence County to Douglas, but received 54 percent of the Alabama vote, including a majority in every congressional district in north Alabama. Even Winston County was in his column.[40]

Abraham Lincoln won the presidency. On December 6, Governor Moore complied with the legislature's convention resolution by issuing a call for an election to take place on December 24 to select delegates to attend a convention he scheduled for January 7, 1861, in Montgomery.[41] At this time, however, Alabama secessionists encountered important impediments to their goal of separate state secession. Concerns about the possibility of civil war became so widespread in north Alabama that only the delegates from that region who stood on a cooperationist platform—one requiring joint and simultaneous action by all the slave states—succeeded in achieving election.[42] The problem this presented for Hubbard and other secessionists was that Virginia and many other Southern states were still reluctant to secede, and waiting for them to go out simultaneously with Alabama might cause the movement to lose momentum and fail altogether.

In an effort to avoid this delay, Governor Moore appointed several prominent Alabamians to visit the other slave states to convince their governments to independently proceed with the mechanics of secession and then join a Southern confederacy to be formed later.[43] Just short of his sixty-ninth birthday, Hubbard was appointed Alabama's commissioner to the state of Arkansas, and he arrived in its capital of Little Rock in late 1860. A majority of the state's voters had voted overwhelmingly for Breck-inridge but, as secessionists had discovered in north Alabama, this did not necessarily mean the people favored secession.[44] According to Hubbard's later report to Governor Moore, he first met with the governor of Arkansas and leading members of its legislature, and they told him that "the people have not yet made up their minds to go out," and at the present time "a majority would vote the Union ticket." Part of their reluctance arose from an old consideration with which Hubbard was well familiar: the presence of Native Americans. "The [Arkansas] counties bordering on the Indian Nations, Creeks, Cherokees, Choctaws, and Chickasaws," Hubbard wrote, "would hesitate greatly to vote for secession, and leave those tribes still under the influence of the Government at Washington, from which they receive such large stipends and annuities."[45]

There was also a belief among leaders in Arkansas that ongoing efforts in Congress to settle the controversy would succeed and make the issue of secession moot. The two houses of the Arkansas legislature nonetheless adopted resolutions inviting Hubbard to address them, and he was questioned by their members regarding how the seceding states would respond if a compromise were reached. Hubbard responded that "no state which had seceded would ever go back, without full power being given to protect themselves by vote against anti-slavery projects and schemes of every kind." That was unlikely, he continued, because "the Northern people were honest, and did fear the Divine displeasure, both in this world and the world to come, by reason of what they considered the national sin of slavery."[46]

The Arkansas legislators, however, still held out hope that compromise was possible if the slave states would cooperate in presenting a united front. Secession was, therefore, unnecessary. The Arkansas senate expressed this position in a resolution adopted on December 28 following Hubbard's address. Although it declared that "Mr. Hubbard is entitled to our respect for the manner in which he has discharged his trust," it believed that "the Southern states should counsel, deliberate, and fully understand each other," i.e., act jointly rather than independently.[47] The Arkansas press, which opposed secession at this point, was therefore generally critical of Hubbard's argument for separate state secession. One editor wrote that Hubbard "failed to make his bad cause even plausible," and would have been better off if he had "looked wise and said nothing." [48]

After Hubbard returned to Alabama and went to Montgomery to attend a special session of the legislature called by Governor Moore, he recognized the existence of some of the same sentiment he had experienced in Arkansas. As the state and national press would soon be reporting, a very heated controversy had erupted in the Alabama secession convention over whether the momentous issue of secession would be submitted for decision by the people in a popular referendum.[49] North Alabama's cooperationists advocated that it should, but when a majority of the delegates voted for separate state secession and against a public referendum, fears rose over the possibility of civil war in north Alabama.[50] George Smith Houston, who had withdrawn from Congress but not formally resigned his seat, was among the leaders of a very active protest movement in Limestone County, where William Yancey was burned in effigy for threatening during the convention to use force to compel the public to acquiesce in the work of the convention, and where the United States flag was hoisted in Athens, the county seat.[51]

Houston's conduct did not surprise Hubbard, who was keeping a close eye on public opinion in north Alabama as resistance continued to manifest itself. In February 1861, after helping orchestrate the Alabama legislature's appropriation of $500,000 for use by the Confederate government,[52] Hubbard returned home to see for himself. A few days later he wrote to Governor Moore confirming that the secession movement was not popular in Lawrence

County with those whom he classified as "Union savers." Without naming names, however, he assured Moore that "the Ambitious who expect to be known throughout the State are not only becoming reconciled but are preparing their followers to be reconciled, and will support the measure as soon as they can do so."[53] In reality, many of those men were only feigning acquiescence, and a movement was already afoot to wrestle the state away from the secessionists in the upcoming state election in August.[54]

The activities of Unionists to reconstruct the Union came to a temporary halt, however, when Confederate forces in South Carolina were ordered to "reduce" Fort Sumter in Charleston Harbor, and President Lincoln raised fears of an attack on the South by calling for volunteers to stamp out the rebellion.[55] As many secessionists had hoped, this also led Arkansas, Tennessee, Virginia, and some other hold-out states to join the .Confederacy.[56] However the outbreak of war also put to the test the promises of Hubbard and others that the people—and their "institutions"—would be protected outside the Union.

As part of the Confederacy's effort to fulfill this promise, its Provisional Congress had created a war department to coordinate raising and deployment of Confederate forces. Rather than selecting an experienced and qualified military man to be secretary of war, however, Jefferson Davis had appointed a political hack: Leroy Pope Walker.[57] Walker's would not be a long tenure. The Confederate Congress had also created a Bureau of Indian Affairs within the War Department with the intention of trying to use conciliation to at least neutralize the threat posed by Native Americans on reservations adjacent to Arkansas, Texas, and Missouri. As the national press reported, however, rather than appointing as commissioner someone who had a proven record for kindness and empathy toward Native Americans, Davis chose a rapacious land speculator: David Hubbard.[58]

Hubbard was slowed in returning to Arkansas and assuming the duties of this post by another serious attack of pneumonia; series of later health problems would dog him for months. In June 1861, he finally did arrive at Fort Smith, Arkansas, a river fort recently abandoned by the federal military that stood on the edge of Indian Territory.[59] His approach to Native Americans was less Jacksonian and more reminiscent of the British efforts

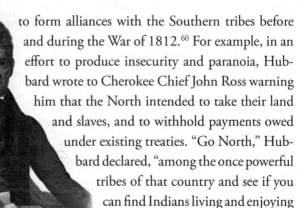

John Ross

to form alliances with the Southern tribes before and during the War of 1812.[60] For example, in an effort to produce insecurity and paranoia, Hubbard wrote to Cherokee Chief John Ross warning him that the North intended to take their land and slaves, and to withhold payments owed under existing treaties. "Go North," Hubbard declared, "among the once powerful tribes of that country and see if you can find Indians living and enjoying power and property and liberty as do your people and the neighboring tribes from the South. If you can," Hubbard concluded, "then say I am a liar, and the Northern States have been better to the Indian than the Southern States."[61] Ross's response to Hubbard indicates that he had a very long memory, one that certainly included the loss of his wife during the infamous death march known as the Trail of Tears.[62] Ross, who was two years older than Hubbard, wrote that he did not believe the federal government would repudiate its treaty obligations. He also saw no real difference between "Northern and Southern philanthropy, as illustrated in their dealings toward Indians within their respective limits" over the years. In particular, the policy of "both sections when extended to the acquisition of Indian lands" was such that" but few Indians now press their feet upon the banks of either the Ohio or the Tennessee." Ross, therefore, announced that the Cherokees would abide by the existing treaty with the federal government and remain "disentangled" from the sectional conflict.[63]

Hubbard returned home to find a number of people in parts of northwest Alabama who also preferred neutrality. On July 4, 1861, residents from Lawrence, Walker, Winston, Fayette, and other north Alabama counties met at a Winston County tavern a few miles south of Hubbard's home to decide on a course of action. There they adopted resolutions declaring secession illegal and requesting that they be "unmolested, that we may work out our political and financial destiny here in the hills and mountains of northwest

Alabama."[64] As had Hubbard when it suited his political strategy over the years, one veteran of the War of 1812 used divisive class rhetoric in an effort to undermine the desire of young men who did not own slaves to fight. He wrote his son that the slaveowners were just trying to use him to fight for their slaves and otherwise cared nothing about him. "After you do their fighting you may kiss their hind parts for all they care."[65]

Neutrality, however, became much more difficult following the bloody Confederate victory on July 21, 1861, at Bull Run near Manassas, Virginia.[66] For many it began to appear that the federal government was impotent to protect Southern Unionists and that the Confederacy would be able to sustain itself and provide protection to its loyal residents. It was no coincidence that the "avalanche" counties of north Alabama then went to the polls in August and voted in a secessionist for governor, John Gill Shorter.[67] It was also no coincidence that by the end of October, the Cherokees and each of the other major tribes had reached treaties with the Confederacy.[68]

The year 1861 was, by far, the zenith of the Confederate era in Alabama.[69] Optimism was so high that peace and Southern independence were near that Hubbard and other Confederates attended another Southern Commercial Convention, this one in Macon, Georgia, in October 1861.[70] The delegates' discussions about postwar economic issues, however, proved to be very premature as a result of changing military strategy by the Union high command. Most significantly, rather than merely concentrating federal military forces in Virginia in an effort to protect, and bring the war to a quick end by taking the Confederate capital at Richmond, the Deep South was designated as another important target.[71] As a result, the war secessionists like Hubbard had brought on would now undermine his life, the lives of his family, and that of all Alabamians.

In early 1862 Union military forces were engaged in joint army and naval operations working their way south through Kentucky and behind Confederate lines there into Tennessee, using the rivers that had been so important to commerce during the antebellum period. The only significant Confederate fortification controlling navigation on the Tennessee River, Fort Henry, was awaiting the approach of Union forces cruising south. Reinforcements from the region were being sent there in an effort to save that undermanned and poorly designed fort and prevent the Union's advance to Alabama and Mississippi.[72]

Among those reinforcements was a group of sixty-five Mississippians called the Chickasaw Rangers, who had been recruited and were being led by David Hubbard's oldest son, David Hubbard Jr.[73] Young Hubbard's wife, Sally, had very recently died, leaving him and their baby boy. He wrote his father a touching letter in late January 1862 while he and his men were aboard a steamship en route to the fort, informing him of Sally's death, the arrangements he had made for the care of the baby, and his profound grief. "I felt and feel as though I had been in companionship with an angel and was found unworthy of it so she was taken from me to a better world of purer spirits. I have but little to live and strive for," he continued, "but will try and do my duty and trust in Providence."[74] Doing his duty appeared to be the quickest way to reunite with his wife. He wrote his father that "the report is that there are 20,000 of the enemy a few miles below and we may form [a] line of battle soon after landing."[75] David Hubbard was very distraught over the loss of his daughter-in-law, and even worse would not know his son's fate for a week or more.

On February 6, Union ironclad gunboats began a fierce bombardment of Fort Henry and two hours later the Confederate commander surrendered unconditionally. David Jr., however, survived and might have been among several Confederates who the fort's commander ordered to leave so they could fight another day.[76] The magnitude of the Confederate loss of Fort Henry quickly became apparent to Alabamians in shocking fashion. On February 8, 1862, Union naval vessels that had been engaged at Fort Henry came unimpeded up the Tennessee River into northwest Alabama chasing Confederate vessels. The Yankees briefly disembarked at Florence where they confiscated Confederate supplies before returning to Tennessee.[77] This incident sent panic through north Alabama, but the worst was yet to come.[78]

Union forces then began moving east toward Fort Donelson, the only Confederate fortification that guarded navigation on the Cumberland River and, therefore, river access to Nashville, Tennessee. That fort surrendered on Sunday, February 16, compelling Confederate forces to abandon Nashville and retreat to a point south of the Tennessee River in north Alabama to avoid being cut off.[79] This, in turn, placed the loyal, but now highly distraught, Confederate civilians residing in Nashville in great jeopardy, one of whom was Hubbard's wife Rebecca's very wealthy widowed niece, Elizabeth McKay Campbell Brown. "Lizinka," as she was nicknamed, had maintained a close relationship with the Hubbards for many years, including fairly frequent correspondence with both. Thus, it was quite natural that she now fled south with her daughter to the Hubbard's home at Kinlock, where they remained for several months. Meanwhile, her Nashville mansion near the state capitol was occupied by a military governor appointed by President Lincoln, her friend and Tennessee Senator Andrew Johnson.[80] As Lizinka's fiancé, and Rebecca Hubbard's nephew, Confederate Brigadier General Richard Ewell, wrote from Virginia, Kinlock was far from being an impregnable sanctuary.[81] The next target for southbound Union forces was the Memphis and Charleston Railroad, of great strategic importance because it was the Confederacy's only continuous east-west rail corridor connecting the eastern portion of the Confederacy with the west.[82]

Before that transportation artery was closed, Hubbard left Kinlock and went to Richmond, Virginia, to meet with Jefferson Davis. One reason for that was to inform Davis of his decision to resign the position of commissioner of Indian Affairs and to recommend another north Alabamian who had been serving as his assistant to replace him. However Hubbard, who suffered another health issue while in Richmond, could have simply mailed Davis a letter and avoided this lengthy and arduous journey.[83] It is likely that the true purpose for his visit was to lobby Davis and the Confederate Congress to quickly and substantially increase the deployment of military assets to north Alabama. Union general Ulysses S. Grant and a huge army had been ferried on troop transports up the Tennessee River on a mission to sever the Confederacy's railroad spine at its junction with the north-south Mobile and Ohio Railroad at Corinth, Mississippi. On March 14, they had disembarked on the west bank of the river at a point approximately sixty land miles northwest of Florence, Alabama, and begun preparing to move south to Corinth.[84]

Despite Hubbard's efforts, Grant would have his foe outnumbered. David Hubbard Jr., and his Chickasaw Rangers were again thrown into the breach as part of a somewhat smaller Confederate army under General Albert Sydney Johnston. The ensuing Battle of Shiloh proved to be the bloodiest conflict of the war up to that timer, with both sides suffering thousands of casualties, among whom was General Johnston.[85] David Jr., however, was not harmed and would ultimately survive the war.[86] The upshot of the battle, which ended in a Union victory on April 7, was that the Union army remained close by and would subsequently occupy Corinth, thereby cutting both key railroads at that point. Closer to home, Union forces from Nashville took Huntsville, Alabama, without a fight on April 11, 1862, and then began consolidating their control of north Alabama. They took Decatur on April 12 and, after moving through Lawrence County, occupied Tuscumbia on April 16.[87]

Joshua Burns Moore, a Tuscumbia lawyer who knew Hubbard, took this opportunity to ridicule the secessionists in his diary. "Where is the boasted chivalry of North Ala. Alas it is fled to the hills and mountains."[88] They, and their sons, however, would soon be forced to fight as a result of the controversial adoption of a conscription law by the Confederate Congress on April 16.[89] Both of Hubbard's other sons were within the age category (1835) subject to the new draft, but he was able to have one of the two, Duncan C. Hubbard, assigned to a "bomb-proof" position on the staff of General P. G. T. Beauregard, who had assumed command of General Johnston's army following Johnston's death.[90] This was quite common for the sons of well-connected families and might have also been a function of influence by Lizinka Brown, whose son Campbell Brown was himself serving as an aide-de-camp on General Ewell's staff. Ewell and his brigade had served under Beauregard at Bull Run.[91]

Safe from harm in his staff position, Campbell Brown wrote to his mother in June 1862 about David Hubbard's youngest son, George, who was married and lived with his wife at Kinlock. Brown teasingly asked: "How does the 'Conscription Act' agree with George Hubbard? He will have to go to the war now in earnest, or else to try a substitute, & *that* I should think he would be ashamed to do."[92] For many young men the social pressure to join the fight was irresistible, and so it was for young George. Unlike Campbell Brown and Duncan Hubbard, however, George followed the course taken by David Hubbard Jr.—and their father before them—and enlisted for service in the field. Unlike them, however, George would not survive the war. He was killed in May 1863 during fighting in west Mississippi in the weeks leading up to the Union siege of Vicksburg.[93]

The Confederacy as a whole was also mortally wounded in 1863, although its death throes would not conclude for almost two years. In July of that year, Vicksburg fell and Confederate forces under General Robert E. Lee that had invaded Pennsylvania were defeated in the equally pivotal Battle of Gettysburg.[94] George's death, coupled with these crushing losses, were obviously reasons for great sorrow to David Hubbard and other family members. One wonders whether he blamed himself for George's demise. There was certainly a great deal of acrimony now being directed by many Alabamians against original secessionists like him who had brought on this terrible war and placed their very survival at risk. This was reflected most graphically in the results of the August 1863 state elections, which resulted in secessionist governor John Gill Shorter being badly beaten in his bid for reelection.[95]

One concern among Alabama Confederates like Hubbard was whether the newly elected governor, prewar Whig Thomas Hill Watts of Montgomery, would move the state toward peace and reconstruction, thereby causing the deaths of many sons like George Hubbard to have been in vain.[96] In his very defiant inaugural address of December 1, 1863, however, which came on the heels of more Confederate setbacks around Chattanooga, Watts vehemently denied any such intention.[97] Hubbard was so grateful that he wrote Watts a thank-you letter from Kinlock, but he also pressed Watts for action: "Let me hope that [your address] means business and government and not palaver. We have been nearly destroyed by words—words and nothing else."[98]

Hubbard was referring to the terrible condition to which north Alabama had devolved since 1861, and the failure of the state and Confederate governments to remedy the plight of loyal Confederate civilians in the region.[99] Shortly after President Lincoln issued his final Emancipation Proclamation on January 1, 1863, Union forces based at Corinth, Mississippi, began a series of punitive and very destructive raids into northwest Alabama that devastated the region and displaced a large number of the residents.[100]

According to one account, "during the occupancy of [Lawrence County] by the federal troops" Hubbard was "shamefully treated, and showed no respect for his gray hairs."[101] The presence of the Union army had also emboldened Alabama Unionists, thousands of whom joined the Union army at Decatur, Alabama, and other federal posts of enlistment.[102] Despite fervent pleas for relief, neither the state nor the Confederate governments took sufficient action to provide protection. This had been another major factor in Governor Shorter's defeat.[103] Since then, Unionist guerrillas had begun a campaign of violent and bloody hit-and-run raids on Confederate conscription officials, jails holding deserters, draft dodgers, and political dissidents, and on Confederate civilians.[104] This type of warfare had intensified when the Confederate desertion rate spiked upwards following more Confederate setbacks in Tennessee in the fall of 1863.[105] It was estimated that almost ten thousand deserters were hiding in the portion of north Alabama south of the Tennessee River, and competing with the civilian population there for food and other necessities.[106]

Contrary to several accounts, Hubbard was never a member of the Confederate Congress and, therefore, had no real ability to directly influence the Confederate government or its military policy.[107] His letter to Watts had been a plea for help. "The mountainous districts of Winston, Walker, parts of Marion, Lawrence and Franklin Counties, have been filled with Tories or Lincolnites and these are robbing and stealing day and night, and the murders, burglaries and robberies [are] receiving but little attention." Hubbard himself had been "burglarized and robbed of between two and three thousand dollars' worth of stock and property and expect to be left entirely destitute, unless some relief and security can be had."[108]

Hubbard acknowledged that the government had deployed "hundreds, nay I may almost say thousands of cavalry" to the region, but he maintained that their sole accomplishment was "eating up the light subsistence made by these poor populations" and thereby impoverishing "the loyal as well as the disloyal." Hubbard's advice to Watts was to have this ineffective Confederate cavalry withdrawn and, in their place, deploy an "active state police, armed and good, reliable police officers from the Military, who will act promptly as a military patrol and who can and *will* punish." These policemen, Hubbard explained, should be stationed in groups of eight to ten at stockades or blockhouses to be constructed at three points along roads used by "these brigands." Hubbard was "satisfied from a knowledge of Indian warfare in early life that for a thinly settled people with bad roads, the 'Block House or Stockade System' of defense with but small consuming occupants is the true one." "Nothing short of this," Hubbard concluded, "will arrest the shocking scenes of arson, murder, [and] burglary, now daily going on."[109]

Whether Governor Watts took Hubbard's dubious suggestion seriously is unknown, but the fact was that Unionist sentiment in north Alabama continued to grow.[110] In March 1864, Unionists conducted public rallies under federal protection in Huntsville and Jackson County, where resolutions were adopted calling for peace and reunion.[111] That same month, Union military forces occupied Moulton, forcing Hubbard and his family to seek refuge elsewhere to avoid capture.[112] Like many north Alabama Confederates, their ultimate destination was Tuscaloosa, but judging from Hubbard's correspondence, they had to take a circuitous route. The Hubbards first fled to Okalona, Mississippi, where the families of David Jr. and Duncan Hubbard lived and where they could board a train to Meridian and then ride east on the Alabama and Mississippi Railroad to Selma. From there they rode the Alabama and Tennessee Rivers Railroad to Montevallo, where they could take a stagecoach to Tuscaloosa. From almost each point along the way he wrote military commanders suggesting measures to redeem north Alabama from the disloyal.[113]

By this time, however, the Confederate military in the region was primarily focused on trying to stop the Union army's move south toward Atlanta, and was stripping north Alabama and other areas of fighting men for that purpose. The effect of this was illustrated in July 1864 when a large Union column that left Decatur and moved south to destroy railroads in east Alabama met only token resistance.[114] Despite the deployment of reinforcements to Georgia, Atlanta fell anyway in September.[115] As 1864 came to an end, the Union military was supreme in north Alabama, most of Mississippi, and Mobile Bay. Only a relatively small number of Confederate troops were left to defend the balance of Alabama from invasions from the north and the south expected to come in the spring of 1865.[116] Among the remaining defenders was David Hubbard Jr., who is said by lore to have become a member of the cavalry corps of Confederate Lieutenant General Nathan Bedford Forrest.[117] Forrest's force was far outnumbered by the anticipated invasion force, but under Forrest's charismatic leadership, they could be counted on to fight despite the odds against them.[118] This was not enough, and the invasion of Alabama resulted in widespread destruction in central and south Alabama.[119]

Hubbard had returned to Tuscaloosa in late March and established a branch of the Society of Loyal Confederates.[120] He and his family might have still been there when elements of the Union invasion force that had been based in north Alabama near Florence destroyed most of The University of Alabama, which he had helped make a reality decades earlier while serving in the legislature.[121] Virtually all of his accomplishments since that early period had been now swept aside or lost, not the least of which was his son, George. But Hubbard's nightmare was not over.

He and his family had a very uncertain and possibly dangerous future ahead. His plantation home at Kinlock had miraculously survived despite being on the route taken by an entire division of the southbound Union invasion force. If he returned to Kinlock, however, he would have to face the enmity and possible violent retribution of bitter north Alabamians who had unsuccessfully opposed him and secession and had now lost all.[122] As Franklin County lawyer-Unionist Joshua Burns Moore put it with men like Hubbard in mind, secessionists had "done more injury" and "caused more suffering" and cost "the lives of more men, than was ever before done by the same number." Furthermore, Moore added triumphantly, those secessionists "have had their run—The Race is over."[123]

Hubbard potentially faced a death sentence or imprisonment for treason, or at the very least governmental confiscation of the remaining property he had succeeded in amassing over the years. Indeed, even before President Lincoln's death, his successor Andrew Johnson had announced that he favored "the halter to intelligent, influential traitors."[124] After the assassination, and Johnson's succession to the presidency, Joshua Burns Moore was sure that the leaders of secession would finally receive the punishment they deserved. Johnson, Moore wrote, "would arrest, try, convict and hang them and confiscate their property to repay Union men what they lost at [their] hands."[125] Even if Hubbard somehow escaped prosecution, it was a foregone conclusion that Alabama's hundreds of thousands of slaves would be freed, raising the specter of all the evils Hubbard had predicted if that day ever came.

It is, therefore, unsurprising that in the years between the end of the war and his death in 1874, David Hubbard strove for obscurity. He and his family remained in Tuscaloosa for several months rather than attempting to travel through Unionist strongholds in north Alabama back to Kinlock. In May 1865, President Johnson issued a proclamation allowing Southerners like Hubbard to apply to him for a pardon, the significance of which was that pardoned individuals would not be subject to criminal prosecution or property confiscation by the federal government, and would be allowed to exercise their suspended political rights.[126] Hubbard submitted his application for a pardon to President Johnson on August 26, 1865, but Johnson did not act on it for several months.[127] This was not uncommon for applicants who had been leading Confederate officials. Johnson was then attempting to reconstruct the Southern states before the Republican-controlled Congress convened in December, and he did not want secessionists involved in the process or to reassume political power. As a consequence, wrote the pro-Johnson editor of the *Huntsville Advocate*, "prominent politicians, who were original secessionists, and the military leaders, will be pardoned very slowly."[128]

Johnson had prescribed a process of reconstruction that called for an election of delegates to a convention to form a revised constitutional framework for the state, and to provide for state elections to elect a new governor and legislature, and representatives to Congress. That convention did not finish its work until September 30, and the state election finally took place in early November.[129] No evidence has been found indicating that Hubbard took even a behind-the-scenes role in this process, but President Johnson still had reason to delay his pardon. There was one very important task for Alabama to accomplish: the ratification of the Thirteenth Amendment formally abolishing slavery. With some reluctance, the Alabama legislature finally performed that duty on December 2, 1865.[130]

By this time David and Rebecca Hubbard had accepted the invitation of Richard and Lizinka Ewell (who had married in 1863) to live with them on Lizinka's large plantation south of Nashville in Spring Hill, Tennessee, approximately thirty miles east of the Hubbard family's old homeplace in middle Tennessee.[131] As another act of kindness, Lizinka wrote Andrew Johnson—with whom she had been a friend before the war—asking him to grant David Hubbard's application for a pardon. She explained that "He & my Aunt are living with us for the present. He has lost all his property [and] his health seems quite feeble—his children scattered & his sources of enjoyment very few." Under these circumstances, she concluded, "I cannot believe you will refuse to grant his application *at once* as it will yield him the assurance he desires that the remnant of his days will be undisturbed."[132]

It was a very common strategy for pardon applicants and their representatives to portray the applicants as harmless individuals who had already been sufficiently punished by the war and were now deserving of mercy. Yet Lizinka's description of David Hubbard's plight might have been accurate. He was seventy-three years old and had periodically suffered from health problems for many years. He had lost his slave property, and the federal Freedmen's Bureau officials might have taken possession of Kinlock and his other property, just as they had Lizinka Ewell's lands until very recently. It was, therefore, reasonable for President Johnson—who had served with Hubbard in Congress years earlier—to assume that Hubbard would probably not live much longer. In any event, Johnson replied to Lizinka that he would grant Hubbard a pardon, and it was finally issued on December 8, 1865.[133]

The evidence regarding David Hubbard's subsequent activities is fragmentary. He and Rebecca lived in the Ewell home until 1867, when they moved into a house on land near the Ewell's plantation.[134] According to one account, Hubbard established a tannery there and, "with the help of his former slaves, succeeded in regaining a part of his lost fortune."[135] After Rebecca, Lizinka, and Richard Ewell were all stricken with a respiratory infection and died in March 1872,[136] Hubbard left Spring Hill and went to live with David Hubbard Jr., who was then residing in Louisiana. He died there on January 20, 1874, at the age of eighty-two from unknown causes.[137]

He would have probably been appreciative that at least a few newspapers around the country took notice of his passing. He would have also been glad that he passed from the scene before George Smith Houston was elected governor of Alabama in late 1874, and later to the United States Senate.[138] Only after Hubbard's death did Houston finally win those races.

15

Epilogue

David Hubbard has been largely forgotten since the Civil War ended. Unlike Alabama secessionists William Lowndes Yancey, C. C. Clay Jr., Leroy Pope Walker, and J. L. M. Curry, he has never been the subject of a biography.[1] There are several possible reasons for this. One is that Hubbard's archived papers in Nashville contain no diary and only a handful of his letters. As a consequence, piecing together his life and activities has required a lengthy search for his other, quite scattered papers, and a painstaking, mostly manual review of newspapers published in Alabama and elsewhere during his life.

In addition, Hubbard, unlike Yancey, Clay, Walker, and Curry, did not come from a prominent family and was not college-educated. He was, therefore, not in the mold of the ideal Southern man—a member of the genteel planter elite—that some early historians preferred to highlight. Hubbard also lacked a dedicated cadre of literate aristocrats or upwardly mobile professionals and businessmen who could be counted on to take steps to perpetuate his memory. He was never an aristocrat and resolutely remained a Jacksonian in terms of focusing his appeal on the common man, many of whom were illiterate.

Hubbard was also a maverick—in his own estimation a Radical Democrat—whose principles regarding national issues never changed with the winds or at the dictation of party leaders. He always placed the interests and needs of the South above those of the Union, even when the smart play might have been to compromise and be rewarded with political preferment. His positions during the nullification crisis of the 1830s and the secession crisis in 1850 and 1851, for example, were entirely consistent, but always cost him in party caucuses and sometimes at the polls.

Hubbard was far ahead of his time in bringing railroad technology to

Alabama, but his positions on state economic issues were opposed by many, particularly in other parts of the state. His controversial efforts to prevent the liquidation and closure of the State Bank to whom he was indebted smacked of self-dealing and were contrary to evolving Democratic Party dogma. His seemingly contradictory opposition to state financial aid for railroad construction enraged business interests throughout the state and probably ended any chance he had to reach the United States Senate or become Alabama's governor. One contemporary member of the south Alabama elite later wrote of Hubbard that, "somehow, the public mind came to regard him as a man of great shrewdness and cunning, and this idea, attaching suspicion to his movements, weakened his position, and no doubt contributed no little to keep him in the background, while his fellows of less substantial attainments were advanced." As a result, he surmised, Hubbard's "ambitious, proud spirit no doubt chaffed under this treatment, and it likely intensified the impatience and bitterness manifested in the latter part of his public life."[2]

Then there was the matter of his oratorical skills. This same observer classified Hubbard as "by no means a pleasant speaker" when he served in the legislature. On the contrary, "his voice was harsh in the extreme, and he soon lost all control of it in the excitement of his feelings." Hubbard had "not the least idea of harmony, taking the vagaries of his voice as a specimen, nor had he any grace of gesture." Rather, Hubbard was "a strong man lashed into fury by a phantom of his own creation, and he dashed off in debate with a headlong speed, which exhaustion and a loss of voice alone could arrest. He then took his seat."[3]

Finally, Hubbard never attained any prestigious position in the Confederate government. Yancey and Clay served in the Confederate Senate, Curry was in the Confederate House, and Walker was the first secretary of war. Hubbard held the most inglorious and thankless position of commissioner of Indian Affairs, which generated almost no press coverage or public interest. Hence, unless they dug far below the surface, historians looking for an interesting subject in the Fire-Eater genre would understandably miss the truly colorful and varied life that David Hubbard led. All of those attributes, however, made him an irresistible topic to me.

Endnotes

Reconstruction in Alabama (Spartanburg, SC: Reprint Company Publishers, 1978), 20.

7   Clarence Phillips Denman, *The Secession Movement in Alabama* (Montgomery: AL) State Department of Archives and History, 1933), 85.

PREFACE

1   Eric H. Walther, *The Fire-Eaters* (Baton Rouge: Louisiana State University Press, 1992), 48–82.

2   Ben H. Severance, *Portraits of Conflict: A Photographic History of Alabama in the Civil War* (Fayetteville: University of Arkansas Press, 2012), 29; Lonnie A. Burnett, "Precipitating a Revolution: Alabama's Democracy in the Election of 1860," in Kenneth W. Noe, ed., *The Yellowhammer War: The Civil War and Reconstruction in Alabama* (Tuscaloosa: University of Alabama Press, 2013), 1516.

3   Eric H. Walther, *William Lowndes Yancey and the Coming of the Civil War* (Chapel Hill: University of North Carolina Press, 2006).

4   J. Mills Thornton III, *Politics and Power in a Slave Society: Alabama, 1800–1860* (Baton Rouge: Louisiana State University Press, 1978), 190; Christopher Lyle McIlwain, Sr., *The Million-Dollar Man Who Helped Kill a President: George Washington Gayle and the Assassination of Abraham Lincoln* (El Dorado Hills, CA: Savas Beatie, 2018).

5   See, e.g., William L. Barney, *The Road to Secession: A New Perspective On the Old South* (New York: Praeger, 1972), 85–100; Thornton, *Politics and Power in a Slave Society*, 333–42; Holt Merchant, *South Carolina Fire-Eater: The Life of Laurence Massillion Keitt, 1824–1864* (Columbia: University of South Carolina Press, 2014), 3.

6   Walter Lynwood Fleming, *Civil War and*

CHAPTER ONE

1   Roy Randolph, *Thomas Hubbard's War* (Decorah, IA: Amundsen Publishing Co., 2014), 1–4, 395–98; Thomas M. Owen, *Revolutionary Soldiers in Alabama* (Montgomery: Brown Print. Co., 1911), 58; James Edmonds Saunders, *Early Settlers of Alabama* (Westminster, MD: Heritage Books, 2009), 95: Thomas McAdory Owen, *History of Alabama and Dictionary of Alabama Biography* (Spartanburg, SC: Reprint Co., 1978), III: 854.

2   Randolph, *Thomas Hubbard's War*, 422–23; Jan Onofrio, *Alabama Biographical Dictionary* (St. Clair Shores, MI: Somerset Publishers, 1998), 178. Compare with Willis Brewer, *Alabama, Her History, Resources, War Record, and Public Men: From 1540 to 1872* (Spartanburg, S.C.: Reprint Co., 1975), 307; Owen, *History of Alabama and Dictionary of Alabama Biography*, III: 854.

3   Thomas O. Ott, *The Haitian Revolution, 1789–1804* (Knoxville: University of Tennessee Press, 1973), 188–90; Edward E. Baptist, *The Half Has Never Been Told: Slavery and the Making of American Capitalism* (New York: Basic Books, 2014), 44–45.

4   David Hackett Fischer and James C. Kelly, *Bound Away: Virginia and the Westward Movement* (Charlottesville: University Press of Virginia, 2000), 208.

5   Douglas R. Egerton, *Gabriel's Rebellion: The Virginia Slave Conspiracies of 1800 and 1802* (Chapel Hill: University

of North Carolina Press, 1993); Alan Taylor, *The Internal Enemy: Slavery and War in Virginia, 1772–1832* (New York: W.W. Norton & Co., Inc., 2013), 94–98.

6   Joseph Cephas Carroll, *Slave Insurrections in the United States, 1800–1865* (Mineola, NY: Dover Publications, Inc., 2004), 58–64; John Hope Franklin and Loren Schweninger, *Runaway Slaves: Rebels on the Plantation* (New York: Oxford University Press, 1999), 11–12.

7   Fischer and Kelly, *Bound Away*, 202–206, 214; Avery Odelle Craven, *Soil Exhaustion as a Factor in the Agricultural History of Virginia and Maryland, 1606–1860* (Columbia: University of South Carolina Press, 2006), 11, 104–105; Arthur Ryker Hall, *Early Erosion-Control Practices in Virginia* (Washington: U.S. Dept. of Agriculture, 1937), 3–16.

8   Robert D. Bush, *The Louisiana Purchase: A Global Context* (New York: Routledge, 2014), 23, 89–92, 96–98; Roger G. Kennedy, *Mr. Jefferson's Lost Cause: Land, Farmers, Slavery, and the Louisiana Purchase* (New York: Oxford University Press, 2003).

9   Alfred H. Conrad and John R. Meyer, *The Economics of Slavery and Other Studies in Econometric History* (Chicago: Aldine Pub. Co., 1964), 76.

10   Fischer and Kelly, *Bound Away*, 138–49.

11   Saunders, *Early Settlers of Alabama*, 95.

12   Composite Deed Book A-F, page 69, Doc. No. 84, Rutherford County, Tennessee, in Helen C. & Timothy R. Marsh, eds., *Land Deed Genealogy of Rutherford County Tennessee: 1804–1813* (Greenville, SC: Southern Historical Press, 2001), I: 15.

13   Terry Weeks, *Heart of Tennessee: The Story & Images of Historic Rutherford County* (Murfreesboro, TN: Courier Printing Co., 1992), 16–17; Robert E. Corlew,

Tennessee: A Short History (Knoxville: University of Tennessee Press, 1981), 12–13.

14   Federal Census, 1810, Rutherford County, Tennessee, 15. See also, Randolph, *Thomas Hubbard's War*, 425.

15   Austin P. Foster, *Counties of Tennessee* (Baltimore: Genealogical Publishing Co., Inc., 1992), 81.

16   Herbert James Lewis, *Clearing the Thickets: A History of Antebellum Alabama* (New Orleans: Quid Pro Quo Books, 2013), 83–84; Tom Kanon, *Tennesseans at War, 1812–1815: Andrew Jackson, the Creek War, and the Battle of New Orleans* (Tuscaloosa: University of Alabama Press, 2014), 59; Donald L. Winters, *Tennessee Farming, Tennessee Farmers: Antebellum Agriculture in the Upper South* (Knoxville: University of Tennessee Press, 1994), 25–27.

17   Kanon, *Tennesseans at War*, 22–23, 66, 181; Frank Lawrence Owsley Jr., *Struggle For the Gulf Borderlands: The Creek War and the Battle of New Orleans 1812–1815* (Gainesville: University Press of Florida, 1981), 18–29.

18   Michael Paul Rogin, *Fathers and Children: Andrew Jackson and the Subjugation of the American Indian* (New York: Alfred Knopf, Inc., 1975), 109; John R. Finger, *Tennessee Frontiers: Three Regions in Transition* (Bloomington: Indiana University Press, 2001), 206; Kanon, *Tennesseans at War*, 63–64.

19   Gordon Thomas Chappell, "The Life and Activities of John Coffee" (Ph.D. diss., Vanderbilt University, 1941), 2–70. Regarding the origins of the war, see Andrew Lambert, *The Challenge: Britain Against America in the Naval War of 1812* (London: Faber and Faber, 2012), and Donald R. Hickey, *The War of 1812: A Forgotten Conflict* (Urbana: University of Illinois Press, 2012).

20   Spencer Tucker, ed., *The Encyclopedia of the War of 1812: A Political, Social, and Military History* (Santa Barbara, CA: ABC-CLIO, 2012), 145; Lorman A Ratner, *Andrew Jackson and His Lieutenants: A Study in Political Culture* (Westport, CT: Greenwood Press, 1997), 41–43; John Buchanan, *Jackson's Way: Andrew Jackson and the People of the Western Waters* (New York: Wiley, 2001); *Nashville Whig*, November 25, 1812, 3; Kanon, *Tennesseans at War*, 44–45; David Hubbard, Compiled Service Records, War of 1812, National Archives (he was at one point a private in the 2d Regiment Mounted Gunmen); Gideon Burnham Hubbard, *The Life and Travels of Gideon Burnham Hubbard* (Burnet, TX: Nortex Press, 1980), 1–2, 5; (Huntsville) *Democrat*, October 15, 1842, 3.

21   Sean Michael O'Brien, *In Bitterness and in Tears: Andrew Jackson's Destruction of the Creeks and Seminoles* (Guilford, CT: Lyons Press, 2005), 64–65; Kanon, *Tennesseans at War*, 70–72; Thomas D. Clark and John D.W. Guice, *The Old Southwest, 1795–1830: Frontiers in Conflict* (Norman: University of Oklahoma Press, 1996), 120; Rickey Butch Walker, *Chickasaw Chief George Colbert: His Family and His Country* (Killen, AL: Bluewater Publications, 2012), 113; William Lindsey McDonald, *Lore of the River: The Shoals of Long Ago* (Killen, AL: Heart of Dixie Publishing Co., 2007), 40–42, 48; Nina Leftwich, *Two Hundred Years at Muscle Shoals* (Tuscumbia, AL: Viewpoint Press, 1935), 19–22.

22   O'Brien, *In Bitterness and in Tears*, 65; Clark, *Old Southwest*, 120–22; Kanon, *Tennesseans at War*, 42–47; Chappell, "Life and Activities of John Coffee," 74.

23   Kanon, *Tennesseans at War*, 108.

24   Kanon, *Tennesseans at War*, 41–47; Finger, *Tennessee Frontiers*, 231.

25   Lewis, *Clearing the Thickets*, 86–91; Clark and Guice, *Old Southwest*, 131–32; Kanon, *Tennesseans at War*, 56, 66–68; William Warren Rogers, Robert David Ward, Leah Rawls Atkins, and Wayne Flynt, *Alabama: The History of a Deep South State* (Tuscaloosa: University of Alabama Press, 2010), 51; Buchanan, *Jackson's Way*, 208–225.

26   Lewis, *Clearing the Thickets*, 91, 102; Clark, *Old Southwest*, 123–24; Kanon, *Tennesseans at War*, 56, 68–69, 71; John E. Grenier, "'We Bleed Our Enemies in Such Cases to Give Them Their Senses': Americans' Unrelenting Wars on the Indians of the Trans-Appalachian West, 1810–1812," in Kathryn E.H. Braund, ed., *Tohopeka: Rethinking the Creek War and the War of 1812* (Tuscaloosa: University of Alabama Press, 2012), 177–79; Robert V. Haynes, *The Mississippi Territory and the Southwest Frontier 1795–1817* (Lexington: University Press of Kentucky, 2010), 303–13; Rogin, *Fathers and Children*, 147–48; Frank L. Owsley, "The Fort Mims Massacre," *Alabama Review* XXIV (July, 1971): 192–204.

27   *Nashville Whig*, September 21, 1813, 1.

28   *Nashville Whig*, September 21, 1813, 1; Kanon, *Tennesseans at War*, 70–71.

29   *Nashville Whig*, September 28, 1813, 3, October 12, 1813, 2; Kanon, *Tennesseans at War*, 71; Davy Crockett, *A Narrative of the Life of Davy Crockett of the State of Tennessee* (Philadelphia: E.L. Carey and A. Hart, 1834), 83–84; Benson John Lossing, *The Pictorial Field-Book of the War of 1812* (New York: Harper & Brothers, 1869), 758; Daniel S. Dupre, *Transforming the Cotton Frontier: Madison County, Alabama 1800–1840* (Baton Rouge: Louisiana State University Press, 1997), 26–41; Rogers, et al, *Alabama*, 44, 61, 67.

30 *Nashville Whig*, October 19, 1813, 3; (New York) *Mercantile Advertiser*, November 16, 1813, 2; (Providence) *Rhode Island American and General Advertiser*, November 23, 1813, 2; K. Randell Jones, *In the Footsteps of Davy Crockett* (Winston-Salem, NC: John F. Blair, 2006), 116–18; Lossing, *Pictorial FieldBook of the War of 1812*, 759.

31 *Nashville Whig*, October 19, 1813, 3; Rogers, *et al., Alabama*, 48; Kanon, *Tennesseans at War*, 72; Herbert J. Lewis, *Lost Capitals of Alabama* (Charleston, SC: History Press, 2014), 101; Kanon, *Tennesseans at War*, 59–64; Buchanan, *Jackson's Way*, 231.

32 *Nashville Whig*, October 19, 1813, 3; Rickey Butch Walker, *Warrior Mountains Folklore: American Indian and Celtic History In the Southeast* (Killen, AL: Bluewater Publications, 2011), 24; Jones, *In the Footsteps of Davy Crockett*, 116–18; O'Brien, *In Bitterness and In Tears,* 69; Saunders, *Early Settlers of Alabama*, 36; Paul Horton, "The Culture, Social Structure, and Political Economy of Antebellum Lawrence County, Alabama," *Alabama Review* XLI (October, 1988): 243–70.

33 William Lindsey McDonald, *A Walk Through the Past: People and Places of Florence and Lauderdale County, Alabama* (Killen, AL: Heart of Dixie Publishing Co., 2003), 95; Adrian G. Daniel, "Navigational Development of Muscle Shoals, 1807–1890," *Alabama Review* XIV (October, 1961): 251–57.

34 Jones, *In the Footsteps of Davy Crockett*, 116–18; Rickey Butch Walker and Lamar Marshall, *Indian Trails of the Warrior Mountains* (Moulton, AL: Lawrence County Schools, 2005), 64–65.

35 Lucille Griffith, ed., *Letters from Alabama 1817–1822* (Tuscaloosa: University of Alabama Press, 2003)

130. Regarding Royall, see also Lucille Griffith, "Anne Royall in Alabama," *Alabama Review* XXI (January, 1968): 53–63.

36 Saunders, *Early Settlers of Alabama*, 36.

37 Lewis, *Lost Capitals of Alabama*, 101; Kanon, *Tennesseans at War*, 72; Lossing, *Pictorial Field-Book of the War of 1812*, 761; Buchanan, *Jackson's Way*, 232–33. Some historians believe the town was in Walker County, but Davy Crockett's account places it at Tuscaloosa.

38 Kanon, *Tennesseans at War*, 72–74; Tom Kanon, "Andrew Jackson's Campaigns in the Creek War Prior to Horseshoe Bend," in Braund, ed., *Tohopeka*, 111–12; Owsley, *Struggle for the Gulf Borderlands*, 63–64; Jones, *In the Footsteps of Davy Crockett*, 116–18.

39 Kanon, *Tennesseans at War*, 76–102; Buchanan, *Jackson's Way*, 240–83; James W. Holland, "Andrew Jackson and the Creek War: Victory at the Horseshoe," *Alabama Review* XXI (October, 1968): 243–75. This might have been when David Hubbard first met his future cousin-in-law, future Republic of Texas president Sam Houston. Hubbard was related to Houston's second wife, Margaret Lea. Sam Houston to Margaret Houston, January 17, 1848, in Madge Thornall Roberts, ed., *The Personal Correspondence of Sam Houston* (Denton: University of North Texas Press, 1995), II: 243.

40 Owsley, *Struggle for the Gulf Borderland*, 72–85; Finger, *Tennessee Frontiers*, 234; Kanon, *Tennesseans at War*, 104; Buchanan, *Jackson's Way*, 283–96.

41 Kanon, *Tennesseans at War*, 105–107, 120–21, 123, 138; Lewis, *Clearing the Thickets*, 102; *Nashville Whig*, May 17, 1814, 5. See also, Buchanan, *Jackson's Way*, 297–302; Annual Message of James Monroe, December 2, 1817,

reprinted in *Huntsville Republican*, January 6, 1818.

42 Lewis, *Clearing the Thickets*, 103–104; Kanon, *Tennesseans at War*, 108–109; Owsley, *Struggle for the Gulf Borderlands*, 86–94.

43 Kanon, *Tennesseans at War*, 110, 120, 125–27; Owsley, *Struggle for the Gulf Borderlands*, 93–105; Buchanan, *Jackson's Way*, 302.

44 Kanon, *Tennesseans at War*, 124–25, 127–30, 132–33; James Monroe to Andrew Jackson, October 21, 1814, in Harold D. Moser, ed., *Papers of Andrew Jackson* (Knoxville: University of Tennessee Press, 1991), 3: 170–71; Buchanan, *Jackson's Way*, 309–12; (Huntsville) *Democrat*, October 15, 1842, 3; Chappell, "The Life and Activities of John Coffee," 109–11.

45 Buchanan, *Jackson's Way*, 312–14.

46 Affidavit of Thomas Williamson, June 16, 1815, in War of 1812 Pension and Bounty Land Warrant Application Files, Record Group 15, National Archives, Washington; (Huntsville) Democrat, October 15, 1842, 3; Saunders, *Early Settlers of Alabama*, 95; Hubbard, *Life and Travels of Gideon Burnham Hubbard*, 2. Regarding this offensive, see Kanon, *Tennesseans at War*, 134, 145, 147, 151–53, 157–87.

47 Eliza Croom Coffee, "Sketch of John Coffee," in Archives of Tennessee Historical Society, Nashville; Burke, *Emily Donelson of Tennessee*, I: 57.

48 *Montgomery Advertiser and State Gazette*, June 16, 1857, 3; (Grove Hill) *Clarke County Journal*, June 25, 1857, 2.

49 Saunders, *Early Settlers of Alabama*, 95.

50 U.S. Congress, *Biographical Directory of the American Congress, 1774–1949* (Washington: U.S. Government Printing Office, 1950), 1340.

51 Kanon, *Tennesseans at War*, 176, 181–83; William S. Coker, "The Last Battle of the War of 1812: New Orleans. Not Fort Boyer," *Alabama Historical Quarterly* XLIII (Spring, 1981): 42–63.

52 Terry L. Jones, ed., *Campbell Brown's Civil War: With Ewell and the Army of North Virginia* (Baton Rouge: Louisiana State University Press, 2004), 56, fn. 55; *Florence Gazette*, July 28, 1849, 2.

53 Kanon, *Tennesseans at War*, 182–86.

54 James David Miller, *South By Southwest: Planter Emigration and the Identity of the Slave South* (Charlottesville: University of Virginia Press, 2002), 3–6, 19; John R. Van Atta, *Securing the West: Politics, Public Lands and the Fate of the Old Republic, 1785–1850* (Baltimore: Johns Hopkins University Press, 2014), 84, 139–46; Adam Rothman, *Slave Country: American Expansion and the Origins of the Deep South* (Cambridge: Harvard University Press, 2005), 183–84.

55 Finger, *Tennessee Frontiers*, 237–38; Owsley, *Struggle for the Gulf Borderlands*, 193.

CHAPTER TWO

1 Murray N. Rothbard, *The Panic of 1819: Reactions and Policies* (New York: Columbia University Press, 1962), 1–3, 159; Clyde A. Haulman, *Virginia and the Panic of 1819: The First Great Depression and the Commonwealth* (London: Routledge, 2008), 910.

2 Rothbard, *Panic of 1819*, 4–7, 9–10, 159; Haulman, *Virginia and the Panic of 1819*, 10–12; Baptist, *Half Has Never Been Told*, 75–78, 82–83.

3 Howard Bodenhorn, *State Banking in Early America: A New Economic History* (New York: Oxford Press, 2003), 49–51; Baptist, *Half Has Never Been Told*, 75–77, 91, 92–114; Thomas P. Abernethy, *The South in the New Nation*

(Baton Rouge: Louisiana State University Press, 1961), 164–65.

4   *Richmond Compiler*, October 15, 1816, reprinted in (Bennington) *Vermont Gazette*, November 5, 1816, 2.

5   (Washington.) *National Intelligencer*, October 22, 1817, 2; *Nashville Clarion*, March 18, 1817, reprinted in (Norfolk, Va.) *American Beacon and Commercial Diary*, April 17, 1817, 4; Malcolm J. Rohrbough, *The Trans-Appalachian Frontier: People, Societies, and Institutions 1775–1850* (Bloomington: Indiana University Press, 2008), 192–217; Stephen P. Brown, *John McKinley and the Antebellum Supreme Court: Circuit Riding in the Old Southwest* (Tuscaloosa: University of Alabama Press, 2012), 31–32; Gene Dattel, *Cotton and Race in the Making of America: The Human Costs of Economic Power* (Lanham, MD: Ivan R. Dee, 2009), 31, 39, 42, 47, 52, 367; Conrad and Meyer, *Economics of Slavery*, 76; Kanon, *Tennesseans at War*, 190; Thomas P. Abernethy, *The Formative Period in Alabama 1815–1828* (Tuscaloosa: University of Alabama Press, 1990), 25; Baptist, *Half Has Never Been Told*, 91–94.

6   New Bern, N.C.) *Carolina Federal Republican*, March 8, 1817, 3; *Richmond Enquirer*, quoted in Leftwich, *Two Hundred Years at Muscle Shoals*, 37.

7   Owen, *History of Alabama and Dictionary of Alabama Biography*, III: 854.

8   Griffith, ed., *Letters from Alabama*, 235. Regarding this process, *see* Paul M. Pruitt Jr., "The Life and Times of Legal Education in Alabama, 1819–1897," *Alabama Law Review* 49 (fall, 1997): 281–321.

9   David Hubbard to Washington D. Miller, November 12, 1836, L.K. Miller Accession, Washington Daniel Miller Papers, Archives and Information Services Division, Texas State Library and Archives Commission.

10 Kanon, *Tennesseans at War*, 191; *New York Herald*, reprinted in *Huntsville Republican*, October 7, 1817, p. 1. Regarding the treaties, see Charles W. Watts, "Colbert's Reserve and the Chickasaw Treaty of 1818," *Alabama Review* 12 (October, 1959): 272–80; *Richmond Compiler*, October 15, 1816, reprinted in (Bennington) *Vermont Gazette*, November 5, 1816, 2.

11 A.P. Hayne to Andrew Jackson, November 27, 1816, January 10, 1817, Andrew Jackson Papers, Library of Congress, and quoted in Rogin, *Fathers and Children*, 176.

12 (New York) *Columbian*, March 11, 1817, 3; (Washington) *National Intelligencer*, July 1, 1817, p. 2; Lewis, *Clearing the Thickets*, 123; Kanon, *Tennesseans at War*, 191; Gordon T. Chappell, "John Coffee: Surveyor and Land Agent," *Alabama Review* XIV (July-October, 1961): 180–95, 243–50.

13 *Huntsville Republican*, January 27, 1818, 2 (publishing an advertisement by some of Coffee's deputy surveyors offering to provide information to prospective buyers for a price); Brown, *John McKinley and the Antebellum Supreme Court*, 34–35; James F. Doster, "Land Titles and Public Land Sales in Early Alabama," *Alabama Review* XVI (April, 1963): 108–24; Rogin, *Fathers and Children*, 175–77; Chappell, "John Coffee," 188–89, 244–45.

14 David Hubbard to John Coffee, March 27, 1816, Dyas Collection, John Coffee Papers, Tennessee State Library and Archives, Nashville, Tennessee. Regarding Hubbard's disability determination, see Certificate of Pension, War of 1812 Pension and Bounty Land Warrant Application Files, Record Group 15, National Archives, Washington.

15　(Huntsville) *Democrat*, October 15, 1842, 3; N.A., "1820 Lawrence County Census," *Old Lawrence Reminiscences* 19 (September, 2005): 21. Regarding Green Kirk Hubbard's military service, see Compiled Service Records, War of 1812, National Archives (he achieved the rank of corporal).

16　(Huntsville) *Democrat*, October 15, 1842, 3; (Huntsville) *Southern Advocate*, July 9, 1857, 3.

17　The sales of all land south of the Tennessee River took place in phases in the summer and fall of 1818. *Nashville Whig and Tennessee Advertiser*, April 25, 1818, 3, September 26, 1818, 2.

18　(Huntsville) *Democrat*, October 15, 1842, 3; (Statesville, NC) *Iredell Express*, reprinted in (Charlotte, NC) *Western Democrat*, September 3, 1861, 2; (Raleigh, N.C.) *Semi-Weekly Standard*, November 6, 1861, 1.

19　Merrill D. Peterson, *The Great Triumvirate: Webster, Clay, and Calhoun* (New York: Oxford University Press, 1987), 55–56; H.W. Brands, *Andrew Jackson: His Life and Times* (New York: Anchor Books, 2005), 327–47; Robert V. Remini, *Andrew Jackson and the Course of American Empire, 1767–1821* (New York; Harper & Row, 1977), 350–68.

20　Matthew Warshauer, *Andrew Jackson and the Politics of Martial Law: Nationalism, Civil Liberties, and Partisanship* (Knoxville: University of Tennessee Press, 2006), 52–53.

21　Margaret Matthews Cowart, *Old Land Records of Lawrence County, Alabama* (Huntsville, AL: NP, 1991), 275 (79.83 acres in W ½ of NE 1/4, T7So., R8W), 276 (160.40 acres in SW ¼, T7So., R8W), 280 (161.34 acres in NW ¼ of T7So., R8W), 372 (80.19 acres in W ½ of SW ¼, T7So., R9W). All land sales in ranges 6, 7, 8, and 9 occurred

in September 1818. *Alexandria* (Va.) *Herald*, April 10, 1818, 3.

22　Cowart, *Old Land Records of Lawrence County*, 165 (stating that he purchased the west ½ of the southwest ¼ of township 7 south, range 7 west). Regarding other land purchases by David Hubbard in 1818, see Ibid, 280 (161.34 acres in SW ¼, Section 18, Township 7 South, Range 8 West), 364 (39.43 ½ acres in SW ¼ of SW ¼ of Township 7 South, Range 9 West), 371 (320.08 acres in the West ½ of Section 22, Township 7 South, Range 9 West). Regarding Moulton and his death, see *Nashville Whig*, May 17, 1814,5; Brewer, *Alabama*, 307.

23　(Natchez) *Mississippi State Gazette*, September 26, 1818, 3, October 3, 1818, 2; *Augusta* (Ga.) *Chronicle*, October 14, 1818, 2; (New York) *Columbian*, October 15, 1818, 2; *Nashville Whig and Tennessee Advertiser*, September 26, 1818, 2, November 14, 1818, 3; *Huntsville Republican*, January 6, 1818, 3.

24　Conrad and Meyer, *Economics of Slavery*, 76; Saunders, *Early Settlers of Alabama*, 42, 96; *Huntsville Republican*, October 14, 1817, 2, November 4, 1817, 2, November 18, 1817, p 2, January 20, 1818, 2; *City of Washington Gazette*, May 12, 1818, 2.

25　(Clarksville, Tenn.) *Weekly Chronicle*, April 8, 1818, 3; Doster, "Land Titles and Public Land Sales in Early Alabama," 118–22.

26　Saunders, *Early Settlers of Alabama*, 96; Dupre, *Transforming the Cotton Frontier*, 42–43; Van Atta, *Securing the West*, 84112 (discussing the later repeal of this credit system in 1820 and the federal land policy that followed); *Richmond Enquirer*, November 13, 1818, 2; (New York) *American*, November 22, 1820, 2;

Doster, "Land Titles and Public Land Sales in Early Alabama," 112, 121.

27   Conrad and Meyer, *Economics of Slavery*, 76; *Nashville Whig*, December 11, 1822, 3; Brian Schoen, *The Fragile Fabric of Union: Cotton, Federal Politics, and the Global Origins of the Civil War* (Baltimore: Johns Hopkins University Press, 2009), 122.

28   Thornton, *Politics and Power in a Slave Society*, 13; Abernethy, *Formative Period in Alabama*, 53; Brown, *John McKinley and the Antebellum Supreme Court*, 35–38; Dupre, *Transforming the Cotton Frontier*, 48–55. Doster, "Land Titles and Public Land Sales in Early Alabama," 123; (Huntsville) *Democrat*, November 2, 1824, 3.

29   Brown, *John McKinley and the Antebellum Supreme Court*, 59–61; Dupre, *Transforming the Cotton Frontier*, 75–97, (Huntsville) *Democrat*, October 14, 1823, 2, November 4, 1823, 2, November 11, 1823, 2, November 25, 1823, 2, December 16, 1823, 2, October 26, 1824, 2, February 9, 1827, 2; Ruth Ketring Nuermberger, "The 'Royal Party' In Early Alabama Politics," *Alabama Review* VI (April and July, 1953): 81–98, 198–212.

30   Griffith, ed., *Letters from Alabama*, 245.

31   Malcolm Cook McMillan, *Constitutional Development in Alabama, 1798–1901: A Study in Politics, the Negro, and Sectionalism* (Chapel Hill: University of North Carolina Press, 1955), 30–33; (Clarksville, Tenn.) *Town Gazette & Farmers Register*, July 19, 1819, 2.

32   *Ala. Const.*, Art. III, § 5 (1819). *See also*, Lewis, *Clearing the Thickets*, 133–42; Thornton, *Politics and Power in a Slave Society*, 12; McMillan, *Constitutional Development in Alabama*, 35–36.

33   *Newport* (Mass.) *Herald*, July 11, 1823, 2; (Huntsville) *Democrat*, November 9,

1824, 2, December 28, 1824, 2; Brown, *John McKinley and the Antebellum Supreme Court*, 61; Thornton, *Politics and Power in a Slave Society*, 16–17, 20.

34   *Ala. Const.*, Art. VI, Slavery, Sec. 1 (1819).

35   Ibid., Sec. 3.

36   Brewer, *Alabama*, 308.

37   Saunders, *Early Settlers in Alabama*, 95; Owen, *History of Alabama and Dictionary of Alabama Biography*, III: 854.

38   Owen, *History of Alabama and Dictionary of Alabama Biography*, III: 854; Saunders, *Early Settlers of Alabama*, 95; McDonald, *A Walk Through the Past*, 25, 186, 189; Griffith, ed., *Letters from Alabama*, 235.

39   Cowart, *Old Land Records of Lawrence County*, 165, 280, 364, 371; Andrew Jackson to James Jackson, August 2, 1821, in Moser, *et al.*, eds., *Papers of Andrew Jackson*, V: 83, n. 4, 91–92; (Huntsville) *Democrat*, February 22, 1828, p. 1; *Huntsville Republican*, September 6, 1822, reprinted in *Providence* (R.I.) *Patriot*, October 30, 1822, 2; Dupre, *Transforming the Cotton Frontier*, 120.

40   Conrad and Meyer, *Economics of Slavery*, 76; *Salem* (Mass.) *Gazette*, January 15, 1822, 2; (Little Rock) *Arkansas Weekly Gazette*, October 8, 1822, 3.

41   Saunders, *Early Settlers of Alabama*, 102; Chappell, "John Coffee," 188. Eliza Campbell was born on May 23, 1788. Spencer A. Waters and Betty R. Waters, *Cemetery Records of Lawrence County, Alabama and Selected Cemeteries in Surrounding Counties* (N.P., 2009), 149. The precise date of their marriage was likely before February 11, 1822, explaining why she later quitclaimed her dower rights to a lot in Moulton that Hubbard had deeded to another man without her signature on that date. *Old*

Lawrence Reminiscences 10 (December, 1996): 136.

42   Saunders, *Early Settlers of* Alabama, 102; Owen, *History of Alabama and Dictionary of Alabama Biography*, III: 854; Hubbard Family File, Lawrence County Archives, Moulton, AL.

43   *Newburyport* (Mass.) *Herald*, December 30, 1822, 3 (eight cents).

44   (Huntsville) *Democrat*, October 15, 1842, 3; Saunders, *Early Settlers of Alabama*, 95–96; McDonald, *Walk Through the Past*, 41.

45   Saunders, *Early Settlers of Alabama*, 96.

46   *New York Advertiser*, April 13, 1820, 2.

47   Saunders, *Early Settlers of Alabama*, 96.

48   *Ala. Acts*, 48–50 (December 17, 1819).

49   The painting was donated to the Alabama Department of Archives and History in 1907 by Hubbard's grandson, George C. Hubbard of Town Creek. *Nashville American*, October 18, 1907, 4. The determination of the time period Hubbard's portrait was likely painted was made by the incomparable Frances O. Robb of Huntsville, Alabama. Her email to me states, *inter alia*, that the clothing he is wearing–"high collar of jacket, fairly high vee of a double-breasted somewhat military coat"–is from the 1820s. The "white vest and jabot," she continued, "are not military." Hubbard's hair "is dressed in a conservative version of the Brutus cut fashionable in England and on the Continent after the Napoleonic wars and worn by Lafayette in his later years." Email to Author, April 6, 2015.

50   Brewer, *Alabama*, 308.

51   Brewer, *Alabama*, 307–308; Garrett, *Reminiscences of Public Men in Alabama*, 298.

52   *Nashville Whig*, December 11, 1822, 3; (Huntsville) *Democrat*, April 27, 1824,

3, January 6, 1827, 2, March 16, 1827, 3, June 8, 1827, 2; Dupre, *Transforming the Cotton Frontier*, 107.

53   *Nashville Whig*, December 11, 1822, 3.

54   (Huntsville) *Democrat*, October 14, 1823, 2–3, October 21, 1823, 3, October 28, 1823, 3, November 4, 1823, 3, November 11, 1823, 2–3, July 20, 1824, 2; Brown, *John McKinley and the Antebellum Supreme Court*, 60; Thornton, *Politics and Power in a Slave Society*, 14, 16–17; Abernethy, *Formative Period in Alabama*, 104, 111–13; Lewis, *Clearing the Thickets*, 178–79.

55   Abernethy, *Formative Period in Alabama*, 173.

56   (Huntsville) *Democrat*, October 28, 1823, 3. The Erie Canal was completed in 1825.

57   (Huntsville) *Democrat*, October 26, 1824, 2.

58   *Ala. Acts*, 3–11 (December 20, 1823). *See also, Owen v. Branch Bank at Mobile*, 3 Ala. 258 (1842); (Huntsville) *Democrat*, January 20, 1824, 1–2, February 10, 1824, 1, July 20, 1824, 2, November 23, 1824, 3; Abernethy, *Formative Period in Alabama*, 114, 117–18, 157–58; Ralph Draughon, "Some Aspects of the History of Alabama Bond Issues," *Alabama Review* VI (July, 1953): 163–74.

59   Regarding the state's efforts to organize the bank, see (Huntsville) *Democrat*, November 23, 1824, 2–3 (publishing the annual message of Governor Israel Pickens), December 28, 1824, 2; William H. Brantley, *Banking in Alabama 1816–1860* (Birmingham: Birmingham Printing Co., 1961), I: 63–135.

60   (Huntsville) *Democrat*, February 24, 1824, 2, April 6, 1824, 3, May 11, 1824, 2, June 8, 1824, 2, June 29, 1824, 2, August 3, 1824, 3, August 24, 1824, 1, November 16, 1824, 2; *Richmond Enquirer*, July 2, 1824, 2;

Nashville Gazette, August 13, 1824, 3; (Bennington) *Vermont Gazette*, October 26, 1824; (Washington) *National Intelligencer*, September 22, 1825, 2, October 4, 1825, 3.

61 Griffith, ed., *Letters from Alabama*, 196. See also, Harry L. Watson, *Liberty and Power: The Politics of Jacksonian America* (New York: Hill and Wang, 1990), 79.

62 *Cahawba Press and Alabama State Intelligencer*, November 22, 1824; Brown, *John McKinley and the Antebellum Supreme Court*, 63; Abernethy, *Formative Period in Alabama*, 132.

63 (Huntsville) *Democrat*, June 29, 1824, 2, July 13, 1824, 3 (publishing a letter from Calhoun to Alabama congressman Gabriel Moore); (Washington) *National Intelligencer*, December 14, 1824, 2 (publishing a report by Calhoun); Daniel, "Navigational Development of Muscle Shoals," 251–58.

64 (Huntsville) *Democrat*, January 19, 1827, 3.

65 *Alabama Senate Journal*, 1827–1828, 54. See also, (Natchez) *Ariel*, January 5, 1827.

66 *Alabama Senate Journal* 1827–1828, 12; (Huntsville) *Democrat*, October 15, 1842, 3; Saunders, *Early Settlers of Alabama*, 48, 96 (Hubbard might have been a partner in the store with a man named Talmadge).

67 Saunders, *Early Settlers of Alabama*, 276; *Richmond Enquirer*, March 3, 1827, 3.

68 *Alabama Senate Journal* 1827–1828, 3–4.; Saunders, *Early Settlers of Alabama*, 96; (Huntsville) *Democrat*, October 15, 1842, 3.

69 Lewis, *Lost Capitals of Alabama*, 108–119.

70 Leftwich, *Two Hundred Years at Muscle Shoals*, 41 (also stating that the road passed south through Kinlock, David Hubbard's future home).

71 *Alabama Senate Journal* 1827–1828, 52, 66–67, 73, 101–10, 121, 148, 156; Robert O. Mellown, "Alabama's Fourth Capital: The Construction of the State House in Tuscaloosa," *Alabama Review* XL (October, 1987) 259–83.

72 *Alabama Senate Journal* 1827–1828, 10, 101–10; *Ala. Acts*, 4–6 (December 18, 1820); Abernethy, *Formative Period in Alabama*, 157–58; Lewis, *Clearing the Thickets*, 195.

73 *Alabama Senate Journal* 1827–1828, 1; (Huntsville) *Democrat*, November 30, 1827, 2–3 (message of Governor John Murphy).

74 *Alabama Senate Journal 1827–1828*, 4–5, 13–14, 16–17. Regarding expressions of sentiment on the tariff in Alabama, see (Huntsville) *Democrat*, June 22, 1827, 2; *Alabama Senate Journal*, 1827–1828, 54–55.

75 *Alabama Senate Journal*, 1827–1828, 54–55.

76 *Ala. Acts*, 6–7 (January 12, 1828); Abernethy, *Formative Period in Alabama*, 118-19.

77 *Alabama Senate Journal* 1827–1828, 116.

78 *Alabama Senate Journal* 1827–1828, 85, 161–65; Dupre, *Transforming the Cotton Frontier*, 110.

79 Saunders, *Early Settlers in Alabama*, 96.

80 *Alabama Senate Journal 1827–1828*, 153–54. Hubbard had attempted to have the University located in north Alabama but was unsuccessful. *Alabama Senate Journal 1827–1828*, 101–10; *Ala. Acts*, 10 (December 29, 1827). It was this legislature that selected the current location of the campus and initiated its construction there. (Huntsville) *Democrat*, April 11, 1828, 3, April 25, 1827, 4.

81   *Alabama Senate Journal 1827–1828*, 155.

82   Abernethy, *Formative Period in Alabama*, 147–48.

83   *Ala. Acts*, Resolutions, January 15, 1828, 169–73; Schoen, *Fragile Fabric of Union*, 130.

84   (Huntsville) *Democrat*, June 22, 1827, 2.

85   4 *Statutes at Large* 290 (May 23, 1828); William W. Freehling, *Prelude to Civil War: The Nullification Controversy in South Carolina* (New York: Oxford University Press, 1965), 134–76; Abernethy, *Formative Period in Alabama,* 146–47; Lewis, *Clearing the Thickets*, 194–95.

86   4 *Statutes at Large* 290 (May 23, 1828). See also (Easton, Md.) *Republican Star and General Advertiser,* July 8, 1828, 1; *Augusta* (Ga.) *Chronicle and Georgia Advertiser,* July 2, 1828, 314. *See generally*, Thornton, *Politics and Power in a Slave Society*, 107–108.

87   Saunders, *Early Settlers of Alabama,* 96; Ruth Ketring Nuermberger, *The Clays of Alabama: A Planter-Lawyer-Politician Family* (Tuscaloosa: University of Alabama Press, 2005), 27–28; Lewis, *Clearing the Thickets*, 194. See also, *Mobile Commercial Register,* August 23, 1828, 2; Thomas Fearn to John Murphy, July 27, 1828, Governor John Murphy Papers, ADAH; (Huntsville) *Democrat*, July 3, 1829, 2.

88   Saunders, *Early Settlers of Alabama,* 7–10; *Memorial Record of Alabama* (Spartanburg, SC: Reprint Company, 1976), 380–81.

89   Saunders, *Early Settlers of Alabama,* 95–96.

90   Brewer, *Alabama*, 307.

91   Saunders, *Early Settlers of Alabama*, 96.

92   Saunders, *Early Settlers of Alabama*, 96.

93   (Huntsville) *Democrat*, February 3, 1831, 3.

94   Saunders, *Early Settlers of Alabama*, 96.

95   (Huntsville) *Democrat*, August 22, 1828, 3.

96   *Natchez Weekly Democrat*, September 28, 1827, 3; (Raleigh) *North Carolina Star*, August 27, 1824, 1 (publishing letter from William Kelly), March 20, 1828, 3.

97   Watson, *Liberty and Power*, 89.

98   Schoen, *Fragile Fabric of Union*, 134; Freehling, *Prelude to Civil War*, 257; William J. Cooper Jr., *The South and the Politics of Slavery, 1828–1856*, (Baton Rouge: Louisiana State University Press, 1978), 12–49; Lynn H. Parsons, *The Birth of Modern Politics: Andrew Jackson, John Quincy Adams, and the Election of 1828* (New York: Oxford University Press, 2009), 158; Merrill D. Peterson, *Olive Branch and Sword: The Compromise of 1833* (Baton Rouge: Louisiana State University Press, 1982), 14–15; Frederic Bancroft, *Calhoun and the South Carolina Nullification Movement,* (Gloucester, MA: P. Smith, 1966), 38–39, 42–47, 122–24.

99   *Charleston Mercury*, October 30, 1828, reprinted in (Washington) *United States Telegraph*, November 7, 1828, 3; (New York) *Evening Post*, November 13, 1828, 2; *Richmond Enquirer*, November 18, 1828,. 1; (Charleston, SC) *City Gazette and Commercial Advertiser,* December 10, 1828, 2, December 13, 1828, 2; *New York Advertiser*, December 8, 1828, 2; *Portland* (ME) *Advertiser*, January 5, 1830, 4. Nullificationists could point to Virginia's purported annulment of the federal Alien and Sedition laws in 1798 as precedent. See generally, Kevin Raeder Gutzman, *Virginia's American Revolution: From Dominion to Republic, 17761840* (Lanham, MD: Lexington Books, 2007), ix, 298. For discussion

of nullification rhetoric in the South Carolina press during this period, see Erika Jean Pribanic-Smith, "Sowing the Seeds of Disunion: South Carolina's Partisan Newspapers and the Nullification Crisis" (PhD. diss., University of Alabama, 2010).

100 South Carolina Exposition and Protest, Reported by the Special Committee of the House of Representatives, on the Tariff (Columbia, SC: NP, 1829).

101 (Tuscaloosa) *Chronicle*, reprinted in *Augusta Chronicle and Georgia Advertiser*, December 3, 1828, 74.

102 *Alabama Senate Journal* 1828–1829, 6–10; Theodore Henley Jack, "Sectionalism and Party Politics in Alabama 1819–1842" (PhD. Diss., University of Chicago, 1919), 24–26.

103 *Livingston (Ala.) Journal*, July 20, 1867, 2; (Tuscaloosa) *Independent Monitor*, March 25, 1868, 2; (Selma) *Alabama State Sentinel*, June 20, 1867, 2..

104 *Alabama Senate Journal* 1828–1829, 13, 54–55.

105 Manisha Sinha, *Counterrevolution of Slavery: Politics and Ideology in Antebellum South Carolina* (Chapel Hill: University of North Carolina Press, 2000), 26; Schoen, *Fragile Fabric of Union*, 134–35; Peterson, *Olive Branch and Sword*, 16.

106 Saunders, *Early Settlers of Alabama*, 285.

107 *Alabama Senate Journal* 1828–1829, 10–11; Dupre, *Transforming the Cotton Frontier*, 118; (Huntsville) *Democrat*, November 28, 1828, 3.

108 *Alabama Senate Journal* 1828–1829, 16–17.

109 *Alabama Senate Journal* 1828–1829, 58, 90.

110 Nuermberger, *Clays of Alabama*, 28.

111 (Huntsville) *Democrat*, June 26, 1829, 3, *See also*, Nuermberger, *Clays of*

Alabama, 28–29; (Huntsville) *Democrat*, June 26, 1829, 3, July 3, 1829, 2, July 10, 1829, 2, July 18, 1828, 3.

112 *Alabama Senate Journal* 1828–1829, 82–83, 85, 90–92, 103, 105, 108–110, 118–19, 125, 132–35; (Tuscumbia, AL) *Tuscumbian*, February 13, 1826, 2–3; Nuermberger, *Clays of Alabama*, 28–29; Abernethy, *Formative Period in Alabama*, 142; Dupre, *Transforming the Cotton Frontier*, 90–91; McMillan, *Constitutional Development in Alabama*, 47–51. Kelly had previously announced his departure to practice law in New Orleans, and so the extent to which he was actually involved in this proceeding in the Senate is unknown. (Huntsville) *Democrat*, June 20, 1828, p.1.

113 *Alabama Senate Journal* 1828–1829, 136.

114 *Alabama Senate Journal* 1828–1829, 138–89, 193–94; Nuermberger, *Clays of Alabama*, 29.

115 *Alabama Senate Journal* 1828–1829, 194.

116 *Alabama Senate Journal* 1828–1829, 205.

117 *Alabama Senate Journal* 1828–1829, 207 (italics added).

118 *Alabama Senate Journal* 1828–1829, 207.

119 *Alabama Senate Journal* 1828–1829, 218, 221; *Ala. Acts*, Joint Resolutions, 101–102 (January 29, 1829).

120 (Huntsville) *Democrat*, February 6, 1829, 3.

121 (Huntsville) *Southern Advocate*, December 19, 1828, quoted in Dupre, *Transforming the Cotton Frontier*, 121–22.

122 *Ala. Acts*, 3–5 (June 20, 1829); Saunders, *Early Settlers of Alabama*, 97.

123 Wayne Cline, *Alabama Railroads* (Tuscaloosa: University of Alabama Press, 1997), 9–16, 274; Ethel Armes,

The Story of Coal and Iron in Alabama (Tuscaloosa: University of Alabama Press, 2011), 36–39; Lucille Griffith, *Alabama: A Documentary History to 1900* (Tuscaloosa: University of Alabama Press, 1968), 213–14; Owen, *History of Alabama and Dictionary of Alabama Biography*, III: 1339–40.

CHAPTER THREE

1 *Richmond Enquirer*, November 21, 1826,4, November 21, 1826, 4, June 8, 1827, 3; (Salem, MA) *Essex Register*, June 11, 1827, 3; (Easton, MD) *Republican Star and General Advertiser*, June 19, 1827, 2; (Keene) *New Hampshire Sentinel*, July 6, 1827, 1; (Washington) *National Intelligencer*, September 18, 1827, 2; (Haverhill, MA *Essex Gazette*, September 6, 1828, 3; *Baltimore Patriot & Mercantile Advertiser*, October 2, 1828, 2.

2 *Moulton Advertiser*, January 14, 1892, 1; A.S. Byars, "Pioneer Days in Lawrence County," *Old Lawrence Reminiscences* 16 (June, 2002): 52; *Montgomery Advertiser*, April 1, 1917.

3 Cline, *Alabama Railroads*, 10; Dorothy Gentry, *Life and Legend of Lawrence County, Alabama* (Tuscaloosa: Nottingham, 1962), 49; Armes, *Story of Coal and Iron in Alabama*, 37. The story of Hubbard making the trip to Pennsylvania entirely by horseback is inaccurate.

4 Conrad and Meyer, *Economics of Slavery*, 76.

5 (Huntsville) *Democrat*, August 28, 1829, 3, October 2, 1829, 3, October 16, 1829, 3, November 6, 1829, 3, November 13, 1829, 3, November 20, 1829, 3, November 27, 1829, 3.

6 (Huntsville) *Democrat*, October 16, 1829, 3, November 27, 1829, 3.

7 Owen, *History of Alabama and Dictionary of Alabama Biography*, IV: 1547–48; Saunders, *Early Settlers of Alabama*, 234.

8 *Tuscumbia Advertiser*, reprinted in (Huntsville) *Democrat*, July 14, 1831, 3; Saunders, *Early Settlers of Alabama*, 233–34; Cline, *Alabama Railroads*, 10; Leftwich, *Two Hundred Years at Muscle Shoals*, 87.

9 (Huntsville) *Democrat*, December 2, 1830, 2.

10 *Alabama Senate Journal* 1829–1830, 154–55, 170–171; *Alabama House Journal* 1829–1830, 221.

11 *Alabama Senate Journal* 1829–1830, 152; *Ala. Acts* 1829–1830, 46 (January 16, 1830); Tubbs and Tubbs, *Colbert County, Alabama Ancestral Homesteads*, 5, 14–18, 22–27, 34–35; Leftwich, *Two Hundred Years at Muscle Shoals*, 87.

12 *Alabama Senate Journal* 1829–1830, 192–95. Regarding Tindall, see Owen, *History of Alabama and Dictionary of Alabama Biography*, IV: 1673.

13 (Huntsville) *Democrat*, October 9, 1829,4 (publishing the results of the public referendum); *Alabama Senate Journal* 1829–1830, 97, 141–42, 144–45; *Ala. Acts* 1829–1830, Joint Resolution, 78–79. See also, Lewis, *Clearing the Thickets*, 201–202; McMillian, *Constitutional Development in Alabama*, 51.

14 Patterson, "Alabama's First Railroad," 33; Brewer, *Alabama*, 191; Cline, *Alabama Railroads*, 10. Regarding Deshler, see Richard C. Sheridan, *Deshler Female Institute: An Example of Female Education in Alabama, 1874–1918* (Birmingham: Birmingham Printing and Publishing Co., 1986), 10–11 (Deshler grew up not far from Mauch Chunk).

15 (Huntsville) *Democrat*, May 7, 1830, 3; *Alabama Senate Journal* 1830–1831, 11.

16   Malcolm J. Rohrbough, *The Land Office Business: The Settlement and Administration of American Public Lands, 1789–1837* (New York: Oxford University Press, 1968), 222; Leftwich, *Two Hundred Years at Muscle Shoals*, 30–31.

17   Gales & Seaton's *Register of Debates in Congress*, 21st Congress, 1st Session, 15; (Huntsvill) *Democrat*, December 2, 1830, 3.

18   (Huntsvill) *Democrat*, April 23, 1830, 3.

19   *Courtland Herald*, April 9, 1830, reprinted in (Huntsville) *Democrat*, May 14, 1830, 2, and July 15, 1830, 3.

20   (Huntsville) *Democrat*, June 3, 1830, 3. See also, (Huntsville) *Democrat*, June 17, 1830, 3, June 24, 1830, 3.

21   Brown, *John McKinley and the Antebellum Supreme Court*, 20–42; (Huntsville) *Democrat*, December 9, 1830, 2.

22   Brown, *John McKinley and the Antebellum Supreme Court*, 42–71. *See also,* (Huntsville) *Democrat*, June 24, 1830, 3.

23   (Huntsville) *Democrat*, July 8, 1830, 3.

24   Brown, *John McKinley and the Antebellum Supreme Court*, 85; (Huntsville) *Democrat*, June 17, 1830, 3, September 9, 1830, 2, November 11, 1830, 2, December 2, 1830, 2, December 9, 1830, 3.

25   Regarding McKinley's speech, see *Florence Gazette*, reprinted in (Huntsville) *Democrat*, July 15, 1830, 2.

26   (Huntsville) *Democrat*, September 16, 1830, 3, September 30, 1830, 2, October 7, 1830, 2, December 2, 1830, 2. *See also,* (Huntsville) *Southern Advocate*, December 11, 1830, 3.

27   *Florence Gazette*, cited in (Huntsville) *Democrat*, October 14, 1830, 3.

28   *Alabama Senate Journal* 1829–1830, 18.

29   (Huntsville) *Democrat*, December 2, 1830, 2, December 9, 1830, 2–3.

30   Andrew Jackson to John Coffee, December 28, 1830, in John Spencer Bassett, ed., *Correspondence of Andrew Jackson* (New York: Kraus, 1969), IV: 215–16.

31   Thornton, *Politics and Power in a Slave Society*, 18. Compare with William S. Powell, ed., *Dictionary of North Carolina Biography* (Chapel Hill: University of North Carolina Press, 1994), 4: 297 (stating that "Moore went to the Senate with much backing from the Jackson men."); Richard E. Ellis, *Union at Risk: Jacksonian Democracy, States' Rights, and the Nullification Crisis* (New York: Oxford University Press, 1987), 70 (agreeing with Thornton but citing only speculation by Andrew Jackson and his supporters).

32   *Alabama Senate Journal* 1830–1831, 14; (Huntsville) *Democrat*, November 25, 1830, 2.

33   Ellis, *Union at Risk*, 42–43; *Richmond Enquirer*, December 30, 1831, January 10, 1832, 3; (Washington) *National Intelligencer*, December 29, 1831. 3; (Huntsville) *Democrat*, December 2, 1830, 2; *Baltimore Patriot & Mercantile Advertiser*, August 27, 1830, 2 (McKinley opposed nullification).

34   (Huntsville) *Democrat*, December 9, 1830, 3; (Huntsville) *Southern Advocate*, December 11, 1830; Doss, "Rise and Fall of an Alabama Founding Father," 170.

35   *Alabama Senate Journal* 1830–1831, 79–80; (Huntsville) *Democrat*, December 30, 1830, 3.

36   *Tuscaloosa Inquirer*, quoted in *Nashville Republican* and reprinted in *Richmond Enquirer*, January 15, 1831, 2.

37   (Huntsville) *Democrat*, December 23, 1830, 3.

38   (Huntsville) *Democrat*, December 23, 1830, 3; Dupre, *Transforming the Cotton Frontier*, 192–94.

39   (Huntsville) *Democrat*, December 23, 1830, 3; Dupre, *Transforming the Cotton Frontier*, 192–94.

40   *Tuscaloosa Inquirer*, reprinted in (Huntsville) *Democrat*, February 3, 1831, 3.

41   *Alabama Senate Journal* 1830–1831, 6, 26, 120–23, 136–37, 147–48, 151–52, 185–86. Regarding Abercrombie, see Thornton, *Politics and Power in a Slave Society*, 24.

42   (Huntsville) *Democrat*, February 3, 1831, 3.

43   *Moulton Advertiser*, October 7, 1880, 2.

44   John Coffee to Andrew Jackson, December 29, 1830, in Feller, Coens, and Moss, eds., *Papers of Andrew Jackson*, VIII: 722.

45   Andrew Jackson to John Coffee, December 28, 1830, in Feller, eds., *Papers of Andrew Jackson*, VIII: 718.

CHAPTER FOUR

1   (Huntsville) *Democrat*, February 17, 1831, 2.

2   (Huntsville) *Democrat*, February 17, 1831, 2. Ironically, the *Democrat* recanted its claims of wrongdoing a year later. (Huntsville) *Democrat*, February 14, 1833, 3, May 30, 1833, 3.

3   Daniel, "Navigational Development of Muscle Shoals," 256.

4   *Tuscumbia Advertiser*, reprinted in (Huntsville) *Democrat*, July 14, 1831, 3; Leftwich, *Two Hundred Years At Muscle Shoals*, 87–88; Cline, *Alabama Railroads*, 10; Patterson, "Alabama's First Railroad," 33.

5   *Tuscumbia Advertiser*, reprinted in (Huntsville) *Democrat*, July 14, 1831, 31 and (Washington) *United States Telegraph*, July 28, 1831.

6   (Little Rock) *Arkansas Gazette*, August 14, 1833 (the festivities also included an oration by David Ligon).

7   Leftwich, *Two Hundred Years at Muscle Shoals*, 43.

8   *Richmond Enquirer*, November 18, 1831, 3; (Milledgeville) *Georgia Journal*, March 8, 1832, 1.

9   (Huntsville) *Southern Advocate*, August 6, 1831, 3.

10   Conrad and Meyer, *Economics of Slavery*, 76. Speculating in Chickasaw land was still not possible. James R. Atkinson, *Splendid Land, Splendid People: The Chickasaw Indians to Removal* (Tuscaloosa: University of Alabama Press, 2004), 227–28; Anthony F.C. Wallace, *The Long Bitter Trail: Andrew Jackson and the Indians* (New York: Hill and Wang, 1993), 76–77.

11   Specie reserves were dropping rapidly. *Alabama Senate Journal* 1831–1832, 20, 164.

12   Brantley, *Banking in Alabama*, I: 240.

13   (Huntsville) *Democrat*, June 23, 1831, 3.

14   (Huntsville) *Democrat*, May 5, 1831, 3, May 12, 1831, 3, June 23, 1831, 3, June 30, 1831, 3; (Huntsville) *Southern Advocate*, November 19, 1831, 3.

15   (Huntsville) *Democrat*, July 21, 1831, 1, November 3, 1831, 3, November 17, 1831, 3.

16   Hubbard and his committee publicly denied the charge. (Huntsville) *Democrat*, November 10, 1831, 3.

17   (Huntsville) *Democrat*, August 11, 1831, 3, December 1, 1831, 2.

18   (Huntsville) *Southern Advocate*, September 10, 1831, 2; (Huntsville) *Democrat*, October 6, 1831, 3, October 20, 1831, 3; Baptist, *Half Has Never Been Told*, 194–95, 206–11; James J.

Magee, *Freedom of Expression* (Westport, CT: Greenwood Press, 2002), 44–45; Freehling, *Road to Disunion*, I: 178–96; David F. Allmendinger Jr., *Nat Turner and the Rising in Southampton County* (Baltimore: Johns Hopkins University Press, 2014); Louis P. Masur, *1831: Year of Eclipse* (New York: Hill and Wang, 2001), 9–62. A contemplated uprising involving a black preacher in possession of copies of the *Liberator* was reportedly discovered in Claiborne County, Alabama. (Easton, Md.) *Republican Star and General Advertiser*, November 15, 1831, 2.

19   *Alabama Senate Journal* 1831–1832, 51–56. The publication was a pro-abolition pamphlet authored by a New Yorker, Sherlock Gregory of Albany. Ibid., 94, 119. See also, (Huntsville) *Southern Advocate*, September 10, 1831 (warning of the danger). Regarding Alabama's growing slave population, see (Huntsville) *Democrat*, January 13, 1831.

20   Ellis, *Union At Risk*, 63, 66–67, 189–94; Schoen, *Fragile Fabric of Union*, 138–41.

21   *Courtland Herald*, reprinted in (Huntsville) *Democrat*, October 20, 1831, 4; (Huntsville) *Southern Advocate*, October 22, 1831, 3, October 29, 1831, 3; Cline, *Alabama Railroads*, 12; *Alabama Senate Journal* 1831–1832, 14; Patterson, "Alabama's First Railroad," 35.

22   Regarding promotion of an eastbound railroad from Memphis, see (Huntsville) *Southern Advocate*, June 4, 1831, 2, reprinted in *Richmond Enquirer*, June 28, 1831, 2; (Huntsville) *Southern Advocate*, November 12, 1831, 2.

23   (Huntsville) *Democrat*, October 27, 1831, 4.

24   *Courtland Herald*, October 21, 1831, reprinted in (Huntsville) *Democrat*, November 3, 1831, 1; (Huntsville)

Southern Advocate, October 29, 1831, 3.

25   Regarding this eventual shift, see Lewy Dorman, *Party Politics in Alabama From 1850 Through 1860* (Tuscaloosa: University of Alabama Press, 1995), 27.

26   *Alabama Senate Journal* 1831–1832, 46–47 (Gayle's address was read on November 26, 1831), 126–27 (regarding efforts by pro-Jackson senators to have a resolution adopted that declared nullification unconstitutional, and endorsed Jackson).

27   (Huntsville) *Democrat*, November 1, 1831, 3; *Alabama House Journal* 1831–1832, 7, 20.

28   Regarding Baker, see Thornton, *Politics and Power in a Slave Society*, 25, 76; (Tuscaloosa) *Alabama State Intelligencer*, December 24, 1831, reprinted in *Richmond Enquirer*, January 1, 1832, 3.

29   *Alabama House Journal* 1831–1832, 21, 32, 34.

30   (Huntsville) *Southern Advocate*, December 17, 1831, 3, reprinted in *Charleston Courier*, January 4, 1832, 2; (Huntsville) *Democrat*, December 22, 1831, 3; (Huntsville) *Southern Advocate*, December 24, 1831, 2.

31   *Alabama House Journal* 1831–1832, 71.

32   (Tuscaloosa) *Alabama State Intelligencer*, December 24, 1831, reprinted in (Huntsville) *Southern Advocate*, December 31, 1831, 2, and *Richmond Enquirer*, January 10, 1832, 3. See also, (Huntsville) *Democrat*, January 5, 1832, 3.

33   (Huntsville) *Democrat*, January 5, 1832, 3.

34   *Alabama Senate Journal* 1831–1832, 48, 52, 62, 64, 68, 73, 81, 86, 101, 103–104, 110.

35   (Huntsville) *Democrat*, December 22, 1831, 2.

36   *Alabama House Journal* 1831–1832, 137, 143–45, 162, 165.

37   *Alabama House Journal* 1831–1832, 38, 67, 237; *Ala. Acts*, 3–7 (January 21, 1832). Baker's motive might have been sinister. (Huntsville) *Democrat*, May 3, 1832, 3 (Baker had defrauded the Tuscaloosa bank), May 10, 1832, 3, May 17, 1832, 3, (Huntsville) *Democrat*, June 7, 1832, 3, June 14, 1832, 3.

38   *Ala. Const.*, Art. VI, § 1 (1819).

39   *Alabama Senate Journal* 1831–1832, 123, 182–84, 189, 198–200; *Alabama House Journal* 1831–1832, 206, 219–22, 229, 237.

40   (Huntsville) *Southern Advocate*, January 21, 1832, 2–3; (Huntsville) *Democrat*, January 19, 1832, 3; Cooper, *South and the Politics of Slavery*, 20.

41   *Alabama House Journal* 1831–1832, 232–35.

42   (Huntsville) *Southern Advocate*, February 11, 1832, 3, February 18, 1832, 2; (Washington) *National Intelligencer*, February 13, 1832, 3, February 15, 1832, 3; *Richmond Enquirer*, February 16, 1832, 2; (Huntsville) *Democrat*, February 23, 1832, 3.

43   Andrew Jackson to John Coffee, January 21, 1832, and January 27, 1832, in Bassett, ed., *Correspondence of Andrew Jackson*, IV: 401–402; Doss, "Rise and Fall of an Alabama Founding Father," 170–71.

44   *Courtland Herald*, February 17, 1832, reprinted in (Huntsville) *Southern Advocate*, February 25, 1832, 3, and (Huntsville) *Democrat*, February 23, 1832, 3; *Richmond Enquirer*, March 3, 1832, 3; (Milledgeville) *Georgia Journal*, March 8, 1832,; (Portland, ME.) *Eastern Argus*, March 16, 1832, 3.

45   Meetings were conducted in Lauderdale, Franklin, Limestone, Lawrence, Morgan, Madison, Jackson, Shelby, Autauga, and Tuscaloosa counties. (Huntsville) *Democrat*, March 1, 1832, 3, March 8, 1832, 3, March 15, 1832, 3, March 29, 1832, 3, April 5, 1832, 1, April 12, 1832, 3, May 10, 1832, 3, May 17, 1832, 3; (Tuscaloosa) *Alabama State Intelligencer*, reprinted in (Washington) *National Intelligencer*, April 2, 1832, 3; *Albany* (N.Y.) *Argus*, April 6, 1832, 2.

46   (Huntsville) *Democrat*, February 23, 1832, 3.

47   (Huntsville) *Democrat*, February 23, 1832, 3. See also, (Huntsville) *Democrat*, March 1, 1832, 3; *Richmond Enquirer*, March 8, 1832, 2; *Mobile Register*, reprinted in (Washington) *Globe*, March 19, 1832.

48   (Huntsville) *Southern Advocate*, February 25, 1832, 2. See also, Leftwich, *Two Hundred Years at Muscle Shoals*, 89–90; Patterson, "Alabama's First Railroad," 35–36.

49   (Memphis) *Western Times*, reprinted in (Milledgeville) *Georgia Journal*, March 8, 1832, 1.

50   John Bell, a deputy surveyor appointed by Andrew Jackson on March 2, 1833, and working under Coffee, oversaw the survey, which began August 28, 1833. C. Albert White, *A History of the Rectangular Survey System* (Washington, U.S. Government Printing Office, 1983), 94.

51   (Huntsville) *Southern Advocate*, March 31, 1832, 6, April 14, 1832, 3; May 26, 1832, 3; (Huntsville) *Democrat*, May 24, 1832, 3.

52   *Florence Gazette*, reprinted in *Huntsville Advocate*, June 23, 1832, 2, reprinted in Cline, *Alabama Railroads*, 11, and Leftwich, *Two Hundred Years at Muscle Shoals*, 88–89. See also, (Huntsville) *Democrat*, June 7, 1832, 3, June 21, 1832, 3; Patterson, "Alabama's First Railroad," 34.

53 Leftwich, *Two Hundred Years at Muscle Shoals*, 89.

54 Patterson, "Alabama's First Railroad," 36–37; Cline, *Alabama Railroads*, 12; Don Dobravolsky, "The Tuscumbia, Courtland & Decatur Railroad," *Historic Huntsville Quarterly* XXI (Spring, 1995): 13; (Huntsville) *Democrat*, May 24, 1832, 3. For a list of many of the stockholders, see *Anniston Star*, December 17, 1934, 4, 6.

55 (Huntsville) *Southern Advocate*, June 9, 1832, 2–3; (Huntsville) *Democrat*, June 7, 1832, 3, June 14, 1832, 3, June 21, 1832, 3, August 23, 1832, 3, September 20, 1832, 3; (Richmond) *Enquirer*, May 25, 1832, 3, May 29, 1832, 6, June 1, 1832, 4; (Tuscaloosa) *Spirit of the Age*, reprinted in (Poughkeepsie, N.Y.) *Independence*, August 1, 1832, 2.

56 (Huntsville) *Democrat*, January 5, 1832, 3; (Washington.) *National Intelligencer*, July 28, 1834, 3. See generally, Maurice G. Baxter, *Henry Clay and the American System* (Lexington: University Press of Kentucky, 2004).

57 (Huntsville) *Southern Advocate,* November 17, 1832, 3.

58 *Charleston Mercury*, reprinted in *Mobile Commercial Register*, and *Macon* (Ga.) *Weekly Telegraph*, June 2, 1832, 1.

59 (Huntsville) *Southern Advocate,* May 19, 1832, 3, June 9, 1832, 3; (Huntsville) *Democrat*, May 3, 1832, 3, May 17, 1832, 3, June 7, 1832, 3, June 14, 1832, 3; (Montgomery) *Alabama Journal,* reprinted in *Richmond Enquirer*, November 17, 1835, 2 (publishing a letter from Baker). Baker later repaid the money. (Tuscumbia) *North Alabamian*, June 16, 1838, 2.

60 (Huntsville) *Democrat*, June 21, 1832, 3, July 19, 1832,. 1, 3.

61 (Huntsville) *Democrat*, July 19, 1832, 3.

62 (Huntsville) *Democrat*, August 16, 1832, 3, November 1, 1832, 3;(Huntsville) *Southern Advocate*, July 28, 1832, 3; Nuermberger, *Clays of Alabama*, 38; Schoen, *Fragile Fabric of Union*, 141; 4 *Statutes At Large* 583; PribanicSmith, "Sowing the Seeds of Disunion," 124–28; Peterson, *Olive Branch and Sword*, 33–40.

63 (Huntsville) *Democrat*, August 16, 1832, 3, September 6, 1832, 5.

64 (Huntsville) *Democrat*, September 20, 1832, 3, November 8, 1832, 3.

65 (Huntsville) *Democrat*, October 18, 1832, 2.

66 (Huntsville) *Democrat*, November 22, 1832, 5; Schoen, *Fragile Fabric of Union*, 141; Ellis, *Union at Risk*, 74–75.

67 Ellis, *Union at Risk*, 74–75; Peterson, *Olive Branch and Sword*, 40–45.

68 (Huntsville) *Democrat*, January 3, 1833, 3.

69 *Alabama House Journal* 1832–1833, 218–19, 221–22.

70 (Huntsville) *Southern Advocate,* December 29, 1832, 3.

71 *Alabama House Journal*, 1832 Special Session, 9, 19, 21; Patterson, "Alabama's First Railroad," 36; (Huntsville) *Democrat*, November 29, 1832, 3.

72 *Alabama Senate Journal*, 1832 Special Session, 5.

73 *Alabama House Journal*, 1832 Special Session, 32, 36–38, 40, 45–46; *Ala. Acts*, 3 (November 16, 1832); (Huntsville) *Democrat*, November 29, 1832, 2, January 3, 1833, 3; Brantley, *Banking in Alabama*, I: 240, 254–56.

74 (Huntsville) *Democrat*, November 29, 1832, 3. *See also*, (Huntsville) *Southern Advocate,* November 17, 1832, 3, November 24, 1832, 3, December 1, 1832, 2, September 10, 1833, 3, September 17, 1833, 3.

75   (Huntsville) *Southern Advocate,* December 8, 1832, 3.

76   The editor later noticed Decatur's connection with the TC&D but dismissed its significance. (Huntsville) *Democrat,* January 3, 1833, 2. The desire of a business community for "independent bank capital uncontrolled by other cities" was common during this period. See *Macon* (GA) *Telegraph,* January 5, 1837, 3.

77   Patterson, "Alabama's First Railroad," 33, 36; *Alabama House Journal* 1832–1833, 16–19, 118; (Huntsville) *Democrat,* October 27, 1831, 4, November 29, 1832, 3; (Huntsville) *Southern Advocate,* October 27, 1831, 4.

78   (Huntsville) *Democrat,* December 27, 1832, 3. *See also,* (Huntsville) *Democrat,* December 13, 1832, 3, January 3, 1833, 2.

79   (Huntsville) *Democrat,* December 13, 1832, 2; (Huntsville) *Southern Advocate,* December 15, 1832, 3; Schoen, *Fragile Fabric of Union,* 141; Ellis, *Union at Risk,* 75–76; Pribanic-Smith, "Sowing the Seeds of Disunion," 139–42.

80   *Alabama House Journal* 1832–1833, 30; (Huntsville) *Democrat,* January 10, 1833, 3. Ormond was an opponent of nullification. (Huntsville) *Democrat,* January 24, 1833, 3.

81   *Alabama House Journal* 1832–1833, 56–57; (Huntsville) *Southern Advocate, December 8, 1832, 3;* (Washington) *National Intelligencer,* December 21, 1832, 3, December 22, 1832, 3. Jackson won 219 electoral votes and Van Buren 129. (Huntsville) *Democrat,* February 28, 1833, 3.

82   *Proclamation of Andrew Jackson, President of the United States, to the People of South Carolina, December 10, 1832* (Harrisburg, PA: Singerly & Myers, 1864), reprinted in (Huntsville) *Democrat,* December 27, 1832, 3. See

also, (Huntsville) *Southern Advocate,* December 29, 1832, 3.

83   (Huntsville) *Democrat,* January 3, 1833, 3, January 10, 1833, 3.

84   *Ala. Acts,* Resolutions, 139–41 (Jan. 12, 1833). See also, *Tuscaloosa Inquirer,* reprinted in (Huntsville) *Southern Advocate,* January 12, 1833, 3; (Huntsville) *Democrat,* January 10, 1833, 3, January 24, 1833, 2; *Richmond Enquirer,* December 28, 1832, 2; (Providence) *Rhode-Island American and Gazette,* January 29, 1833, ; Schoen, *Fragile Fabric of Union,* 141–42; Ellis, *Union at Risk,* 159.

85   *Alabama House Journal* 1832–1833, 218–19; (Huntsville) *Democrat,* January 10, 1833, 3.

86   *Alabama House Journal* 1832–1833, 222–24.

87   (Huntsville) *Democrat,* March 21, 1833, 2–3; Schoen, *Fragile Fabric of Union,* 142–43; Freehling, *Prelude to Civil War,* 284–85.

88   Saunders, *Early Settlers of Alabama,* 97.

89   *Ala. Acts,* Resolutions, 141–42 (January 12, 1833). See also, (Huntsville) *Democrat,* April 18, 1833, 2; Ellis, *Union at Risk,* 159.

90   (Huntsville) *Democrat,* January 24, 1833, 3, February 21, 1833, 4; (Huntsville) *Southern Advocate,* February 16, 1833, 3.

91   (Huntsville) *Democrat,* February 28, 1833, 3, March 7, 1833, 3; (Huntsville) *Southern Advocate,* March 2, 1833, 2; (Tuscaloosa) *Alabama State Intelligencer,* March 2, 1833, 2–3. See generally, Ellis, *Union at Risk,* 165–77; Freehling, *Prelude to Civil War,* 292–93.

92   (Huntsville) *Democrat,* March 7, 1833, 3.

93   (Montgomery) *Alabama Journal,* quoted in (Huntsville) *Democrat,* March

14, 1833, 3.

94 4 US Statutes at Large 629 and 632; (Huntsville) *Democrat,* March 14, 1833, 3, March 21, 1833, 2–3, March 28, 1833, 3, April 11, 1833, 2; (Huntsville) *Southern Advocate,* April 20, 1833, 3.

95 (Huntsville) *Democrat,* May 30, 1833, 3.

96 Walther, *William Lowndes Yancey and the Coming of the Civil War,* 24–32.

97 *Florence Gazette,* November 2, 1850, 1.

98 *Newport* (R.I.) *Mercury,* February 16, 1833, 3.

99 *Ala. Acts,* 17–18 (December 19, 1832); (Huntsville) *Democrat,* January 10, 1833, 3; James P. Pate, ed., *The Reminiscences of George Strother Gaines: Pioneer and Statesman of Early Alabama and Mississippi, 1805–1843* (Tuscaloosa: University of Alabama Press, 1998), 19.

100 (Huntsville) *Southern Advocate,* March 4, 1834, 3, March 25, 1834, 3, November 11, 1834, 3, November 18, 1834, 3; (Keene) *New Hampshire Sentinel,* January 17, 1833, 3; *Salem* (MA) *Gazette,* October 30, 1832, 2; *New York Courier,* reprinted in *Portsmouth* (NH) *Journal and Rockingham Gazette,* November 24, 1832, 2; Pate, ed., *Reminiscences of George Strother Gaines,* 21.

101 (Huntsville) *Southern Advocate,* December 29, 1832, 3, April 20, 1833, 2–3, May 14, 1833, 3, June 4, 1833, 3, June 18, 1833, 2, August 13, 1833, 3, November 26, 1833, 2.

102 (Huntsville) *Southern Advocate,* June 4, 1833, 3, July 23, 1833, 3.

103 (Huntsville) *Southern Advocate,* July 9, 1833, 2.

104 (Huntsville) *Southern Advocate,* July 30, 1833, 3, September 17, 1833, 4.

105 *Alabama Senate Journal,* 1839–1840, 233–34, 314–14; Brantley, *Banking in Alabama,* I: 23–24, 101–102; Leftwich,

Two Hundred Years at Muscle Shoals, 91; (Huntsville) *Southern Advocate,* August 27, 1833, 3, December 17, 1833, 3. Horton, "Culture, Social Structure, and Political Economy of Antebellum Lawrence County, Alabama," 263.

106 *Moulton Democrat,* August 13, 1858, 1.

107 (Huntsville) *Southern Advocate,* December 3, 1833, 3, December 10, 1833, 2, March 18, 1834, 3.

108 Leftwich, *Two Hundred Years at Muscle Shoals,* 90; Patterson, "Alabama's First Railroad," 36–37; Cline, *Alabama Railroads,* 12–13.

CHAPTER FIVE

1 Atkinson, *Splendid Land Splendid People,* 228–31; Grant Foreman, *Indian Removal: The Emigration of the Five Civilized Tribes of Indians* (Norman: University of Oklahoma Press, 1932), 198–200; Amanda L. Paige, Fuller L. Bumpers, and Daniel F. Littlefield Jr., *Chickasaw Removal* (Ada, OK: Chickasaw Press, 2010), 53.

2 (Huntsville) *Democrat,* April 12, 1832, 3; (Huntsville) *Southern Advocate,* April 21, 1832, 2; John T. Ellisor, *The Second Creek War: Interethnic Conflict and Collusion on a Collapsing Frontier* (Lincoln: University of Nebraska Press, 2010), 47–96; Ronald N. Satz, *American Indian Policy in the Jacksonian Era* (Norman: University of Oklahoma Press, 2002), 105.

3 (Montgomery) *Alabama Journal,* August 10, 1833, reprinted in (Washington) *National Intelligencer,* August 21, 1833, 3; *Columbus* (GA) *Enquirer,* reprinted in (Washington) *National Intelligencer,* August 23, 1833, 3, and *Richmond Enquirer,* August 27, 1833, 4; *Newport* (RI) *Mercury,* September 14, 1833, 2, October 5, 1833, 2; *Salem*

(MA) *Gazette*, October 8, 1833, 3; *Richmond Enquirer*, October 18, 1833, 2, November 8, 1833, 3; (Washington) *National Intelligencer*, October 26, 1833, 2, October 29, 1833 3.

4   (Huntsville) *Southern Advocate*, December 29, 1832, 3, October 1, 1833, 2, October 15, 1833, 1–3, October 22, 1833, 3, October 29, 1833, 2–3, November 5, 1833, 1–2, November 12, 1833, 1–3, November 26, 1833, 2–3, December 3, 1833, 3, December 10, 1833, 3, December 31, 1833, 3, January 28, 1834, 3; (Huntsville) *Democrat*, May 3, 1832, 3; (Washington) *National Intelligencer*, December 17, 1832, 3; *Salem* (MA) *Gazette*, September 4, 1832, 3. See generally, Michael D. Green, "Federal-State Conflict In the Administration of Indian Policy: Georgia, Alabama, and the Creeks, 1824–1834" (PhD diss., University of Iowa, 1973), 273–83.

5   (Huntsville) *Southern Advocate*, November 26, 1833, 3, December 31, 1833, 3; (Washington) *National Intelligencer*, November 11, 1833, 3. See also, Nuermberger, *Clays of Alabama*, 42; Thornton, *Politics and Power in a Slave Society*, 28–30; Green, "Federal-State Conflict In the Administration of Indian Policy," 278–83; Lewis, *Clearing the Thickets*, 204–206; Frank L. Owsley Jr., "Francis Scott Key's Mission to Alabama in 1833," *Alabama Review* XXIII (July, 1970): 181–92; Ellisor, *Second Creek War*, 91–95.

6   Conrad and Meyer, *Economics of Slavery*, 76; Draughon, "Some Aspects of the History of Alabama Bond Issues," 165; Joshua D. Rothman, *Flush Times and Fever Dreams: A Story of Capitalism and Slavery in the Age of Jackson* (Athens: University of Georgia Press, 2012); Rogers, *et al.*, *Alabama*, 136; (Huntsville) *Southern Advocate*, August 20, 1833, 3, September 10, 1833, 3, October

22, 1833, 3, November 12, 1833, 3, November 26, 1833, 2, December 31, 1833, 3.

7   *Richmond Enquirer*, reprinted in (Washington) *National Intelligencer*, November 11, 1833, 3.

8   Proclamation of Andrew Jackson, December 17, 1833, reprinted in *Richmond Enquirer*, December 31, 1833, 4.

9   (Milledgeville) *Georgia Journal*, reprinted in *Baltimore Patriot & Mercantile Advertiser*, February 3, 1834, 2.

10   *Moore v. Hubbard*, 4 Ala. 187 (June Term, 1842).

11   Henry W. Collier to S.W. Mardis, October 24, 1833, reprinted in *Richmond Enquirer*, October 24, 1833, 2.

12   Mary E. Young, "The Creek Frauds: A Study in Conscience and Corruption," *Mississippi Valley Historical Review* 42 (December, 1955): 412–14; Foreman, *Indian Removal*, 129–34; Rogin, *Fathers and Children*, 231–33; Ellisor, *Second Creek War*, 95–101. But accusations of fraud were also likely sometimes inspired by President Jackson's political enemies within the relatively new and growing Whig Party to embarrass his administration before the 1836 presidential election. *New York Advertiser*, April 24, 1835, reprinted in (Hartford) *Connecticut Courant*, April 27, 1835, 2; (Keene) *New Hampshire Sentinel*, May 14, 1835, 2; (Washington,) *National Intelligencer*, June 2, 1835, 3; (Montgomery) *Alabama Journal*, reprinted in *Richmond Enquirer*, June 16, 1835, 2.

13   John James Abert to David Hubbard, November 22, 1834, Papers of David Hubbard, Tennessee State Library and Archives. See also, Young, "Creek Frauds," 423–24; Ellisor, *Second Creek War*, 100–101 (speculators based in Columbus, Georgia, also offered Abert a bribe).

14   *Baltimore Patriot and Mercantile Adver-*
     tiser, June 13, 1834, 3, July 5, 1834, 2;
     Columbus (GA) *Sentinel,* reprinted in
     (Huntsville) *Southern Advocate,* June
     17, 1834, 3.

15   *Huntsville Southern Mercury,* reprinted
     in *Nashville Republican & State Gazette,*
     January 30, 1834, 3; (Huntsville) *South-*
     ern Advocate, April 15, 1834, 2, May 13,
     1834, 3; *Baltimore Patriot & Mercantile*
     Advertiser, June 13, 1834, 3; *American*
     Railroad Journal and Advocate of Internal
     Improvements III (February 22, 1834):
     97.

16   *Nashville Republican & State Gazette,*
     February 4, 1834, 2; (Huntsville)
     Southern Advocate, March 11, 1834,
     3, April 1, 1834, 2, July 22, 1834, 2,
     September 9, 1834, 3, September 23,
     1834, 3; *New Bedford* (MA) *Mercury,*
     October 10, 1834, 1

17   (Huntsville) *Southern Advocate,* June
     24, 1834, 3, August 15, 1834, 1.

18   (Tuscumbia) *North Alabamian,* reprint-
     ed in (Huntsville) *Southern Advocate,*
     August 5, 1834, 1.

19   David Deshler to Editor, August 19,
     1834, *American Railroad Journal and*
     Advocate of Internal Improvements III
     (October 4, 1834), 610; (Huntsville)
     Southern Advocate, November 8, 1836,
     3; Leftwich, *Two Hundred Years at Mus-*
     cle Shoals, 91. The Fulton was designed
     by an English civil engineer, Edward
     Bury, and constructed at his Clarence
     Foundry in Liverpool. P.S. Bury, *Recol-*
     lections of Edward Bury By His Widow
     (Windermere: John Garnett, 1860).
     The TC&D acquired two more engines
     in 1835, and another in 1836. Cline,
     Alabama Railroads, 14–15; (Huntsville)
     Southern Advocate, November 8, 1836,
     3.

20   Paige, *et al., Chickasaw Removal,* 36.

21   Paige, *et al., Chickasaw Removal,* 53–55;

Foreman, *Indian Removal,* 200; Atkinson, *Splendid Land Splendid People,*
230–31; *Florence Gazette,* reprinted in
(Huntsville) *Southern Advocate,* August
5, 1834, 3; (Huntsville) *Southern Advo-*
cate, September 16, 1834, 1 (publishing
the revised treaty).

22   Larry Schweikart, *Banking in the*
     American South From the Age of Jackson to
     Reconstruction (Baton Rouge: Louisiana
     State University Press, 1987), 60; East,
     "Land Speculation in the Chickasaw
     Cession," 7–8, 59; Mary Elizabeth
     Young, *Redskins, Ruffleshirts and Red-*
     necks: Indian Allotments in Alabama
     and Mississippi, 1830–1860 (Norman:
     University of Oklahoma Press, 1961),
     118; Wiggins and Truss, eds., *Journal*
     of Sarah Haynsworth Gayle, 311, 313,
     315; Dennis East, "New York and Mis-
     sissippi Land Company and the Panic
     of 1837," *Journal of Mississippi History*
     33 (November, 1971): 299–331.

23   Paige, *et al., Chickasaw Removal,* 60–61.

24   Report of Banking Commissioners,
     November 8, 1834, reprinted in (Hunts-
     ville) *Southern Advocate,* December 16,
     1834, 1.

25   (Huntsville) *Southern Advocate,* Febru-
     ary 3, 1835, 2.

26   *Decatur Clarion,* November 14, 1834,
     reprinted in (Huntsville) *Southern Ad-*
     vocate, November 18, 1834, 3; (Hunts-
     ville) *Southern Advocate.* November
     25, 1834, 3; (Huntsville) *Democrat,*
     reprinted in *National Banner and*
     Nashville Whig, December 1, 1834, 2;
     Leftwich, *Two Hundred Years at Muscle*
     Shoals, 91–93.

27   *Decatur Clarion,* December 19, 1834,
     reprinted in (Huntsville) *Southern Ad-*
     vocate, December 30, 1834, 3, *National*
     Banner and Nashville Whig, January 5,
     1835, 2, and *Richmond Enquirer,* Janu-
     ary 22, 1835, 1.

28   (Huntsville) *Southern Advocate,* January 20, 1835, 3, February 10, 1835, 1.

29   *Ala. Acts,* No. 44, 43 (January 9, 1836); *Selma Free Press,* January 16, 1836, 2, February 6, 1836, 3.

30   Isham Harrison to Thomas Harrison, October 14, 1834, James Harrison Papers, Southern Historical Collection, University of North Carolina, Chapel Hill; Thomas Dorsey to J. Beiller, April 15, 1835, Alonzo Snyder Papers, Lower Louisiana and Mississippi Valley Collections, Louisiana State University, Baton Rouge.

31   (Decatur, AL) *Morgan Observer,* reprinted in (Huntsville) *Democrat,* November 10, 1838, 3.

32   East, "New York and Mississippi Land Company," 303–304.

33   David Hubbard to J.D. Beers and Co., March 7, 1835, March 25, 1835, Papers of the New York and Mississippi Land Company, State Historical Society of Wisconsin (hereinafter "NYMLC Papers"); East, "Land Speculation in the Chickasaw Cession," 8, 59; Young, *Redskins, Ruffleshirts and Rednecks,* 118–41; Sven Beckert, *Empire of Cotton: A Global History* (New York: Vintage Books, 2014), 107; *Delafield v. Anderson,* 15 Miss. 630 (1846).

34   East, "Land Speculation in the Chickasaw Cession," 11–25, 37.

35   *Niles v. Anderson,* 6 Miss. 365 (1841).

36   East, "Land Speculation in the Chickasaw Cession," 44–50, 58. This was a commonly used tactic. Don H. Doyle, *Faulkner's County: The Historical Roots of Yoknapatawpha* (Chapel Hill: University of North Carolina Press, 2001), 62–63.

37   (Tuscaloosa) *Alabama Intelligencer and State Rights Expositor,* August 22, 1835, 3.

38   *Portsmouth* (NH) *& Great Falls Journal of Literature & Politics,* April 29, 1837, 2.

39   (Washington) *National Intelligencer,* February 13, 1835, 3; *Newport* (RI) *Mercury,* May 2, 1835, 2; (Macon) *Georgia Weekly Telegraph,* May 21, 1835, 2; *Richmond Whig,* June 12, 1835, 2; (Huntsville) *Southern Advocate,* June 30, 1835, 2.

40   *National Banner and Nashville Whig,* June 1, 1835, 2; Joel H. Silbey, *Storm Over Texas: The Annexation Controversy and the Road to Civil War* (New York: Oxford University Press, 2005), 6–25.

41   Baptist, *Half Has Never Been Told,* 266–67.

42   (Huntsville) *Southern Advocate,* June 30, 1835, 2, August 11, 1835, 3, October 6, 1835, 3, October 27, 1835, 2; (Tuscaloosa) *Alabama Intelligencer and State Rights Expositor,* July 25, 1835, 2, August 29, 1835, 3, September 19, 1835, 2–3.

43   (Tuscaloosa) *Alabama Intelligencer and State Rights Expositor,* November 7, 1835, 1, November 14, 1835, 3; (Montgomery) *Alabama Journal,* reprinted in *Richmond Enquirer,* November 17, 1835, 2.

44   Regarding the Red Rovers, see Gary Brown, *Hesitant Martyr in the Texas Revolution: James Walker Fannin* (Plano: Republic of Texas Press, 2000), 133–37; William Kennedy, *Texas: The Rise, Progress, and Prospects of the Republic of Texas* (London: R. Hastings, 1841), II: 165–67, 215–16; William H. Jenkins, "The Red Rovers of Alabama," *Alabama Review* 18 (April, 1965): 106–12; James E. Harris, "Remember Goliad!" *Alabama Heritage* 5 (Summer, 1987): 2–19.

45   Claude Elliott, "Alabama and the Texas Revolution," *Southwestern Historical Quarterly* L (January, 1947): 315–28.

46   (Huntsville) *Southern Advocate,*

November 3, 1835, 3 (publishing Houston's appeal for volunteers). See also, Haley, *Sam Houston*, 87–110; *National Banner and Nashville Whig*, April 18, 1836, 2 (regarding the authorization for bounty land grants); (Tuscumbia) *North Alabamian*, June 23, 1837, 3.

47   Some charged that the Texas independence movement was a ploy by land speculators. (Amherst, N.H.) *Farmers' Cabinet*, May 6, 1836, 2.

48   East, "Land Speculation in the Chickasaw Cession," 44–50.

49   East, "Land Speculation in the Chickasaw Cession," 59.

50   (Huntsville) *Southern Advocate*, February 23, 1836, 3–4.

51   (Huntsville) *Southern Advocate*, May 3, 1836, 3, May 24, 1836, 3, May 31, 1836, 3, June 7, 1836, 3; *Richmond Enquirer*, May 20, 1836, 3; Ellisor, *Second Creek War*, 180–226; Christopher D. Haveman, *Rivers of Sand; Creek Indian Emigration, Relocation, and Ethic Cleansing in the American South* (Lincoln: University of Nebraska Press, 2016), 180.

52   *Natchez Courier*, reprinted in (Huntsville) *Southern Advocate*, March 22, 1836, 3.

53   (Huntsville) *Southern Advocate*, April 5, 1836, 2, April 12, 1836, 3, April 19, 1836, 3, April 26, 1836, 2–3, May 3, 1836, 3, May 10, 1836, 3, May 17, 1836, 3, May 31, 1836, 2, July 19, 1836, 3, July 26, 1836, 3.

54   (Huntsville) *Southern Advocate*, May 10, 1836, 3.

55   David Hubbard to Lewis Curtis, April 29, 1836, Papers of the New York and Mississippi Land Company, State Historical Society of Wisconsin.

56   (Huntsville) *Southern Advocate*, May 17, 1836, 3. See also, (Huntsville) *Southern*

Advocate, May 24, 1836, 3, May 31, 1836, 2.

57   (Huntsville) *Southern Advocate*, May 24, 1836, 3.

58   (Huntsville) *Southern Advocate*, September 6, 1836, 3, October 18, 1836, 2, October 25, 1836, 3, January 17, 1837, 3, January 24, 1837, 3, February 28, 1837, 3; (Huntsville) *Democrat*, September 22, 1838, 3, September 22, 1838, 3.

59   (Huntsville) *Southern Advocate*, May 3, 1836, 3, August 23, 1836, 3, August 30, 1836, 3, October 14, 1836, 3; (Tuscumbia) *North Alabamian*, July 14, 1837, 2; (Huntsville) *Democrat*, December 8, 1838, 3.

60   Portsmouth (NH) *Journal of Literature & Politics*, June 25, 1836, 2.

61   (Huntsville) *Advocate*, June 21, 1836, 3; Baptist, *Half Has Never Been Told*, 267–268.

62   (Huntsville) *Southern Advocate*, July 26, 1836, 2.

63   (Huntsville) *Southern Advocate*, July 5, 1836, 3, September 6, 1836, 2; *National Banner and Nashville Whig*, June 17, 1836, 2; *Richmond Enquirer*, September 6, 1836, 2.

64   *Savannah Georgian*, April 2, 1837, reprinted in *Pittsfield* (MA) *Sun*, April 13, 1837, 3; (Huntsville) *Southern Advocate*, February 7, 1837, 2, February 14, 1837, 3, February 28, 1837, 1; *Mobile Commercial Register and Patriot*, March 20, 1837, 2; (Tuscumbia) *North Alabamian*, February 24, 1837, 2.

65   James Silver, "Land Speculation Profits in the Chickasaw Cession," *Journal of Southern History* 10 (February, 1944): 84–92.

CHAPTER SIX

1   *New York Commercial Advertiser*,

reprinted in *Richmond Whig*, July 22, 1836, 4, July 27, 1836; *Albany* (NY) *Advertiser*, reprinted in *Richmond Whig*, July 27, 1836, 1; (Washington) *National Intelligencer*, July 28, 1836, 3; (Keene) *New Hampshire Sentinel*, August 25, 1836, 3. Regarding the text of the specie circular, which was issued on July 11, 1836, see (Huntsville) *Southern Advocate*, July 26, 1836, 3. See generally, Watson, *Liberty and Power*, 136–38, 140–50, 163–64, 174.

2   (Huntsville) *Southern Advocate*, July 26, 1836, 3; (Concord) *New Hampshire Patriot and State Gazette*, July 25, 1836, 2; Baptist, *Half Has Never Been Told*, 272.

3   *New York Commercial Advertiser*, reprinted in *Richmond Whig*, July 22, 1836, 4; *Richmond Whig*, July 29, 1836, 2.

4   *New York Transcript*, reprinted in (Concord) *New Hampshire Patriot and State Gazette*, August 22, 1836, 2; *New York Journal of Commerce*, August 6, 1836, reprinted in (Huntsville) *Southern Advocate*, August 30, 1836, 3.

5   *Boston Atlas*, cited in *Richmond Whig*, July 29, 1836, 1; (Washington) *Globe*, reprinted in *Richmond Enquirer*, August 26, 1836, 1.

6   (Washington) *Globe*, reprinted in *Richmond Enquirer*, August 26, 1836, 1.

7   Jessica M. Lepler, *The Many Panics of 1837: People, Politics, and the Creation of a Transatlantic Financial Crisis* (New York: Cambridge University Press, 2013), 37–41; Baptist, *Half Has Never Been Told*, 272–74.

8   David Hubbard to John Bolton, January 11, 1836, NYMLC Papers, State Historical Society of Wisconsin; Lepler, *Many Panics of 1837*, 67. See also, (Keene) *New Hampshire*, August 25, 1836, 3; *Richmond Enquirer*, August 26,

1836, 1; (Washington) *National Intelligencer*, November 7, 1836, 2; *Ithaca* (NY) *Herald*, December 21, 1836, 2.

9   Henry Watson to Father, December 15, 1836. Henry Watson Papers, David M. Rubenstein Rare Book & Manuscript Library, Duke University.

10   (London) *Times*, April 4, 1836, 5, April 25, 1836, 5, May 7, 1836, 2, May 9, 1836, 2, May 10, 1836, 5, May 16, 1836, 5, May 17, 1836, 3, May 20, 1836, 3, May 21, 1836, 5; (London) *Times*, reprinted in (London) *Standard*, August 1, 1836, 1; Lepler, *Many Panics of 1837*, 53.

11   Sellers, *Market Revolution*, 353–55; Lepler, *Many Panics of 1837*, 54; Jay Sexton, *Debtor Diplomacy: Finance and American Foreign Relations in the Civil War Era 1837–1873* (Oxford: Oxford University Press, 2005), 22–25; Andreas Andreades, *History of the Bank of England: 1640 to 1903* (New York: A.M. Kelley, 1966), 264–66; Peter Temin, *The Jacksonian Economy* (New York: W.W. Norton, 1969), 113–47, 172–77; Edward J. Balleisen, *Navigating Failure: Bankruptcy and Commercial Society in Antebellum America* (Chapel Hill: University of North Carolina Press, 2001), 22–24; Reginald Charles McGrane, *The Panic of 1837: Some Financial Problems of the Jacksonian Era* (Chicago: University of Chicago Press, 1965), 145–76; Baptist, *Half Has Never Been Told*, 272–73; (Huntsville) *Southern Advocate*, October 25, 1836, 2; (Washington) *National Intelligencer*, September 30, 1836, 3, October 12, 1836, 3, October 15, 1836, 3, November 7, 1836, 2; *Richmond Enquirer*, October 14, 1836, 2, October 21, 1836, 4.

12   *Coopwood v. Bolton*, 26 Miss. 212 (1853); *Delafield v. Anderson*, 15 Miss. 630 (1846); (Pontotoc) *Chickasaw*

Union, reprinted in *Richmond Enquirer*, November 8, 1836, 2, and (Huntsville) *Southern Advocate*, November 1, 1836, 3; East, "Land Speculation in the Chickasaw Cession," 66–69; Young, *Redskins, Ruffleshirts and Rednecks*, 141–42.

13   (Huntsville) *Southern Advocate*, October 25, 1836, 2.

14   (Pontotoc) *Chickasaw Union*, November 2, 1836, reprinted in *Richmond Enquirer*, November 25, 1836, 2.

15   (Washington) *National Intelligencer*, September 8, 1836, 3, September 12, 1836, 3.

16   (Tuscumbia) *North Alabamian*, October 7, 1836, reprinted in (Huntsville) *Southern Advocate*, October 14, 1836, 3, *Richmond Enquirer*, November 1, 1836, 2, and (Salisbury, NC) *Carolina Watchman*, October 29, 1836, 1.

17   *Worchester* (MA) *Palladium*, reprinted in *Richmond Enquirer*, November 8, 1836, 2.

18   (Little Rock) *Arkansas Times*, reprinted in (Washington) *National Intelligencer*, October 17, 1836, 3; (Hartford) *Connecticut Courant*, October 22, 1836, 2.

19   (Pontotoc) *Chickasaw Union*, reprinted in (Huntsville) *Southern Advocate*, November 1, 1836, 3, reprinted in *Richmond Enquirer*, November 8, 1836, 2 and (Washington) *Globe*, November 9, 1836. See also, (Pontotoc) *Chickasaw Union*, reprinted in *Macon Georgia Telegraph*, December 1, 1836, 2.

20   (Pontotoc) *Chickasaw Union*, November 2, 1836, reprinted in *Richmond Enquirer*, November 25, 1836, 2.

21   David Hubbard to Lewis Curtis, November 24, 1836, NYMLC Papers. See also, East, "Land Speculation in the Chickasaw Cession," 69; Young, *Redskins, Ruffleshirts and Rednecks*, 142.

22   East, "Land Speculation in the Chickasaw Cession," 83; (Washington) *Globe*, March 20, 1837; (Tuscumbia) *North Alabamians*, April 7, 1837, 2–3, April 14, 1837, 2. Regarding the collapse, see Lepler, *Many Panics of 1837*, 95–112.

23   H.P. Watson to A.B. Springs, January 24, 1836, Springs Family Papers, Southern Historical Collection, University of North Carolina, Chapel Hill.

24   David Hubbard to Washington Miller, March 13, 1837, L.K. Miller Accession, Washington Daniel Miller Papers, Archives and Information Services Division, Texas State Library and Archives Commission.

25   (New Orleans) *True American*, March 22, 1837, reprinted in *Richmond Enquirer*, April 4, 1837, 2.

26   (Tuscumbia) *North Alabamian*, December 16, 1836, 2 (Van Buren won Alabama); (Huntsville) *Southern Advocate*, February 7, 1837, 3, February 28, 1837, 2; Donald B. Cole, *Martin Van Buren and the American Political System* (Princeton, NJ: Princeton University Press, 1984), 275–84; Sellers, *Market Revolution*, 351.

27   (Washington) *National Intelligencer*, April 28, 1837, 3; (Tuscumbia) *North Alabamian*, July 7, 1837, 1.

28   (Tuscaloosa) *Alabama State Intelligencer*, reprinted in (Huntsville) *Southern Advocate*, January 31, 1837, 3; (New Orleans) *Picayune*, March 7, 1837, 2, March 8, 1837, 2, March 26, 1837, 2, April 1, 1837, 2, April 5, 1837, 2, April 6, 1837, 2.

29   Richard Bolton to Lewis Curtis, April 14, 1837, Papers of the NYMLC, State Historical Society of Wisconsin.

30   *Macon* (GA) *Telegraph*, April 27, 1837, 3.

31   Conrad and Meyer, *Economics of Slavery*, 76.

32   *Augusta* (GA) *Chronicle*, January 24, 1840, 2.

33   (Huntsville) *Democrat*, January 26, 1839, 1; (Huntsville) *Southern Advocate*, November 8, 1836, 3 (listing the TC&D's expenditures); *Anniston Star*, December 17, 1934, 6; *New Decatur Advertiser*, December 23, 1915, 1.

34   *Richmond Enquirer*, April 21, 1837, 3.

35   (Tuscumbia) *North Alabamian*, May 19, 1837, 2.

36   *Mobile Commercial Register and Patriot*, March 27, 1838, 2; (New Orleans) *Picayune*, May 13, 1837, 2, May 14, 1837, 2; (Tuscaloosa) *Flag of the Union*, May 17, 1837, 2; (Tuscumbia) *North Alabamian*, May 19, 1837, 2, May 26, 1837, 2.

37   (Tuscumbia) *North Alabamian*, May 19, 1837, 2, May 26, 1837, 2.

38   *Richmond Enquirer*, June 30, 1837, 3.

39   *Macon* (GA) *Telegraph*, May 16, 1837, 3; (Tuscumbia) *North Alabamian*, May 19, 1837, 2.

40   *Macon* (GA) *Telegraph*, May 16, 1837, 3; Edward Kaplan, *Bank of The United States and the American Economy* (Westport, CT: Greenwood Press, 1999), 156.

41   (Tuscumbia) *North Alabamian*, December 16, 1836, 2.

42   *Macon* (GA) *Telegraph*, May 16, 1837, 3.

43   *Portsmouth* (NH) *& Great-Falls Journal of Literature & Politics*, April 1, 1837. See also, *Richmond Enquirer*, May 26, 1837, 2; *Little Rock* (AR) *Times*, reprinted in (Tuscumbia) *North Alabamian*, October 6, 1837, 3.

44   (Washington) *National Intelligencer*, February 18, 1840, 3.

45   (Huntsville) *Democrat*, June 8, 1839; Lepler, *Many Panics of 1837*, 137; Baptist, *Half Has Never Been Told*, 288.

46   (Tuscumbia) *North Alabamian*, September 15, 1837, 2.

47   (New Orleans) *Picayune*, April 1, 1836, 2, April 14, 1837, 2, May 12, 1837, 2, May 13, 1837, 2, May 20, 1837, 2, May 25, 1837, 2, June 18, 1837, 2; (Cahawba) *Southern Democrat*, quoted in (Tuscaloosa) *Flag of the Union*, March 7, 1838, 2; (Tuscaloosa) *Flag of the Union*, November 6, 1839, 1; *Mobile Commercial Register and Patriot*, April 6, 1838, 2, June 28, 1841, 2.

48   (Tuscaloosa) *Flag of the Union*, May 17, 1837, 3 (publishing a May 6, 1837 letter to Clay); (New York) *Herald*, May 1, 1837; Thornton, *Politics and Power in a Slave Society*, 78–79.

49   (New Orleans) *Picayune*, April 14, 1837, 2.

50   (New Orleans) *Picayune*, April 13, 1837, 2. *See also,* (New Orleans) *Picayune*, April 15, 1837, 2, April 18, 1837, 2; Lepler, *Many Panics of 1837*, 150.

51   (New Orleans) *Picayune*, May 14, 1837, 2. *See also,* Thornton, *Politics and Power in a Slave Society*, 3538, 48, 78–79.

52   (Tuscumbia) *North Alabamian*, April 14, 1837, 2. *See also,* (Tuscumbia) *North Alabamian*, May 19, 1837, 2.

53   (Tuscaloosa) *Flag of the Union*, May 17, 1837, 2; (Tuscumbia) *North Alabamian*, May 26, 1837, 2.

54   *Macon* (GA) *Telegraph*, June 20, 1837, 3. See also, (Tuscumbia) *North Alabamian*, May 26, 1837, 2.

55   *Portsmouth* (NH) *& Great-Falls Journal of Literature & Politics*, June 24, 1837, 2.

56   *Delafield v. Anderson*, 15 Miss. 630 (1846); *Coopwood v. Bolton*, 26 Miss. 212 (1853).

57   *Richmond Enquirer*, July 21, 1837, 2.

58   *Ala. Acts*, No. 16, 9–15 (June 30, 1837); (Tuscumbia) *North Alabamian*, July 7, 1837, 2; (Huntsville) *Democrat*,

November 17, 1838, 3.

59   (Huntsville) *Democrat*, January 28, 1843, 3; *Mobile Register and Journal*, May 10, 1845, 2, May 14, 1845, 2, May 15, 1845, 2, May 16, 1845, 2; (Tuscumbia) *North Alabamian*, July 4, 1845, 2, July 11, 1845, 2, December 25, 1845, 2.

60   (Tuscaloosa) *Independent Monitor*, January 15, 1841, 3; *Mobile Commercial Register and Patriot*, January 20, 1841, 2, July 28, 1841, 2; (Tuscumbia) *North Alabamian*, July 4, 1845, 2.

61   *Augusta* (GA) *Chronicle*, February 12, 1840, 2; (Huntsville) *Democrat*, reprinted in (Tuscaloosa) *Flag of the Union*, July 21, 1841, 3; (Tuscumbia) *North Alabamian*, July 4, 1845, 2; *Mobile Register and Journal*, December 25, 1845, 2. *See also*, Brantley, *Banking in Alabama* II: 216, 236.

62   (Tuscaloosa) *Flag of the Union*, June 21, 1837, 2 (The seat was open because of the resignation of John McKinley, whom President Van Buren had appointed to the United States Supreme Court.) (Tuscumbia) *North Alabamian*, July 7, 1837, 2.

63   *See also*, (Tuscaloosa) *Flag of the Union*, June 14, 1837, 3 (reporting that Arthur Francis Hopkins resigned from the Alabama Supreme Court and John James Ormond was elected to replace him).

64   *Selma Free Press*, January 13, 1838, 3; *New York Times*, March 30, 1837, reprinted in *Richmond Enquirer*, April 4, 1837, 2.

65   Regarding emigrating Native Americans during this period, see (Tuscumbia) *North Alabamian*, December 16, 1836, 2, March 17, 1837, 2, July 14, 1837, 2, November 10, 1837, 3; *Pittsfield* (MA) *Sun*, August 3, 1837, 2; *Little Rock* (AR) *State Gazette*, reprinted in *Ithaca* (NY) *Herald*, August 30, 1837, 3, June 16, 1838, 2; (Washington) *National Intelligencer*, September 22, 1837, 3, December 28, 1837, 3; *Newport* (RI) *Mercury*, December 2, 1837, 2, July 20, 1838, 2; (Huntsville) *Democrat*, August 25, 1838, 3, November 17, 1838, 3.

66   Steve Inskeep, *Jacksonland: President Andrew Jackson, Cherokee Chief John Ross, and a Great American Land Grab* (New York: Penguin Press, 2015), 312–13, 323, 335, 342–43.

67   *Ala. Acts*, No. 16, §§ 1, 26 (June 30, 1837); (Tuscumbia) *North Alabamian*, July 7, 1837, 3 (publishing this law); *Mobile Advertiser*, reprinted in *Richmond Enquirer*, July 21, 1837, 2; (Huntsville) *Democrat*, December 1, 1838, 3; *Bates v. Bank of the State of Alabama*, 2 Ala. 451 (1841); *Sale v. Branch Bank of Decatur*, 1 Ala. 425 (1840).

68   (Tuscumbia) *North Alabamian*, July 7, 1837, 1; (Washington) *National Intelligencer*, May 18, 1838, 3; Michael Holt, *Rise and Fall of the American Whig Party: Jacksonian Politics and the Onset of the Civil War* (New York: Oxford University Press, 1999), 60–69. See generally, Robert V. Remini, *Andrew Jackson and the Bank War: A Study in the Growth of Presidential Power* (New York: W.W. Norton, 1967); Kaplan, *Bank of the United States and the American Economy*, 124–25; Robert V. Remini, *Daniel Webster: The Man and His Time* (New York: W.W. Norton, 1997), 471–73.

69   *New York Express*, reprinted in (Keene) *New Hampshire Sentinel*, December 12, 1838, 2; Baptist, *Half Has Never Been Told*, 231–32.

70   John Niven, *John C. Calhoun and the Price of Union: A Biography* (Baton Rouge: Louisiana State University Press, 1988), 227–32; Clyde N. Wilson, ed., *The Papers of John Calhoun* (Columbia: University of South Carolina Press,

1980), XIII: 557–58, 560–63, 574–81, 586–87, 592–616; Holt, *Rise and Fall of the American Whig Party*, 65; Irving H. Bartlett, *John C. Calhoun: A Biography* (New York: W.W. Norton, 1993), 236–39; Peterson, *Great Triumvirate*, 271; Sellers, *Market Revolution*, 356–57.

71   Irving H. Bartlett, *John C. Calhoun: A Biography* (New York: W.W. Norton, 1993), 236, 239–40; (Huntsville) *Democrat*, September 22, 1838, 3, October 6, 1838, 2–3. Many Alabama politicians shared Calhoun's concerns. *Montgomery Advertiser*, reprinted in *Macon* (GA) *Telegraph*, July 30, 1838, 3.

72   *Richmond Enquirer*, October 6, 1837, 3; Sellers, *Market Revolution*, 357.

73   (Pontotoc) *Chickasaw Union*, reprinted in *Macon* (GA) *Telegraph*, November 13, 1837, 2.

74   *Charleston Mercury*, reprinted in (Huntsville) *Democrat*, July 14, 1838, 3; H. Roger Grant, *The Louisville Cincinnati & Charleston Rail Road: Dreams of Linking North and South* (Bloomington: Indiana University Press, 2014), 44–57, 83–85; Niven, *John C. Calhoun and the Price of Union*, 216; Peterson, *Great Triumvirate*, 262–64.

75   *Sherrod v. Rhodes*, 5 Ala. 683 (1843).

76   David Hubbard to John Bolton, October 16, 1837 and David Hubbard to Lewis Curtis, February 2, 1838, February 24, 1838, NYMLC Papers, State Historical Society of Wisconsin. See also, East, "Land Speculation in the Chickasaw Cession," 88–89.

77   David Hubbard to Washington Miller, December 17, 1837, February 12, 1838, L.K. Miller Accession, Washington Daniel Miller Papers, Archives and Information Services Division, Texas State Library and Archives Commission. The auction sales in Pontotoc were

scheduled to begin on January 8, 1838. *Richmond Enquirer*, October 24, 1837, 4 (publishing President Van Buren's proclamation).

78   *Newport* (R.I.) *Mercury*, February 17, 1838, 2; Remini, *Daniel Webster*, 474–76.

79   Wilson, ed., *Papers of John Calhoun*, XIV: 11–15, 22–23. See also, Remini, *Daniel Webster*, 474–76; William Lee Miller, *Arguing About Slavery: The Great Battle in the United States Congress* (New York: Vintage, 1996), 277–83.

80   It was common for Southerners to vacation in the North in the summertime after the spring planting season was completed. (Concord) *New Hampshire and State Gazette*, August 27, 1838, 1.

81   David Hubbard to Dixon H. Lewis, April 21, 1838, April 26, 1838, May 14, 1838, Papers of Dixon Hall Lewis, Special Collections Library, Clemson University, Clemson, South Carolina.

82   D.H. Lewis to David Hubbard, April 12 and 14, 1838, David Hubbard Papers, Tennessee State Library and Archives.

83   David Hubbard to Dixon H. Lewis, April 21, 1838, Papers of Dixon Hall Lewis, Special Collections Library, Clemson University. See generally, Remini, *Daniel Webster*, 97–99, 108, 114, 122–23, 127–31. Sergeant was Clay's running mate in the 1832 presidential election.

84   David Hubbard to Dixon H. Lewis, May 14, 1838, Papers of Dixon Hall Lewis, Special Collections Library, Clemson University.

85   (Huntsville) *Democrat*, December 22, 1838, 3; Lepler, *Many Panics of 1837*, 159; Baptist, *Half Has Never Been Told*, 229, 277.

86   David Hubbard to Nicholas Biddle, (N.D.), Papers of Nicholas Biddle, Library of Congress, Washington;

Nicholas Biddle to David Hubbard, August 29, 1841, Papers of David Hubbard, Tennessee State Library and Archives, Nashville, Tennessee. See also, Young, *Redskins, Ruffleshirts and Rednecks*, 143; East, "New York and Mississippi Land Company and the Panic of 1837," 322; East, "Land Speculation in the Chickasaw Cession," 89.

87   David Hubbard to Dixon H. Lewis, April 21, 1838, Papers of Dixon Hall Lewis, Special Collections Library, Clemson University. See also, David Hubbard to Dixon H. Lewis, April 26, 1838, Papers of Dixon Hall Lewis.

88   David Hubbard to Dixon H. Lewis, April 26, 1838, Papers of Dixon Hall Lewis, Special Collections Library, Clemson University.

89   (Huntsville) *Democrat*, December 22, 1838, 3.

90   (Huntsville) *Democrat*, November 24, 1838, 2, January 5, 1839, 3.

91   J.C. Calhoun to David Hubbard, June 15, 1838, Wilson, ed., *Papers of John C. Calhoun*, XIV: 344–45.

CHAPTER SEVEN

1   (Belfast, ME) *Waldo Patriot*, July 13, 1838, 3; (Huntsville) *Democrat*, September 8, 1838, 3.

2   (Huntsville) *Democrat*, September 8, 1838, 3, December 29, 1838, 3, January 19, 1839, 2, March 23, 1839, 3; (Huntsville) *Southern Advocate*, March 28, 1839, 2.

3   (Huntsville) *Democrat*, March 23, 1839, 3.

4   (Huntsville) *Democrat*, December 8, 1838, 2, January 19, 1839, 3, January 26, 1839, 1, April 6, 1839, 3. See also, *Pittsfield* (MA) *Sun*, April 25, 1839, 3, (New Orleans) *Times Picayune*, October

27, 1839, 2; *Tuscumbia, Courtland and Decatur Rail Road Co. v. Rhodes*, 8 Ala. 206 (1845) (insolvency).

5   (Huntsville) *Democrat*, July 27, 1839, 2.

6   (Huntsville) *Democrat*, March 23, 1839, 3.

7   Ibid.

8   Ibid.; (Huntsville) *Democrat*, July 27, 1839, 2; (New Orleans) *Picayune*, August 22, 1839, 2. Regarding the term "Locofocoism," see Sellers, *Market Revolution*, 352.

9   *Decatur(AL) Register*, quoted in *Jacksonville* (AL) *Republican*, reprinted in (Huntsville) *Democrat*, June 8, 1839, 2.

10   Saunders, *Early Settlers of Alabama*, 221–22; (Tuscumbia) *North Alabamian*, July 7, 1837, 1, August 11, 1837, 2, August 25, 1837, 2, July 4, 1845, 21; James Benson Sellers, *The Prohibition Movement in Alabama*, 1702 to 1943 (Chapel Hill: University of North Carolina Press, 1943), 22.

11   (Tuscumbia) *North Alabamian*, July 7, 1837, 1.

12   (Huntsville) *Democrat*, May 25, 1839, 3; *Vicksburgh Sentinel*, May 11, 1839; (Amherst, NH) *Farmer's Cabinet*, July 5, 1839, 3. See also, (Huntsville) *Democrat*, June 8, 1839, 2.

13   (Huntsville) *Democrat*, June 15, 1839, 3; Sellers, *Market Revolution*, 355, 358; Baptist, *Half Has Never Been Told*, 277.

14   *Athens* (AL) *Republican*, reprinted in (Huntsville) *Democrat*, July 27, 1839, 2.

15   David Hubbard to Martin Van Buren, November 20, 1837, Papers of Martin Van Buren, Library of Congress.

16   (Huntsville) *Democrat*, July 27, 1839, 2.

17   John C. Calhoun to Andrew Pickens Calhoun, May, 1840, in Wilson, ed.,

Papers of John C. Calhoun, XV: 194–95.

18   *Huntsville Democrat*, July 27, 1849, 2.

19   Saunders, *Early Settlers of Alabama*, 222.

20   (Huntsville) *Democrat*, August 10, 1839, 3, August 17, 1839, 3; *Moulton* (AL) *Banner and Lawrence Enquirer*, August 21, 1839, 2; (Washington) *National Intelligencer*, August 21, 1839, 3; (New Orleans) *Times Picayune*, August 22, 1839, 2.

21   (Newport) *Rhode Island Republicans*, August 28, 1839, 2.

22   *Mobile Advertiser*, October 8, 1839, reprinted in (Washington) *National Intelligencer*, October 17, 1839, 3.

23   (Tuscaloosa) *Flag of the Union*, November 7, 1840, 2. See generally, Reinhard O. Johnson, *The Liberty Party, 1840–1848: Antislavery Third-Party Politics in the United States* (Baton Rouge: Louisiana State University Press, 2009).

24   Harvey M. Watterson to James K. Polk, November 29, 1839, in Wayne Cutler, ed., *Correspondence of James K. Polk* (Nashville: Vanderbilt University Press, 1979), V: 319.

25   Cave Johnson to James K. Polk, November 28, 1839, in Cutler, ed., *Correspondence of James K. Polk*, V:317.

26   Peterson, *Great Triumvirate*, 453.

27   Cave Johnson to James K. Polk, November 28, 1839, in Cutler, ed., *Correspondence of James K. Polk*, V: 316–17. The other Southerners were Cave Johnson, Aaron Brown, and Harvey Watterson, all of Tennessee.

28   (New York) *Journal of Commerce*, reprinted in *New Bedford* (MA) *Mercury*, November 28, 1839, 1; Sellers, *Market Revolution*, 360.

29   *Congressional Globe*, 26th Cong., 1st Session, 252–56. See also, Jeffery A. Jenkins and Charles Haines Stewart, *Fighting For the Speakership: The House*

and the Rise of Party Government (Princeton, NJ: Princeton University Press, 2012), 115–26, Cave Johnson to James K. Polk, December 16, 1839, in Cutler, ed., *Correspondence of James K. Polk*, V: 343–44.

30   *Congressional Globe*, 26th Cong., 1st Session, 88; (Tuscaloosa) *Flag of the Union*, January 22, 1840, 3.

31   (Tuscaloosa) *Flag of the Union*, December 18, 1839, 3; *Wetumpka Argus*, March 25, 1840, 3. See also, Holt, *Rise and Fall of the American Whig Party*, 100–105; Baptist, *Half Has Never Been Told*, 278.

32   (Tuscaloosa) *Flag of the Union*, January 1, 1840, 1, June 17, 1840, 2, September 23, 1840, 1.

33   *Selma Reporter*, October 3, 1839, 1.

34   *Wetumpka Argus*, March 25, 1840, 3.

35   (Tuscaloosa) *Flag of the Union*, February 19, 1840, 1; *Richmond Whig*, February 4, 1840, 4; Miller, *Arguing About Slavery*, 360–72.

36   (Huntsville) *Democrat*, August 24, 1839, 3, August 31, 1839, 3, September 7, 1839, 3, October 3, 1839, 2; (Tuscaloosa) *Flag of the Union*, May 22, 1839, 3, September 11, 1839, 2, September 25, 1839, 2, October 2, 1839, 2, October 9, 1839, 2; (Nashville) *Republican Banner*, September 27, 1839, 2; *Moulton* (AL) *Banner and Lawrence Enquirer*, August 21, 1839, 3; Saunders, *Early Settlers of Alabama*, 12–13.

37   James K. Polk to David Hubbard, February 7, 1840, in Cutler, ed., *Correspondence of James K. Polk*, V: 386389.

38   James K. Polk to David Hubbard, February 7, 1840, in Cutler, ed., *Correspondence of James K. Polk*, V: 386–87.

39   David Hubbard to James K. Polk, February 23, 1840, Cutter, ed., *Correspondence of James K. Polk*, V: 392–93.

40   Cooper, *South and the Politics of Slavery*,

86, 130–32.

41 *Congressional Globe*, 26th Cong., 1st Session, 181, 255.

42 See, e.g., (New Orleans) *Picayune*, February 7, 1839, 2 (regarding an incident in Tuscaloosa County); *Augusta* (GA) *Chronicle*, March 19, 1840, 1 (regarding another incident in Tuscaloosa County).

43 Dupre, *Transforming the Cotton Frontier*, 64.

44 Robert Carson to John Forsyth, August 30, 1839, John Forsyth Papers, David M. Rubenstein Rare Books and Manuscripts Library, Duke University, Durham, North Carolina.

45 *Newport* (R.I.) *Mercury*, April 11, 1840, 2 (referring to proceedings on April 6).

46 The Senate adopted the bill on June 25, but it was tabled in the House on July 7 over the objection of David Hubbard and the rest of the Alabama delegation. *Congressional Globe*, 26th Cong., 1st Session, 512.

47 (Mobile) *Banner of Reform*, August 10, 1840, 1.

48 ( ) *Globe*, May 3, 1840, reprinted in (Tuscumbia) *North Alabamian*, May 9, 1840, 1. See also, Brantley, *Banking in Alabama*, II: 118–19.

49 Pierce B. Anderson to James K. Polk, May 6, 1840, in Cutler, ed., *Correspondence of James K. Polk*, V: 439; *Proceedings of the National Democratic Convention, held in Baltimore, on the 5th of May, 1840* (Baltimore: Office of Blair & Rives, 1840); (Keene) *New Hampshire Sentinel*, May 13, 1840, 3; (Tuscaloosa) *Flag of the Union*, May 27, 1840, 2; (Concord) *New Hampshire Patriot and State Gazette*, May 18, 1840, 1; (Washington) *National Intelligencer*, May 11, 1840, 3; (Raleigh) *North Carolina Standard*, May 13, 1840, 3; Sellers, *Market Revolution*, 361; Cooper, *South and the Politics of Slavery*, 132.

50 David Hubbard to James K. Polk, May 7, 1840, in Cutler, ed., *Correspondence of James K. Polk*, V: 441.

51 (Baltimore) *Pilot and Transcript*, May 21, 1840, 2, May 28, 1840, 2; *Richmond Whig*, May 22, 1840, 1; (Washington) *National Intelligencer*, June 2, 1840, 3; (Nashville) *Republican Banner*, June 13, 1840, 2.

52 *Remarks of Mr. Hubbard of Alabama in the House of Representatives, May 24, 1840: On the bill granting pre-emption rights to settlers on the public lands* (S.I.: s.n., 1840), in Hoole Special Collections Library, University of Alabama, Tuscaloosa, Alabama.

53 *Congressional Globe*, 26th Cong., 1st Session, 420–21.

54 *Congressional Globe*, 26th Cong., 1st Session, 490; *Richmond Whig*, July 3, 1840, 1.

55 5 U.S. Statutes at Large 385–92; (Washington) *National Intelligencer*, July 11, 1840, 3.

56 *Charleston Courier*, July 20, 1840, reprinted in *Edgefield* (SC) *Advertiser*, August 6, 1840, 2; (Concord) *New Hampshire Patriot and State Gazette*, August 10, 1840, 3; (Baltimore.) *Pilot and Transcript*, July 29, 1840, 2; *Burlington* (VT) *Free Press*, August 7, 1840, 2; *Camden* (SC) *Journal*, August 1, 1840, 3; (Raleigh) *North Carolina Standard*, August 5, 1840, 3, August 12, 1840, 4; (Stroundsburg, PA) *Jeffersonian Republican*, August 7, 1840, 2. The wreck of the *North Carolina* was not identified until 1996. Among the artifacts discovered were a number of gold coins. *Marex Intern.m, Inc. v. Unidentified, Wrecked and Abandoned Vellel*, 952 F. Supp. 825 (S.D. Ga., 1997).

57 Thornton, *Politics and Power in a Slave Society*, 93.

58 (Tuscaloosa) *Flag of the Union*, October

28, 1840, 3; *Mobile Commercial Register and Patriot*, November 4, 1840, 2.

59   (Tuscaloosa) *Independent Monitor*, November 13, 1840, 2; *Mobile Commercial Register and Patriot*, November 17, 1840, 2; (Tuscaloosa) *Flag of the Union*, November 18, 1840, 2, February 3, 1841, 1; *Florence Enquirer*, November 28, 1840, 3; David I. Durham, *A Southern Moderate in Radical Times: Henry Washington Hilliard, 1808–1892* (Baton Rouge: Louisiana State University Press, 1997), 63, note 48;

CHAPTER EIGHT

1   *Congressional Globe*, 26th Cong., 2nd Session, 16; Peterson, *Great Triumvirate*, 297–301, 304–308.

2   *Congressional Globe*, 26th Congress, 2nd Session, 134; *New York Herald*, reprinted in *Portsmouth* (NH) *Journal of Literature and Politics*, February 6, 1841, 3.

3   *Richmond Whig*, March 16, 1841, 1; *New York Herald*, reprinted in *Pittsfield* (MA) *Sun*, March 18, 1841, 3.

4   David Hubbard to George S. Houston, February 24, 1841, George S. Houston, Paper, David M. Rubenstein Rare Books and Manuscripts Library, Duke University, Durham, North Carolina.

5   *Ibid.*

6   1860 Federal Census, Lawrence County, Alabama, 65.

7   Conrad and Meyers, *Economics of Slavery*, 76.

8   (Tuscaloosa) *Flag of the Union*, December 23, 1840, 2, December 30, 1840, 1, January 27, 1841, 1, 3. David Hubbard's name had also been mentioned as a possible candidate for governor. *Florence Enquirer*, November 28, 1840, 3.

9   (Tuscaloosa) *Flag of the Union*, June 30, 1841, 2. See also, Thornton, *Politics and Power in a Slave Society*, 49; Lewis,

Clearing the Thickets, 220–21.

10   Nuermberger, *Clays of Alabama*, 91.

11   (Tuscaloosa) *Flag of the Union*, January 27, 1841, 3; Brantley, *Banking in Alabama*, II: 217.

12   *Alabama Senate Journal* 1839–1840, 233–34, 314–15. See also, Thornton, *Power and Politics in a Slave Society*, 107.

13   *Mobile Journal of Commerce*, reprinted in *Selma Free Press*, reprinted in *Macon* (GA) *Telegraph*, December 15, 1840, 3; *Mobile Commercial Register and Patriot*, January 20, 1841, 2; (Tuscaloosa) *Flag of the Union*, January 20, 1841, 1; (Concord) *New Hampshire Patriot and State Gazette*, April 9, 1841, 2; Thornton, *Politics and Power in a Slave Society*, 49.

14   (Huntsville) *Democrat*, November 19, 1842, 2.

15   David Hubbard to George S. Houston, February 24, 1841, George S. Houston Papers, David M. Rubenstein Rare Books and Manuscripts Library, Duke University, Durham, North Carolina. See also, Thornton, *Politics and Power in a Slave Society*, 54.

16   David Hubbard to George S. Houston, February 24, 1841, George S. Houston Papers.

17   Owen, *History of Alabama and Dictionary of Alabama Biography*, III: 848, 1831; (Tuscaloosa) *Flag of the Union*, April 28, 1841, 3; (Huntsville) *Democrat*, June 1, 1843, 3.

18   (Tuscaloosa) *Flag of the Union*, March 3, 1841, 3, March 31, 1841, 2, April 28, 1841, 3; Durham, *Southern Moderate in Radical Times*, 66–67.

19   (Russellville, AL) *Franklin Democrat*, reprinted in (Tuscaloosa) *Flag of the Union*, April 28, 1841, 2. See also, *Florence Gazette*, July 21, 1849, 2.

20   Ibid. See also, *Mobile Commercial Register and Patriot*, April 22, 1841, 2.

21 (Washington) *Globe*, reprinted in (Tuscaloosa) *Flag of the Union*, April 28, 1841, 2. See generally, Edward P. Crapol, *John Tyler: The Accidental President* (Chapel Hill: University of North Carolina Press, 2006); Peterson, *Great Triumvirate*, 301–302.

22 (Tuscaloosa) *Flag of the Union*, June 2, 1841, 2.

23 Waters and Waters, *Cemetery Records of Lawrence County*, 149.

24 (Nashville) *American*, December 27, 1876, 4; Thomas Hubbard Estate File, Morgan County Orphans Court, Morgan County, Alabama.

25 5 U.S. Statutes At Large 439 (August 13, 1841); Peterson, *Great Trumvirate*, 305.

26 5 U.S. Statutes At Large 440 (August 19, 1841); (Tuscaloosa) *Flag of the Union*, September 1, 1841, 3, September 8, 1841, 2.

27 (Tuscaloosa) *Flag of the Union*, August 18, 1841, 3, October 13, 1841, 3; Thornton, *Politics and Power in a Slave Society*, 38, 49; Nuermberger, *Clays of Alabama*, 89.

28 License to practice law issued May 1, 1841, in David Hubbard Papers, Tennessee State Library and Archives.

29 (Tuscaloosa) *Flag of the Union*, August 25, 1841; Peterson, *Great Triumvirate*, 308.

30 David Hubbard to James K. Polk, September 17, 1841, in Cutler, ed., *Correspondence of James K. Polk*, V: 758.

31 David Hubbard to John Calhoun, October 14, 1841, in Wilson, ed., *Papers of John C. Calhoun*, XV: 793–94.

32 *Alabama House Journal*, 1840–1841, 67–73; (Tuscaloosa) *Independent Monitor*, November 17, 1841; (Tuscaloosa) *Flag of the Union*, November 24, 1841, 2; (New Orleans) *Picayune*, November 21, 1841, 2.

33 (Tuscumbia) *North Alabamian*, reprinted in *Cleveland Herald*, December 3, 1841, and (Nashville) *Republican Banner*, November 24, 1841, 2; *Wetumpka Argus*, November 24, 1841, 4.

34 Nuermberger, *Clays of Alabama*, 64; *Wetumpka Argus*, December 1, 1841, 2; (Tuscaloosa) *Flag of the Union*, November 24, 1841, 3, December 1, 1841, 2, December 8, 1841, 3.

35 (Tuscaloosa) *Flag of the Union*, August 18, 1841, 3, September 15, 1841, 3, October 13, 1841, 3.

36 (New York) *Tribune*, reprinted in (Ossining, NY) *Hudson River Chronicle*, January 4, 1842, 3. See also, (New Orleans) *Jeffersonian*, May 30, 1842, 92.

37 (Tuscaloosa) *Flag of the Union*, December 1, 1841, 3. See also, (Tuscaloosa) *Flag of the Union*, January 5, 1842, 1, February 9, 1842, 1.

38 (Tuscaloosa) *Flag of the Union*, December 8, 1841, 3. See also, (Huntsville) *Democrat*, October 1, 1842, 3, October 29, 1842, 2.

39 (Washington) *National Intelligencer*, January 17, 1842, 4.

40 (Tuscaloosa) *Flag of the Union*, December 29, 1841, 3.

41 *Augusta* (GA) *Chronicle*, June 30, 1842, 2.

42 (Tuscaloosa) *Flag of the Union*, May 18, 1842, 3.

43 Ibid; ; (New Orleans) *Jeffersonian*, May 30, 1842, 92; (Huntsville) *Democrat*, June 11, 1842, 2, July 9, 1842, 2, August 6, 1842, 3; *Florence Enquirer*, reprinted in (Huntsville) *Democrat*, July 2, 1842, 4.

44 (Pontotoc, MS) *Spirit of the Times*, April 30, 1842, 2.

45 *DeJarnett v. Haynes*, 23 Miss. 600 (1852).

46   (Huntsville) *Democrat*, March 4, 1843, 2.

47   (Huntsville) *Democrat*, June 11, 1842, 2.

48   (Huntsville) *Democrat*, August 20, 1842, 4. See also, (Huntsville) *Democrat*, January 28, 1843, 3.

49   (Huntsville) *Democrat*, November 19, 1842, 2.

50   (Huntsville) *Democrat*, November 19, 1842, 2.

51   (Huntsville) *Democrat*, October 15, 1842, 3.

52   (Huntsville) *Democrat*, August 6, 1842, 3; *Wetumpka Argus*, August 17, 1842, 2; Saunders, *Early Settlers of Alabama*, 97.

53   (Huntsville) *Democrat*, October 15, 1842, 3.

54   (Huntsville) *Democrat*, November 19, 1842, 2.

55   Ibid.

56   Ibid.; *New York Herald*, December 1, 1842.

57   Ibid.

58   Peterson, *Great Triumvirate*, 252.

59   William Garrett, *Reminiscences of Public Men in Alabama for Thirty Years* (Atlanta: Plantation Publishing Co. Press, 1872), 297.

60   David Hubbard to James K. Polk, September 17, 1841, in Cutler, ed., *Correspondence of James K. Polk*, V: 758–59.

61   (Huntsville) *Democrat*, November 26, 1842, 2.

62   Garrett, *Reminiscences of Public Men in Alabama*, 297. See also, Robert Royal Russel, "Economic Aspects of Southern Sectionalization, 1840–1861" (PhD. diss., University of Illinois, 1922), 90 and note 74.

63   *Alabama House Journal* 1842–1843, 3, 92; (Tuscaloosa) *Flag of the Union*, reprinted in (Huntsville) *Democrat*, December 17, 1842, 3; (Huntsville) *Democrat*, December 24, 1842, 3, December 31, 1842, 3.

64   *Alabama House Journal* 1842–1843, 93–94; (Huntsville) *Democrat*, December 10, 1842, 2, December 31, 1842, 3.

65   *Alabama House Journal* 1842–1843, 139, 145, 156, 160, 184; *Wetumpka Argus*, January 18, 1843, 2.

66   *Ala. Acts* No. 53, 53–56 (January 21, 1843) (Decatur), No. 37, 37–40 (January 25, 1843) (Montgomery), No. 49, 47–50 (February 4, 1843) (Huntsville); (Huntsville) *Democrat*, December 17, 1842, 3 (Mobile); Nuermberger, *Clays of Alabama*, 91–92. See also, (Huntsville) *Democrat*, January 21, 1843, 3, January 28, 1843, 3, February 4, 1843, 3.

67   (Huntsville) *Democrat*, January 28, 1843, 3.

68   (Huntsville) *Democrat*, December 17, 1842, 3, January 28, 1843, 3.

69   *Ala. Acts*, No. 1, 3–9 (February 13, 1843); (Huntsville) *Democrat*, February 25, 1843, 2. See also, Grady McWhiney, Warner O. Moore Jr., and Robert F. Pace, eds., "*Fear God and Walk Humbly*": *The Agricultural Journal of James Mallory, 1843–1877* (Tuscaloosa: University of Alabama Press, 1997), 3, 492 n. 3.

70   (Huntsville) *Democrat*, March 4, 1843, 2.

71   (Huntsville) *Democrat*, January 28, 1843, 3.

72   (New Orleans) *Times Picayune*, January 12, 1843, 2; (Philadelphia) *Pennsylvania Inquirer and National Gazette*, January 23, 1843; *Alabama House Journal* 1842–1843, 176.

73   *Ala. Acts*, No. 47, 45–46 (February 13, 1843); *Alabama House Journal* 1842–1843, 164, 375, 396–398; (Huntsville) *Democrat*, February 18, 1843, 3; *Richmond Whig*, March 10, 1843, 1, June 6,

1843, 4; Garrett, *Reminiscences of Public Men*, 191, 246–50; Nuermberger, *Clays of Alabama*, 90–91; Dorman, *Party Politics in Alabama from 1850 Through 1860*, 96; Saunders, *Early Settlers of Alabama*, 97; Carlton L. Jackson, "The White Basis System and the Decline of Alabama Whiggery," *Alabama Historical Quarterly* 25 (fall and winter 1963): 246–53; McWhiney, *et al.*, eds. *"Fear God and Walk Humbly*," 3.

74   Stephen F. Miller, *Heads of the Alabama Legislature at the Session of 1842–3* (Tuscaloosa: M.D.J. Slade, 1843), 57–59.

75   (Huntsville) *Democrat*, February 11, 1843, 3.

76   (Huntsville) *Democrat*, March 14, 1843, 2.

77   *Moulton* (AL) *Flag*, reprinted in (Huntsville) *Democrat*, April 8, 1843, 3.

78   (Washington) *National Intelligencer*, May 2, 1843, 3; (New Orleans) *Picayune*, May 12, 1843, 2; (Huntsville) *Democrat*, May 25, 1843, 2.

79   *Mobile Advertiser*, reprinted in *Richmond Whig*, June 6, 1843, 4.

CHAPTER NINE

1   (Huntsville) *Democrat*, May 4, 1843, 3.

2   *Mobile Register*, quoted in (Concord) *New Hampshire Patriot and State Gazette*, May 4, 1843, 2; (Huntsville) *Democrat*, September 28, 1843, 3, October 19, 1843, 4. Cotton was selling for 7.5 cents a pound in 1843. Conrad and Meyer, *Economics of Slavery*, 76.

3   *Wetumpka Argus*, August 22, 1843, 2.

4   (Huntsville) *Democrat*, December 7, 1843, 2; *Mobile Register and Journal*, December 6, 1843, 2.

5   David Hubbard to D.J. Goodlett, *et al.*, November 20, 1843, reprinted in

(Huntsville) *Democrat*, December 7, 1843, 2.

6   (Huntsville) *Democrat*, December 14, 1843, 2–3.

7   *Mobile Register and Journal*, December 6, 1843, 2.

8   (Huntsville) *Democrat*, December 7, 1843, 2.

9   (Huntsville) *Democrat*, December 14, 1843, 3; *Macon* (GA) *Telegraph*, December 26, 1843, 2; (Washington) *National Intelligencer*, December 28, 1843, 3; *Richmond Whig*, January 2, 1844, 1.

10   (Washington) *National Intelligencer*, reprinted in (Huntsville) *Democrat*, July 31, 1844, 2.

11   *Selma Free Press*, May 23, 1840, 3; Joan M. Hartwell, "Margaret Lea of Alabama: Mrs. Sam Houston," *Alabama Review* 17 (October, 1964): 271–79.

12   William W. Freehling, *The Road to Disunion: Secessionists at Bay 1776–1854* (New York: Oxford University Press, 1990), 364–68; Silbey, *Storm Over Texas*, 8–17.

13   Washington Miller to John Tyler, January 30, 1843 and September 16, 1843, L.K. Miller Accession, Washington Daniel Miller Papers, Archives and Information Services Division, Texas State Library and Archives Commission. See also, Friend, *Sam Houston*, 122–23; Sibley, *Storm Over Texas*, 17, 36.

14   *Mobile Tribune*, reprinted in (Huntsville) *Democrat*, November 9, 1843, 3; *Columbia Tennessee Democrat*, reprinted in (Huntsville) *Democrat*, November 16, 1843, 2. See also, (New York) *Journal of Commerce*, reprinted in (Huntsville) *Democrat*, December 7, 1843, 2.

15   *Alabama House Journal* 1843–1844, 26, 141; (Huntsville) *Democrats*, December 14, 1843, 2.

16   *Alabama House Journal* 1843–1844, 30.

17   *Alabama House Journal* 1843–1844, 57.

18   Andrew Johnson to David T. Patterson, February 27, 1844, in Leroy P. Graf and Ralph W. Haskins, eds., *The Papers of Andrew Johnson* (Knoxville: University of Tennessee Press, 1967), I: 154.

19   *Alabama House Journal* 1843–1844, 238.

20   *Ala. Acts*, Joint Resolutions, 196 (January 17, 1844).

21   This legislature adjourned on January 17, 1844. *Alabama House Journal* 1843–1844, 202; (Huntsville) *Democrat*, January 25, 1844, 3.

22   *Richmond Whig*, March 26, 1844, 1; (Washington) *National Intelligencer*, April 12, 1844, 1; *Mobile Register and Journal*, March 16, 1844, 2, March 28, 1844, 2, April 11, 1844, 2; Andrew Johnson to David T. Patterson, February 27, 1844, in Graf and Haskins, eds., *Papers of Andrew Johnson*, I: 154–55.

23   (New Orleans) *Picayune*, April 13, 1844, 2.

24   William L. Barney, *The Secessionist Impulse: Alabama and Mississippi in 1860* (Tuscaloosa: University of Alabama Press, 2004), 138–39 (quoting a speech by Clement Clay).

25   Crapol, *John Tyler*, 205; Freehling, *Road to Disunion*, 418–23.

26   (Tuscaloosa) *Independent Monitor*, October 30, 1840, 3.

27   Friend, *Sam Houston*, 126–27; Crapol, *John Tyler*, 190–91, 194–207; Robert W. Merry, *A Country of Vast Designs: James K. Polk, the Mexican War, and the Conquest of the American Continent* (New York: Simon & Schuster, 2009), 67, 71–73; Sibley, *Storm Over Texas*, 30–32.

28   *Mobile Register and Journal*, March 16, 1844, 2, March 28, 1844, 2 and April 11, 1844, 2; Friend, *Sam Houston*, 126–27.

29   Friend, *Sam Houston*, 129–30, 135; James L. Haley, *Passionate Nation: The Epic History of Texas* (New York: Free Press, 2006), 243–48.

30   Friend, *Sam Houston*, 137; (Huntsville) *Southern Advocate*, April 26, 1844, 3; (Huntsville) *Democrats*, May 15, 1844, 1 (publishing a copy of the treaty); Crapol, *John Tyler*, 207–13; Silbey, *Storm Over Texas*, 38–46.

31   See, e.g., *Boston Courier*, reprinted in (Washington) *National Intelligencer*, April 23, 1844, 2; Silbey, *Storm Over Texas*, 52–63.

32   Martin Van Buren to William H. Hammett, April 20, 1844, Martin Van Buren Papers, Library of Congress; Arthur M. Schlesinger Jr., ed., *History of American Presidential Elections, 1789–1968* (New York: Chelsea House, 1971), 1: 822. See also, Joel H. Silbey, *Martin Van Buren and the Emergence of American Popular Politics* (Lanham, MD: Roman & Littlefield Publishers, 2002), 172–78; Cole, *Martin Van Buren and the American Political System*, 390–94.

33   David Hubbard to Fellow Citizens, reprinted in *Florence Gazette*, July 21, 1849, 2.

34   Henry Clay to the editors, (Washington) *National Intelligencer*, April 17, 1844; Melba Porter Hay, ed., *The Papers of Henry Clay* (Lexington: University Press of Kentucky, 1991), 10: 41–46; (Huntsville) *Democrat*, May 22, 1844, 2. See also, Justin H. Smith, *The Annexation of Texas* (New York: MacMillan Co., 1911), 239–42; David S. Heidler and Jeanne T. Heidler, *Henry Clay: The Essential American* (New York: Random House, 2010), 381–87.

35   James K. Polk to Salmon P. Chase, April 23, 1844, in Cutler, ed., *Correspondence of James K. Polk*, VII: 99; (Huntsville)

Democrat, May 15, 1844, 4; (Huntsville) *Southern Advocate,* May 29, 1844, 4; Merry, *Country of Vast Designs,* 75–96; Cole, *Martin Van Buren,* 394–98; Silbey, *Storm Over Texas,* 68–72.

36 *Mobile Register and Journal,* June 17, 1844, 2; Avery Craven, *The Coming of the Civil War* (Chicago: University of Chicago Press, 1942), 195, 199; Silbey, *Storm Over Texas,* 46–55.

37 The resolution was adopted by the Methodists on June 1, 1844, and the treaty was rejected by the Senate on June 8. (Huntsville) *Democrat,* June 19, 1844, 2, July 31, 1844, 2, September 25, 1844, 3, October 2, 1844, 3, May 14, 1845, 3.

38 *Macon* (GA) *Telegraph,* June 4, 1844, 2. See also, *Mobile Register and Journal,* reprinted in (New Orleans) *Picayune,* June 6, 1844, 2 (publishing portions of a letter from Lewis). King had accepted appointment as ambassador to France, and Lewis's brother-in-law, Governor Benjamin Fitzpatrick, appointed Lewis to replace King.

39 (Huntsville) *Democrat,* June 19, 1844, 3. See also, (Huntsville) *Southern Advocate,* August 22, 1844, 2 (referring to another speech by Hubbard in Moulton on July 29 favoring the annexation of Texas or disunion), August 2, 1844, 2; (Huntsville) *Democrat,* July 10, 1844, 3 (referring to defections); (Columbus) *Weekly Ohio Statesman,* July 17, 1844 (same).

40 *Richmond Whig,* July 30, 1844, 1, August 6, 1844, 2, August 20, 1844, (Washington) *National Intelligencer,* August 3, 1844, 3; (Pittsfield, MA) *Berkshire County Whig,* August 29, 1844, 4; (Huntsville) *Southern Advocate,* July 5, 1844, 3, September 11, 1844, 3; (Washington) *Niles Register,* LXVI, 405; (Huntsville) Democrat, July 17, 1844,

2, September 11, 1844, 3, September 25, 1844, 3. See also, Page Smith, *A People's History of the Antebellum Years: The Nation Comes of Age* (New York, McGraw-Hill, 1981) IV: 204–205. Newspaper comments regarding this very controversial and widely reported resolution indicate that David Hubbard was present but do not identify the militia members who offered this resolution other than to say that it was a mixture of Whigs and Democrats. Given his future course, one of the likely suspects is Leroy Pope Walker, who then held the rank of brigadier general. (Huntsville) *Southern Advocate,* September 11, 1844, 3, (Huntsville) *Democrat,* September 25, 1844, 3; Garrett, *Reminiscences of Public Men in Alabama,* 507. See generally, *Moulton* (AL) *Democrat,* November 14, 1856, 2 (apparently referring to this meeting, and stating that Walker and Hubbard were present).

41 (Huntsville) *Democrat,* July 24, 1844, 3; *Mobile Register and Journal,* July 24, 1844, 2; (Tuscumbia) *North Alabamian,* July 26, 1844, 2.

42 (Huntsville) *Democrat,* July 24, 1844, 4; (Tuscaloosa) *Independent Monitor,* August 28, 1844, 2; *Mobile Register and Journal,* quoted in (Columbus) *Weekly Ohio Statesman,* July 17, 1844;

43 (Tuscumbia) *North Alabamian,* July 19, 1844, 2; (Huntsville) *Democrat,* July 17, 1844, 3; *Mobile Register and Journal,* July 22, 1844, 2; Nuermberger, *Clays of Alabama,* 117. Alabama Democrats made good use of these defections. Peters's decision and those of like-minded Alabama Whigs were published in Democrat organs throughout the state and as far away as New York. The *Mobile Register and Journal* reprinted an editorial from the *Franklin Democrat* announcing that "Thomas M. Peters, Esq. of Lawrence County, a talented

lawyer, the most influential Whig in the county, and appointed one of the Whig sub-electors for this district, has determined to support Polk and Dallas because Clay's policy is not the true policy of this Union." *Brooklyn Eagle,* July 17, 1844, p.2; *Mobile Register and Journal,* July 22, 1844, 2. See also, (Huntsville) *Democrat,* July 17, 1844, 3; *Montgomery Advertiser,* quoted in *Greenville* (SC) *Mountaineer,* July 26, 1844; (Columbus) *Weekly Ohio Statesman,* July 17, 1844.

44   (Tuscumbia) *North Alabamian,* reprinted in (Huntsville) *Southern Advocate,* August 2, 1844, 2, July 23, 1844, 2, *Mobile Advertiser,* July 23, 1844, 2, (Washington) *National Intelligencer,* August 3, 1844, and *Richmond Whig,* August 6, 1844, 2, August 20, 1844, 4.

45   *Augusta* (GA) *Chronicle,* reprinted in (Washington) *National Intelligencer,* August 3, 1844, 3, and *Richmond Whig,* August 6, 1844, 2. See also, *Richmond Whig,* August 9, 1844, 1 (indicating this editorial was read during a "Clay Club" meeting in Richmond), August 23, 1844, 4; (Washington) *National Intelligencer,* August 15, 1844, 2.

46   *Pittsfield* (MA) *Sun,* September 5, 1844, 2.

47   (Huntsville) *Democrat,* August 14, 1844, 3.

48   *Mobile Register and Journal,* August 12, 1844, 2, August 14, 1844, 2, August 21, 1844, 2; (Macon) *Georgia Telegraph,* August 20, 1844, 2; *Brooklyn Eagle,* August 14, 1844; Walther, *William Lowndes Yancey and the Coming of the Civil War,* 30–32, 57, 70–73.

49   See, e.g., (Huntsville) *Democrat,* January 22, 1845, 3.

50   Walther, *William Lowndes Yancey and the Coming of the Civil War,* 26–49.

51   Walther, *William Lowndes Yancey and*

the Coming of the Civil War, 30, 226–27. Newspaper editor John Witherspoon DuBose, an admirer of Yancey, wrote the first biography, which was published in 1892,

52   David Hubbard to John Calhoun, August 22, 1844, in Meriwether, et al., eds., *Papers of John Calhoun,* XIX: 627–28.

53   (Huntsville) *Democrat,* August 28, 1844, 3.

54   Jeannette Tillotson Acklen, *Tennessee Records: Tombstone Inscriptions and Manuscripts, Historical and Biographical* (N.P.: Clearfield Co., 1992), 27; Donald Pfanz, *Richard S. Ewell: A Soldier's Life* (Chapel Hill: University of North Carolina Press, 1998), 516–17.

55   (Huntsville) *Southern Advocate,* reprinted in (Washington) *National Intelligencer,* August 27, 1844, 3.

56   (Huntsville) *Democrat,* October 16, 1844, 3; *Mobile Register and Journal,* October 11, 1844, 2.

57   (Huntsville) *Democrat,* October 16, 1844, 3.

58   (Huntsville) *Democrat,* October 16, 1844, 2.

59   David Hubbard to James K. Polk, October 11, 1844, quoted in James K. Polk to Cave Johnson, October 14, 1844, in Cutler, ed., *Correspondence of James K. Polk,* VIII: 184–85, 506.

60   (Huntsville) *Democrat,* November 27, 1844, 3, December 11, 1844, 3; Schlesinger Jr., *History of American Presidential Elections,* I: 747–861 (1971); George Rawlings Poage, *Henry Clay and the Whig Party,* (Chapel Hill: University of North Carolina Press, 1936), 106–51; Robert V. Remini, *Henry Clay: Statesman For the Union* (New York: Norton & Co., 1991), 65963; (Tuscaloosa) *Independent Monitor,* November 16, 1848, 3; New Orleans) *Picayune,* December

8, 1844, 2; (New York: Norton & Co., 1991).

61 Henry Mayer, *All On Fire: William Lloyd Garrison and the Abolition of Slavery*, (New York: W.W. Norton, 1998), 190, 336–40; Freehling, *Road to Disunion*, 435–39; Amy S. Greenberg, *A Wicked War: Polk, Clay, Lincoln, and the 1846 U.S. Invasion of Mexico* (New York: Vintage Books, 2012), 60.

62 *Congressional Globe*, 28th Congress, 2nd Sess., 2, 7; Miller, *Arguing About Slavery*, 476–87, 500.

63 *Congressional Globe*, 28th Congress, 2nd Sess., 102.

64 *Congressional Globe*, 28th Congress, 2nd Sess., 100–102; (Washington) *National Intelligencer*, January 10, 1845, 1–2; (Huntsville) *Democrat*, February 17, 1845, 1, March 12, 1845, 2.

65 (Washington) *National Intelligencer*, January 14, 1845, 4, January 15, 1845, 1–2.

66 *Mobile Advertiser*, December 9, 1844, 2.

67 Hilliard M. Judge to John Calhoun, December 6, 1844, in Wilson, ed., *Papers of John Calhoun*, XX: 487–88; *Alabama House Journal* 1844–1845, 44–45.

68 David Hubbard to Fellow Citizens, in *Florence Gazette*, July 21, 1849, 2.

69 (Huntsville) *Democrat*, March 6, 1845, 2.

70 (Tuscaloosa) *Independent Monitor*, March 12, 1845, 4; *Mobile Register and Journal*, March 8, 1845, 2, March 10, 1845, 2, March 12, 1845, 2; (Huntsville) *Democrat*, March 12, 1845, 2.

71 David Hubbard to Lewis Curtis, May 2, 1844, Papers of the NYMLC, State Historical Society of Wisconsin.

72 East, "Land Speculation in the Chickasaw Cession," 118–25.

73 (Washington) *National Intelligencer*, October 29, 1849, 3.

74 Edythe Whitley, *Marriages of Davidson County, Tennessee, 1789–1847* (Baltimore: Genealogical Publishing Co., 1981), 203. Hubbard might have attended the funeral of Andrew Jackson, which occurred in Nashville in June 1845. (Huntsville) *Democrat*, June 18, 1845.

75 (Huntsville) *Democrat*, November 20, 1844, 3.

76 Walker, *Warrior Mountains Folklore*, 308; Saunders, *Early Settlers of Alabama*, 102; Robert G. Pasquill, *The Conservation Corps in Alabama, 1833–1942: A Great and Lasting Good* (Tuscaloosa: University of Alabama Press, 2008), 38–39; *New York Times*, October 22, 1933, RE2.

77 Alabama Writers Program, *Alabama: A Guide to the Deep South* (New York: R.R. Smith, 1941).

78 *Moulton Democrat*, February 23, 1856, 3, July 17, 1857, 4, April 28, 1887, 1, May 25, 1909, 3. *Albany-Decatur* (AL) *Daily*, January 27, 1917, 2; Owen, *History of Alabama and Dictionary of Alabama Biography*, III: 854.

79 *Alabama House Journal* 1845–1846, 219–20, 237–38.

80 (Huntsville) *Democrat*, February 26, 1845, 3, May 14, 1845, 3.

81 (Huntsville) *Democrat*, January 29, 1845, 2, February 17, 1845, 2–3, May 14, 1845, 3, May 21, 1845, 1.

82 (Huntsville) *Democrat*, April 16, 1845, 3, June 25, 1845, 3, August 13, 1845, 3, September 24, 1845, 2, September 29, 1845, 2; Thornton, *Politics and Power in a Slave Society*, 49–50.

83 (Tuscaloosa) *Independent Monitor*, August 13, 1845, 2, December 17, 1845, 1; (Huntsville) *Democrat*, August 13,

1845, 3.

84   *Alabama House Journal* 1845–1846, 90–95.

85   *Mobile Register and Journal*, December 22, 1845, 2.

86   (Tuscaloosa) *Independent Monitor*, December 24, 1845, 3; (Greensboro) *Alabama Beacon,* December 13, 1845, 2; *Mobile Advertiser*, December 19, 1845, 2. *See also,* Brantley, *Banking in Alabama*, II: 254.

87   *Alabama House Journal* 1845–1846, 368–79; *Ala. Acts* No. 24, 28 (January 21, 1846); *Mobile Register & Journal*, December 16, 1845, 2, January 20, 1846, 2; (Tuscaloosa) *Independent Monitor*, December 17, 1845, 2, January 14, 1846, 2–3.

88   *Alabama House Journal* 1845–1846, 256, 367–68; *Ala. Acts*, No. 311, 216 (January 31, 1846); *Mobile Register and Journal*, January 22, 1846, 2, January 28, 1846, 2, January 31, 1846, 2, February 2, 1846, 2, February 5, 1846, 2; (Tuscaloosa) *Independent Monitor*, February 4, 1846, 3. Relief bills of this type were later ruled to be invalid. *Haley v. Clark*, 26 Ala. 439 (1855).

89   *Alabama House Journal* 1845–1846, 408–43.

90   *Ala. Acts* No. 2, 5–8 (February 4, 1846). See also, *Mobile Register & Journal*, February 11, 1846, 2.

91   *Ala. Acts* No. 1, 3–5 (February 5, 1846). See also, (Huntsville) *Democrat*, January 21, 1846, 3, February 25, 1846, 3. The tax burden fell most heavily on taxpayers in Mobile, Greene, Montgomery and Dallas counties. *Montgomery Flag and Advertiser*, reprinted in (New Orleans) *Picayune*, July 12, 1849, 1.

92   *Jacksonville Republican*, reprinted in (Huntsville) *Democrat,* March 4, 1846, 2.

93   *Florence Gazette*, reprinted in (Huntsville) *Democrat*, March 4, 1846, 2.

94   *Ala. Acts*, No. 27, 31–32 (February 4, 1846).

CHAPTER TEN

1   (Huntsville) *Democrat*, May 13, 1846, 3, May 20, 1846, 2, May 27, 1846, 1, June 3, 1846, 3.

2   (Huntsville) *Democrat*, July 15, 1846, 1.

3   (Huntsville) *Democrat*, November 11, 1846, 2.

4   Ibid.

5   *Speech of Mr. Calhoun, of South Carolina, on his resolutions in reference to the war with Mexico* (Washington, DC: J.T. Towers, 1848); Freehling, *Road to Disunion*, I: 456–57.

6   Clyde Norman Wilson, ed., *The Essential Calhoun: Selections from Writings, Speeches, and Letters* (New Brunswick: Transaction Publishers, 1992), 132.

7   (Huntsville) *Democrat*, November 11, 1846, 2.

8   Ibid.

9   *Congressional Globe*, 29th Congress, 1st Sess., 1214–15; Charles Buxton Going, *David Wilmot, Free-Soiler: A Biography of the Great Advocate of the Wilmot Proviso* (Gloucester, MA: P. Smith, 1966), 11, 86, 94–98, 14654, 642; Chaplain W. Morrison, *Democratic Politics and Sectionalism: The Wilmot Proviso Controversy* (Chapel Hill: University of North Carolina Press, 1967), 18–19, 27, 180–81.

10   (Russellville, AL) *Franklin Democrat*, reprinted in (Huntsville) *Democrat*, October 21, 1846, 2, and (Tuscaloosa) *State Journal and Flag of the Union*, October 16, 1846, 2.

11   Walther, *William Lowndes Yancey and*

the Coming of the Civil War, 97–110.

12 (Tuscaloosa) State Journal and Flag of the Union, October 16, 1846, 2.

13 Selma Reporter, reprinted in Montgomery Flag and Advertiser, March 21, 1847, 1.

14 (Huntsville) Democrat, May 26, 1847, 1.

15 Cooper, South and the Politics of Slavery, 235–36.

16 (Huntsville) Democrat, November 11, 1846, 3.

17 (Huntsville) Southern Advocate, July 30, 1847, 3. See also, Mobile Register & Journal, April 24, 1847, 2.

18 John Barnwell, Love of Order: South Carolina's First Secession Crisis (Chapel Hill: University of North Carolina Press, 1982), 46, 68–69.

19 George S. Houston to Howell Cobb, June 26, 1846, in Ulrich B. Phillips, ed., The Correspondence of Robert Toombs, Alexander H. Stephens, and Howell Cobb (American Historical Association, 1913), 166–67; Ralph B. Draughon Jr., "George Smith Houston and Southern Unity, 1846–1849," 19 Alabama Review (July, 1966): 186, 190–95.

20 Franklin (County, AL) Democrat, reprinted in Montgomery Flag and Advertiser, July 30, 1847, 2.

21 (Huntsville) Southern Advocate, July 30, 1847, 3.

22 (Huntsville) Southern Advocate, August 20, 1847, 3; (Huntsville) Democrat, August 11, 1847, 3, August 18, 1847, 3, August 25, 1847, 2.

23 (Montgomery) Alabama Journal, reprinted in Augusta (GA) Chronicle, July 20, 1847, 2; (Tuscumbia) North Alabamian, reprinted in (Huntsville) Democrat, September 29, 1847, 3; Ala. Acts, No. 98, 146 (1848). Regarding the operating condition of TC&D at this point, see (Pittsfield, MA) Berkshire County Whig, September 14, 1848, 1; (Nashville) Republican Banner, September 30, 1851, 2. There is evidence the railroad was still in operation in 1850. See (New Orleans) Picayune, May 9, 1850, 2.

24 Florence Gazette, August 25, 1849, 1, in David Hubbard Papers, Tennessee State Library and Archives, Nashville, Tennessee.

25 Mobile Register and Journal, October 27, 1845, 2, November 1, 1845, 2, November 20, 1845, 2, November 21, 1845, 2, November 24, 1845, 2, November 28, 1845, 2.

26 (Huntsville) Southern Advocate, January 15, 1848, 3.

27 Ala. Acts, No. 1, 1 (1848); (Huntsville) Democrat, March 29, 1848, 1; Florence Gazette, August 11, 1849, 2, December 22, 1849, 2, and January 26, 1850, 1.

28 Mobile Register and Journal, February 21, 1848, 2, February 26, 1848, 2.

29 (Huntsville) Democrat, December 7, 1843, 2.

30 Walther, William Lowndes Yancey and the Coming of the Civil War, 109–10; David M. Potter, The Impending Crisis: 1848–1861 (New York: Harper & Row, Publishers, Inc., 1976), 80–81.

31 (Natchez) Mississippi Free Trader, November 22, 1848, 1. See also, (Montgomery) Tri-Weekly Flag and Advertiser, July 1, 1848; Cahawba Gazette, reprinted in Mobile Register and Journal, June 12, 1848, 2; Mobile Register and Journal, October 4, 1848, 2.

32 Durham, Southern Moderate in Radical Times, 98.

33 New York Times, January 3, 1853, 1. See also, Philip S. Foner, A History of Cuba and its Relations With the United States, 1845–1895 (New York: International Publishers, 1963), II: 20–28.

34   *Florence Gazette*, September 7, 1850,
1; *Congressional Globe, 31st Congress, 1st
sess., Appendix*, 947–50. Hubbard likely
did not realize that the gold fields in
California were all *north* of the Missouri
Compromise line.

35   Marion (AL) *Review*, quoted in (Concord) *New Hampshire Patriot & State
Gazette*, August 17, 1848, 2.

36   Potter, *Impending Crisis*, 81.

37   *Florence Gazette* and (Huntsville)
Democrat, quoted in (Concord) *New
Hampshire Patriot & State Gazette*,
July 20, 1848, 2; (Huntsville) *Southern
Advocate*, July 29, 1848, 3, August 5,
1848, 3.

38   (Tuscaloosa) *Independent Monitor*, June
18, 1848, 3, November 10, 1848, 2,
November 16, 1848, 3; (Greensboro)
Alabama Beacon, November 18, 1848,
2; Potter, *Impending Crisis*, 81–82.

39   *Mobile Register and Journal*, January 4,
1849, 2.

40   *Congressional Globe*, 30th Congress 2d
Sess., 38, 83–84; *Mobile Register and
Journal*, January 4, 1849, 2.

41   Potter, *Impending Crisis*, 83–84.

42   "The Address of Southern Delegates In
Congress, To Their Constituents," in
Wilson and Cook, eds., *Papers of John
C. Calhoun*, XXVI: 225–43; *Mobile
Register and Journal*, January 29, 1849,
2, February 1, 1849, 2, February 5,
1849, 2, February 6, 1849, 2. For an
example of negative commentary in
the South on the address, see *Augusta
Chronicle*, July 23, 1849, 2.

43   (Huntsville) *Southern Advocate*, Feb-
ruary 9, 1849, 3, March 9, 1849, 2;
Florence Gazette, reprinted in *Augusta
Chronicle*, June 16, 1849, 2; Potter,
Impending Crisis, 85–88.

44   (Athens) *Herald*, quoted in *Augusta
(GA) Chronicle*, March 30, 1849, 2;

(Montgomery) *Weekly Flag and Advertiser*, April 20, 1849, 2. For additional
criticism of Houston, see *Cahaba Gazette*, January 23, 1857, 2.

45   (Huntsville) *Southern Advocate*, April
13, 1849, 3; (Macon) *Georgia Telegraph*,
May 8, 1849, 2; (Montgomery) *Weekly
Flag and Advertiser*, May 4, 1849, 1.
One staunch, consistent defender of
Houston was the *Florence Gazette*.
Florence Gazette, reprinted in *Augusta
Chronicle*, June 16, 1849, 2.

46   *Florence Gazette*, July 21, 1849, 3,
November 3, 1849, 2.

47   John T. Trezevant to John Calhoun,
June 7, 1849 and September 6, 1849,
in Wilson and Cook, eds., *Papers of John
Calhoun*, XXVI: 427, and XXVII: 44.

48   (Huntsville) *Southern Advocate*, March
9, 1849, 3; Nuermberger, *Clays of Alabama*, 109.

49   John Calhoun to Citizens of Memphis,
May 26, 1849 in Wilson and Cook,
eds., *Papers of John C. Calhoun*, XXVI:
408–10; (Greensboro) *Alabama Beacon*, June 30, 1849, 2; *Mobile Register
and Journal*, June 14, 1849, 2; *Augusta
Chronicle*, June 21, 1849, 2.

50   *Mobile Register and Journal*, June 4,
1849, 2; *Augusta Chronicle*, June 13,
1849, 2, August 17, 1849, p. 2.

51   *Florence Gazette*, June 2, 1849, 2; *Mobile
Register and Journal*, June 4, 1849, 2.

52   (Wetumpka) *State Guard*, April 18,
1849, 2, April 24, 1849, 1; (Eufaula)
Spirit of the South, April 24, 1849, 1;
(Greensboro) *Alabama Beacon*, May 5,
1849, 2.

53   (Montgomery) *Weekly Flag and Advertiser*, May 18, 1849, 3; *Florence Gazette*,
June 2, 1849, 2; *Augusta Chronicle*, June
13, 1849, 2.

54   George S. Houston to Howell Cobb,
June 26, 1849, in Phillips, ed., "The

Correspondence of Robert Toombs, Alexander H. Stephens, and Howell Cobb," II: 166.

55   *Florence Gazette*, June 14, 1849, 2, July 28, 1849, 2.

56   *Florence Gazette*, July 231, 1849, 2.

57   *Florence Gazette*, July 21, 1849, 2.

58   George S. Houston to Howell Cobb, August 10, 1849, in Phillips, ed., "Correspondence of Robert Toombs, Alexander H. Stephens, and Howell Cobb," 173; *Florence Gazette*, August 11, 1849, 2, August 18, 1849, 2, August 25, 1849, 2; Dorman, *Party Politics in Alabama*, 34, 36. Hubbard won 49 percent of the 9,341 votes cast. *Richmond Whig*, August 28, 1849, 2.

59   *Augusta Chronicle*, August 17, 1849, 2.

60   *Florence Gazette*, November 3, 1849, 2; Nuermberger, *Clays of Alabama*, 105–106.

CHAPTER ELEVEN

1   K. Jack Bauer, *Zachary Taylor: Soldier, Planter, Statesman of the Old Southwest* (Baton Rouge: Louisiana State University Press, 1993), 277, 298; Foner, *History of Cuba and Its Relations with the United States,* 45–54; *Florence Gazette*, June 15, 1850, 2.

2   *Cal. Const.*, Art. 1, § 18 (1849). Regarding the "gold rush" of population to California and the making of the constitution, see Leonard L. Richards, *The California Gold Rush and the Coming of the Civil War* (New York: Vintage, 2008), 37, 91, 129.

3   (Huntsville) *Democrat*, January 10, 1850, 3, February 7, 1850, 3; *Pittsfield* (MA) *Sun*, January 31, 1850, 2; Michael A. Morrison, *Slavery and the American West: The Eclipse of Manifest Destiny and the Coming of the Civil War* (Chapel Hill: University of North Carolina Press,

1997), 104–105.

4   *Montgomery Flag and Advertiser,* reprinted in *Augusta Chronicle*, November 20, 1849, 2; Potter, *Impending Crisis,* 87–88.

5   John Calhoun to Henry S. Foote, August 3, 1849, reprinted in (Huntsville) *Democrat*, June 26, 1851, 2; (Huntsville) *Democrat*, December 26, 1849, 3, January 17, 1850, 3, January 24, 1850, 3; *Richmond Whig*, May 14, 1850, 1.

6   (Huntsville) *Democrat*, January 31, 1850, 3.

7   *Congressional Globe*, 31st Congress, 1st sess., 62.

8   *Congressional Globe*, 31st Congress, 1st sess., 1–66; John E. Simpson, "Prelude to Compromise: Howell Cobb and the House Speakership Battle of 1849," *Georgia Historical Quarterly* 58 (Winter, 1974): 389–99. For press coverage of these efforts, see (Huntsville) *Democrat*, December 12, 1849, 3; *Florence Gazette*, December 22, 1849, 2; (New Orleans) *Times Picayune*, December 26, 1849, 2. For further discussion of Cobb and the election of speaker, see Elbert B. Smith, *The Presidencies of Zachary Taylor & Millard Fillmore* (Lawrence: University Press of Kansas, 1988), 105–107; John Eddins Simpson, *Howell Cobb: The Politics of Ambition* (Chicago: Adams Press, 1973), 59–60; William B. McCash, *Thomas R. R. Cobb: The Making of a Southern Nationalist* (Macon, GA: Mercer University Press, 1983), 137 and n. 13; Anthony Gene Carey, *Parties, Slavery, and the Union in Antebellum Georgia* (Athens: University of Georgia Press, 2012), 158–59; Morrison, *Slavery and the American West*, 105.

9   David Hubbard, *et al.* to H.W. Collier, December 14, 1849, reprinted in (Natchez) *Mississippi Free Trader*, January 2, 1850, 2; *Richmond Whig*, January

4, 1850, 2; (Amherst, N.H.) *Farmer's Cabinet*, January 10, 1850, 2, January 17, 1850, 2; New Orleans) *Picayune*, December 26, 1849, 2; (Huntsville) *Democrat*, January 2, 1850, p., 3; Thornton, *Politics and Power in a Slave Society*, 184.

10 *Congressional Globe*, 31st Congress, 1st sess., 3–66; Fergus M. Bordewich, *America's Great Debate: Henry Clay, Stephen A. Douglas, and the Compromise that Preserved the Union* (New York: Simon & Schuster, 2012), 107–108, 114–21; Morrison, *Slavery and the American West*, 105.

11 *Congressional Globe*, 31st Congress, 1st sess., 65–66, 88. See also, (Huntsville) *Democrat*, January 2, 1850, p. 3.

12 *Florence Gazette*, December 22, 1849, 2.

13 *Congressional Globe*, 31st Congress, 1st sess., 69–72; (Huntsville) *Democrat*, January 2, 1850, 2.

14 (Greensboro) *Alabama Beacon*, January 19, 1850, 2.

15 (Greensboro) *Alabama Beacon*, February 2, 1850, 2; (Huntsville) *Southern Advocate*, May 1, 1850, 3; Nuermberger, *Clays of Alabama*, 106, 109–10; Thornton, *Politics and Power in Slave Society*, 180, 186.

16 *Florence Gazette*, February 9, 1850, 1.

17 Ibid.; (Huntsville) *Democrat*, February 7, 1850, 2. See also, (New Orleans) *Picayune*, February 20, 1850, 5.

18 Hay, ed., *The Papers of Henry Clay*, 10: 655–58; Morrison, *Slavery and the American West*, 108–109; (Huntsville) *Democrat*, February 7, 1850, 2; Bordewich, *America's Great Debate*, 134–44.

19 (Huntsville) *Democrat*, February 14, 1850, 3.

20 (Huntsville) *Democrat*, February 7, 1850, 3.

21 *Mobile Advertiser*, June 25, 1850, 2.

22 *Mobile Register*, February 11, 1850, 2; *Florence Gazette*, February 23, 1850, 2; (Huntsville) *Democrat*, February 28, 1850, 3; (Macon) *Georgia Telegraph*, February 19, 1850, 2; ( ) *National Intelligencer*, March 11, 1850, 3; (New Orleans) *Picayune*, March 30, 1850, 2; Thornton, *Politics and Power in a Slave Society*, 185; Thelma Jennings, *The Nashville Convention: Southern Movement for Unity, 1848–1850* (Memphis, TN: Memphis State University Press, 1980, 62–64.

23 (Montgomery) *Alabama Journal*, March 1, 1850, 2.

24 (Huntsville) *Democrat*, January 17, 1850, 3, January 31, 1850, 3, February 14, 1850, 3, October 24, 1850, 3, October 31, 1850, 3.

25 David Hubbard to Editor of the *Montgomery Atlas*, February 10, 1850, reprinted in the *Montgomery Atlas*, reprinted in the *Florence Gazette*, March 2, 1850, 2.

26 Wilson and Cook, eds., *Papers of John C. Calhoun*, XXVII: 187–211; *Congressional Globe*, 31st Congress, 1st sess., 451–56. See also, (Huntsville) *Democrat*, March 14, 1850, 2–3 (publishing and praising the speech), March 21, 1850, 3; Bordewich, *America's Great Debate*, 156–58.

27 *Richmond Whig*, March 8, 1850, 1.

28 *Mobile Register*, reprinted in *Pittsfield* (MA) *Sun*, March 14, 1850, 2.

29 (Greensboro) *Alabama Beacon*, March 23, 1850, 2; *Mobile Register*, April 27, 1850, 2. Regarding Webster's speech, see Bordewich, *America's Great Debate*, 165–70.

30 *Florence Enquirer*, reprinted in the *Florence Gazette*, March 23, 1851, 1.

31 *Florence Gazette*, March 30, 1850, 1.

32 (Greensboro) *Alabama Beacon*, April 6, 1850, 2; (Huntsville) *Democrat*, April 11, 1850, 3.

33 Bordewich, *America's Great Debate*, 221; Potter, *Impending Crisis*, 103.

34 *Florence Gazette*, May 18, 1850, 1 (emphasis added).

35 *Mobile Advertiser*, June 4, 1850, 2; (Huntsville) *Southern Advocate*, May 29, 1850, 3. Regarding the Committee of Thirteen's report, see Bordewich, *America's Great Debate*, 223–27.

36 (Huntsville) *Southern Advocate*, June 19, 1850, 3; *Florence Gazette*, June 8, 1850, 1–2,

37 Thornton, *Politics and Power in a Slave Society*, 187–88.

38 (Huntsville) *Southern Advocate*, May 15, 1850, 3.

39 Nuermberger, *Clays of Alabama*, 106, 109–10; (Huntsville) *Southern Advocate*, May 15, 1850, 1.

40 David Hubbard to M.C. Gallaway, May 28, 1850, in *Florence Gazette*, June 8, 1850, 2, and July 11, 1850, 2, and (Jackson) *Mississippian*, August 9, 1850.

41 *Florence Gazette*, June 1, 1850, 1.

42 *Florence Gazette*, June 1, 1850, 2.

43 Ibid.

44 Ibid. See also, *Mobile Advertiser*, June 11, 1850, 2 (referring to this letter); (Montgomery) *Alabama Journal*, June 14, 1850, 2 (same).

45 (Huntsville) *Southern Advocate*, July 3, 1850, 1; (Huntsville) *Democrat*, August 1, 1850, 1.

46 *Congressional Globe*, 31st Congress, 1st sess., Appendix,. 947–50; Morrison, *Slavery in the American West*, 115–17. See also, Sellers, *Slavery in Alabama*, 348–49.

47 See generally, *Mobile Advertiser*, June 14, 1850, 2; *Florence Gazette*, June 15, 1850, 2; (Huntsville) *Southern Advocate*, June 12, 1850, 3, June 19, 1850, 1, 3; June 26, 1850, 3; Dorman, *Party Politics in Alabama From 1850 Through 1860*, 44; Jennings, *Nashville Convention*, 122–23, 137–57; Bordewich, *America's Great Debate*, 256–58.

48 Ibid., 947–49.

49 Ibid., 949–950. See also, (Huntsville) *Democrat*, September 26, 1850, 1, *Florence Gazette*, September 7, 1850, 1; (Savannah, GA) *Morning News*, August 23, 1850; Morrison, *Slavery and the American West*, 115–17.

50 (Huntsville) *Democrat*, May 23, 1850, 3, May 30, 1850, 2, July 18, 1850, 3; (New Orleans) *Picayune*, May 22, 1850, 1.

51 *Florence Gazette*, June 15, 1850, 2–3.

52 (Washington) *Southern Press*, reprinted in *Richmond Whig*, July 2, 1850, 2. The two communications may be found in *Florence Gazette*, June 8, 1850, 2 and June 15, 1850, 2; Ritchie did not pass through this episode unscathed. Several months later he stepped down as editor of the *Union*. (Huntsville) *Democrat*, March 27, 1851, 3, April 3, 1851, 3.

53 Other Southerners used the same tactics as Hubbard. Durham, *Southern Moderate in Radical Times*, 113.

54 (Huntsville) *Democrat*, July 18, 1850, 3; (Montgomery) *Alabama Journal*, July 12, 1850, 2; Bordewich, *America's Great Debate*, 276–78.

55 (Huntsville) *Southern Advocate*, June 5, 1850, 3; (Montgomery) *Alabama Journal*, July 3, 1850, 2.

56 (Huntsville) *Southern Advocate*, July 10, 1850, 3,

57 *Mobile Advertiser*, June 25, 1850, 2; *Florence Gazette*, July 13, 1850, 2, August 3, 1850, 2; (Huntsville) *Southern Advocate*, July 3, 1850, 3,

58 (Montgomery) *Alabama Journal*,

August 5, 1850, 2; *Florence Gazette*, August 10, 1850, 2; *Florence Gazette*, reprinted in *Mobile Advertiser*, June 11, 1851, 2; Potter, *Impending Crisis*, 107–108; Bordewich, *America's Great Debate*, 289–302.

59 William R. King to Morgan Smith, June 13, 1850, cited in John William McIntosh, "Alabama and the Compromise of 1850" (Master's Thesis, University of Alabama, 1932), 46 and n.2. See also, (Huntsville) *Southern Advocate*, June 5, 1850, 2 (discussing an earlier letter from King to Morgan Smith of Lowndes County also complaining of divisions among Southerners).

60 Potter, *Impending Crisis*, 108–11.

61 *Florence Gazette*, July 13, 1850, 2.

62 *Florence Gazette*, September 7, 1850, 2; *Mobile Advertiser*, September 19, 1850, 2; (Huntsville) *Southern Advocate*, September 11, 1850, 3; (New Orleans) *Picayune*, September 23, 1850, 3.

63 *Congressional Globe*, 31st Congress, 1st sess., 1769–76, (W.R.W. Cobb voted for it); Potter, *Impending Crisis*, 111–13; Robert W. Johannsen, *Stephen A. Douglas* (Urbana: University of Illinois Press), 294–98; Martin H. Quitt, *Stephen A. Douglas and Antebellum Democracy* (Cambridge: Cambridge University Press, 2012), 113–17; Bordewich, *America's Great Debate*, 303–16, 335–46. Hubbard voted for the revised fugitive slave law. *Congressional Globe*, 31st Congress, 1st sess., 1807.

64 Potter, *Impending Crisis*, 111–12; (Montgomery) *Alabama Journal*, September 13, 1850, 2; (Huntsville) *Southern Advocate*, September 18, 1850, 3; (Huntsville) *Democrat*, September 19, 1850, 2.

65 *Florence Gazette*, November 2, 1850, 1.

66 *Mobile Register*, quoted in *Savannah (GA) Republican*, September 30, 1850, 2.

67 Athens (AL) *Herald*, reprinted in (Huntsville) *Southern Advocate*, October 9, 1850, 2. See also, (Greensboro) *Alabama Beacon*, reprinted in (Montgomery) *Alabama Journal*, October 15, 1850.

68 (Huntsville) *Democrat*, November 7, 1850, 2–3; (Greensboro) *Alabama Beacon*, November 9, 1850, 1–2 (publishing Collier's October 22, 1850, letter); (New Orleans) *Picayune*, November 5, 1850, 2.

69 Weekly (Montgomery) *Alabama Journal*, November 9, 1850, 1; (Montgomery) *Advertiser and State Gazette*, February 19, 1851, 2; Thornton, *Politics and Power in a Slave Society*, 189.

70 (Huntsville) *Democrat*, September 19, 1850, 2, September 26, 1850, 1, October 10, 1850, 3, February 13, 1851, 3.

71 (Huntsville) *Democrat*, February 13, 1851, 3.

72 *Florence Gazette*, reprinted in (Montgomery) *Alabama Journal*, April 1, 1851, 2.

73 *Mobile Register*, December 18, 1850, 2.

74 *Mobile Advertiser*, February 22, 1851, 2; (Huntsville) *Democrat*, February 13, 1851, 3.

75 *Florence Gazette*, reprinted in *Mobile Advertiser*, February 28, 1851, 2. See also, *Florence Gazette*, reprinted in *Mobile Daily Advertiser*, April 30, 1851, 2, and *Augusta (GA) Chronicle*, May 9, 1851, 2.

76 New York *Tribune*, April 8, 1851, 3; (Brattleboro, VT) *Semi-Weekly Eagle*, May 29, 1851, 2; (New Orleans) *Picayune*, June 13, 1851, 2; (New Orleans) *Picayune*, June 13, 1851, 2; July 11, 1851, 2, July 17, 1851, 2; (Huntsville) *Southern Advocate*, April 9, 1851, 3; (Tuscaloosa) *Independent Monitor*, May

1, 1851, 2; (Greensboro) *Alabama Beacon*, April 19, 1851, 2; *Mobile Advertiser*, June 27, 1851, 2; (Huntsville) *Democrat*, June 5, 1851, 3.

77 *Mobile Advertiser*, April 13, 1851, 2. Accord, *Mobile Advertiser*, June 21, 1851, 2.

78 (Tuscaloosa) *Independent Monitor*, May 1, 1851, 2.

79 *Mobile Register*, June 6, 1851, 2.

80 (Huntsville) *Democrat*, April 17, 1851, 3.

81 Johnson Jones Hooper, *Adventures of Captain Simon Suggs* (Philadelphia: T.B. Peterson, 1848), 12.

82 (Huntsville) *Southern Advocate*, April 23, 1851, 3. See also, *Mobile Advertiser*, July 8, 1851, 2. Regarding the Georgia Platform, see (Huntsville) *Democrat*, December 26, 1850, 3.

83 Athens (AL) *Herald*, quoted in *Mobile Advertiser*, July 8, 1851, 2.

84 *Mobile Advertiser*, July 8, 1851, 2.

85 (Montgomery) *Alabama Journal*, July 9, 1851, 2.

86 (Huntsville) *Southern Advocate*, June 25, 1851, 3; (Tuscaloosa) *Independent Monitor*, July 17, 1851, 2.

87 (Huntsville) *Southern Advocate*, July 16, 1851, 2–3; (New Orleans) *Picayune*, July 30, 1851, 2. See also, (Huntsville) *Democrat*, July 17, 1851, 3; (New Orleans) *Picayune*, August 6, 1851, 2 (reporting that Houston had withdrawn).

88 *Florence Gazette* reprinted in (Huntsville) *Southern Advocate*, May 14, 1851, 3 and *Mobile Advertiser*, April 1, 1851, 2.

89 (Huntsville) *Southern Advocate*, May 14, 1851, 3, reprinted in *Florence Gazette*, May 17, 1851, 2. See also, *Mobile Register*, November 13, 1850, 2.

90 *Mobile Advertiser*, June 27, 1851, 2, June 28, 1851, 2.

91 Athens (AL) *Herald*, reprinted in (Huntsville) *Southern Advocate*, July 16, 1851, 2.

92 *Florence Gazette*, reprinted in (Huntsville) *Southern Advocate*, July 16, 1851, 2.

93 (Huntsville) *Southern Advocate*, July 16, 1851, 3.

94 (Huntsville) *Southern Advocate*, August 20, 1851, 3.

95 (Huntsville) *Democrat*, quoted in (Huntsville) *Southern Advocate*, August 20, 1851, 3. See also, (Huntsville) *Southern Advocate*, April 23, 1851, 3 (criticizing the *Democrat's* defense of Hubbard).

96 (Hartselle) *Alabama Enquirer*, March 20, 1890, 1.

97 Dorman, *Party Politics in Alabama*, 58.

98 (Tuscumbia) *North Alabamian*, quoted in *Mobile Advertiser*, August 16, 1851, 2.

99 *Mobile Advertiser*, August 12, 1851, 2, August 14, 1851, 2, August 23, 1851, 2; (New Orleans) *Picayune*, August 11, 1851, 2, August 12, 1851, 2, August 15, 1851, 2, August 17, 1851, 2; Dorman, *Party Politics in Alabama*, 58. See also, (Tuscaloosa) *Independent Monitor*, August 28, 1851, 2. Hubbard's success in Lawrence County is somewhat curious. The three men elected there to the legislature—all incumbents—were each classified by press accounts as Unionists. In fact, so were all of the legislators from Franklin County. *Mobile Advertiser*, August 16, 1851, 2, August 21, 1851, 2

100 (Greensboro) *Alabama Beacon*, August 16, 1851, 2.

CHAPTER TWELVE

1 (Huntsville) *Southern Advocate*, reprinted in *Mobile Advertiser*, October

7, 1851, 2, December 19, 1851, 2. See also, Paul Harncourt, *The Planter's Railway: Excitement and Civil War Years* (Arab, AL: Heritage, 1995), 77–83.

2   *Mobile Advertiser*, October 12, 1851, 2; (Huntsville) *Southern Advocate*, October 15, 1851, 3.

3   (Huntsville) *Democrat*, reprinted in *Augusta* (GA) *Chronicle*, January 28, 1851, 2.

4   See generally, *Mobile Advertiser*, November 8, 1851, 2, November 27, 1851, 2 (reporting a railroad convention in Cherokee County); (Greensboro) *Alabama Beacon*, November 15, 1851, 3 (same); Weekly (Mobile) *Herald and Tribune*, December 27, 1851.

5   *Mobile Advertiser*, November 19, 1851, 2; (Tuscaloosa) *Independent Monitor*, November 20, 1851, 2.

6   See generally, *Mobile Advertiser*, November 25, 1851, 2, November 26, 1851, 2, December 6, 1851, 2, January 23, 1852, 2; (Tuscaloosa) *Independent Monitor*, December 4, 1851, 2; (Huntsville) *Southern Advocate*, January 21, 1852, 3; (Huntsville) *Democrat*, December 4, 1851, 3; (Montgomery) *Alabama Journal*, April 26, 1852, 2.

7   *Mobile Advertiser*, January 6, 1852, 2; Weekly (Mobile) *Herald and Tribune*, December 27, 1851, January 23, 1852.

8   *Mobile Advertiser*, January 6, 1852, 2; Weekly (Mobile) *Herald and Tribune*, January 10, 1851.

9   (Huntsville) *Southern Advocate*, January 21, 1852, 3; *Mobile Advertiser*, January 24, 1852, 2; Weekly (Mobile) *Herald and Tribune*, January 24, 1852.

10   Weekly (Mobile) *Herald and Tribune*, February 4, 1852.

11   Weekly (Mobile) *Herald and Tribune*, February 13, 1852; (Washington) *National Intelligencer*, February 21, 1852,

3.

12   *Mobile Advertiser*, March 11, 1852, 2.

13   *Mobile Advertiser*, April 14, 1852, 2.

14   *Mobile Advertiser*, August 4, 1852, 2 (discussing efforts by promoters of the Selma and Tennessee Railroad to sell twenty year bonds); Harncourt, *Planter's Railway*, 111, 124 (the Memphis and Charleston's Board of Directors decided to sell bonds on April 7, 1852).

15   *Proceedings of the Democratic National Convention Held at Baltimore, June 1–5, 1852* (Washington: Robert Armstrong, 1852).

16   Walther, *William Lowndes Yancey and the Coming of the Civil War*, 142–43; Nuermberger, *Clays of Alabama*, 113.

17   Weekly (Mobile) *Herald and Tribune*, November 20, 1852; (Huntsville) *Southern Advocate*, December 1, 1852, 3 (in Lawrence County, Pierce received 588 votes, Scott 512, and Troup 4).

18   (Huntsville) *Southern Advocate*, December 1, 1852, 3 (Troup received only a handful of votes in Franklin, Lawrence, Randolph, Talladega, and Tuscaloosa counties, and nineteen in Tallapoosa County); (Huntsville) *Democrat*, October 28, 1852, 2, December 2, 1852, 2.

19   Weekly (Mobile) *Herald and Tribune*, June 5, 1853, June 7, 1853, July 9, 1853; (Huntsville) *Southern Advocate*, June 15, 1853, 2, August 3, 1853, 3; *Moulton Democrat*, reprinted in (Montgomery) *Advertiser and State Gazette*, April 9, 1853, p 2; *Florence Gazette*, reprinted in (Huntsville) *Southern Advocate*, June 15, 1853, 2.

20   Thomas Owen, *History of Alabama and Dictionary of Alabama Biography*, IV: 1790; (Tuscaloosa) *Independent Monitor*, April 30, 1857, 2; (Huntsville) *Southern Advocate*, July 13, 1853, 3. Regarding Winston, see Glenn Nolen

Sisk, "John Anthony Winston: Alabama's Veto Governor" (Masters Thesis, University of Alabama, 1934), 1, 3, 16–17, 21.

21 Sisk, "John Anthony Winston," 4; *Mobile Register*, May 5, 1851, 2, May 31, 1851, 2. See also, *Mobile Register*, July 9, 1853, 2 (reporting Winston's attendance at a "Railroad Jubilee" in Montevallo).

22 In 1844, Hubbard and his son purchased land at what later became Iuka, Mississippi.

23 *Mobile Register*, July 30, 1853, 2.

24 (Montgomery) *Advertiser and State Gazette*, May 14, 1853, 2 (emphasis added).

25 See, e.g., (Montgomery) *Advertiser and State Gazette*, May 24, 1853, 2 (referring to the *Moulton Democrat*), May 17, 1853, 3; (Huntsville) *Southern Advocate*, June 15, 1853, 2 (quoting the *Florence Gazette*). See also, Sisk, "John Anthony Winston," 21–22.

26 (Montgomery) *Advertiser and State Gazette*, July 9, 1853, 2. See also, (Huntsville) *Southern Advocate*, June 29, 1853, 3, July 13, 1853, 3; *Weekly* (Mobile) *Herald and Tribune*, July 13, 1853.

27 *Alabama House Journal* 1853–1854, 68–69.

28 (Huntsville) *Southern Advocate*, April 6, 1853, 3, July 13, 1853, 3, August 10, 1853, 3; (Montgomery) *Advertiser and State Gazette*, August 6, 1853, 2.

29 (Huntsville) *Southern Advocate*, August 10, 1853, 3, August 24, 1853, 3; Nuermberger, *Clays of Alabama*, 115–17.

30 (Huntsville) *Southern Advocate*, August 3, 1853, 3, August 10, 1853, 3; (Montgomery) *Advertiser and State Gazette*, August 16, 1853, 2.

31 (Huntsville) *Southern Advocate*,

August 3, 1853, 3, August 17, 1853, 3; *Louisville* (KY) *Courier*, August 23, 1853, 2; *Glasgow* (MO) *Weekly Times*, September 8, 1853, 1; (Montgomery) *Advertiser and State Gazette*, October 8, 1853, 2; (New Orleans) *Picayune*, October 15, 1853, 2; (Montgomery) *Alabama Journal*, November 2, 1853, 2; Nuermberger, *Clays of Alabama*, 116.

32 Nuermberger, *Clays of Alabama*, 116.

33 (Huntsville) *Southern Advocate*, October 12, 1853, 3.

34 (Huntsville) *Southern Advocate*, November 9, 1853, 3, October 26, 1853, 2.

35 (Huntsville) *Southern Advocate*, November 30, 1853, 3; (Montgomery) *Advertiser and State Gazette*, November 23, 1853, 2; *Weekly* (Mobile) *Herald and Tribune*, November 27, 1853; *Alabama House Journal* 1853–1854, 92–95.

36 *Weekly* (Mobile) *Herald and Tribune*, November 27, 1853.

37 *Weekly* (Mobile) *Herald and Tribune*, November 27, 1853.

38 *Mobile Advertiser*, reprinted in (Huntsville) *Southern Advocate*, December 28, 1853, 3.

39 (Montgomery) *Advertiser and State Gazette*, October 18, 1853, 2; (Huntsville) *Southern Advocate*, October 19, 1853, 3; Dorman, *Party Politics in Alabama*, 93–94; Nuermberger, *Clays of Alabama*, 117.

40 Nuermberger, *Clays of Alabama*, 117.

41 (Huntsville) *Southern Advocate*, November 30, 1853, 3; *Weekly* (Mobile) *Herald and Tribune*, November 26, 1853; (Montgomery) *Advertiser and State Gazette*, November 30, 1853, 3; Nuermberger, *Clays of Alabama*, 117–18.

42 Dorman, *Party Politics in Alabama*, 91.

43 *Alabama House Journal* 1853–1854, 111–13; *Weekly* (Mobile) *Herald and*

Tribune, December 2, 1853; (Cahawba) *Dallas Gazette*, December 2, 1853, 2.

44   (Montgomery) *Advertiser and State Gazette*, November 23, 1853, 3, November 30, 1853, 3; *Weekly* (Mobile) *Herald and Tribune*, December 8, 1853, December 24, 1853, January 26, 1854, January 28, 1854, February 4, 1854; (Huntsville) *Southern Advocate*, February 8, 1854, 2, February 15, 1854, 2.

45   *Ala. Acts,* No. 424, 298–305 (1853). See generally, Cline, *Alabama Railroads,* 43.

46   *Ala. Acts,* No. 407, 270–280 (1853).

47   *Ala. Acts,* No. 434, 318–320 (1853). See Cline, *Alabama Railroads,* 38; Wiggins, *Scalawag in Alabama Politics,* 43–45.

48   *Weekly* (Mobile) *Herald and Tribune*, December 1, 1853, December 24, 1853.

49   *Weekly* (Mobile) *Herald and Tribune*, December 8, 1853.

50   *Weekly* (Mobile) *Herald and Tribune*, December 24, 1853, January 28, 1854, February 4, 1854; (Huntsville) *Southern Advocate*, February 15, 1854, 2.

51   *Mobile Advertiser*, reprinted in (Huntsville) *Southern Advocate*, December 28, 1853, 3; *Alabama House Journal* 1853–1854, 194, 201.

52   *Weekly* (Mobile) *Herald and Tribune*, December 23, 1853; (Huntsville) *Southern Advocate*, January 4, 1854, 3. See also, Sisk, "John Anthony Winston," 24–25.

53   (Washington) *National Intelligencer,* March 3, 1854 (most of the bonds were owned by foreign investors).

54   *Mobile Advertiser*, reprinted in (Huntsville) *Southern Advocate*, December 28, 1853, 3.

55   *Weekly* (Mobile) *Herald and Tribune*, February 4, 1854.

56   *Weekly* (Mobile) *Herald and Tribune*, February 4, 1854.

57   *Moulton Democrat*, August 13, 1858, 1.

58   (Huntsville) *Southern Advocate*, February 8, 1854, February 22, 1854, 3; *Weekly* (Mobile) *Herald and Tribune*, February, 1854.

59   *Ala. Acts,* No. 26, 36 (1853); (Huntsville) *Southern Advocate*, February 22, 1854, 3; *Weekly* (Mobile) *Herald and Tribune*, March 4, 1854, March 7, 1854; Sisk, "John Anthony Winston," 28.

60   See, (Montgomery) *Advertiser and State Gazette*, February 4, 1854, 3, March 18, 1854, 2; (Huntsville) *Southern Advocate*, February 1, 1854, 2, February 8, 1854, 3, February 15, 1854, 3, February 22, 1854, 2, March 1, 1854, 2, August 29, 1855, 2.

61   (Huntsville) *Democrat*, reprinted in (Montgomery) *Alabama Journal*, reprinted in (Washington) *National Intelligencer*, March 15, 1854, 5.

62   (Huntsville) *Southern Advocate*, May 17, 1854, 3 (emphasis added).

63   (Huntsville) *Southern Advocate*, November 7, 1855, 2. See also, (Huntsville) *Democrat*, May 31, 1855.

64   (Montgomery) *Advertiser and State Gazette*, March 29, 1854, 1; Nuermberger, *Clays of Alabama,* 123–25.

65   (Montgomery) *Advertiser and State Gazette*, July 11, 1854, 2.

66   See, e.g., *Weekly* (Mobile) *Herald and Tribune*, July 14, 1854; (Washington) *National Intelligencer*, July 6, 1854; Nuermberger, *Clays of Alabama,* 125–26.

67   Nuermberger, *Clays of Alabama,* 125.

68   (Huntsville) *Southern Advocate*, November 22, 1854, 2. See generally, Arthur Charles Cole, *The Whig Party in the South* (Gloucester, MA: P. Smith, 1962), 277–308.

69   *Boston Atlas*, September 19, 1854, November 13, 1854; (Washington)

National Intelligencer, November 13, 1854; *Cleveland Herald,* May 14, 1855; *Ripley* (OH) *Bee,* June 23, 1855.

70   Cole, *Whig Party in the South,* 305–308.

71   (Huntsville) *Southern Advocate,* June 14, 1854, 2. Accord, *Weekly* (Mobile) *Herald and Tribune,* June 20, 1854; *Richmond Whig,* July 24, 1855, 1.

72   (Huntsville) *Southern Advocate,* July 25, 1855, 2.

73   See, e.g., (Montgomery) *Advertiser and State Gazette,* March 29, 1854, 2; *Mobile Register,* cited in *Weekly* (Mobile) *Herald and Tribune,* June 20, 1854 and June 22, 1854. See also, Jeff Frederick, "Unintended Consequences: The Rise and Fall of the Know-Nothing Party in Alabama," *Alabama Review* 55 (January, 2002): 3. *See generally,* Cole, *Whig Party in the South,* 306–16; W. Darrell Overdyke, *The Know-Nothing Party in the South* (Baton Rouge: Louisiana State University Press, 1968), 63.

74   *Moulton Democrat,* August 16, 1855, 1; See also, (Huntsville) *Southern Advocate,* May 2, 1855, 3 (reporting the establishment of the *Lawrence County Independence,* a campaign newspaper).

75   Notable among this group were legislative candidates Jeremiah Clemens, (Huntsville) *Southern Advocate,* July 18, 1855, 2–3, September 26, 1855, 1 and 2, October 17, 1855, 1, October 31, 1855, 2; Dorman, *Party Politics in Alabama,* 117; David Peter Lewis, *Moulton Democrat,* July 5, 1855, 3 (also stating that Dr. Francis W. Sykes was an American Party candidate for the legislature), (Huntsville) *Southern Advocate,* December 5, 1855, 3; Dorman, *Party Politics in Alabama,* 117; Luke Pryor, a Limestone County lawyer, and Robert Coman Brickell, the law partner of Leroy Pope Walker. (Huntsville) *Southern Advocate,* July 18, 1855, 3; *Montgomery*

Advertiser and State Gazette, July 7, 1855, 2. Although he denied joining the new party, even George Smith Houston, who was then serving as chairman of the House Ways and Means Committee, revealed that he was sympathetic to some of its goals, particularly those relating to tightening immigration and naturalization laws. This may in part explain why Houston ran unopposed during this particular election cycle. See (Huntsville) *Southern Advocate,* July 11, 1855, 3; *Montgomery Advertiser and State Gazette,* July 17, 1855, 2–3. See also, *Moulton Democrat,* August 14, 1857, 2 (publishing letters connecting Houston to the American Party). Regarding Houston's candidacy, see (Huntsville) *Southern Advocate,* March 28, 1855, 2; *Montgomery Advertiser and State Gazette,* March 29, 1855, 2; *Moulton Democrat,* July 5, 1855, 3.

76   Compare *Moulton Democrat,* February 3, 1855, 2 with July 5, 1855, 2 and July 12, 1855, 2. Regarding Shortridge, see Owen, *History of Alabama and Dictionary of Alabama Biography,* IV, 1555; Thornton, *Politics and Power in a Slave Society,* 325–27; Dorman, *Party Politics in Alabama,* 106–19; Sellers, *Prohibition Movement in Alabama,* 36.

77   *Ala. Acts* No. 424, 298–305 (1853).

78   See, e.g., *Moulton Democrat,* February 3, 1855, 2.

79   *Moulton Democrat,* reprinted in *Montgomery Advertiser and State Gazette,* January 16, 1855, 3.

80   *Montgomery Advertiser and State Gazette,* February 13, 1855, 3.

81   *Montgomery Advertiser and State Gazette,* June 9, 1855, 2 (italics added).

82   See, e.g., *Montgomery Advertiser and State Gazette,* May 26, 1855, 4, June 28, 1855, 2; (Huntsville) *Southern Advocate,* June 6, 1855, 2, July 11, 1855, 2.

83   *Jacksonville Republican,* quoted in (Huntsville) *Southern Advocate,* June 20, 1855. See also, (Huntsville) *Southern Advocate,* July 7, 1855, 2; *Montgomery Advertiser and State Gazette,* June 21, 1856, 2.

84   *Montgomery Advertiser and State Gazette,* June 17, 1855, 2.

85   *Montgomery Advertiser and State Gazette,* August 14, 1855, 2; (Huntsville) *Southern Advocate,* August 15, 1855, 3; *Moulton Democrat,* August 16, 1855, 1.

86   (Huntsville) *Southern Advocate,* August 29, 1855, 2.

87   (Huntsville) *Southern Advocate,* August 29, 1855, 3.

88   *Montgomery Advertiser and State Gazette,* March 11, 1856, 3.

89   See (Greensboro) *Alabama Beacon,* August 31, 1855, 2.

90   *Mobile Register,* November 20, 1855, 2; (Huntsville) *Southern Advocate,* November 21, 1855, 2.

91   (Huntsville) *Southern Advocate,* November 21, 1855, 3; *Mobile Register,* November 29, 1855, 2; *Memphis Appeal,* November 24, 1855, 2.

92   (Huntsville) *Southern Advocate,* November 21, 1855, 3.

93   *Montgomery Advertiser and State Gazette,* December 8, 1855, 2; *Mobile Register,* December 11, 1855, 3, December 18, 1855, 2.

94   *Mobile Register,* December 18, 1855, 2; *Montgomery Advertiser and State Gazette,* December 19, 1855, 2.

95   *Mobile Register,* January 15, 1856, 2.

96   *Mobile Register,* January 15, 1856, 2.

97   *Mobile Register,* January 15, 1856, 2.

98   *Montgomery Advertiser and State Gazette,* January 10, 1856, 2.

99   *Montgomery Advertiser and State Gazette,* January 10, 1856, 2, January 15, 1856, 2; *Mobile Register,* January 13, 1856, 2, January 19, 1856, 3, January 23, 1856, 2.

100   *Ala. Acts* No. 16, 10–11 (January 12, 1856); *Mobile Register,* January 19, 1856, 3, (Huntsville) *Southern Advocate,* January 23, 1856, 2,

101   *Montgomery Advertiser and State Gazette,* January 24, 1856, 2. See also, *Montgomery Advertiser and State Gazette,* February 19, 1856, 2 (the first mention of the "Veto Governor" moniker), April 3, 1856, 2.

102   *Ala. Acts* No. 18, 12 (January 21, 1856); *Ala. Acts* No. 20, 13–14 (January 21, 1856).

103   *Montgomery Advertiser and State Gazette,* January 24, 1856, 2, June 21, 1856, 2 (Winston's letter explaining his rationale); *Mobile Register,* January 25, 1856, 2; (Huntsville) *Southern Advocate,* January 30, 1856, 3.

104   *Montgomery Advertiser and State Gazette,* April 3, 1856, 2.

105   *Montgomery Advertiser and State Gazette,* June 21, 1856, 2.

CHAPTER THIRTEEN

1   *Montgomery Advertiser and State Gazette,* January 12, 1856, 2. See also, (Huntsville) *Southern Advocate,* January 23, 1856, 2 (reporting a meeting in Huntsville on January 19, 1856, in which similar sentiments were expressed).

2   (Huntsville) *Southern Advocate,* February 27, 1856, 3.

3   *Moulton Democrat,* March 27, 1856, 2; (Huntsville) *Southern Advocate,* March 26, 1856, 3; *Montgomery Advertiser and State Gazette,* April 24, 1856, 2.

4   *Charleston Mercury,* February 7, 1856, 2; *Bangor* (ME) *Whig and Courier,* March 17, 1856; *Montgomery Advertiser*

and State Gazette, March 27, 1856, 2; (Huntsville) *Southern Advocate*, April 9, 1856, 2,

5 (Huntsville) *Southern Advocate*, March 19, 1856, 3.

6 (Huntsville) *Southern Advocate*, March 12, 1856, 3, March 19, 1856, 3, June 11, 1856, 3. See also, (Huntsville) *Southern Advocate*, April 9, 1856, 2 (reporting the attendance of South Carolinians at a Huntsville railroad meeting).

7 *Montgomery Advertiser and State Gazette*, May 29, 1856, 2, June 5, 1856, 2, June 10, 1856, 4, June 12, 1856, 2, June 21, 1856, 2; September 11, 1856, 2.

8 (Huntsville) *Southern Advocate*, June 4, 1856, 3. See also, *Montgomery Advertiser and State Gazette*, May 31, 1856, 2, June 10, 1856, 2; Potter, *Impending Crisis*, 209–10; Nuermberger, *Clays of Alabama*, 143; Potter, *Impending Crisis*, 259–60. See also, Eric Foner, *Free Soil, Free Labor, Free Men: The Ideology of the Republican Party Before the Civil War* (Oxford: Oxford University Press, 1995), 162; *Cahaba Gazette*, September 12, 1856, 2, October 31, 1856, 2; Nuermberger, *Clays of Alabama*, 142.

9 *Cahaba Gazette*, January 18, 1856, 2; *Official Proceedings of the National Democratic Convention* (Dayton, OH: *Daily Journal Book and Job Rooms*, 1882), 51 (listing Alabama's delegates). See also, Charles Edward Cauthen, *South Carolina Goes to War, 1860–1882* (Columbia: University of South Carolina Press, 2005), 8–9; *Montgomery Advertiser and State Gazette,* June 10, 1856, 2; Nuermberger, *Clays of Alabama*, 143; Potter, *Impending Crises*, 259–60. See also, Eric Foner, *Free Soil, Free Labor, Free Men: The Ideology of the Republican Party Before the Civil War* (Oxford: Oxford University Press, 1995), 2; *Cahaba Gazette*, September 12, 1856,

2, October 31, 1856, 2; Nuermberger, *Clays of Alabama*, 142.

10 John F. Kvach, *DeBow's Review: The Antebellum Vision of a New South* (Lexington: University Press of Kentucky, 2013), 85; Elizabeth H. Varon, *Disunion! The Coming of the American Civil War, 1789–1859* (Chapel Hill: University of North Carolina Press, 2008), 292–93; Herbert Wender, "The Southern Commercial Convention at Savannah, 1856," *Georgia Historical Quarterly* 15 (June, 1931): 173–91.

11 "Southern Convention at Savannah" in J.D.B. DeBow, ed., *DeBow's Review and Industrial Resources, Statistics, etc.* (New Orleans: DeBow, 1857), XXII: 85, 89, 94, 96; *Montgomery Advertiser and State Gazette*, December 18, 1856, 2.

12 (Montgomery) *Confederation*, May 18, 1858, 2; (Savannah, GA) *Morning News*, May 21, 1858.

13 (Mobile) *Weekly Herald and Tribune*, March 22, 1853, April 1, 1853, April 7, 1853, April 23, 1853; *Montgomery Advertiser and State Gazette*, May 18, 1857, 2.

14 *Moulton Democrat*, February 6, 1857, 2, March 20, 1857, 2.

15 (Huntsville) *Southern Advocate*, March 26, 1857, 3; *Mobile Register*, March 27, 1857, 2; *Montgomery Advertiser and State Gazette*, March 31, 1857, 2.

16 *Moulton Democrat*, July 17, 1857, 1; (Huntsville) *Southern Advocate*, April 30, 1856, 2–3.

17 (New Orleans) *Picayune*, May 27, 1857, 1, May 28, 1857, 1 and 4, May 29, 1857, 3, May 31, 1857, 1, June 4, 1857, 1; Junius P. Rodriguez, ed., *Slavery in the United States: A Social, Political, and Historical Encyclopedia* (Santa Barbara, CA: ABC-CLIO, 2007), I: 502–503.

18 (Huntsville) *Southern Advocate*, April 30, 1857, 3.

19   Ibid.

20   Ibid. See also, *Mobile Register*, May 7, 1857, 2; *Montgomery Advertiser and State Gazette*, May 7, 1857, 2; *Moulton Democrat*, May 29, 1857, 2; *Cahaba Gazette*, May 8, 1857, 2.

21   (Huntsville) *Southern Advocate*, April 2, 1857, 3, April 30, 1857, 3.

22   *Montgomery Advertiser and State Gazette*, May 7, 1857, 2.

23   *Montgomery Advertiser and State Gazette*, May 29, 1857, 2.

24   *Montgomery Advertiser and State Gazette*, June 1, 1857, 3, June 7, 1857, 2, June 9, 1857, 3; (Huntsville) *Southern Advocate*, June 11, 1857, 3; (Tuscaloosa) *Independent Monitor*, June 11, 1857, 2.

25   *Moulton Democrat*, July 17, 1857, 1.

26   *Moulton Democrat*, July 17, 1857, 1.

27   Potter, *Impending Crisis*, 299–315.

28   Potter, *Impending Crisis*, 315–16.

29   *Moulton Democrat*, July 3, 1857, 1 (emphasis added); *Montgomery Advertiser and State Gazette*, June 1, 1857, 3.

30   *Cahaba Gazette*, July 17, 1857, 2.

31   (Huntsville) *Southern Advocate*, July 9, 1857, 3; (Washington) *Star*, July 15, 1857, 2; *Moulton Democrat*, July 10, 1857, 2; (Huntsville) *Southern Advocate*, July 30, 1857, 3; *Memphis Appeal*, July 14, 1857, 2; (Washington) *Star*, July 15, 1857, 2; (Shreveport) *South-Western*, August 5, 1857, 2; (New Orleans) *Times-Picayune*, July 22, 1857, 1.

32   "To the Voters of the 5th Congressional District," in David Hubbard Papers, Tennessee State Library and Archives, Nashville, Tennessee.

33   Ibid.

34   *Mobile Register*, August 14, 1857, 3; *Moulton Democrat*, July 24, 1857, 2, August 14, 1857, 2; (Huntsville) *Southern Advocate*, August 6, 1857, 3; *Montgomery Advertiser and State Gazette*, August 10, 1857, 2, August 12, 1857, 2; (Washington) *Star*, August 10, 1857, 2, August 11, 1857, 2; *Nashville Union and American*, August 15, 1857, 2; (Tuscaloosa) *Independent Monitor*, August 13, 1857, 2; Dorman, *Party Politics in Alabama*, 140–41.

35   *Nashville Union and American*, August 28, 1857, 2, September 9, 1857, 2; *Yorkville* (SC) *Enquirer*, September 3, 1857, 1.

36   (Washington) *National Intelligencer*, September 4, 1857, 2; (New Orleans) *Times-Picayune*, September 11, 1857, 1; (Richmond) *Dispatch*, September 12, 1857, 1; *Montgomery Advertiser and State Gazette*, September 14, 1857, 2.

37   *Montgomery Advertiser and State Gazette*, November 26, 1857, 2; (Tuscaloosa) *Independent Monitor*, November 19, 1857, 2.

38   Thomas M. Peters to George S. Houston, December 7, 1857, George S. Houston Papers, Southern Historical Collection, University of North Carolina.

39   *Mobile Register*, November 24, 1857, 2; Nuermberger, *Clays of Alabama*, 155–156.

40   (Huntsville) *Southern Advocate*, December 24, 1857, 2.

41   *Ala. Acts*, No. 306, 318 (January 28, 1858).

42   *Ala. Acts*, Joint Resolutions, pp,. 426–27 (January 22, 1858).

43   (Tuscaloosa) *Independent Monitor*, February 4, 1858, 2.

44   *Moulton Democrat*, April 23, 1858, 2.

45   *Montgomery Advertiser and State Gazette*, April 16, 1858, 2, April 21, 1858, 2; (Huntsville) *Southern Advocate*, April 22, 1858, 3; *Moulton Democrat*, April 23, 1858, 2; *Memphis Appeal*, April 29, 1858, 1.

46 *Moulton Democrat*, May 21, 1858, 1.

47 (Montgomery) *Confederation*, May 18, 1858, 2. For discussion of this Convention, see Vicki Vaughn Johnson, *The Men and the Vision of the Southern Commercial Conventions, 1845–1871* (Columbia: University of Missouri Press, 1992), 146–54.

48 *Moulton Democrat*, August 13, 1858, 1; *Memphis Appeal*, September 7, 1858, 1; *Montgomery Advertiser and State Gazette*, September 14, 1858, 2.

49 See, for example, (Huntsville) *Southern Advocate*, May 20, 1858, 3; *Montgomery Advertiser and State Gazette,* May 8, 1858, 3; *Memphis Appeal,* May 19, 1858, 1; (Montgomery) *Confederation*, May 11, 1858, 2, May 18, 1858, 2.

50 W.L. Yancey to James S. Slaughter, June 15, 1858, reprinted in *Moulton Democrat*, July 16, 1858, 1.

51 *Montgomery Advertiser and State Gazette*, June 15, 1858, 2.

52 (Montgomery) *Confederation*, October 25, 1858, 1.

53 (Huntsville) *Southern Advocate*, November 25, 1858, 3.

54 (Huntsville) *Southern Advocate*, December 23, 1858, 3, January 13, 1859, 3.

55 David Hubbard to Stephen A. Douglas, December 26, 1858, Stephen A. Douglas Papers, 1858, Box 22, Folder 22, Special Collection Research Center, University of Chicago Library.

56 *Charleston Mercury*, November 9, 1859, 1.

57 David Hubbard to Wm. F. Samford, February 28, 1859, reprinted in *Montgomery Advertiser and State Gazette*, March 26, 1859, 4.

58 (Jackson) *Mississippian*, April 8, 1859.

59 *Montgomery Advertiser and State Gazette*, April 20, 1858, 2.

60 Henry A. Wise to David Hubbard, January 3, 1859, reprinted in (Huntsville) *Southern Advocate*, April 7, 1859, 2. See also, Craig M. Simpson, *A Good Southerner: The Life of Henry A. Wise of Virginia* (Chapel Hill: University of North Carolina Press, 1985), 226.

61 *Montgomery Advertiser and State Gazette*, July 20, 1859, 2. See also, *Mobile Register*, July 21, 1859, 2, August 9, 1859, 2; (Montgomery) *Confederation*, August 7, 1859, 2; (Huntsville) *Southern Advocate*, August 11, 1859, 2.

62 (Montgomery) *Mail*, reprinted in *Athens Herald*, reprinted in (Montgomery) *Confederation*, August 16, 1859, 2; *Montgomery Advertiser and State Gazette*, August 31, 1859, 2, October 19, 1859, 1; (Troy) *Southern Advertiser*, reprinted in (Montgomery) *Confederation*, September 6, 1859, 2.

63 *Montgomery Advertiser and State Gazette*, August 31, 1859, 2.

CHAPTER FOURTEEN

1 *Montgomery Mail*, June 2, 1860, 2; (Marion) *South Western Baptist*, December 22, 1859, 2.

2 *Charleston Mercury*, November 30, 1859, 1.

3 *Montgomery Advertiser*, January 8, 1917, 4.

4 Walther, *William Lowndes Yancey and the Coming of the Civil War*, 236.

5 *Tuskegee Republican*, December 8, 1859, 2.

6 *Montgomery Advertiser and State Gazette*, October 19, 1859, 1.

7 *Montgomery Advertiser and State Gazette*, December 7, 1859, 1.

8 Walther, *William Lowndes Yancey and the Coming of the Civil War*, 236.

9 Saunders, *Early Settlers of Alabama*, 98–99.

10 *Alabama House Journal 1859–1860*, 109

(December 1, 1859); Thornton, *Politics and Power in a Slave Society*, 380.

11 Saunders, *Early Settlers of Alabama*, I: 98–99.

12 Ibid.

13 *Montgomery Advertiser and State Gazette*, December 14, 1859, 1.

14 *Alabama Senate Journal 1859–1860* (December 2, 1859), 88; *Montgomery Advertiser and State Gazette*, December 7, 1859, 2–3, December 21, 1859, 1–2.

15 Walther, *William Yancey and the Coming of the Civil War*, 237; Lonnie A. Burnett, *The Pen Makes a Good Sword: John Forsyth of the Mobile Register* (Tuscaloosa: University of Alabama Press, 2006), 106–107.

16 Walther, *William Yancey and the Coming of the Civil War*, 237–38.

17 *Montgomery Advertiser and State Gazette*, October 19, 1859, 2.

18 *Charleston Mercury*, January 18, 1860, 1.

19 (Washington) *Star*, January 16, 1860, 2; (Baltimore) *Exchange*, January 17, 1860, 1; *Augusta Chronicle*, January 17, 1860, 1; *Richmond Whig*, January 17, 1860, 3.

20 *Mobile Register*, May 22, 1860, 2.

21 (Selma) *Alabama State Sentinel*, reprinted in *Mobile Register*, January 26, 1860, 1.

22 *Montgomery Advertiser and State Gazette*, December 14, 1859, 1.

23 *Montgomery Advertiser and State Gazette*, December 14, 1859, 1; *Alabama House Journal, 1859–1860*, 151 (December 10, 1859).

24 (Montgomery) *Alabama State Journal*, November 30, 1859, 1; *Montgomery Advertiser and State Gazette*, November 30, 1859, 2; (Tuscaloosa) *Independent Monitor*, December 10, 1859; (Huntsville) *Southern Advocate*, December 7, 1859, 3.

25 *Montgomery Weekly Advertiser* (December 21, 1859), 1; (Huntsville) *Southern Advocate*, December 21, 1859, 3.

26 *Ala. Acts*, No. 203, 292 (December 15, 1859).

27 *Ala. Acts*, No. 31, 25 (February 23, 1860). *See* (Tuscaloosa) *Independent Monitor*, March 10, 1860, 2.

28 *Ala. Acts*, Nos. 68,54 (February 18, 1860), No. 39, 31 (February 24, 1860) and No. 132, 110 (February 24, 1860).

29 *Ala. Acts*, No. 45, 36 (February 24, 1860); (Huntsville) *Southern Advocate*, February 29, 1860, 3; (Greensboro) *Alabama Beacon*, March 2, 1860, 2; *Mobile Register*, February 28, 1860, 2.

30 *Ala. Acts*, Joint Resolutions (February 24, 1860) (emphasis added).

31 *Montgomery Mail*, February 21, 1860, 2.

32 (Tuscaloosa) *Independent Monitor*, February 25, 1860, 2.

33 James Leonidas Murphy, "Alabama and the Charleston Convention of 1860," in *Studies in Southern and Alabama History*, George Petrie, ed., 239–66 (Montgomery, AL: Alabama Historical Society, 1905).

34 Walther, *William Lowndes Yancey and the Coming of the Civil War*, 238–51; Burnett, *Pen Makes a Good Sword*, 107–14; Margaret M. Storey, *Loyalty and Loss: Alabama's Unionists in the Civil War and Reconstruction* (Baton Rouge: Louisiana State University Press, 2004), 24–25; William Best Hesseltine, *Three Against Lincoln: Murat Halstead Reports the Caucuses of 1860* (Baton Rouge: Louisiana State University Press, 1960).

35 *Richmond Whig*, August 28, 1860, 1.

36 (Montgomery) *Confederation*, June 2, 1860, 2; (Huntsville) *Southern Advocate*, August 21, 1860, 4; (Huntsville) *Independent*, reprinted in *Richmond Whig*,

September 18, 1860, 2.

37   (Wheeling, VA) *Intelligencer*, June 4, 1860, 2; (Port Allen, LA) *Sugar Planter*, June 9, 1860, 2; *St. Cloud* (MN) *Democrat*, June 28, 1860, 1. See also, *Newbern* (NC) *Weekly Progress*, October 9, 1860, 2 ("I would tear this government to atoms.").

38   *Nashville Patriot*, July 10, 1860, 2, July 19, 1860, 2. See also, Saunders, *Early Settlers of Alabama*, 100.

39   (Huntsville) *Southern Advocate*, October 3, 1860, 3.

40   Thornton, *Politics and Power in a Slave Society*, 403–404; Dorman, *Party Politics in Alabama*, 176–77.

41   *Montgomery Advertiser and State Gazette*, December 12, 1860, 1; Walther, *William Lowndes Yancey and the Coming of the Civil War*, 274–75.

42   (Huntsville) *Southern Advocate*, cited in *Montgomery Weekly Post*, January 2, 18612, 4. See also, Burnett, *Pen Makes a Good Sword*, 125–26; Joseph W. Danielson, *War's Desolating Scourge: The Union's Occupation of North Alabama* (Lawrence: University Press of Kansas, 2012), 5–15; Thornton, *Politics and Power in a Slave Society*, 344. Moulton lawyer David Peter Lewis later wrote Thomas Hill Watts that over 90 percent of the voters in Lawrence County were opposed to secession. D.P. Lewis to T.H. Watts, February 9, 1863, Papers of Governor Thomas Hill Watts, Alabama Department of Archives and History, Montgomery, Alabama.

43   Charles B. Dew, *Apostles of Disunion: Southern Secession Commissioners and the Causes of the Civil War* (Charlottesville: University Press of Virginia, 2001), 51–58. Dew's otherwise excellent book inexplicably omits mention of David Hubbard.

44   Fleming, *Civil War and Reconstruction*

in Alabama, 46; (New Orleans) *Picayune*, January 3, 1861,6; A.B. Moore to Gentlemen of the Convention, January 8, 1861, Official Records, Series IV, Vol. I, 3; Durward Long, "Alabama's Secession Commissioners," *Civil War History* 9 (March, 1963): 55–66; Thomas A. DeBlack, *With Fire and Sword: Arkansas, 1861–1874* (Fayetteville: University of Arkansas Press, 2003), 18.

45   David Hubbard to Governor Andrew B. Moore, January 3, 1860, Papers of Governor Andrew Barry Moore, Alabama Department of Archives and History, Montgomery, Alabama. See also, David Hubbard to John Pettus, January 5, 1861, RG 27, vol. 36, Papers of Governor John Pettus, Mississippi Department of Archives and History, Jackson, Mississippi; David Hubbard to Isham Harris, February 25, 1861, Papers of Governor Isham Harris, Tennessee State Library and Archives, Nashville, Tennessee.

46   Ibid.

47   Arkansas Senate Resolution, December 28, 1860, in David Hubbard Papers, Tennessee State Library and Archives, Nashville, Tennessee.

48   (Little Rock) *Arkansas Gazette*, December 20, 1860, reprinted in (Washington) *National Intelligencer*, January 9, 1861.

49   *Nashville Banner*, reprinted in (Washington) *National Intelligencer*, January 22, 1861, 3. See generally, Danielson, *War's Desolating Scourge*, 15–17.

50   (Tuscumbia) *North Alabamian*, reprinted in (Washington) *National Intelligencer*, March 14, 1861, 3; Faye Acton Axford, ed., *The Journals of Thomas Hubbard Hobbs* (Tuscaloosa: University of Alabama Press, 1976), 225–31.

51   Axford, ed., *Journals of Thomas Hubbard Hobbs*, 228–33; McIlwain, *Civil War Alabama*, 50–51.

52 *Journal of the Congress of the Confederate States of America*, 24, 32.

53 David Hubbard to Andrew B. Moore, February 23, 1861, Papers of Governor Andrew Barry Moore, quoted in Thornton, *Politics and Power in a Slave Society*, 438. See generally, Danielson, *War's Desolating Scourge*, 20–21.

54 Lang C. Allen to Dr. F.H. Anderson, January 24, 1861, reprinted in (Tuscumbia) *North Alabamian, Montgomery Advertiser*, and (Washington) *National Intelligencer*, March 14, 1861, 3 (letter from a Marion County delegate in the secession convention); (Montgomery) *Alabama State Journal*, September 8, 1872, p. 2 (letter from a Lawrence County delegate). See generally, McIlwain, *Civil War Alabama*, 34–52.

55 *Charleston Mercury*, April 13, 1861, 1, April 15, 1861, 3, April 18, 1861, 3.

56 DeBlack, *With Fire and Sword*, 27–28 (Arkansas seceded on May 6, 1861).

57 *Charleston Mercury*, February 22, 1861, 3; George C. Rable, *The Confederate Republic: A Revolution Against Politics* (Chapel Hill: University of North Carolina Press, 1994), 72; William C. Harris, *Leroy Pope Walker: Confederate Secretary of War* (Tuscaloosa, AL: Confederate Pub. Co., 1962); Rick Halperin, "Leroy Pope Walker and the Problems of the Confederate War Department, 1861" (Ph.D. Diss., Auburn University, 1978).

58 (New Orleans) *Picayune*, March 17, 1861, 3; (Columbus) *Ohio Statesman*, March 18, 1861, 3; *Charleston Mercury*, March 18, 1861, 3; (Greensboro) *Alabama Beacon*, March 22, 1861, 3; *New York Herald*, March 22, 1861, 8; Annie Heloise Abel, *The American Indian as Slaveholder and Secessionist: An Omitted Chapter in the Diplomatic History of the Southern Confederacy* (Cleveland, OH; Arthur H. Clark Company, 1915), 110,

128; *Journal of the Congress of the Confederate States of America, 1861–1865*, I: 154.

59 David Hubbard to L.P. Walker, June 2, 1861, Official Records, Series 1, Vol. 3, 589–90. Regarding Fort Smith, see Edwin C. Bearrs and Arrell Morgan Gibson, *Fort Smith: Little Gibraltar on the Arkansas* (Norman: University of Oklahoma Press, 1988).

60 That might have been the result of directions given Hubbard by Secretary of War Walker. See L.P. Walker to David Hubbard, May 14, 1861, Official Records, Series I, Vol. 3, 576–78.

61 David Hubbard to John Ross, June 12, 1861, Official Records, Series I, Vol. 13, 497–99.

62 Inskeep, *Jacksonland*, 342–43.

63 John Ross to David Hubbard, June 17, 1861, Official Records, Series I, Vol. 13, 498–99. Hubbard also oversaw the selection of Indian agents to liaise with the tribes on a day-to-day basis on behalf of the Confederacy, and to make the payments required by treaties. One who had formerly served as a federal agent later wrote that Hubbard "requested me to return to the Agency, and take charge of the Indians, try to keep them quiet, and satisfied, and still endeavor to learn them something of the habits and customs of civilized men." The man accepted Hubbard's proposal. Richard B. McCaslin, Donald E. Chipman, Andrew J. Torget, and Randolph B. Campbell, eds., *This Corner of Canaan: Essays On Texas in Honor of Randolph B. Campbell* (Denton: University of North Texas Press, 2013), 191.

64 Wesley S. Thompson, *The Free State of Winston: A History of Winston County, Alabama* (Winfield, AL: Pareil Press, 1968), 3–4; Donald B. Dodd and Wynelle S. Dodd, *Winston: An Antebellum*

and Civil War History of a Hill County of North Alabama (Jasper, AL: C. Elliott, 1972), 88.

65   James Bell to Henry Bell, April 21, 1861, Papers of Governor Andrew Barry Moore, Alabama Department of Archives and History, Montgomery, Alabama. Regarding militant Unionist activities during this period, see Storey, *Loyalty and Loss*, 59–62, 64.

66   *Mobile Advertiser and Register*, July 24, 1861, 1, August 8, 1861, 1.

67   *Montgomery Weekly Advertiser*, August 31, 1861,4; Malcolm Cook McMillan, *Disintegration of a Confederate State: Three Governors of Alabama's Wartime Home Front, 1861–1865* (Macon, GA: Mercer Press, 1986), 32–33.

68   David A. Nichols, *Lincoln and the Indians: Civil War Policy and Politics* (Urbana: University of Illinois Press, 2000), 32.

69   McWhiney, *et al.*, eds., *"Fear God and Walk Humbly,"* 289.

70   *Richmond Examiner*, October 19, 1861, 3.

71   Jack H. Lepa, *Grant's River Campaign: Fort Henry to Shiloh* (Jefferson, NC: McFarland & Company, Inc., 2014), 20–23; William B. Feis, *Grant's Secret Service: The Intelligence War from Belmont to Appomattox* (Lincoln: University of Nebraska Press, 2004), 53–64; Danielson, *War's Desolating Scourge*, 26.

72   Jack H. Lepa, *The Civil War in Tennessee, 1862–1863* (Jefferson, NC: McFarland & Co., 2007), 14–15.

73   *Confederate Veteran* XIII (February, 1905): 84. Regarding the river forts in Tennessee, see Kendall D. Gott, *Where the South Lost the War: An Analysis of the Fort Henry–Fort Donelson Campaign, February 1862* (Mechanicsburg, PA: Stackpole Books, 2003).

74   David Hubbard Jr., to David Hubbard, circa January, 1862, David Hubbard Papers, Tennessee State Library and Archives, Nashville, Tennessee.

75   Ibid. See also, (Huntsville) *Democrat*, January 16, 1862, 3.

76   *Montgomery Weekly Advertiser*, February 7, 1862, February 9, 1862, and March 15, 1862. See generally, Lepa, *Civil War in Tennessee*, 15–17.

77   *Tuscumbia Constitution*, February 12, 1862, reprinted in *Montgomery Weekly Advertiser*, February 15, 1862; *Memphis Appeal*, reprinted in (Huntsville) *Democrat*, February 19, 1862,4, (New Orleans) *Picayune*, February 14, 1862, 1, and (Richmond) *Dispatch*, February 17, 1862, 2; Edwin C. Bearss, "A Federal Raid Up the River," *Alabama Review* 17 (October, 1964): 261–70.

78   Diary of Miss Catherine M. Fennell, 26, in Huntsville-Madison County Public Library, Huntsville, AL; Daily Journal of Joshua Burns Moore, 27–28, in Alabama Department of Archives and History, Montgomery, AL; (Huntsville) *Democrat*, February 12, 1862, 3.

79   *Montgomery Weekly Advertiser*, February 23, 1862; (Huntsville) *Democrat*, February 19, 1862, 3; *Selma Reporter*, February 22, 1862, 2. See generally, Lepa, *Civil War in Tennessee*, 18–28; Lepa, *Grant's River Campaign*, 68–71; B. Franklin Cooling, *Forts Henry and Donelson–The Key to the Confederate Heartland* (Knoxville: Easton Press, 1987).

80   Pfanz, *Richard S. Ewell*, 81, 84, 87–88, 149; Donald C. Pfanz, ed., *The Letters of General Richard S. Ewell: Stonewall's Successor* (Knoxville: University of Tennessee Press, 2012), 100, 142, 183, 185, 187, 193–94; Terry Jones, ed., *Campbell Brown's Civil War: With Ewell and the Army of Northern Virginia* (Baton

Rouge: Louisiana State University Press, 2004), 6, 56, 70–71, 161, 180.

81   Richard Ewell to Lizinka Brown, March 16, 1862, in Pfanz, ed., *Letters of General Richard S. Ewell*, 197–98.

82   L.P. Walker to J.P. Benjamin, February 17, 1862, Official Records, Series 1, Vol. 7, 888–89; Robert C. Black, *The Railroads of the Confederacy* (Chapel Hill: University of North Carolina Press, 1998), 139.

83   David Hubbard to Jefferson Davis, April 4, 1862, in Confederate Papers Relating to Citizens or Business Firms, 1861–65, Record Group 109, Roll 911, National Archives, Davis accepted Hubbard's recommendation and appointed Huntsville lawyer-secessionist Sutton Selwyn Scott in his place. Owen, *History of Alabama and Dictionary of Alabama Biography*, 4: 1514–15.

84   *Montgomery Weekly Advertiser*, March 22, 1862; (New Orleans) *Picayune*, March 6, 1862, 2, March 12, 1862, 2, March 14, 1862, March 20, 1862, 3, March 21, 1862, 2.

85   *Mobile Advertiser and Register*, April 6, 1862, 2, April 8, 1862, 1–2, April 9, 1862, 1–2, April 11, 1862, 1.

86   *Confederate Veteran* XIII (Feb., 1905): 84.

87   *Mobile Advertiser and Register*, April 17, 1862, 1–2, April 22, 1862, 2, May 13, 1862, 2; Daily Journal of Joshua Burns Moore, 33–36; Paul Horton, "Submitting to the Shadow of Slavery: The Secession Crisis and Civil War in Alabama's Lawrence County," *Civil War History* 44 (June, 1998): 111, 121–27; Danielson, *War's Desolating Scourge*, 26–30.

88   Daily Journal of Joshua Burns Moore, 33–36.

89   Rable, *Confederate Republic*, 139–44; Storey, *Loyalty and Loss*, 56–58.

90   *Confederate Veteran* XIII (February, 1905): 84.

91   Jones, ed., *Campbell Brown's Civil War*, 12, 15–16, 73.

92   Campbell Brown to Lizinka Brown, June 17, 1862, in Papers of Campbell Brown and Richard S. Ewell, Tennessee State Library and Archives, Nashville, TN..

93   *Confederate Veteran* XIII (Feb., 1905): 84.

94   Winston Groom, *Vicksburg, 1863* (New York: Alfred A. Knopf, 2009); Clifford Dowdey, *Death of a Nation: The Story of Lee and His Men at Gettysburg* (New York: Knopf, 1958).

95   McMillan, *Disintegration of a Confederate State*, 80.

96   *Huntsville Confederate*, reprinted in *Mobile Advertiser and Register*, October 10, 1863, 1.

97   McMillan, *Disintegration of a Confederate State*, 84; Danielson, *War's Desolating Scourge*, 139.

98   David Hubbard to Thomas H. Watts, December 19, 1863, Papers of Governor Thomas Hill Watts, Alabama Department of Archives and History, Montgomery, AL.

99   George C. Bradley and Richard L. Dahlen, *From Conciliation to Conquest: The Sack of Athens and the Court-Martial of Colonel John B. Turchin* (Tuscaloosa: University of Alabama Press, 2006).

100   (Greensboro) *Alabama Beacon*, April 3, 1863, 2; *Huntsville Advocate*, reprinted in *Montgomery Advertiser*, March 8, 1863, 1 and 3; R.J. Oglesby to Gen. S.A. Hurlburt, May 3, 1863, Official Records, Series 1, Vol. 23 (Part I), 245; Danielson, *War's Desolating Scourge*, 120–24.

101   Brewer, *Alabama*, 308.

102   Alan Sewell, "Dissent: The Free State of

Winston," *Civil War Times Illustrated* 20 (December, 1981): 30, 35–36; Storey, *Loyalty and Loss*, 39, 41, 88, 97–99, 102–106.

103 Danielson, *War's Desolation Scourge*, 118–127.

104 *Huntsville Confederate*, April 23, 1863, in (Washington) *National Intelligencer*, May 13, 1863; B.J. Hill to Col. E.J. Harvie, March 24, 1864, Official Records, Series 1, Vol. 32 (Part III), 681–82; Storey, *Loyalty and Loss*, 74–85, 159–68.

105 *Mobile Advertiser and Register*, August 15, 1863, 2, August 26, 1863, 2, December 10, 1863, 1, February 17, 1864, 2; *Huntsville Confederate*, October 29, 1863, 1; *Talladega Reporter*, reprinted in *Columbus* (GA) *Enquirer*, October 14, 1863, 2. See also, Bessie Martin, *A Rich Man's War, A Poor Man's Fight: Desertion of Alabama Troops from the Confederate Army* (Tuscaloosa, University of Alabama Press, 2003), 26–27, 33, 244–45.

106 Danielson, *War's Desolating Scourge*, 124–26, 144–45.

107 The congressman from Hubbard's district was Thomas Jefferson Foster. Owen, *History of Alabama and Dictionary of Alabama Biography*, III: 606.

108 David Hubbard to Thomas Hill Watts, December 19, 1863, Papers of Governor Thomas Hill Watts, Alabama Department of Archives and History, Montgomery, AL..

109 Ibid.

110 In effect, Hubbard maintained that twenty-five to thirty men could hold off thousands of Unionists and deserters.

111 *Selma Reporter*, March 23, 1864, 2; *Mobile Advertiser and Register*, April 23, 1864, 1; (Washington) *National Intelligencer*, March 14, 1864, 2; Danielson, *War's Desolating Scourge*, 132.

112 G.M. Dodge to Lt. Col. Bowers, March

11, 1864, Official Records, Series 1, Vol. 32 (Part I), 492.

113 David Hubbard to P.G.T. Beauregard, May (day unknown) 1862 (from Okalona), David Hubbard to Lt. Gen. Leonidas Polk, May 10, 1862 (from Montevallo), and David Hubbard to Lt. Gen. Leonidas Polk, May 20, 1862 (from Jasper, AL), in Confederate Papers Relating to Citizens or Business Firms, 1861–65, Record Group 109, National Archives

114 *New York Times*, July 26, 1864, 1, July 31, 1864, 6, August 3, 1864, 8.

115 *Mobile Advertiser and Register*, September 6, 1864, 1, September 10, 1864, 1.

116 (Montgomery, AL) *Memphis Appeal*, reprinted in *Mobile Advertiser and Register*, February 18, 1865, 2; Danielson, *War's Desolating Scourge*, 148–55.

117 *Confederate Veteran* XIII (February, 1905): 84 (stating that Hubbard served under Forrest until the end of the war.

118 Perry D. Jamieson, *Spring 1865: The Closing Campaigns of the Civil War* (Lincoln: University of Nebraska Press, 2015), 205–207; Jack Hurst, *Nathan Bedford Forrest: A Biography* (New York: Random House, 1994), 24255.

119 *Mobile Advertiser and Register*, April 8, 1865, 2.

120 *Tuscaloosa Observer*, March 8, 1865, 2.

121 James Pickett Jones, *Yankee Blitzkrieg: Wilson's Raid Through Alabama* (Lexington: University Press of Kentucky, 2000), 60–62, 145–52.

122 Regarding the desire of Unionists for violent retribution, see Storey, *Loyalty and Loss*, 191–92.

123 Daily Journal of Joshua Burns Moore, 95–96.

124 *Washington Chronicle*, April 4, 1865, reprinted in *Cleveland Leader*, April 6, 1865, 2.

125   Daily Journal of Joshua Burns Moore, 84–85.

126   Johnathan Truman Dorris, *Pardon and Amnesty Under Lincoln and Johnson: The Restoration of the Confederates to Their Rights and Privileges, 1861–1898* (Chapel Hill: University of North Carolina Press, 1977), 111–13; Michael Perman, *Reunion Without Compromise: The South and Reconstruction: 1865–1868* (New York: Cambridge University Press, 1973), 122.

127   Paul H. Bergeron, ed., *The Papers of Andrew Johnson*, (Knoxville: University of Tennessee Press, 1991), 9: 465, n 3, 466.

128   *Huntsville Advocate*, July 26, 1865, 3.

129   Sarah Woolfolk Wiggins, *The Scalawag in Alabama Politics, 1865–1881* (Tuscaloosa: University of Alabama Press, 1991), 10–14; J. Mills Thornton, "Alabama Emancipates," in Raymond Arsenault and Orville Burton, eds., *Dixie Redux: Essays in Honor of Sheldon Hackney*, (Montgomery, AL: NewSouth Books, 2013), 80; Robert S. Rhodes, "The Registration of Voters and the Election of Delegates to the Reconstruction Convention in Alabama," *Alabama Review* 8 (April, 1955): 119–42.

130   J. Mills Thornton, "Alabama's Presidential Reconstruction Legislature," in Gary W. Gallagher and Rachel A. Sheldon, eds., *A Political Nation: New Directions in Mid-Nineteenth Century American Political History* (Charlottesville: University of Virginia Press, 2012), 173.

131   Pfanz, *Ewell*, 275–76, 474; Pfanz, ed., *Letters of Richard S. Ewell*, 404–405, 405 n. 467.

132   L.C. Ewell to Andrew Johnson, December 4, 1865, in Bergeron, ed., *Papers of Andrew Johnson*, 9: 465.

133   Ibid., at note 3.

134   Pfanz, ed., *Letters to General Richard S. Ewell*, 404, 405 n. 3.

135   Owen, *History of Alabama and Dictionary of Alabama Biography*, 854. Hubbard probably operated this tanyard in conjunction with the Ewell's large stock farm.

136   (Nashville) *Republican* Banner, March 27, 1872,4; Pfanz, *Richard S. Ewell*, 494.

137   *New Orleans Republican*, January 25, 1874; (New Orleans) *Times-Democrat*, January 27, 1874,4; Saunders, *Early Settlers of Alabama*, 100.

138   Rogers, *et al.*, *Alabama*, 264.

Chapter Fifteen

1   See Nuermberger, *Clays of Alabama;* Harris, *Leroy Pope Walker;* Walther, *William Lowndes Yancey and the Coming of the Civil War;* William Ewart Gladstone, *J.L.M. Curry* (Richmond: B.V. Johnson, 1891); John J. Chodes, *Destroying the Republic: Jabez Curry and the Re-education of the Old South* (New York: Algora Pub., 2005); Jessie Pearl Rice, *J.L.M. Curry: Southerner, Statesman and Educator* (New York: King's Crown Press, 1949).

2   Garrett, *Reminiscences of Public Men in Alabama*, 298.

3   Garrett, *Reminiscences of Public Men in Alabama*, 298.

Image Credits

Index

Bradley, Joseph 182
Breckinridge, John xii, 181–183
Britain, British ix, 4, 7–10, 11, 13, 22,
    30, 41, 53, 56, 64, 76, 77, 81, 84, 88,
    101, 103, 105, 106, 107, 119, 140,
    165, 166, 168, 172, 185
Brooks, Preston 163
Brown, Aaron 230
Brown, Campbell 190
Brown, Elizabeth McKay Campbell
    "Lizinka" 189, 190
Brown, John x, 174, 179, 181
Buchanan, James 164, 166
Bynum, Oakley H. 160, 169, 182

C

Cahaba, Alabama xi, 19, 121
Calhoun County, Alabama 54, 169
Calhoun, James M. 98
Calhoun, John Caldwell xi, 18, 23, 35,
    38, 42, 50, 71–75, 92, 96, 97, 98,
    101, 105, 109, 110, 112, 119, 121,
    122, 124–127, 129, 133, 135, 148,
    153, 169, 175, 181, 228
California x, 124, 128–130, 132,
    135–137, 139, 143, 242
Campbell, Duncan (father-in-law) 15
Campbell, Elizabeth (wife) 15, 89, 92,
    207
Campbell, George Washington 15, 110
Campbell, John Archibald 97, 98
canals 18, 21, 24, 26, 27, 28, 36, 37,
    64, 76, 80, 139, 208
Cass, Lewis 60, 123, 124
Chambers County, Alabama 54
Chapman, Reuben 39, 58, 80, 84, 154
Charleston Mercury 44, 178
Charleston, South Carolina 38, 46, 56,
    72, 85, 122, 178, 179, 181, 185
Chattanooga, Tennessee 74, 191
Cherokees 12, 183, 186, 187
Chickasaws 5, 10, 12, 29, 30, 43, 54,
    57, 59–61, 66, 78, 79, 183, 214
Chickasaw Land Company 57, 59

Chickasaw Rangers 188, 189
Chickasaw Union 65, 72
Choctaws 183
Cincinnati, Ohio 72, 161, 163, 164
Civil War 185–194
Clay, Clement Claiborne, Jr. 98, 126,
    136, 152–154, 161, 198, 199
Clay, Clement Comer xii, 24, 26,
    68–70, 84, 92, 93, 95, 96, 147, 151,
    157, 158, 164, 169
Clay, Henry 31, 44, 50, 73, 88, 91, 101,
    105–108, 110, 111, 132, 134, 135,
    238
Clay, Matthew 19
Clayton-Bulwer Treaty 166
Clemens, Jeremiah 126, 142, 147, 251
Clitherall, Alexander 175, 176
Cobb, Howell 127, 129, 130
Cobb, Williamson R. W. 126, 127, 136,
    138, 152
Coffee, John 4–8, 12, 15, 16, 20, 34,
    42, 43, 55, 205, 216
Colbert County, Alabama 16, 33, 38,
    48, 57, 148, 192, 194
Colbert, George 5
Collier, Henry Watkins 129, 143, 149
Columbia, Tennessee 113
Comanches 61
Compromise of 1850 x, 143, 146, 147,
    150, 151
Confederacy x, 185–194, 258
Congressional Globe 73, 85
Connecticut 11
Cooper, William 182
Coopwood, Thomas Benton 33, 37, 40,
    46, 58
Coosa County, Alabama 54
Corinth, Mississippi 189, 190, 191
cotton ix, 3, 11, 12, 13–15, 16, 17, 18,
    27, 37, 38, 51, 53, 55, 57, 59, 60–62,
    63, 64, 65, 66, 68, 70, 72, 78, 89,
    101, 105, 114, 115, 122, 124, 131,
    133, 152, 166
Courtland, Alabama 38, 42, 43, 53, 56,